POSTWAR
REVISITED

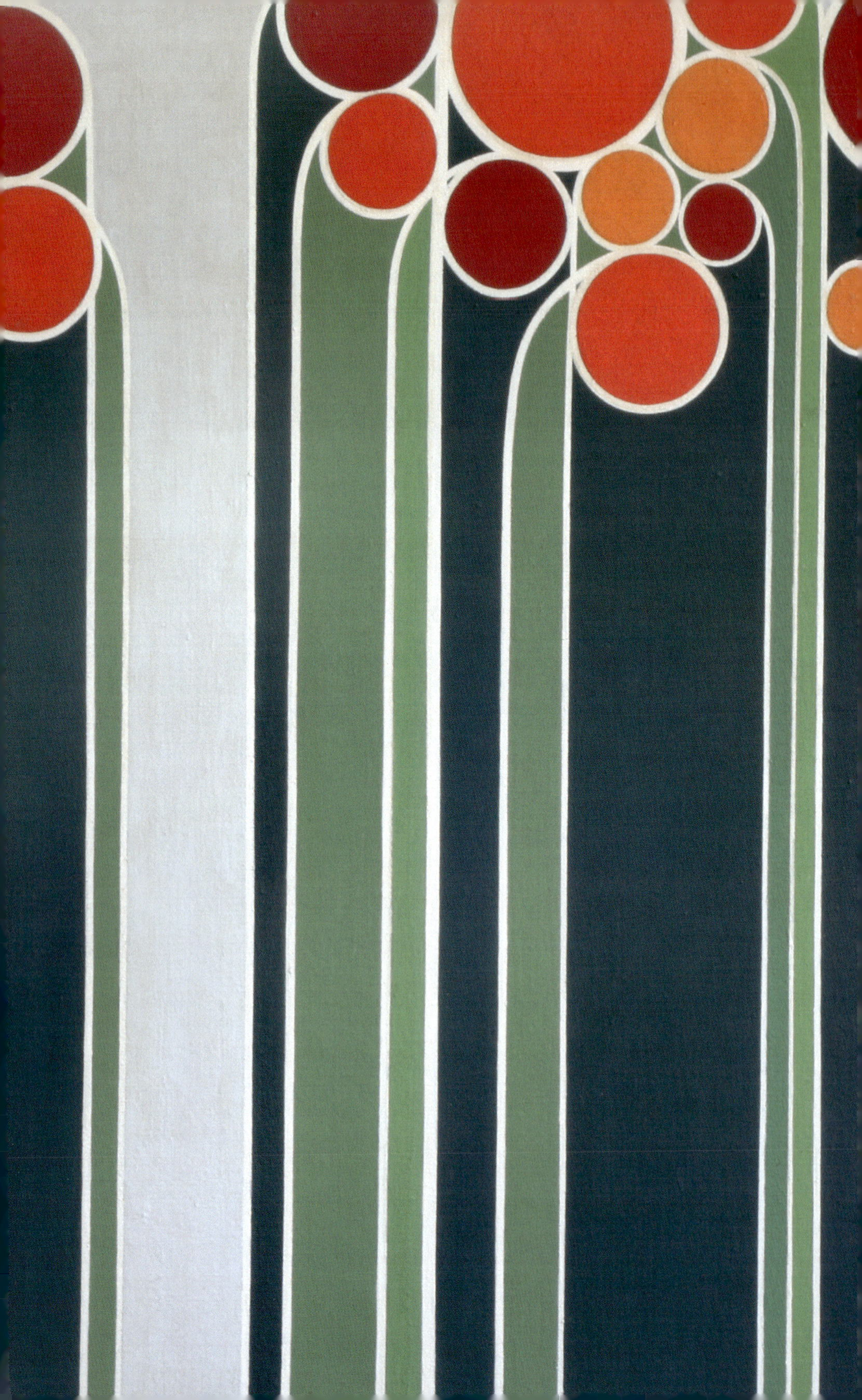

POSTWAR REVISITED

A Global Art History

• • •

Okwui Enwezor and
Atreyee Gupta, EDITORS

Duke University Press · *Durham and London* · 2025

Printed in the United States of America on acid-free paper ∞
Project Editor: Livia Tenzer
Designed by Courtney Leigh Richardson
Typeset in Garamond Premier Pro, Real Head Pro, and Clarendon
by Westchester Publishing Services

Library of Congress Cataloging-in-Publication Data
Names: Enwezor, Okwui, editor. | Gupta, Atreyee, editor.
Title: Postwar revisited : a global art history / Okwui Enwezor
and Atreyee Gupta, editors.
Description: Durham : Duke University Press, 2025. | Includes
bibliographical references and index.
Identifiers: LCCN 2024033258 (print)
LCCN 2024033259 (ebook)
ISBN 9781478031451 (paperback)
ISBN 9781478028222 (hardcover)
ISBN 9781478060437 (ebook)
Subjects: LCSH: Art, Modern—20th century. | Modernism (Art) |
Art—History. | Decolonization in art. | Art and globalization.
Classification: LCC N6490 .P678 2025 (print) | LCC N6490 (ebook) |
DDC 709.04/5—dc23/eng/20241212
LC record available at https://lccn.loc.gov/2024033258
LC ebook record available at https://lccn.loc.gov/2024033259

IN MEMORY OF

Okwui Enwezor (1963–2019)

Contents

Part III
PACIFIC PASSAGES, ATLANTIC OSCILLATIONS

Part IV
DECOLONIZING CONSTELLATIONS

Illustrations

Preface

The task of writing a preface for this book is complicated as much by the fact that it was a long time in the making as by its state of incompletion at the time of Okwui Enwezor's passing. *Postwar Revisited: A Global Art History* is the book that Enwezor referenced in an interview with Ulrike Knöfel published in *Der Spiegel* in the fall of 2018, shortly after Enwezor's separation from Haus der Kunst, Munich.[1] At the time, Enwezor and I were working unremittingly to complete the final draft of the manuscript for this book, a task that was disrupted by his faltering health and was completed after his passing. The ideas behind this book had emerged five years earlier within the context of Enwezor's research and exhibition project titled *Postwar: Art between the Pacific and the Atlantic, 1945–1965*, which began with a four-day international conference in May 2014.[2]

This was a conference that I—then the inaugural Goethe Postdoctoral Fellow at Haus der Kunst, with a newly minted PhD—coordinated and convened with Enwezor and the then chief curator, Ulrich Wilmes, at Haus der Kunst. Enwezor imagined the conference to be central to the research process leading up to the *Postwar* exhibition, which he cocurated two years later with Katy Siegel and Wilmes. The forty speakers who participated in the 2014 conference included Sam Bardaouil, Nicholas Cullinan, Iftikhar Dadi, Federico Deambrosis, Alessandro Del Puppo, Lara Demori, Burcu Dogramaci, Nikolas Drosos, Patrick Flores, Éva Forgács, Alessio Fransoni, Jacopo Galimberti, Walter Grasskamp, Boris Groys, Serge Guilbaut, Sohl Lee, Gregor H. Lersch, Vivian Li, Paula Barreiro López, Tara McDowell, Abigail McEwen, Armin Medosch, Gerardo Mosquera, Majella Munro, Alexandra Munroe, Susanne Neubauer, Chika Okeke-Agulu, Mari Carmen Ramírez, Amanda Katherine Rath,

Dorothea Schöne, Nada Shabout, Devika Singh, Terry Smith, Ming Tiampo, Reiko Tomii, Isobel Whitelegg, Midori Yamamura, and Lingling Amy Yao. Just as he had hoped, the incredible body of intellectual ideas that the 2014 conference brought to the fore shaped Enwezor's own thinking about the 2016 *Postwar* exhibition in substantial ways; several conference participants also contributed to the sumptuous catalog that accompanied the exhibition. At the time, this book was imagined as a volume of conference proceedings, a companion piece to the catalog accompanying the *Postwar: Art between the Pacific and the Atlantic, 1945–1965* exhibition.[3]

But as is often the case with projects that evolve over time, this book, too, underwent several incarnations in the years that followed. Enwezor's own vision and aspiration for this book had shifted by 2018 as he confronted what he perceived to be a growing detrition in Germany and elsewhere of commitment to global dialogue, intellectual cultures of curiosity and openness, and the ethics and politics of diversity and inclusion.[4] For my part, I took up a tenure-track position merely months after Donald Trump became the forty-fifth president of the United States, began teaching at a time of rising xenophobia around the world, and, among other things, became increasingly invested in the conjunction of perspectives gained from postcolonial theory with debates on global modernisms in particular and global art history more generally. Thus, by 2018, some years after the 2014 conference and the 2016 exhibition, this book had assumed a very different task: standing in a politically embattled present, it sought to grasp *postwar* as a collective horizon in the time of decolonization and reassess its implications for a global art history in the present. It is this theme that the title of the book—*Postwar Revisited: A Global Art History*—also indexes.

To be sure, this book is not yet another revisionist attempt, nor did we aim to stop with tracing the simultaneous presence of many modernisms across the world. The foundations of the larger *Postwar* research, exhibition, and publication project to which this book belongs can in fact be traced back to an essay that Enwezor wrote in 2003 and repeatedly referred to in the course of our work on this book nearly a decade later. The essay in question was "The Postcolonial Constellation: Contemporary Art in a State of Permanent Transition."[5] A lucid statement of Enwezor's curatorial philosophy, this essay had always struck me as simultaneously invigorating and challenging because the postcolonial condition that it invoked was not one that mapped onto the historical matrix of colonialism and decolonization in any simple sense. Categorically delineating the "postcolonial constellation" as "the site for the expansion of the definition of what constitutes contemporary culture," here Enwezor had sketched out a provocative picture of the twentieth century that emphasized the epistemological and hermeneutic violence that constituted global cultural modernity as such.[6] The artistic and intellectual "subjectivities that emerge directly from the convergences and proximities wrought by imperialism," Enwezor insisted, "direct us to the postcolonial," which annotates subterranean convolutions in the history of twentieth-century modernism as a whole.[7] His was an unambiguous indictment, not just of modern art history "with roots in imperial discourse" but also of contemporary curatorial procedures derived, as Enwezor saw it, "with the unambiguous sanction of [this] historical and imperial precedent."[8] What he instead insisted upon amounted to a dismantling of the epistemic Westernism of art history and its allied institutions of knowledge production. In this, the "postcolonial constellation" had an important role to play, as he conceived of the postcolonial not merely as the time after decolonization but as a necessary critical intellectual frame for understanding the "social and cultural temporality of late modernity."[9]

Tellingly, Enwezor returned with alacrity to this "postcolonial constellation"—whose form, he had already acknowledged in 2003, was shaped by the "series of structural, political, and cultural restructuring since after World War II and which include[d] movements of decolonization, civil rights, feminist, gay/lesbian, [and] antiracist" positions[10]—in his tripartite intervention in the global history of modern and contemporary art, beginning with the *Postwar* project. *Postwar* was slated to be followed by two five-year research and exhibition projects: one focusing on the concept of the postcolonial, circa 1965–85, and the other focusing on postcommunism from 1985 to the present. Of the trio, only the first was completed during Enwezor's lifetime. Whereas postcolonial art has often been conflated with the story of newly independent nation-states, Enwezor had intended to shift our focus to the emergence of a revolutionary consciousness among nonstate actors in the face of repressive states, military dictatorships, and human rights violations in the second exhibition. He had provisionally titled this exhibition *The Postcolonial Constellation: Art, Culture, Sovereignty, 1960–1985*, as he had related to me during our conversations. Like Frantz Fanon, he understood that a revolutionary consciousness could sometimes turn toward violence to achieve its goals; the historical movements that he intended to think through in this exhibition therefore included the Italian Red Brigades, the Japanese Red Army, and the Indian Naxalites.[11] This exhibition was installed posthumously, in accordance with Enwezor's wishes, in an altered form at the 2023 Sharjah Biennial. To our loss, the third iteration of the magisterial trio of historically dense exhibitions that Enwezor envisaged is destined to remain unrealized.

As for this book, Enwezor remained keenly involved in its structuring and organization, especially as our vision for the book evolved from a volume of conference proceedings to a reader on global postwar art. In the end, only nine of the fourteen chapters in this book were drawn from papers presented at the 2014 conference (by Iftikhar Dadi, Patrick Flores, Boris Groys, Vivian Li, Tara McDowell, Alexandra Munroe, Nada Shabout, Terry Smith, and Ming Tiampo), while five were contributed by authors who enthusiastically responded to our invitation to write chapters at a later juncture (Hal Foster, Atreyee Gupta, Elizabeth Harney, Jennifer Josten, and Jenni Sorkin). However, even though the editorial decisions that shaped the book were made together, Enwezor was no longer present at the time of this book's completion. *Postwar Revisited* then also conveys an unbearable intimacy with Enwezor's absence.

The Editors—these were the words with which Enwezor and I signed off an early draft of the introduction to this book on October 29, 2017. That introduction had taken a long time to craft; I would put together a draft, which Enwezor would edit and add to in between his incessant travels and numerous exhibitions. It is here that Enwezor's absence is also most palpable to me because the introduction, as it now stands, bears no resemblance to the one that we wrote together. This is because the present text of the introduction was rewritten in its entirety in response to generative feedback we received from the anonymous reviewers of the manuscript. I began writing the introduction in late 2018 in conversation with Enwezor at a time when he himself could no longer engage in sustained writing; I completed it long after his passing.

The words in the introduction are all mine. Nonetheless, the thrust of the argument grew out of the discussions that we had about this book between 2014 and 2019, and, by way of inserting Enwezor's voice without ventriloquizing, I have consistently tried to draw on his ideas as they are stated in his own writings. We had no substantial difference in opinion regarding the primary themes, but if anything, the text is now more invested in tracing an art historical genealogy for the postwar era than Enwezor perhaps had in mind. This is because I find it impossible to remove my historian's hat; Enwezor had the poetic imagination, the political will, and the intellectual acumen to transform the allegedly known and the proverbially familiar into something astonishing and revelatory in a matter of a few bold gestures, as I discovered in the process of writing with him collaboratively. For this reason, completing this book after his death has involved the agonizing realization that we will never know how he would have ultimately shaped it. And no words can compensate for this fact.

Many others played an important role in the making of this book. This book would have never seen the light of day if not for Ken Wissoker at

Duke University Press, who greeted the project with enthusiasm when we first brought the idea to him in 2017 and whose support was even more crucial after Enwezor's passing. Also crucial was Chika Okeke-Agulu's support in his role as the executor of Enwezor's intellectual property. Equally crucial are the color illustrations without which this book would have been visually impoverished; these were made possible through Alexandra Munroe and Jane DeBevoise's unstinting generosity. Institutional homes are essential, and mine has been the History of Art Department at the University of California, Berkeley, for most of this book's making. I am tremendously grateful for the intellectual comradery of my colleagues as well as history of art graduate students.

This book is with Okwui, this book is for Okwui.

Atreyee Gupta
June 20, 2024
Berkeley, California

NOTES

1. Knöfel, "Es ist eine Beleidigung, ja."
2. For the video documentation of the conference, see Haus der Kunst, "Postwar—Art between the Pacific and Atlantic, 1945–1965," accessed September 1, 2022, http://postwar-conference.hausderkunst.de.
3. See curator's acknowledgments in Enwezor, Siegel, and Wilmes, *Postwar*, 17.
4. See Knöfel, "Es ist eine Beleidigung, ja."
5. Enwezor, "Postcolonial Constellation," 57–82.
6. Enwezor, "Postcolonial Constellation," 77.
7. Enwezor, "Postcolonial Constellation," 59.
8. Enwezor, "Postcolonial Constellation," 59.
9. Enwezor, "Postcolonial Constellation," 77.
10. Enwezor, "Postcolonial Constellation," 59.
11. See Fanon, *Wretched of the Earth*, chap. 1.

Introduction

ATREYEE GUPTA

I am not burying myself in a narrow particularism. But neither do I want to lose myself in an emaciated universalism. There are two ways to lose oneself: walled segregation in the particular or dilution in the "universal." My conception of the universal is that of a universal enriched by all that is particular, a universal enriched by every particular: the deepening and coexistence of all particulars.—AIMÉ CÉSAIRE, "Letter to Maurice Thorez," October 24, 1956

The term *postwar* in the book's title refers to the first two decades that followed the conclusion of the Second World War, a period that, in Okwui Enwezor's words, "inspired a profound reflection on how to assimilate the lessons of the war and the invidious statecraft of colonialism, while also recognizing, without equivocation, the quest of the colonized for the end of colonial empires and imperial dominions."[1] As such, the historical period under consideration is bookended by the conclusion of the Second World War and the emergence and consolidation of a tripartite world order in the backdrop of the Cold War in the first half of the 1960s. At the same time, the conception of the book remains embedded within the present, a time when old empires have been replaced by new ones. Relentless processes of globalization cohabit today with equally global calls to tighten borders and render national cultures distinct, mitigate freedom of speech and action with circumspect censorship, and re-inscribe otherness onto bodies that are unlike and therefore deemed expendable.[2] If the repeated comparison of numerous contemporary political leaders to Adolf Hitler and the global return of fascism in a multitude of guises is a sign, then we have traveled the full circle.[3] This book is a return of a very different kind. Standing in an embattled present, a time that provokes a keen despair in many of us, but one to which we must not succumb, the book returns, with great urgency, to postwar as a historical period when the end of the Second World War and the eclipse of colonial empires precipitated efforts to reimagine the world in a future tense.

It is worth highlighting, at the very onset, that *Postwar Revisited: A Global Art History* does not seek to cast this historical period only in terms of an aftermath of war. Neither does the period between 1945 and 1965 figure here as a time of peace, precarious or otherwise;[4] nor does the book seek to resuscitate the story of the proverbial battle between abstraction and realism.[5] The collective will and cultural energies of decolonization that manifested in this period to shape something like a political aesthetic do not allow for such recursive gestures. Moreover, not only were the experiences and aspirations of artists in Axis nations and Axis-occupied territories and those in the Allied contexts distinct, but the connotation of the Second World War shifted in contexts of colonial recruitment. Likewise, the postwar decades signified something rather different in countries that had remained neutral in the Second World War and in Europe's peripheries. Given this dissonance, it necessarily follows that the story of the two decades after the conclusion of the Second World War must be sketched onto an expansive multimodal canvas if we are to confront the globality of the postwar years as a historical period. Ultimately, accounting for the vastly different territories of practice and politics within which artistic cultures unfolded produces an understanding of postwar as a collective horizon onto which new ideals of humanism, emancipation, and decolonization were projected.

As a discipline, art history has been primarily concerned with objects and artifacts produced through human labor, centralizing, in turn, the figure of the human—the human creator—as the principal protagonist of the story. To grasp postwar as a collective global horizon, it is then also essential to enter the postwar decades by way of the cultural and philosophical debates on humanism that the period engendered. In this regard, the argument between Jean-Paul Sartre, who posited his own take on existentialism as a form of postwar humanism, and Martin Heidegger is well known.[6] As is Theodor Adorno's condemnation of the traditions of post-Enlightenment humanism internal to his initial description of the act of writing poetry after Auschwitz as a form of "barbarism," which he subsequently qualified in relation to lyric poetry.[7] Reflecting on the origins of totalitarianism, Hannah Arendt, for her part, discerned that the convergences between the ideology of race and its management were "actually made on the Dark Continent. Race was the emergency explanation of human beings whom no European or civilized man could understand and whose humanity so frightened and humiliated the [European] immigrants."[8] Cosmopolitans of color such as Aimé Césaire, W. E. B. Du Bois, C. L. R. James, Mulk Raj Anand, and George Padmore also recognized Nazism and fascism not as an exception to but as part and parcel of the legacy of colonialism authorized by post-Enlightenment civilizational discourses. Writing from Paris in 1950, Césaire would thus insist that Europe "is morally, spiritually indefensible. And today the indictment is brought against it not by the European masses alone, but on a world scale, by tens of millions of men, who, from the depths of slavery, set themselves up as judge."[9]

Césaire's *Discourse on Colonialism*, we may recollect, was written shortly after the United Nations General Assembly adopted the Universal Declaration of Human Rights in 1948—the same year that W. E. B. Du Bois was dropped from the United States' delegation to the United Nations because he rejected an outline for a global government in which a substantial part of the world had neither agency nor rights.[10] Yet what Césaire proposed in *Discourse on Colonialism* was not tantamount to a wholesale rejection of the ideal of human rights as articulated in the Universal Declaration of 1948. Rather, for Césaire and others, the conclusion of the Second World War presented the very condition of possibility for the emergence of a significantly more profound humanism that they believed only decolonization could fully materialize. The figure of the human was inseparable from these deliberations, as a protracted traction between the abstract figure of a (European) universalism and the seeming provincialism of a (non-European) particularity remained implicit in postwar political and intellectual arrangements. As Césaire wrote by way of a response in 1956: "I am not burying myself in a narrow particularism. But neither do I want to lose myself in an emaciated universalism. There are two ways to lose oneself: walled segregation in the particular or dilution in the 'universal.' My conception of the universal is that of a universal enriched by all that is particular, a universal enriched by every particular: the deepening and coexistence of all particulars."[11] It is with these deliberations in mind that the book returns to the vexed question of the postwar in/and global art history.

Postwar in/and Global Art History

The year 1945 had long prefigured in art history as a rupture, an ostensible break with the art of the past and the beginning of new modes of experimentation temporally and conceptually welded to the aftermath of the Second World War.[12] Marked out as early as 1958 in the edited volume *Neue Kunst nach 1945*, the first survey text on the postwar art of Europe and the United States, the idea of 1945 as a pivot in the trajectory of twentieth-century art was further concretized the very next year, during the second iteration of Documenta in Kassel, Germany, when curator Arnold Bode chose *Kunst nach 1945* as the exhibition's theme and subtitle.[13] Arguably, if the curatorial emphasis in the 1959 Documenta programmatically centralized postwar abstraction, the 1958 book edited by the influential German modernist art historian Will Grohmann made an analogous discursive move by conjoining an ideation of newness—*neue*—to art since 1945.[14] Indeed, most European and North American art historians and critics of the time conceded that there was something radically new about postwar as an art historical period. And, as Amelia Jones has noted, by the end of the 1970s, taking the postwar decades as significant in marking a key point in North Atlantic history, art history departments in Britain and North America also began to explore the possibility of teaching courses on art made after 1945.[15] Over the subsequent decades, "since 1945" came to be institutionally embedded within art history as a discrete epoch.[16] Although subsequent critics debated the extent to which the art of this period retained contiguities with the one that had preceded it, postwar's historical specificity as an epoch in art and history was never a point of contention.[17]

What was also not a point of contention was the period's geocultural delineation. Deliberations about postwar art both began and ended in the North Atlantic worlds—in other words, worlds shaped by the North Atlantic Alliance. As Terry Smith has observed, this would change only in the late 1980s, with the arrival of another discrete cultural field, called contemporary art, after modernism's formal energies were seemingly evacuated in the North Atlantic worlds and under pressure from neoliberal economies and globalization.[18] As art worlds expanded exponentially with the creation of international contemporary art biennials in formerly peripheral locations such as Havana, Gwangju, and Dakar, they also rendered distant places proximate.[19] Established geocultural frames of reference mutated in the face of rapid economic, political, and cultural globalization as artists, curators, and scholars both uncovered new convergences and divergences and excavated traces of historical flows and exchanges. "Where in the past such critical tools or paradigms as 'neo-avant-garde' or 'postmodernism' could illuminate or explain substantial aspects of Western contemporary art, now they clearly have little critical purchase in the crowded—and, one might add, resplendent—space that has become global contemporary art," wrote Chika Okeke-Agulu in response to the 2009 "Questionnaire on 'The Contemporary'" circulated by the editors of *October*.[20]

Paradoxically, it is precisely at this juncture of neoliberal globalization and disciplinary expansion that another art historical rift surfaced, one that marked the global out as the exemplary realm of ultimate alterity. Two distinct strands shaped this discursive delegation. Squarely appending the global to neoliberal globalization, the first strand demarcated contemporary art—defined within this discursive matrix as art produced in the age of post-1989 globalization—as the only proper domain of global art.[21] Hans Belting, for instance, affirmed that "global art" had "emerged, like a phoenix from the ashes, from modern art. . . . It is by definition contemporary." Global contemporary art, Belting also noted, "differs from modernity whose self-appointed universalism was based on a hegemonial notion of art."[22] However nuanced in its attention to the uneven cartography of twentieth-century art, such a positioning of the global nonetheless relegated modernism to North Atlantic frontiers, delegitimizing, in the process, postwar modernism's multimodal habitations, manifestations, and *créolité*. The unintended effect was the unconditional reinscription of a center/periphery model that once again posited Europe as the originating locus of modernism, the center from which modernism as an aesthetic discourse was transmitted to the rest of the world, traveling slowly, arriving late, almost inevitably marked by a temporal lag, a delay, and a certain belatedness that had allegedly been upended only in the post-1989 arena of global contemporary art. Is the post-1989 globalization then the only cipher for comprehending the global in art history? Arguably not.

The second discursive strand took seriously the countermodels through which the displaced—those formerly placed on the margins of European modernity—entered modernism by producing experimental cultures that engaged long histories of imperialism, colonialism, enslavement, and indenture. Many art history departments in North America and Western Europe did precisely this by instituting new faculty positions and initiating programs with a designated emphasis on artistic and cultural modernisms outside of North Atlantic traditions.[23] For the North Atlantic strands of art history, the "global turn" registered as something like a punctum signaling a crisis within the discipline itself.[24] University curricula changed and new readers appeared to address the discipline's expansion beyond Westernist frontiers; in some instances, new faculty lines for Global Modern Art or Global Modernism were also created.[25]

Art history was finally alert to the demands of the formerly marginalized. Or so it appeared. But, ironically, this progressive move was weighed down by a Westernist conceptual hubris that seamlessly supplanted the "non-West," an older and much beleaguered descriptor, with the "global." In effect, this otherwise self-reflexive effort yet again ended up compacting "Western modernism" into a self-referential contained category, with "global modernisms" as its privileged mode of counternarration. By now ingrained within everyday forms of thought and expression, this conceptual collocation of the "global" and the "non-Western" seems to have acquired the fixity of common sense.[26] Was the North Atlantic modern *not* global? Is the global within the modern necessarily only a sign of alterity, of otherness, the *non*? Then what, the discerning reader will no doubt ask, is at stake in returning to *postwar* as a means of constructing a *global art history*?

If the second discursive strand outlined above reparatively marks non-Western modernisms as the proper domain of the global via delimitating geocultural binaries, the first positions post-1989 economic globalization as the sole arbitrator in the production of a global contemporary, disarticulating, with equal alacrity, the much longer ontology of the global already prefigured in the postwar decades. The resultant conceptual opacity is what underwrites with urgency the project of returning to the end of the Second World War to write a global art history. The global political processes of the postwar years had a profound impact on "art since 1945," the authors in this book collectively show, as artists across the world grappled not only with aesthetic and formal issues of artistic creation but also with debates on conformity or individualism, subjectivity or collectivity, and localism or internationalism in art. Dissimilarities abound, but what is important to underscore is the coproduction of the global that made the postwar decades distinctive from the post-1989 economic globalization, as economic and political histories have already shown.[27] We must begin again.

The Global in the Time of Postwar

When the word *globalization* entered general dictionaries around 1961, it did not carry the connotation of an integrated global economic market but signaled the emerging consciousness of an expansive, and interdependent, social whole, as economic historians have shown.[28] Writing in 1958 from New York, Arendt may have already sensed a thickening of worldly cultural interdependence when she described the emergence of an incipient postwar society "whose members at the most distant points of the globe need less time to meet than the members of a nation a generation ago."[29] Just four years later, in his visionary early work on postwar media technologies, the social theorist Marshall McLuhan predicted the future of the world as a global village, a unitary social structure connected by the electric synapses of media technology and inhabited by the typographic man.[30] McLuhan's prophetic vision for the future is eerily close to the digital present that we now inhabit, although the liberatory potentialities of cyborg life have not manifested in the time of late capitalism in quite the same way as the Canadian social theorist predicted. Arendt, in contrast, was not fundamentally invested in technology as the harbinger of a new human society. Rather, she had come to understand the most crucial Western developments of modern times, such as the rise of capitalism, imperialism, and totalitarianism, as paradigms that were fundamentally global.[31]

No doubt the political internationalism of the postwar decades left an impression on such global cultural imaginaries. If McLuhan and Arendt intuited the cultural contours of the postwar era beyond the strictures of West/non-West and center/periphery models, the intersecting histories of the United Nations and the Bandung conference of 1955 were yet another arena where the international dimension of postwar interdependence was amplified during the Cold War. Recollect that although the United Nations was formally established in 1945, the United States, the Soviet Union, China, Great Britain, and twenty allied nations signed the Declaration of the United Nations in 1942, well before the end of the war.[32] Plans for instituting the World Bank and the International Monetary Fund were also initiated at the invitation of the United States in 1944.[33] However, the systems of international governance that the United Nations inaugurated were not yet available to close to half of the colonies and former colonies, whose leaders gathered in Bandung, Indonesia, on April 24, 1955, to lay the foundation for the principle of nonalignment and to speak about postwar international relations, sovereignty, universal human rights, and development from the perspective of the still marginalized.

Collectively, the Bandung contingent represented more than one-third of the world's population; "this was a meeting of almost all of the human race living in the main geopolitical center of gravity of the earth," in cultural critic and civil rights activist Richard Wright's words.[34] Their verdict, as documented in the "final communiqué," was unambiguous: "The Asian-African Conference having considered the dangerous situation of international tension existing and the risks confronting the whole human race from the outbreak of *global* war in which the destructive power of all types of armaments, including nuclear and thermo-nuclear weapons, would be employed, invited the attention of all nations to the terrible consequences that would follow if such a war were to break out."[35] Explicitly, the communiqué interjected in debates unfolding in the United Nations. Implicitly, the conversations at Bandung centered on "the question of whether or how a global conversation of humanity could genuinely acknowledge cultural diversity without distributing such diversity over a hierarchical scale of civilization—that is to say, an urge toward cross-cultural dialogue without the baggage of imperialism," as historian Dipesh Chakrabarty has pointed out.[36] Both the Bandung conference of 1955 and the Non-Aligned Movement that it helped initiate in 1961 were replete with internal tensions.[37] Yet the political multilateralism launched at Bandung nonetheless rendered a deep fissure in the monopoly of Westernism, not just over the definition of the global but also in the discursive delineation of postwar humanism, as Wright was quick to discern in 1955.[38] It was a claim to the global that served as the ground from which to resist the epistemological violence of Westernism; it is also within this discursive and political matrix of the global that the idea of an intellectual Third World accrued definition as part and parcel of the processes of decolonization in the postwar world. The contending political and geocultural imaginations that emerged during the postwar decades through the intersecting histories of the United Nations and the Bandung conference of 1955 then unsettle any sedimentary conception of the global as either the exclusive domain of the non-Western modern or entirely buoyed by post-1989 economic globalization.

Proceeding with an image of postwar as a collective conceptual horizon within which a global was coproduced, this book takes up the task of remapping the postwar decades from within the field of art history. Mappings, of course, have always subtended art history's disciplinary unconscious, and we would do well to recollect cultural geographers Steve Pile and Nigel Thrift's words: "Maps are not empty mirrors, they at once hide and reveal the hand of the cartographer. Maps are fleshly: of the body and of the mind of the individuals that produce them, they draw the eye of the map-reader."[39] Even before the birth of art history as a discipline, maps legitimized the operation of power and allocated meaning within boundaries. And, in twentieth-century art history, maps separated proverbial metropolitan centers from alleged provincial peripheries, assigning artistic value on a hierarchical sliding scale of imagined civilizational fullness or lack. A project of critical remapping must then trace against this grain, with and through differences, dialectically projecting contiguities and disjunctures onto the very contours of the globe simultaneously. This book is concerned with such a remapping—within the practical compunctions of an edited volume—of postwar art history.

The Book

The past two decades have seen a tectonic shift in scholarly approaches to art produced in the second half of the twentieth century. A complex picture of postwar American art has emerged in the aftermath of scholarly initiatives to read into the formal aspects of abstraction, minimalism, and conceptual art multivalent dimensions of artistic labor and civil rights struggles in the United States during the turbulent 1960s.[40] Seeking to provincialize Europe from within, scholars of European art, too, have both situated modernism at the intersection of metropolitan and colonial projects and brought into sharper focus precarious intersections between postwar political and aesthetic economies.[41] In tandem, new art historical scholarship on Asia, Africa, South America, and the Middle East has discursively stretched the field of postwar art far beyond its older, Westernist limits.[42] The deep-rooted heterogeneities that structure the global field of modernism have been substantially foregrounded with these transformations. Now, taking up the expansive possibilities offered by the framework of an edited volume and proceeding from the premise that postwar modernism was a worldwide, albeit heterogenous, phenomenon, this book undertakes a second and equally pressing intellectual work of *localizing* postwar—that is, the years between 1945 and 1965—through sketching out a series of encounters across an uneven *global* terrain by way of punctuating recursive histories with declarative disjunctures. The hope is that the attendant ruptures that materialize in the pages of this book will provoke new ways of thinking, engaging, and narrating a global art history of postwar.[43]

The trajectories of such a project are necessarily replete with material and conceptual conundrums. On the one hand, there exist a range of postwar artistic practices in the former peripheries but limited critical history for these even in the present. It necessarily follows that the relationship to the intellectual and artistic gambits of the postwar period remains messy, incomplete, and unresolved, perhaps more in some parts of the world than others. The historical reality of artistic processes and their attendant archives in diverse parts of the globe then still require close analytic attention. As literary historians Laura Doyle and Laura Winkiel have succinctly put it: "So much depends on which modernism, written when and why and from what place—which city, which hillside, which seat on the train, which new nation or colony, and before, after, or during which war."[44] On the other hand, a critical inquiry aligned along strict geographic or regional demarcations—Asia, Africa, America, Australia, and so on, or even studies of specific urban cultural ecologies of particular cities—cannot bring to the surface similarities and differences, elective affiliations and innate affinities, and singularities and serialities that dialogically unfolded along the axis of a global cross-hatching.

Among other possibilities, Enwezor and I considered recovering dialogic cross-hatchings by comparatively approaching clusters of themes, artistic movements, concepts, and terminologies that were well established within postwar Anglophone art history's critical vocabulary but accrued dissonant densities when mobilized outside it. Revisionist motives notwithstanding, such a comparative approach might have performed a codifying function at its best; at its worst, this could have served to recentralize Europe as the model for all histories once again. Both fell far short of the critical discursive work that we felt this book needed to perform. At the same time, the global artistic movements under scrutiny here not only flummoxed conventional geographic demarcations but also proved to be substantially more malleable than conventional art historical wisdom would have it. In the end, we opted to divide the book into four broad geocultural clusters that position postwar art within intersecting domains of practice and affiliations, both national and transnational, by way of holding together the many vital particularities that vividly contoured imaginations of postwar's globality in the years between 1945 and 1965.

The first cluster—"Europe in Transition"—traces political and cultural transformations in Europe, lingering in particular on fractures that render obsolete any sedimented notion of centers or peripheries as well as universalisms or particularisms. In the opening chapter, Hal Foster proposes we read the monstrous figures of Cobra—the collective whose name derived from the first letters of Copenhagen, Brussels, and Amsterdam, where the group's founding members lived—as creatures spawned by a crisis that rendered a deep fissure within Europe itself. Ming Tiampo's discussion on artists from Asia and Africa in the Slade School of Fine Art, in London, settles the proverbial peripheries at the very heart of metropolitan Europe. Here, the place of enunciation—Europe—matters as much as that which is enunciated, and we find that this sense of place hovers between belonging and dispersal.

The second cluster—"The Soviet Bloc and Communist China"—shifts between local complexities and global arrangements that unfolded across socialist and communist worlds. The symbolic economy of Soviet culture, Boris Groys writes, substantially shaped all forms of artistic practice, state supported and dissident, in the USSR. Consequently, movements such as Moscow conceptualism, too, must be situated within this matrix, compounding assumed distinctions between realism and conceptualism, Groys argues. We are still far more attuned to the abstraction/realism dialogic in postwar art as it transpired in the United States and the USSR. The recalcitrant trajectories of postwar China, however, open up a substantially different configuration of representation and politics in Vivian Li's focused discussion of the *Rent Collection Courtyard*. The instability of art historical categories also receives sharp emphasis in the *Rent Collection Courtyard*—the "atomic bomb of the art world"—as Li maps the art of postrevolutionary China onto the postwar axis, on which this artistic trajectory has largely remained absent. Collectively, the juxtaposition of discrepant local histories of socialism and communism alters the scale of analysis, bringing to the surface a shifting web of global relations, both representational and otherwise. Reading regional and transregional scales of geopolitics into art then offers one way to confront the multiscalar nature of the postwar global.

The focus of the next cluster—"Pacific Passages, Atlantic Oscillations"—is the parenthetical area of the bodies of water, the Pacific and Atlantic Oceans, through which an art historical passage from north to south and east to west becomes conceivable. Spanning East Asia, Southeast Asia, and the Americas, the chapters in this cluster traverse a vast cultural geography. Collectively, they foreground postwar's Pacific theaters as it stretched from Japan (Alexandra Munroe) to the US West Coast (Tara McDowell) and from the Philippines (Patrick Flores) to Australasia (Terry Smith). Connecting Europe to North America and North America to South America and Latin America (Jenni Sorkin and Jennifer Josten), chapters in this cluster also highlight cultural oscillations that emerged in the Atlantic through the circulation of objects, ideas, and people. Thus "Pacific Passages, Atlantic Oscillations" situates artistic practices within continuums and interregnums among prewar arrangements and postwar cultural networks. To be sure, the transatlantic movement of artists before and during the Second World War has received scholarly attention; we need only to recollect the primacy given to the migration of Bauhaus artists and architects to the United States in histories of European and North American art. The chapters gathered here, in contrast, significantly complicate "the traditional circuitry of the transatlantic movement of prewar ideas," to use Sorkin's words, embedding, in turn, cultural practices within the intricate web of political and socioeconomic forces that impelled them. To this end, the authors in this section take up different postwar motifs of trauma and transcendence, religious beliefs and political theologies, discrepant traditionalisms and processes of modernization, and Indigenous artistic productions and their appropriations. "The entire array of these interacting forces needs to be taken into account, and their relativities plotted," Smith writes, "if we are to develop an art historical approach that, while acknowledging the historical impact of the Westernist model, supersedes it."

The changes wrought by transitions to new forms of national institutions and new domains of living and belonging define the fourth cluster, "Decolonizing Constellations," which focuses broadly on Asia (Atreyee Gupta), Africa (Elizabeth Harney), and the Middle East (Iftikhar Dadi and Nada Shabout). Here, representation does not simply signal forms of creative practice but quite literally becomes the name for a political awareness of identity that compenetrates the formal field of representation. As a framework for analysis, the national then had a very specific resilience in decolonizing contexts. Yet artistic and intellectual projects "retained critical affiliations and differences from metropolitan modernisms that were not merely local or national but gestured toward imagining broader regional concerns that were aesthetic, as well as social and political," as Dadi writes. Attached to these are ideas of a postwar decolonized modernity that is bound up with notions of modernization, development, and progress, as Gupta shows. "Decolonizing Constellations" then prompts us to, in Gupta's words, "read the postwar archive against its grain, not only to open it up to plural desires but also to confront the art historical epistemic ruptures that such a reading necessarily engenders."

Individual chapters within the book's four sections address postwar from a single locale or through case studies. But the reader will discover that this address finds dynamic and often unpredictable equivalents in other chapters, in other locales, and in other practices. Vibrant political and artistic intersections fundamentally undergirded the years under consideration. But these remain invisible unless postwar is confronted as a global epoch. Take, for example, the intersecting histories of race, gender, representation, and the atomic. In art history, the question of race has rarely transected the question of the atomic. Yet race had always been internal to the atomic: in the atomic cities of the Manhattan Project, it was the question of race that presented the most complex challenges, not only undermining the military economy of obedience and efficiency but also threatening to subvert the very goal of weapon production, as Peter B. Hales has shown elsewhere.[45] Furthermore, in Munroe's chapter, the atomic accrues a different density as the author reads the postwar production of a "pacified, effeminized, and contemplative Japan" alongside the phenomenon of the radioactive monster Godzilla awakened from the depths of the ocean. It is as if the liberal humanist symbolic universe has met its absolute other, not just in the monstrous colored body redolent with atomic energy but also in the conflation of the racialized defeated body with effeminacy. The racialized effeminized body then layers Sorkin's reading of the feminist labor of weaving in Anni Albers's and Sheila Hicks's artistic practices by superimposing race and gender as intersecting categories of art historical analysis. Other points of global intersections are presented by institutions such as the Slade School of Fine Art, in London, which serves as the unpredictable, but critical, backdrop for scenes of decolonization for Dadi, Shabout, and Tiampo. These, of course, are only a few points of transversal reading that surface in this anthology; the reader will no doubt discover many others. Indeed, the editors hope that the material, conceptual, and methodological conjunctions and disjunctures a book such as this brings into view will open up horizons for future research, in turn inflecting the postwar global—"a universal enriched by every particular," as Césaire would have it—that we have inherited and continue to inhabit.[46]

NOTES

Epigraph: Césaire, "Letter to Maurice Thorez," 152.

1. Okwui Enwezor, foreword to Enwezor, Siegel, and Wilmes, *Postwar*, 13.

2. Donald Trump's presidency in the United States, the Brexit referendum in the United Kingdom, the growing popularity of the Patriotic Europeans Against the Islamization of the Occident (Pegida) in Germany, and the right-wing Bharatiya Janata Party's spectacular electoral victories in India are only symptomatic of the global rise of exclusionist nationalisms.

3. For an extended discussion on this analogy, see Snyder, *Road to Unfreedom*; and Banaji, *Fascism*. Some examples of news articles that explore this theme include Applebaum, "Warning from Europe"; Browning, "Suffocation of Democracy"; and Ross, "Frankfurt School."

4. Interpreting the *post* of *postwar* literally, art historians have often read the decades after the conclusion of the Second World War as a time of peace after war. As Hannah Feldman writes: "Whereas the field of modern European art history circumscribes these decades as being 'post-war,' their reality was anything but, especially in France. Indeed, it was during these decades that France fought the longest wars of the twentieth century, wars that were, not coincidentally . . . intended to preserve a dwindling colonial empire." Feldman, *From a Nation Torn*, 1–2.

5. For this history, see Guilbaut, *How New York Stole the Idea of Modern Art*.

6. See Sartre, *Essays in Existentialism*; and Heidegger, "Letter on Humanism."

7. Theodor Adorno, who spent the war years in Los Angeles, wrote: "Even the most extreme consciousness of doom threatens to degenerate into idle chatter. Cultural criticism finds itself faced with the final stage of the dialectic of culture and barbarism. To write poetry after Auschwitz is barbaric. And this corrodes even the knowledge of why it has become impossible to write poetry today. Absolute reification, which presupposed intellectual progress as one of its elements, is now preparing to absorb the mind entirely. Critical intelligence cannot be equal to this challenge as long as it confines itself to self-satisfied contemplation." Adorno, *Prisms*, 34. For the qualification in relation to lyric poetry, see Adorno, "From 'Commitment,'" 71–72.

8. Arendt, *Origins of Totalitarianism*, 185.

9. Césaire, *Discourse on Colonialism*, 32.

10. See Lewis, *W. E. B. Du Bois*.

11. Césaire, "Letter to Maurice Thorez," 152.

12. See Belting, *Art History after Modernism*, 37–53.

13. See *Documenta '59*.

14. See Grohmann, *Neue Kunst nach 1945*. The book was translated and published simultaneously in Britain, France, and the United States. For the US edition, see Grohmann, *Art since 1945*.

15. See Jones, "Writing Contemporary Art," 3–16.

16. For a retrospective assessment of this history, see Siegel, *Since '45*; Meyer, *What Was Contemporary Art?*; and Blocker, *Becoming Past*.

17. Precipitated by the 1974 publication of Peter Burger's *Theory of the Avant-Garde*, the debate centered around the question of the avant-garde and the neo-avant-garde. See Burger, *Theory of the Avant-Garde*; Buchloh, "Theorizing the Avant-Garde"; Krauss, *Originality of the Avant-Garde*; and Foster, "What's Neo about the Neo-Avant-Garde?"

18. "This shift," Terry Smith writes, "has been occurring since the decline of modernism in the 1980s and has appeared in institutional naming—of galleries, museums, auction house departments, academic courses, and textbook titles—which, however, tend to use contemporary as a soft signifier of current plurality." T. Smith, *What Is Contemporary Art?*, 701.

19. See Enwezor, "Mega-exhibitions and the Antinomies of a Transnational Global Form."

20. Okeke-Agulu, "Questionnaire on 'The Contemporary,'" 45. This questionnaire was specifically framed for scholars and curators working in Europe and North America, a fact that led the Asia Art Archive, one of the most prominent nonprofit research entities in the field of modern and contemporary art of Asia, to circulate a questionnaire to art historians, critics, and curators from South, Southeast, and East Asia. See "The And: An Expanded Questionnaire on The Contemporary." The questions, however, have persisted, and since then, several similar questionnaires on the idea of the global have been published. See, e.g., Joyeux-Prunel, "Art History and the Global Challenge."

21. See, e.g., Stallabrass, *Art Incorporated*; Harris, *Global Contemporary Art World*; and Zarobell, *Art and the Global Economy*.

22. Belting, "Contemporary Art as Global Art."

23. See Jones and Nelson, "Global Turns in US Art History." Notably, the critical and intellectual unfolding of the global described in this introduction is specific to art history. In the domain of literary studies, the trajectory has unfolded differently. See Wollaeger, introduction to Wollaeger and Eatough, *Oxford Handbook of Global Modernisms*.

24. As Aruna D'Souza noted in her introduction to an edited volume published in conjunction with the 2011 conference at the Clark Art Institute "In the Wake of the Global Turn": "For art historians and art history departments in North America, there seems a particular urgency to 'deal with' the reality that the twenty-first-century world seems much bigger than the one our discipline has imagined for itself since its formation in European universities at the turn of the last century." D'Souza, introduction to D'Souza and Casid, *Art History in the Wake of the Global Turn*, viii. The perceived disciplinary "crisis" also led to the publication of several edited volumes on the subject, including Elkins, *Is Art*

History Global?; and Zijlmans and van Damme, *World Art Studies*. In the process, the term *global art history* became a subject of debate. For critical positions in this regard, see Davis, "World without Art"; Carroll, "Art and Globalization"; and Juneja, "Global Art History and the 'Burden of Representation.'" The perception of "crisis," however, was specific to a North Atlantic art history. For a perspective on the discipline from outside the North Atlantic context, see Gupta and Ray, "Is Art History Global?"

25. See Chiem and Colburn, "Global Foundations for a World Art History" and Nelson, "Map of Art History."

26. Consider, e.g., a review of the exhibition *The Progressive Revolution: Modern Art for a New India* at the Asia Society, New York, in September 2018. Writing in *Art in America*, critic Prajna Desai observed: "Yet even as the show provided an opportunity to reflect on the mirage of India's secular multiculturalism—ratified at Partition if discredited in later years—the presentation equated the works' aesthetic complexity with a diagnosis of national conditions. This thesis hewed to the common expectation in Euro-American contexts that global modern art histories are first and foremost narratives about nation and identity rather than formal propositions about the processes and practice of art, that they are always practice before theory." The substance of Desai's critique notwithstanding, the taken-for-granted sliding of "global modern art histories" into modernist practices outside of Euro-American contexts only highlights the place that the "global" has come to assume within "modern art histories." Desai, "Other Than Nation," 50.

27. Reflecting on globalization from the vantage point of 2014, Paul James and Manfred B. Steger write: "After a few tentative and disparate uses across the mid-twentieth century, it erupted in the 1990s with explosive energy in both public and academic discourses that sought to make sense of momentous social change." The post-1990s usage of the term, however, was quite distinct, for in the postwar decades, the term "did not mean the extension of economic relations across the globe, as Europe remained the focus," as James and Steger show. Contemporary globalization is a period "like no other in human history," Enwezor, too, had observed in 1997. James and Steger, "Genealogy of 'Globalization,'" 426; Enwezor, "Travel Notes," 12.

28. This point is discussed extensively in James and Steger, "Genealogy of 'Globalization.'"

29. Arendt, *Human Condition*, 257.

30. McLuhan, *Gutenberg Galaxy*, 31.

31. See Benhabib, *Reluctant Modernism*, 78.

32. See Hoopes and Brinkley, *FDR and the Creation of the U.N.*, 45.

33. See Steil, *Battle of Bretton Woods*.

34. Wright, *Color Curtain*, 12.

35. C. Lee, "Final Communiqué of the Asian African Conference," 100 (emphasis added). For a discussion on what the "global" signified for the Bandung contingent, see C. Lee, "At the Rendezvous of Decolonization."

36. Chakrabarty, "Legacies of Bandung," 75.

37. See Hongoh, "Asian-African Conference (Bandung)"; Prashad, *Darker Nations*; Westad, *Global Cold War*; and McMahon, *Cold War in the Third World*.

38. See Wright, *Color Curtain*.

39. Pile and Thrift, "Mapping the Subject," 48.

40. See, e.g., P. Lee, *Chronophobia*; Bryan-Wilson, *Art Workers*; and English, *1971*.

41. See, e.g., Feldman, *From a Nation Torn*; Mansoor, *Marshall Plan Modernism*; Medosch, *New Tendencies*; López, *Avant-garde Art and Criticism*; and Galimberti, *Individuals against Individualism*.

42. See, e.g., Harney, *In Senghor's Shadow*; Shabout, *Modern Arab Art*; Dadi, *Modernism and the Art of Muslim South Asia*; Tiampo, *Gutai*; Kee, *Contemporary Korean Art*; Okeke-Agulu, *Postcolonial Modernism*; Tomii, *Radicalism in the Wilderness*; and Bardaouil, *Surrealism in Egypt*.

43. This makes the present anthology both analogous to and dissonant from edited volumes such as *The Oxford Handbook of Global Modernisms* and *Geomodernisms: Race, Modernism, Modernity*, which remain grounded in the methods and methodologies of literary studies and include discussions on art and cinema only by way of intersections. Wollaeger and Eatough, *Oxford Handbook of Global Modernisms*; Doyle and Winkiel, *Geomodernisms*. Likewise, the temporal frame used in this volume makes it conceptually analogous to but materially distinct from the four groundbreaking anthologies exploring alternative modernisms that were published in the series Annotating Art's Histories: Cross-cultural Perspectives in the Visual Arts, edited by Kobena Mercer, which broadly examined the period from the nineteenth century to the mid-twentieth century. Another major intervention was *Antinomies of Art and Culture: Modernity, Postmodernity, Contemporaneity*, which took up the question of the contemporary. See Mercer, *Exiles, Diasporas and Strangers*; Mercer, *Pop Art and Vernacular Cultures*; Mercer, *Discrepant Abstraction*; Mercer, *Cosmopolitan Modernisms*; T. Smith, Enwezor, and Condee, *Antinomies of Art and Culture*.

44. Doyle and Winkiel, introduction to *Geomodernisms*, 1.

45. See Hales, *Atomic Spaces*.

46. Césaire, "Letter to Maurice Thorez," 152.

Part I

EUROPE IN TRANSITION

1

Creaturely Cobra

HAL FOSTER

In the aftermath of the Second World War, young artists in Copenhagen, Brussels, and Amsterdam began to insist, at first separately and then together, on the necessity of a new approach to the brutal conditions of the time. They did so under the name "Cobra," an abbreviation of the names of the three cities where they were based as well as a tribute to the snake they took up as an emblem. In Copenhagen a group of painters and sculptors had already formed around the magazine *Helhesten* (Hell horse), edited by the precocious Asger Jorn. Encouraged by the Copenhagen example, three young artists in Amsterdam—Constant Nieuwenhuys, Karel Appel, and Corneille—launched "the Experimental Group in Holland" in July 1948 with a magazine of their own called *Reflex*. Finally, in Brussels, where surrealism lingered as a force, writers directed the scene—especially Christian Dotremont, who would soon edit the eponymous magazine *Cobra*.

Jorn met Constant (who went by one name) in the fall of 1946 and contacted Dotremont the next summer; by late 1948 the three were able to forge a coalition, which was as fragile as it was intense, lasting little more than three years. Despite ample evidence of the Stalinist purges, the three refused to abandon communism, and they insisted on dialectical materialism as essential to artistic experiment. They were linked, too, in their opposition to both functionalist and formalist positions, with Jorn reacting against his early training in Paris under Fernand Léger and Le Corbusier, and Constant turning against his Dutch forebears in de Stijl. At the same time, Jorn and Constant wanted to depart from surrealism, aspects of which—a painterly automatism above all—they appropriated nonetheless. "By means of this irrational spontaneity," Jorn wrote in the first issue of *Cobra*, with this automatist technique in mind, "we get closer to the vital source of life."[1]

Does the aim of "the vital source of life" make Cobra another belated expressionism, one inflected by primitivism and surrealism, or is there a distinctive program to be extracted from its different practices, a Cobra idea? Its concerns with the art of tribal peoples, children, and the mentally ill (which the Nazis had declared "degenerate" only a decade before) are familiar from prewar avant-gardes. And its involvement with folk culture does not adequately specify Cobra either (Jorn, in particular, was fascinated by Nordic myths, Viking monuments, medieval frescoes, and rural churches). However, one attribute might distinguish it: its special penchant for the animal, or better, the creaturely. Such is the hypothesis I want to explore here.[2]

Consider *The Cry of Freedom* (1948) by Appel. As often occurs in his work, the painting presents a figure full in the canvas, barely contained by the cage of the frame, and made up of a patchwork of hot reds, yellows, oranges, and pinks relieved only by swatches of cool blues and greens. The schematic head, its simple features blocked out in flat black, confronts us directly; the asymmetrical arms are deformed and useless (they resemble stubby wings wrapped around the figure, which they fail to protect); and the creature is propped up on three spindly legs. Neither human nor animal nor bird, it is all three: a newfangled beast whose "cry of freedom" seems to announce a damaged past as much as a transformed future—as if the famous *Angelus Novus* (1920), produced by Paul Klee after the First World War, had been reborn, after the Second World War, as a mutant phoenix.[3]

Or consider *Erotic Moment* by Constant, a watercolor produced in 1949, the year of his polemic "It's Our Desire That Makes the Revolution," published in the fourth issue of *Cobra*. A lewd picture dominated by fecal browns, it seems to show two figures commingled sexually, in an eroticism that transforms discrete bodies into charged parts that are ecstatically exchanged. A wild-eyed creature raises its arms exultantly (one arm ends in a paw of three digits, the other begins as an obscene nose), while its partner, head thrown back, sticks a penile tongue into its mouth—even as this aggressive figure is also gendered female by the large vulva located at its center and the long wave of hair down its back. Although gender ambiguity is a staple in the work of Marcel Duchamp, Alberto Giacometti, and others, the force of this confusion is entirely different here: not a frustrated search for the lost object of sexual desire à la surrealism but an unbridled expression of revolutionary passion à la Cobra.

How to understand such figures? A first clue can be found in a 1948 manifesto by Constant, who frames the postwar situation, in dialectical terms, as a "total collapse" that might permit a "new freedom," as long as artists "find their way back to the first point of origin of creative activity."[4] In this regard Constant champions the usual "expressions from the untaught" (again, the familiar trio of the primitive, the child, and the insane) but then refers enigmatically to postwar man as "a creature," delivering this striking formula: "A painting is not a construction of colors and lines, but an animal, a night, a scream, a human being, or all of these."[5] Here Constant overturns the formalist formula of modernist painting presented sixty years earlier by Maurice Denis ("Remember that a painting—before it is a battle horse, a nude model, or some anecdote—is essentially a flat surface covered with colors assembled in a certain order") and intimates that the creaturely is a cipher of the confused aftermath of the war—of a "broken down" condition in which "limitations . . . are dissolved."[6] Jorn rises to the challenge: "We must portray ourselves as human beasts," he writes to Constant in 1950.[7]

In this light Cobra can be seen as an artistic intervention in the debate about humanism after the war, one that engaged the preeminent philosophers of the time, above all Jean-Paul Sartre, who insisted that his existentialism was a humanism, and Martin Heidegger, who dismissed both concepts as metaphysical.[8] For far too long, Heidegger argues, Western philosophy has defined the human in its difference from the animal (man possesses language, reason, and so on), and this "anthropological machine" has made the world all too human—that is, too subject to instrumental abuse. At the same time, Heidegger refuses any celebration of the animal as a counterterm; in a well-known formula he insists that whereas the stone is worldless and the animal is poor in world, the human alone is world-making. And elsewhere he charges Rainer Maria Rilke with the gross misunderstanding, expressed in his eighth Duino elegy, that animals are closer to Being than man is.[9] If Heidegger had known Cobra, he would have condemned it on the same grounds, for it, too, values the animal as more immediate to "the vital source of life": the untamed expression in *The Cry of Freedom*, the primal ecstasy in *Erotic Moment*, and the powerful symbol of the coiled cobra all proclaim as much.

Yet the becoming-animal of the human in Cobra is no simple recovery of a lost nature, for it also attests to the denaturalization produced by the Second World War and the Holocaust. Cobra creatures sometimes signify this irredeemable anguish, which is felt everywhere in Jorn. For example, *Wounded Beast II* (1951) is another misshapen bird from the Cobra menagerie, also painted full in the frame and pressed close to the picture plane. With a large head atop a little body, it appears in profile under a black sun, its whiskered beak haggard, its yellow eye crazed, its feathers limp like so many flaps of dead flesh. This is not the only painting in which Jorn turns the eagle, the emblem of state par excellence, into a terror-struck bird of prey; in this version, however, it is the world at large that appears wounded. Here Jorn answers the call for a painting as "an animal, a night, a scream, a human being, or all of these"; indeed, this definition (if anything so antiformal can be called a definition) speaks to his Cobra practice in general.

Jorn often frames his work of this period in an expressionist way—that is, as an attempt to reclaim a primal unity, both natural and communal, before psychic repression and social division. And in the conventional manner of the Freudo-Marxism of the time he associates this fall from unity with bourgeois class culture. Yet finally his Cobra painting is not expressionist—his gestures already suggest their own futility—and his philosophy, a patchwork creature of its own, is anything but conventional.[10]

The bad object of this philosophy is monolithic enough: "the classical tradition," by which Jorn means all European culture given over to Apollonian form (here he follows the familiar opposition laid down by Friedrich Nietzsche in *The Birth of Tragedy*). Yet his good objects are multiple: though Jorn sometimes calls it Dionysian rhythm, he is just as likely to associate it with primitive art or folk culture, Taoist philosophy or dialectical materialism, and so on. First and last, however, Jorn advocates any expression that advances materialist vitality over idealist fixity. In this regard he acts in the name of Scandinavian culture above all. In his view the Scandinavian is the great other to the classical, at once marginal to it and subversive of it; in particular he champions the pagan vernacular of the North in opposition to the official Christianity of the South, imported by the nobility. It is this commitment that drives not only his Cobra practice, both visual and textual, but also his project to reclaim the idea of the Nordic from its racist abuse by the Nazis. He envisioned this project to consist of twenty-eight volumes devoted to "10,000 Years of Nordic Art," only six of which were completed (and only one in his lifetime). It also involved his founding of the Scandinavian Institute of Comparative Vandalism; the vandal, especially the Viking, is his great anticlassical hero.[11]

It is this passionate anticlassicism that accounts for the apparent ugliness of his art, which Jorn pits, with great delight, against classical beauty. Already in a 1947 text titled "Apollo or Dionysus" Jorn proposes Dionysian rhythm as a counter to Apollonian form in such a way that the Apollonian is not only underwritten by the Dionysian but also undone by it—a line of thought that follows directly from Nietzsche, for whom Apollo is "the marvelous divine image of the *principium individuationis*" and Dionysus its "shattering." If "individuation is the root of all evil" for Nietzsche in *The Birth of Tragedy*, so too is it for Jorn.[12] This is evident not only in his philosophy—his critique of all bourgeois distinctions in society and culture and his advocacy of all collective forms of art—but also in his painting, where he often stages his own modernist deconstruction of figure and ground, the "principle of individuation" in image-making.

In fact, all his Cobra production is a concerted attack on classical aesthetics. Well before his situationist reworkings of found flea-market paintings, known as "modifications" and "disfigurations," Jorn practiced a programmatic deformation of the classical tableau, and he did so primarily through the creaturely. What I mean by *the classical tableau* is simple enough. "A well-composed tableau is a whole contained under a single point of view," Denis Diderot writes in his essay on composition for his *Encyclopédie* (1751–72), "in which the parts work together to one end, and form by their mutual correspondence a unity as real as that of the members of the body of an animal; so that a piece of painting made up of a large number of figures thrown at random on to the canvas, with neither proportion, intelligence nor unity, no more deserves to be called a *true composition* than scattered studies of legs, nose and eyes on the same cartoon deserve to called a *portrait* or even a *human figure*."[13] It is against this idealist model of the integrated painting (which, significantly here, turns on the analogy of "the body of an animal") that Jorn poses his materialist pictures of disruptive creatures.

Two points should be stressed right away. First, this critique is not about a lack of skill: schooled in composition under Léger, Jorn performs a calculated deskilling of the tableau, to which end he puts his own brand of painterly automatism. Like his Danish predecessors Egill Jacobsen and Richard Mortensen, Jorn releases color from drawing, and his liberated palette favors Nordic obscurity over Mediterranean clarity.[14] In general Jorn paints a sublunary world of nocturnal creatures, as seen in the 1951 work *The Moon and the Animals*; sometimes, too, as in *Wounded Beast II*, he places his formless figures under a cold sun. This is to advance another basic confusion, here of day and night, and another *détournement* of the classical, here of its (Apollonian) heliotropism. Second, this critique is not a nihilistic attack: Jorn launches it largely from within the tableau format, for only there can it be truly incisive. This is to say that as much as he challenges the tableau tradition, he is also invested in it: "The future is made through relinquishing or sacrificing the past," Jorn writes in "Peinture détournée" (Detourned painting; 1959). "I want to rejuvenate European culture. I begin with art. Our past is full of becoming. One needs only to crack open the shells."[15] In short, already at the moment of Cobra, his goal is *détournement*, not destruction. And yet this *détournement* is a thorough one, involving most of the classical criteria noted by Diderot: single point of view, pictorial integration, "true composition," and so on. It also targets most of the academic genres of traditional painting.

The creaturely disruption of the landscape genre is already announced—in composition, color, and title—in *Obtrusive Creatures Whose Right to Exist Is Proved by Their Existence* (1939–40), in which Jorn attempts to turn the idioms of Pablo Picasso and Joan Miró to his own ends. Yet this subversion is more radical, more original, a decade later in *Shameful Pastoral* (1952), where any ordering of space is undone by the amorphous animals that swarm through it. Various homunculi and monsters, most painted with the pink of human flesh and all given too many heads, legs, or wings, enact the "shameful pastoral" of the title in a way that indicates the final rotting of this classical ideal of rural life. Traditionally the pastoral designates a scene in which common folk serve as foils for elevated subjects, but here there is only a commingling of perverse hybrids.[16]

Jorn undoes the exalted genre of history painting from within, too, most directly in his *Historical Pictures* series (1949–50). He mocks the nobility of grand actions in titles such as *Nelson Orders the Bombardment of Copenhagen in 1807* and *Foreign Ambassador Presents a Jet Fighter to the Nation as a Gift*. These scenes derange the ideal figures of history painting as well: in *Nelson*, faces are plunged into bodies (which are topped by fanged mouths), while the protagonists of *Foreign Ambassador* evoke so many harpies. Although both paintings call to mind a monstrous crucifixion by Hieronymus Bosch reborn as an abstract expressionist, *Guernica* (1937) is the proximate precedent; yet the sense of history here is even more brutal than in Picasso, precisely because it lacks any redemptive pathos (the sense of humor is also scabrous). This is true, too, of *The Retreat at Dybbol, 1864*, a muddy mess of a painting in which the putative scene, the retreat of the Danish army during the Second War of Schleswig, is imaged as an animalistic regression. As the mad gazes of the creatures suggest, this dark world is given over to an atavistic fear, a primal paranoia of predator and prey. The *War Visions* series from the same years (again, 1949–50) is no less horrific. Like *Wounded Beast II*, *The Eagle's Share I* transforms this emblem of state, which cuts across the different ideologies of the mid-twentieth century, into a multiheaded dragon, all eyes, talons, and teeth.

In 1957 Jorn began *Stalingrad, No Man's Land or the Mad Laughter of Courage*, which he toiled over intermittently till 1972; at three by five meters, it is his largest painting. The title refers to an early turning point in the Second World War—the catastrophic battle of attrition waged between Nazi and Soviet forces outside Stalingrad—and the painting shows a scarred terrain of strokes and scribbles, in which the bright yellow and blue scribbles only highlight the icy white and black grounds. Here the horror of twentieth-century history has rendered history painting as such null and void, for *Stalingrad* is a world scored and scratched into illegibility, a painting pushed to the point where abstraction *is* destruction and vice versa.[17] And yet, paradoxically, it is in this very illegibility that *Stalingrad* succeeds precisely as a history painting—that is, as a credible document of historical experience, or rather, as a document of the withering away of such experience.[18] In a sense Jorn executes a double *détournement* here: on the one hand, history painting is both canceled and preserved; on the other hand, abstract expressionism is compelled to evoke the very history that it otherwise evades.[19]

Given the importance of the human figure to the classical tableau—which is also to say the importance of the implicit relation between the ideal composition of the painting and the ideal composure of the viewer—it is in this genre that Jorn does his greatest damage, and here again it comes largely through the creaturely. This is evident, for example, in *Space Woman* (1953), a grotesque female form that looms like a comic ghost, with multiple breasts topped by a misshapen head with yellow eyes. Our gaze is sluiced around the picture along with the paint in a Dionysian rhythm that roils any Apollonian form, and the figure is almost inchoate as a result. (The thing at her feet, also in yellow, suggests a withered offspring; Jorn often includes such homunculi, again as if to mock any "principle of individuation.") Even more creaturely is the figure in *You'll Never Get Me Alive* (1954), an amorphous monster with a huge maw that is barely contained by the frame. Here as elsewhere Jorn pushes proper form toward an obscene formlessness.[20]

It is not only through the *informe* of these creatures that Jorn undoes the academic genre of the figure; also subversive is the intensity of their gazes. This is programmatic in *Yellow Eyes* (1953), a swirl of acrid colors punctuated by the shrill organs of the title, but it also occurs in other beasts whose crazy look renders our aesthetic contemplation impossible. In Lacanian terms, it is as though these pictures were stripped of the protective "image-screen" of cultural representation as such, and so thrown open, via the creaturely, to the wild gaze of the world.[21] Such an effect is already intimated in *The Face of the Earth* (1948), where the exalted head, the paragon of form in traditional painting, the seat of pure vision and lofty intellection, becomes an inchoate ground where form is undone.

Finally, the creaturely in Jorn often calls up the foul. Some beasts are given generic names like "Troll" and "Brute," but he also invents mythical terms such as "Didaska," "Falbo," and "Aganak." In the eponymous series (1950–51), Aganak shape-shifts, appearing as a pig, tortoise, alligator, and beetle. That is, this creature suggests a lowly being of pollution, one subject to ritual prohibition. "Holiness requires that individuals shall conform to the class to which they belong," Mary Douglas writes in *Purity and Danger*, her classic text on the operations of taboo. "And holiness requires that different classes of things shall not be confused."[22] Such confusion abounds in Jorn, who seems to take Leviticus as a script for his creature-making. Taboo is reserved for things that frustrate classification, Douglas tell us, and she gives us pertinent examples: "Eels and worms inhabit water, though not as fish; reptiles go on dry land, though not as quadrupeds; some insects fly, though not as birds. There is no order in them. Recall what the prophecy of Habakkuk says of them: 'For those makest men like the fish of the sea, like crawling things that have no ruler.'"[23] In a sense Jorn carries this prophecy further with his mutant beings. For example, in *The Moon and the Animals*, the bird is semireptilian, with scales on its head, while the animal is semihuman, bipedal as it appears to be; in *Shameful Pastoral*, the human seems to combine with the animal and both with fish and/or vegetable—a violation of the most basic orders of all.

What animates Jorn to produce such creatures? Already toward the end of the war his paintings are dominated by creaturely masks, which he associates generally with tribal art. In order "to express psychic experiences in dramatic form," Jorn writes at this time, primitive artists "bring before the face a mask, which is wholly different from a face. A totally new creature comes into being, neither animal nor human."[24] At this point Jorn still refers such representations to "human psychic needs"; in other words, he sees them in existential, even ontological, terms. Yet his motives are more particular, more personal. "The folk tales and myths speak of monsters, fantastic animals and signs," Jorn writes in the 1950 letter to Constant mentioned above. "They are always symbols of people, of real phenomena." Certainly, the Cobra period was a time of great private stress for Jorn: in extreme poverty, he developed tuberculosis, which kept him in a sanatorium from May 1951 to October 1952. It was also a period of great historical tension: the eruption of the Korean War pointed to yet another world war, one that threatened to be final because of nuclear weapons. Jorn evokes both registers of crisis through his creatures.

On this score his key text is "The Human Animal" (1950–51).[25] The ancients of Egypt, India, Persia, America, and even Europe represented gods as "half human, half animal," Jorn notes, yet in the Middle Ages these same figures were transformed into "devilish representatives of evil."[26] What motivated the reversal? "Why does the dragon continue to be the holy sign of China and the Orient," Jorn asks, "while *the dragon killer* has become the most popular symbol of the West, the symbol of the struggle against 'evil'?" The truth of the human animal, he insists, resides in "a continuous movement from state to state, from good to evil and back again," and though occluded, this truth is nonetheless suggested by some writers: for example, certain Franz Kafka characters, especially ones who fail to love, are changed "into an animal state." According to Jorn, this is not strictly a punishment for Kafka; it is also a matter of "pleasure, even redemption," which Jorn calls a release from "the curse of the good." He terms such creaturely transformation a "positive negation" of the human, and it is one that he performs in his work too; in fact it is his primary response to the Cobra call to tap "the vital source of life" and to touch "the origin of creative activity." Yet Jorn answers this call in a manner that makes clear that this paradise is not only impossibly remote but also necessarily distorted.

I WANT TO focus on "positive negation" now through two brief juxtapositions. First, I will position Jorn on the human animal alongside Georges Bataille on a similar subject in the same years; then I will consider Jorn in light of contemporary reflections on the creaturely as a symptom of a crisis in the symbolic order. The two concerns converge on the question of origins—of the human, of sovereignty, and of law.

Jorn never cites Bataille, but he did know of some of his writings, and the two renegades do share certain positions: a challenge to the classical, in part through the *informe*; a critique of all idealisms (which for Bataille included the idea of surrealism advanced by André Breton, and for Jorn the painting of surrealism associated with René Magritte); a notion of art as excess (if Bataille theorized this surplus, Jorn practiced it—his output of paintings alone is enormous); and so on.[27] More salient here is their common fascination with the human animal. For Bataille this interest was reignited in the early 1950s by the publication of *Four Hundred Centuries of Cave Art* by the Abbé Henri Breuil, which prompted Bataille to write several texts on the topic. In the prehistoric images in southern France and northern Spain, Bataille argues, we see not only "the birth of art" but also "the passage from animal to man" (the latter phrase served him as the title of a 1953 essay).[28] Yet this "decisive step" is a paradoxical one, Bataille insists, for humanity is "not clearly distinguish[ed] from animality" in the caves, or more precisely, early man "disguised" humanity at the very moment he claimed it.[29] As evidence Bataille notes that the stick man in Lascaux has the face of a schematic bird, and that the horned men at Les Trois-Frères possess the heads and hooves of bison and stags. "What seems to be fundamental is the rejection of our face," Bataille continues; Paleolithic man "masked the face of which we are proud, and he flaunted that which our clothes conceal"—that is, his sex. Man "had now prevailed" over the animal, Bataille concludes, but in this very instant "he apologized" for the domination and blurred the difference.[30]

In a further text, titled "The Cradle of Humanity," Bataille elaborates on this ambivalence of early man about his humanity. For Paleolithic man, the animal is not only below the human, as it were, but also above it; indeed, the animal is considered "more holy [than the human]—more holy, which is to say more sacred, more divine."[31] Bataille reiterates that "nothing is more common" in prehistoric art than the representation of "a god in the form of an animal": for early man "the animal had . . . [a] divine quality that the human form could not have expressed."[32] This ambiguous connection between animal and god is a leitmotif in Bataille, fascinated as he is by the shared alterity of beast and sovereign to man. Yet Bataille tends to frame this "heterogeneity" in ontological terms. So too, as we have seen, does Jorn; recall his statement that the "truth" of man resides in "a continuous movement from state to state" (Jorn terms this movement "relativity," while Bataille calls it "alteration"). Yet in both cases historical pressures motivated these ontological propositions.[33] Just as Bataille turned to sovereignty during the period of fascism (it is pronounced in his seminars for the Collège de Sociologie, conducted in Paris in the late 1930s), so too did Jorn foreground the creaturely in his Cobra years, soon after the catastrophes of the war and the Holocaust and in the midst of the everyday terror of the Cold War—which is also to say during the failure of a European humanism still tied to "the classical tradition" to address these disasters. It was this predicament that led Jorn to seek "a new, true foundation" for artistic culture and human society alike.

So much for the human animal in the 1950s. What about the creaturely in contemporary discourse? Over the last few decades, the question of the connection between animal and god, beast and king, has returned. Why? As developed by Jacques Derrida and Giorgio Agamben, this discourse is concerned with the origin of law and the nature of sovereignty (both are markers of "the passage from animal to man," and Bataille is a key precedent for these theorists).[34] More precisely, this discourse is concerned with the *lack* of any solid basis for these institutions, at least any basis that is not founded in violence, the sheer violence of self-authorized power. It is this paradox that intrigues these thinkers: that the beginnings of sovereignty and law might lie in an exception to the just rule that they otherwise purport to secure and to represent.

Before his death in 2004, Derrida devoted his final seminars to the beast and the sovereign.[35] What interests Derrida here is that, even as the two are opposites—the one lowly, the other supreme, the one beneath the law, the other above it—they are also alike in this very exteriority to human society, and they are often represented thus, in the guise of each other: the prince as wolf, the beast as king, and so on. The celebrated instance of this unexpected convergence is the representation of the ruler as Leviathan in the 1651 tract of the same name by Thomas Hobbes, though Bataille might point to cave paintings and Jorn to tribal masks or Scandinavian carvings.[36] In any case, it is in this "mutual attraction" of beast and sovereign that Derrida searches for a key to the greater mystery of the foundation of law or, again, the absence of any such foundation.[37]

Here Derrida is close to Agamben, whose reflections on "bare life" and sovereign power are elaborated in his influential *Homo sacer* (1995). "Bare life," Agamben writes in a now-familiar phrase, is "the life of *homo sacer* (sacred man), who *may be killed and yet not sacrificed*."[38] This man is sacred only in the antithetical sense lost to us—that is, he is accursed, at the mercy of all. Indeed, in Roman society *homo sacer* was the lowest of the low, yet as such he was also the complement of the highest of the high. "At the two extreme limits of the order," Agamben writes, "the sovereign and *homo sacer* present two symmetrical figures that have the same structure and are correlative: the sovereign is the one with respect to whom all men are potentially *homines sacri*, and *homo sacer* is the one with respect to whom all men act as sovereigns."[39] Essentially, then, what the doubling of beast and sovereign is in Derrida, the doubling of *homo sacer* and sovereign is in Agamben—a riddle that points to how power is founded in a primordial yoking of violence and law. And it is this "knot"—the ruler as "the point of indistinction between violence and law," "the threshold on which violence passes over into law and law passes over into violence"—that both theorists attempt to tease out.[40]

This is not a new riddle. It is central to Western political thought: from Aristotle on, man as the political animal; through Thomas Hobbes and Jean-Jacques Rousseau on the passage from the state of nature to the commonwealth and the social contract, respectively; to Bataille on the heterogeneous status of the sovereign, Walter Benjamin on the origin of violence, and above all, Carl Schmitt on "the state of exception" to the law that founds the law.[41] In Schmitt, the state of exception is not a primordial act lost in the mists of time; it recurs whenever a government declares a "state of emergency" and suspends its own judicial codes. This is why we have seen a Schmittian turn in political theory and cultural criticism in recent decades, for once again we seem to live in a time when the state of emergency threatens to become the norm.

Yet where is the creaturely in this discourse? As Eric Santner defines it, the eruption of the creaturely in art or literature might signal a decreation in the human order, a crisis in which life appears "abandoned to the state of exception/emergency."[42] This is close to Agamben on bare life, yet uniquely in this discourse, Santner imagines this condition from the position of *homo sacer*, from the place of the beast, as it were, on "the threshold where life takes on its specific biopolitical intensity, where it assumes the cringed posture of the creature."[43] For Santner this cringe is produced by "exposure to a traumatic dimension of political power," when life becomes a direct matter of politics and politics penetrates the very matter of life.[44] This exposure is obscene, to be sure, but it can also reveal faults in the social order, "fissures or caesuras in the space of meaning," gaps in the symbolic order that might be turned into places of purchase where power can be resisted or at least rethought, where "new social links" might be imagined.[45]

"What I am calling creaturely life," Santner writes, "is the life that is, so to speak, called into being, *ex-cited*, by exposure to the peculiar 'creativity' associated with this threshold of law and nonlaw."[46] This creativity can also take the form of criticality. Certainly this was the case for the aforementioned philosophers, who witnessed the workings of power during times of crisis: Hobbes labored on *Leviathan* during the English Civil War (again, his book appeared in 1651); Rousseau conceived *The Social Contract* as the authority of European kings and princes began to crumble (his text was published in 1762); Benjamin wrote his "Critique of Violence" in 1921, in the wake of the destroyed Reich and in the midst of the *Freikorps* rampages; and, again, Bataille debated the nature of sovereignty as fascism spread through Europe. It is also no accident that the reflections of Agamben, Derrida, and Santner developed mostly in the George W. Bush years, a period that saw controversial electoral results, the deception of the Iraq War and the debacle of the occupation, Abu Ghraib, Guantánamo Bay, rendition to torture camps, and all the rest. During this time, for all the discussion of "failed states" elsewhere, our own governments came to operate, routinely and destructively, as "rogues" (a rogue, Derrida reminds us, is one "who does not even respect the law of the animal community, of the pack, the horde, of its kind"), and in this capacity they threatened us all.[47]

The historical conditions for the recent discourse on the beast and the sovereign are thus clear enough. But what are its implications for our understanding of Jorn in particular and Cobra in general? If the creatures in Kafka are prewar examples of "the peculiar 'creativity' associated with this threshold of law and nonlaw," so too do the creatures in Jorn stand as postwar instances; they are "crawling things that have no ruler." Indeed, as announced in the totem of the snake, this excited animality is active in Cobra at large, where, as we have seen, its force is ambiguous—both a sign of "total collapse" and a portent of "new freedom."

Born into this extreme situation, Cobra died with it. As the Cold War escalated and a society of spectacle emerged, Jorn and Constant moved on to found the Situationist International with Guy Debord. Yet we should conclude here with Cobra and draw out a moral that bears on modernist studies in general. At the outset I mentioned the familiar fascination among prewar avant-gardes with the art of the primitive, the child, and the insane. For the most part we modernists have charted this exploration in terms of the unconscious and the other, that is, in terms of psychoanalysis and anthropology. This approach is not wrong as far as it goes, but to the extent that it registers a disruption to the Western subject by these alterities, it assumes a stability given to this subject in the first place. The creatures of Cobra allow us to see another possibility: that some of these expressions also point to "fissures in the space of meaning," opened up by "exposure to a traumatic dimension of political power." In this light it is less a question of *where* such creatures are—again, we have names for those spaces, such as the unconscious or the other—and more a question of *when* they appear. Potentially this is right now, or whenever the symbolic order cracks under political pressure. Such was the moment of Cobra, and for a time Jorn was able to force this crack into an opening—an opening, via the creaturely, to new social links.[48]

1. Jorn, "Discours aux pingouins," 8. Unless otherwise noted, all translations are by the author.

2. Jorn and company hardly invented this idiom. As Guy Atkins writes, "What is now regarded as the typically 'Cobra' inventory of forms: strange birds, beasts, wizards, masks, a general melee of zoomorphic and human shapes—such motifs had figured in the paintings of Egill Jacobsen and others since the late thirties." Atkins, *Jorn in Scandinavia*, 86. The Atkins volumes remain fundamental; I have also benefited from Birtwistle, *Living Art*.

3. The Klee-Cobra connection is explored in Baumgartner, Fineberg, and Fuchs, *Klee and Cobra*.

4. Constant, "Manifesto," 167.

5. Constant, "Manifesto," 168, 171.

6. Constant, "Manifesto," 171. The Denis formula is from Denis, "Definition of Neotraditionism."

7. Part of Jorn's letter to Constant appears in facsimile in Stokvis, *Cobra*, 243.

8. See Sartre, *Existentialism Is a Humanism*; and Heidegger, "Letter on Humanism," in which he responds to Sartre.

9. See Heidegger, *Fundamental Concepts of Metaphysics*, 185; Heidegger, *Parmenides*, 150–60; Rilke, *Duino Elegies*. These reflections were first given as lectures in 1929–30 and 1942–43, respectively. Also see Agamben, *Open*, 49–62. Agamben develops the phrase *anthropological machine* in a chapter of that title in *Open*, 33–38.

10. His situationist painting of the late 1950s and early 1960s, Karen Kurczynski writes, "demonstrates an explicit irony in relation to the painterly gesture," with its "direct parody in the form of caricature or vandalism." Kurczynski, "Ironic Gestures," 110, 113.

11. Jorn was especially taken by Didrik the Knight, a legendary figure of Scandinavian strength who derives from Theodoric the Great, the king of the Ostrogoths from 475 to 526 (Jorn devoted his last publication project to Didrik). Already with *Helhesten*, the name of which was taken from the three-legged beast of death in the Edda, Jorn and company moved to reclaim Nordic mythology from the Nazis.

12. Nietzsche, *Birth of Tragedy*, 22, 67. "Apollo embodies the transcendent genius of the *principium individuationis*; through him alone is it possible to achieve redemption in illusion. The mystical jubilation of Dionysus, on the other hand, breaks the spell of individuation and opens a path to the maternal womb of being." Nietzsche, *Birth of Tragedy*, 97.

13. Diderot, quoted in Barthes, *Image-Music-Text*, 71.

14. Jorn writes that Jacobsen and Mortenson "provoked a salutary crisis . . . the downfall of drawing in favor of color, triumphant, effulgent." Jorn, *Lettres à plus jeune*, 89. Although this suggests an affinity with Romantic art, Jorn would include it in the classical tradition, as is clear enough from the many "Romantic" canvases that he "detourns."

15. Jorn, "Peinture détournée," n.p. Jorn continues: "Painting is over. You might as well finish it off. Detourn. Long live painting." In his view, then, does painting, like the medieval king, have two bodies, only one of which is mortal?

16. The Christian meaning of the pastoral as spiritual guidance seems mocked here as well. Indeed, the painting is also a *détournement* of "the peaceable kingdom" as imagined

in Isaiah 11:6: "The wolf shall also dwell with the lamb, and the leopard shall lie down with the kid; and the calf and the young lion and the fatling together; and a little child shall lead them."

17. This suggests "Le chef-d'oeuvre inconnu" (The unknown masterpiece) by Honoré de Balzac (whom Jorn greatly admired), with history painting substituted for the nude in the story. See Balzac, *Unknown Masterpiece*.

18. On such withering, see Benjamin, "Experience and Poverty." Might *Stalingrad* also be considered a document of the "positive barbarism" Benjamin proposes in the same essay?

19. For more on *Stalingrad*, see Kurczynski, "No Man's Land."

20. Around the creature in *You'll Never Get Me Alive* Jorn inscribed the French title, which might also be translated as "Over My Dead Body." This is more in keeping with the note that Jorn, along with Dotremont, scrawled on the back of the painting: "To our families and adorable fiancées, to priests, merchants, and all other sharks, we have the pleasure of informing you, in all modesty, of our refusal to participate in the struggle for existence." There is a close affinity here, if not a direct connection, to Georges Bataille as philosopher of the *informe* (especially in his texts on the mouth, the big toe, etc.), as discussed in the final section of this chapter.

21. On this tearing of the image-screen, see Foster, *Prosthetic Gods*, chap. 7.

22. Douglas, *Purity and Danger*, 53.

23. Douglas, *Purity and Danger*, 56.

24. Jorn, quoted in Kurczynski and Pezolet, "Primitivism, Humanism, and Ambivalence."

25. See the English translation of Jorn's "Menneskedyret" ("The Human Animal") in the special issue of *October* on Asger Jorn (no. 141 [Summer 2012]); the translation here is my own. Jorn's essay was prompted by reviews that compared him to Franz Kafka, some of whose stories he translated into Danish. Jorn opposed the existentialist account of Kafka that was already then dominant. For Jorn what truly plagues Kafka characters is a failure to love—a failure, we might say, in the social bond.

26. "We perceived the transformation based on the assumptions of Pinocchio," Jorn writes here, "based on a fear of the bestial. I no longer had this fear." Sigmund Freud and Georges Bataille were also interested in this transformation of god to devil, which bears on the relation of sovereign and beast that I take up later in this chapter.

27. Jorn must have seen Bataille's magazine *Documents*, and later texts by Bataille appear in the library assembled for Jorn's Scandinavian Institute of Comparative Vandalism. Of course, Bataille was also a key figure for the situationists.

28. Breuil, *Four Hundred Centuries of Cave Art*. See the essays collected in Bataille, *Cradle of Humanity*. Also see Bataille, *Prehistoric Painting*. Jorn alludes to cave paintings in his writings, mostly to note that though Denmark lacks the caves of France and Spain, it does possess animal sculptures; he also posits the possibility of prehistoric sand inscriptions. Thanks to Karen Kurczynski for this information.

29. Bataille, *Cradle of Humanity*, 55.

30. Bataille, *Cradle of Humanity*, 169, 61.

31. Bataille, *Cradle of Humanity*, 165.

32. Bataille, *Cradle of Humanity*, 165, 169.

33. "For us," too, Bataille writes enigmatically in *Prehistoric Painting*, "a new but indefinite time is being born. . . . The world within us is altering" (26).

34. "Bataille's merit," Agamben writes, "is to have brought to light the hidden link between bare life and sovereignty." However, "in his thought life still remains entirely bewitched in the ambiguous circle of the sacred." Agamben, *Homo sacer*, 113.

35. See Derrida, *Beast and the Sovereign*.

36. In his volume on stone sculpture in southern Sweden, Jorn includes a photograph of a representation of a king bitten by two snakes, which might be read as a figure of the state attacked by a symbol of the people—or as an image of belonging together in opposition of sovereign and beast.

37. Derrida, *Beast and the Sovereign*, 1:17.

38. Agamben, *Homo sacer*, 8.

39. Agamben, *Homo sacer*, 84.

40. Agamben, *Homo sacer*, 32.

41. See Benjamin, "Critique of Violence"; and Schmitt, *Political Theology*.

42. Santner, *On Creaturely Life*, 22. Also see Foster, "I Am the Decider."

43. Santner, *On Creaturely Life*, 35.

44. Santner, *On Creaturely Life*, 12.

45. Santner, *On Creaturely Life*, xv.

46. Santner, *On Creaturely Life*, 15.

47. Derrida, *Beast and the Sovereign*, 1:19.

48. To take up how Jorn imagined these links would require another essay. Suffice it to say here that, in this moment and beyond, these links are implicit in his different experiments in collaboration and community, in avant-garde projection and historical recovery, from the Cobra murals through the founding of the Imaginist Bauhaus and the Situationist International to the proposal for the Scandinavian Institute of Comparative Vandalism.

2

Decolonizing Modernism/s

Transversal Histories and the Slade School of Fine Art

MING TIAMPO

In 1863, five young Japanese aristocrats, later known as the "Chōshū Five," left Japan illegally in defiance of the Tokugawa shogunate's *sakoku*, or seclusion policy. Disguised as English sailors, the five first boarded a ship bound for Shanghai, then took refuge on an opium storage ship before dividing into two groups to sail around the Cape of Good Hope to London. They sailed as anonymous apprentice seamen, and as one observer noted, they were tasked with "washing decks, working pumps, and spreading sails," as no one was aware of their aristocratic status.[1] Once in London, the five enrolled at University College London (UCL), where they had been sent by Chōshū leaders to study Western military technology and practices in an undercover plot to build Chōshū strength, contest foreign aggression, and eventually overthrow the Tokugawa shogunate.[2]

Upon their return to Japan, the Chōshū Five took on major leadership roles in the Meiji government and were protagonists in Japan's struggle to repel Western imperialism and colonization. The five included Itō Hirobumi, who would become Japan's first prime minister, and Inoue Kaoru, who became the secretary of state for foreign affairs. The three others were also instrumental in modernizing Japan: Endō Kinsuke established a unified currency in Japan and founded the mint; Yamao Yōzō founded Japan's first Institute of Technology; and Nomura Yakichi established the Japanese railways. Under their leadership, the new Meiji government embraced a policy of *bunmei kaika*, or civilization and enlightenment, appropriating Western knowledge in fields as diverse as engineering, law, medicine, philosophy, and art in order to rapidly build a modern nation-state that could resist the incursions of European and American imperialism and colonialism. Prior to their voyage, the Chōshū Five had been exclusionists, supportive of Japan's isolation policies. During their time abroad, however—having landed in opium-drenched Shanghai and seen firsthand the terrible power of European imperialism, then learned its intellectual infrastructure at UCL—they developed strategies of engagement that appropriated and transformed European technologies and ways of thinking as a vehicle for resistance.

It is no accident that the Chōshū Five studied at UCL in particular. Founded in 1826 as London University, UCL was the first university in England to admit students from around the world, regardless of race or religion.[3] As a result, it became an important site for the education of students from the colonized world, an institution of imperial education that nevertheless became a fruitful contact zone for many future leaders of the postcolonial world. This chapter explores the history of one school within UCL as a site of global microhistory for understanding the ways in which London and other colonial and imperial metropolises, such as Paris or New York, functioned as crossroads for diasporic and global histories to activate and connect decolonizing movements in the visual arts. The school in question is the Slade School of Fine Art, established in 1871, which not only admitted students from around the world regardless of race and religion but also offered equal opportunities to male and female students. This phenomenon intensified after the end of the Second World War, when, with the rise of independence movements throughout Asia and Africa, ambitious students seeking to build new national futures pursued higher education and endeavored to put their learning toward postcolonial futures. Concurrently, the UK also began to consider its own postimperial futures and sought to train a "successor generation" of elites in formerly colonized nations, increasing the number of overseas students from ten thousand to fifty thousand between 1950 and 1960.[4] It is this generation—the beneficiaries of postcolonial and postimperial education policies—that I examine in this chapter, considering how the specific conditions at the Slade during this period created a complex site of negotiation and encounter, which produced several different but related approaches to decolonizing modernism/s.

Significantly, the Slade was established with a mandate to provide fine art training within the context of a liberal education. Under the direction of William Coldstream (1949–75), the school developed a discursive pedagogical method to foster intellectualism, inquiry, and, after the 1960 Coldstream report, interdisciplinarity in its students.[5] In addition to pursuing an art curriculum that centered on figure-drawing from life (in the "life room"), students studied art history, an addition to the program that enabled them to see the systemic failures of European art history's claims to universality and made the Slade a particularly interesting site of meaning-making in the context of decolonization. The parallel tracks, friendships, and networks that these students forged against the backdrop of global independence movements created a social, cultural, intellectual, and political environment that nurtured the emergence of decolonizing discourses that were articulated transnationally, spanning diasporas and independence movements on multiple continents.[6]

Taking the Slade School of Fine Art as a contact zone and site of entanglement, this chapter proposes a transnational cultural history of decolonization, which I define as the historical processes of political, economic, and epistemic liberation from colonialism. Although the national histories of the artists addressed in this chapter follow slightly different timelines of decolonization, liberation, and independence, I argue that their discourses are co-constitutive of a transversal phenomenon of decolonizing modernism/s. I understand *decolonizing modernism/s* as the articulation of modernism/s in the context of decolonization as well as the operation of decolonizing modernism/s, and I have chosen to render modernism's pluriversality (not its universality or its multiplicity) with a slash—a diagonal line that both connects and separates, much like a transversal.[7]

In order to track the history of decolonizing modernism/s as a discourse that traversed multiple national contexts rather than as separate, disconnected, "multiple modernisms," this chapter uses the notion of transversals: connecting lines that in Euclidean geometry create equal angles at their points of intersection with parallel lines on the same plane. It traces the histories of artists from multiple decolonizing contexts at corresponding points of intersection—geographical (London), institutional (Slade), pedagogical (life room, Ernst Gombrich), historical (decolonization), and aesthetic (modernism)—in order to draw transversals that reveal shared conceptual structures and also act as points of connection and relationality. This transversal analysis allows us to surface the relationships between decolonizing modernism/s from their earliest moments and thus to historicize the antecedents of solidarity movements such as the Black Arts Movement.[8]

The horizon of this transversal analysis is not to narrate a unified, singular history of global modernisms but rather to propose a model of history writing that accounts for the multiple epistemologies, temporalities, and histories of decolonizing territories while also addressing their entanglements, resonances, and solidarities—not just with the metropolis but with *each other*, along transversals through colonial centers. I conduct this transversal analysis of decolonizing modernism/s through a global microhistory that brings together the questions of global history with the methodologies of microhistory, allowing for the writing of more precise histories of the global through smaller scales of transnational and transcultural ecosystems such as the Slade.[9] This global microhistory both traces the condensed context of a shared cultural infrastructure at the Slade and beyond and also maps entanglements and common experiences.[10] As a cultural analysis, it also thinks about poetics and draws from Shu-mei Shih's notion of "relational comparison," which seeks to understand the historical and theoretical relationships that undergird apparently parallel cultural formations, in this case decolonizing modernism/s, which I argue is a transnational and multi-sited phenomenon and not a collection of "multiple modernisms." As Shih contends, "Apparent parallelisms are not historical accidents," a statement borne out in this chapter through the transversal analyses of artists concerned with nation-building and world-building.[11]

This chapter will focus on two major decolonizing discourses that a transversal approach reveals across national contexts: nation-building and world-building. The first discourse, which I examine by focusing on Ben Enwonwu from Nigeria and Zainul Abedin from Bangladesh as case studies, considers how both artists approach the problem of decolonizing modernism/s in the context of nation-building, which included the construction of national cultural infrastructures as well as the formulation of modern artistic practices identified with nation. The second discourse, which I consider by analyzing work by Ibrahim El-Salahi from Sudan and Anwar Jalal Shemza from Pakistan as case studies, ponders how both artists, who permanently settled in Britain, engaged in decolonizing practices that asserted modernism as a contrapuntal and globally co-constituted phenomenon that decentered European universalism.[12] Although when interpreted from the perspective of Western modernism these two strategies are viewed as oppositional poles between particularism and universalism, I argue that when taken within the context of decolonization, these discourses are in fact complementary and necessary options that seek to undo the hegemony of European modernism and colonialism in both former colonies and the former metropolis.

The goal of this analysis is to demonstrate how decolonizing modernism/s became a transversally linked yet distributed set of discourses that move beyond bilateral histories that focus on the relationships between colonizer and (de)colonized. By identifying the relationships between decolonizing discourses across regions as well as their roles in co-constituting larger narratives of global modernisms, this research refutes existing narratives about the dissemination of knowledge and culture from center to periphery, argues for the transnationality and entanglement of both metropolitan and decolonizing art histories, and proposes conceptual structures for understanding the visual languages of decolonization transversally.

Nation-Building as Decolonizing Strategy

In the immediate postwar period, many of the artists who went to the Slade from decolonizing or newly independent nations were fired up with the ambition of nation-building, both institutionally and culturally. Much like the Chōshū Five, they went to the Slade with the explicit aim of taking part in their countries' nation-building projects. In some cases, artists in this group had already achieved a level of artistic success in their home countries before going to the Slade and, in a few cases, visited the Slade as part of a larger, transnational research initiative to build institutions in their countries of origin, demonstrating how postcolonial nationhood was constituted transnationally.

In this section on nation-building as a decolonizing strategy, I focus primarily on two figures who gained great prominence as both arts administrators and artists, looking in particular at the ways in which they interacted with the British arts establishment in order to forge decolonizing pathways that were premised upon the foundation of new national cultures: Ben Enwonwu (Slade, 1946–47), from the then British colony of Nigeria, and Zainul Abedin (Slade, 1951–52), from the territory known then as East Pakistan, present-day Bangladesh.

Ben Enwonwu's time in London was a struggle between colonial expectations and anticolonial awakenings. When he arrived in 1944, he was already an established artist with an exhibition record and reputation in Nigeria. Upon his arrival on a Shell Petroleum Company–British Council scholarship in London, he was required to enroll in two semesters of remedial studies in drawing, basic painting, and art history, what art historian Sylvester Ogbechie describes as a "short but concentrated lesson in ideological reorientation."[13] It was during this time that Enwonwu made his first acquaintance with the politics of African nationalism at the West African Student Union, although he quickly distanced himself from them out of fear of losing his scholarship.[14] At the Slade, Enwonwu was classically trained through courses in drawing, sculpture, painting, human anatomy, and European art history, which he later supplemented with a year of postgraduate work on West African ethnography.[15]

While in England, Enwonwu became Nigeria's most internationally prominent artist, putting on exhibitions and earning major commissions even while a student, but he battled against the ways in which African art was framed in British narratives.[16] On completion of his postgraduate work, Enwonwu was offered the position of art supervisor in the Information Services Department of the Colonial Office in Nigeria. He eagerly took up the post in 1948, hoping to devise a national cultural policy for modern Nigerian art and expand the country's art education program. Unfortunately for Enwonwu, his powers in the Nigerian civil service were severely curtailed by the colonial government, which used him as a mere figurehead and a symbol of benevolent colonial rule, without granting him any resources or even an office from which to engage in any projects to construct a national culture beyond his own artistic practice. It was in this capacity that in 1958, two years after Nigeria gained provisional independence from Britain, Enwonwu wrote to Slade principal William Coldstream regarding the Slade's planned role in developing art institutions in Nigeria, inquiring in particular about its partnership with the Nigerian College, Zaria.[17] Imagining that Enwonwu was seeking his advice, Coldstream responded that "if there is anything you would like to discuss concerning art education, I would be very pleased to have a talk."[18]

By this point, Enwonwu had become involved in the pan-African Négritude movement around the Présence Africaine group in Paris, even delivering a speech at the 1956 Congress of Black Artists and Writers, in which he stated:

> I know that when a country is suppressed by another politically, the native traditions of the art of the suppressed begin to die out. Then the artists also begin to lose their individuality and the values of their own artistic idiom. Art, under this situation is doomed. What follows is an artistic vacuum that may be prolonged for even a century. By this of course, I do not mean that no more art can be created by the artists, but much of what they could, and did do in the past, can be denied them and those who follow them.[19]

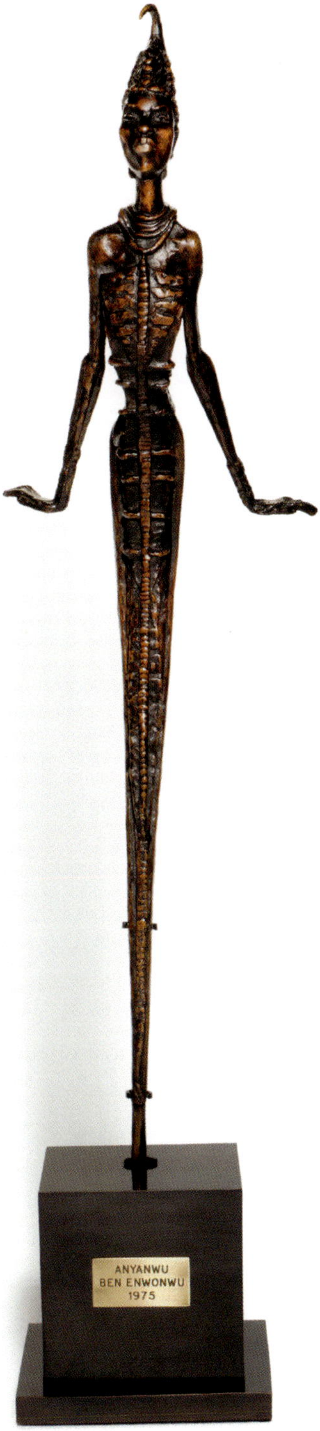

FIGURE 2.1. Ben Enwonwu, *Anyanwu*, 1954–55. Bronze, h. 210 cm. Private collection. © The Ben Enwonwu Foundation. Photograph courtesy Sotheby's.

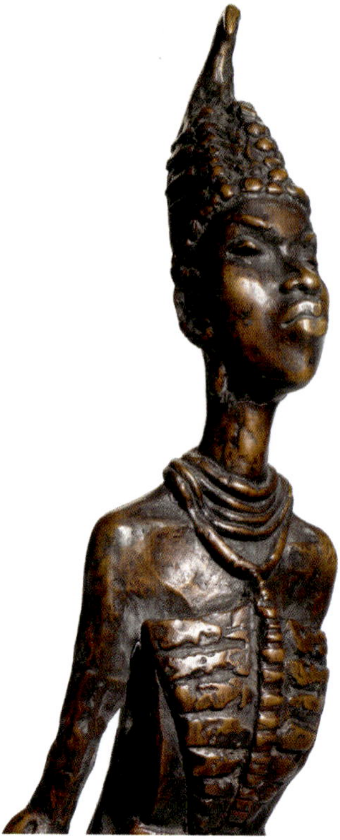

FIGURE 2.2. Ben Enwonwu, *Anyanwu*, 1954–55 (detail). Bronze, h. 210 cm. Private collection. © The Ben Enwonwu Foundation. Photograph courtesy Sotheby's.

No longer needing to wear the mask of the colonial subject, Enwonwu expressed views that had been growing since his student days in London, where he had sought to counter the Slade's Eurocentrism with his study of West African anthropology, only to discover the colonial epistemologies of that discipline, too.[20] In the years after his graduation, Enwonwu developed a more vociferous anticolonial discourse thanks to his alliances with pan-Africanists in Paris, the optimism of early decolonization in Nigeria, and his studio practice in works such as the 1954–55 *Anyanwu* (figs. 2.1 and 2.2), considered his most important work and the epitome of his "search for a modern artistic expression of Igbo aesthetics and metaphysics."[21] As Ogbechie argues, this sculpture synthesizes Igbo aesthetics and metaphysics with idioms derived from Meta Warrick Fuller's Harlem Renaissance sculpture in order to create a work replete with his vision for modern African aesthetics. As Enwonwu himself commented with regard to this sculpture, "my aim was to symbolize our rising nation."[22]

Four days after Coldstream had written, on September 20, 1958, with his offer to discuss art education, Enwonwu responded: "There seems to be no particular need for a discussion on this subject." He continued:

> I am to make recommendations to my Government on Nigerian Art and Culture generally and want to explore, in accordance with your own scheme, how much [the] Western system of Art Education may be helpful in achieving the cultural and artistic rebirth which we are working for. If our Art does not express African characteristics, then it can play no significant role in our development as a Nation. I am not sure that the entire influence of the Slade School would be a good thing.[23]

Enwonwu's acerbic response was a comment on what he saw as far too much British interference in the development of national culture in Nigeria, in particular at the Nigerian College, Zaria. It was there that the Zaria Art Society was formed in 1958, a group that under Uche Okeke advocated a "natural synthesis" of European modernist and African visual vocabularies. From the society's perspective, Enwonwu's vision of modernizing African aesthetics did not take a sufficiently critical perspective on primitivism, and they saw Enwonwu's embrace of Négritude as a colonial hangover.[24] Enwonwu, on the other hand, perceived the Zaria Art Society as overly influenced by expatriate European art critics such as the German Jewish writer Ulli Beier and sought to decolonize art institutions by building pan-African rather than European ties.[25] In 1966, Enwonwu led the official Nigerian delegation at the 1966 First World Festival of Negro Arts in Dakar, Senegal, and although he left Nigeria during the Nigerian-Biafran war (1967–70), he returned to his government post at the war's end. In 1971, he was appointed professor of fine arts at the University of Ife, the first Nigerian to hold the post, and in 1975 he left the job to serve as director and special consultant to the International Secretariat of the Second World Festival of Black Arts and Culture, or FESTAC, which took place in Lagos in 1977.

WHEREAS ENWONWU EXPERIENCED his anticolonial awakening while a student, Zainul Abedin was already a major figure in the postindependence cultural bureaucracy of Pakistan when he went to the Slade. As with Enwonwu, Abedin's Slade study was instrumentalized by British narratives, which sought to maintain British leadership over its former colonies through the Commonwealth. Abedin's 1951–52 visit to the Slade was chronicled by *Commonwealth Today* in an article titled "Zainul Abedin: Pakistan Artist Studying in London."[26] Here, Abedin is portrayed intently observing artists

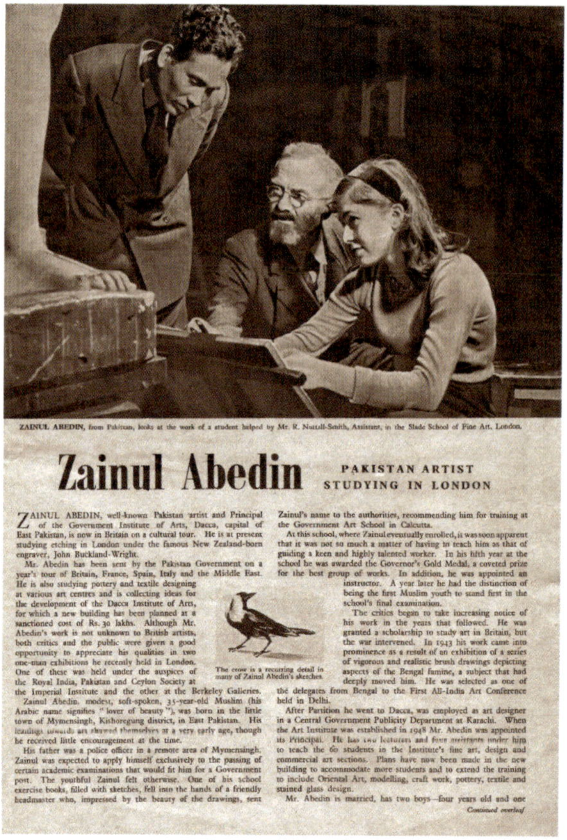

ZAINUL ABEDIN, from Pakistan, looks at the work of a student helped by Mr. R. Nuttall-Smith, Assistant, in the Slade School of Fine Art, London.

Zainul Abedin

PAKISTAN ARTIST STUDYING IN LONDON

ZAINUL ABEDIN, well-known Pakistan artist and Principal of the Government Institute of Arts, Dacca, capital of East Pakistan, is now in Britain on a cultural tour. He is at present studying etching in London under the famous New Zealand-born engraver, John Buckland-Wright.

Mr. Abedin has been sent by the Pakistan Government on a year's tour of Britain, France, Spain, Italy and the Middle East. He is also studying pottery and textile designing at various art centres and is collecting ideas for the development of the Dacca Institute of Arts, for which a new building has been planned at a sanctioned cost of Rs. 30 lakhs. Although Mr. Abedin's work is not unknown to British artists, both critics and the public were given a good opportunity to appreciate his qualities in two one-man exhibitions he recently held in London. One of these was held under the auspices of the Royal India, Pakistan and Ceylon Society at the Imperial Institute and the other at the Berkeley Galleries.

Zainul Abedin, modest, soft-spoken, 35-year-old Muslim (his Arabic name signifies "lover of beauty"), was born in the little town of Mymensingh, Kishoregung district, in East Pakistan. His leanings towards art showed themselves at a very early age, though he received little encouragement at the time.

His father was a police officer in a remote area of Mymensingh. Zainul was expected to apply himself exclusively to the passing of certain academic examinations that would fit him for a Government post. The youthful Zainul felt otherwise. One of his school exercise books, filled with sketches, fell into the hands of a friendly headmaster who, impressed by the beauty of the drawings, sent Zainul's name to the authorities, recommending him for training at the Government Art School in Calcutta.

At this school, where Zainul eventually enrolled, it was soon apparent that it was not so much a matter of having to teach him as that of guiding a keen and highly talented worker. In his fifth year at the school he was awarded the Governor's Gold Medal, a coveted prize for the best group of works. In addition, he was appointed an instructor. A year later he had the distinction of being the first Muslim youth to stand first in the school's final examination.

The critics began to take increasing notice of his work in the years that followed. He was granted a scholarship to study art in Britain, but the war intervened. In 1943 his work came into prominence as a result of an exhibition of a series of vigorous and realistic brush drawings depicting aspects of the Bengal famine, a subject that had deeply moved him. He was selected as one of the delegates from Bengal to the First All-India Art Conference held in Delhi.

After Partition he went to Dacca, was employed as art designer in a Central Government Publicity Department at Karachi. When the Art Institute was established in 1948 Mr. Abedin was appointed its Principal. He has two lecturers and four assistants under him to teach the 60 students in the Institute's fine art, design and commercial art sections. Plans have now been made in the new building to accommodate more students and to extend the training to include Oriental Art, modelling, craft work, pottery, textile and stained glass design.

Mr. Abedin is married, has two boys—four years old and one

Continued overleaf

The crow is a recurring detail in many of Zainul Abedin's sketches.

FIGURE 2.3. "Zainul Abedin: Pakistan Artist Studying in London," *Commonwealth Today* 1, no. 10 (ca. 1951–52). Collection: Slade School of Fine Art, University College London Archives. © The Estate of Zainul Abedin. Photograph courtesy Slade School of Fine Art, University College London.

at work: drawing, painting, printmaking, and teaching (fig. 2.3). In all of the photographs save one, Abedin is depicted in postures of close study and absorption, communicating the tutelage he was receiving from his hosts. This impression is underscored by the article, which describes him as being "now in Britain on a cultural tour" and "studying etching in London under the famous New Zealand–born engraver, John Buckland Wright." Describing Abedin as a "well-known Pakistan artist and Principal of the Government Institute of Arts, Dacca," the article explains that he is "collecting ideas . . . for the development of the Dacca Institute of Arts," thereby emphasizing the continued prestige of British leadership and education as well as its developmentalist role in the Commonwealth, an organization that, although founded in 1931, was reimagining itself in the wake of postwar independence movements.

Significantly, the article's author neglects to comment on the works by Abedin reproduced in the article and makes only cursory mention of one of the two solo

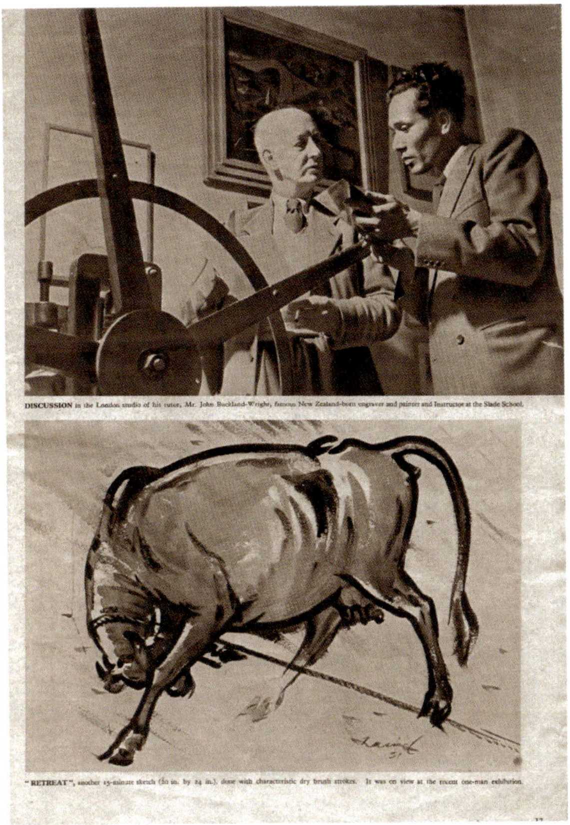

FIGURE 2.4. (*top*) Zainul Abedin with John Buckland Wright, his tutor at the Slade School; (*bottom*) Zainul Abedin, *Retreat*, ca. 1951–52. From "Zainul Abedin: Pakistan Artist Studying in London," *Commonwealth Today* 1, no. 10 (ca. 1951–52). Collection: Slade School of Fine Art, University College London Archives. © The Estate of Zainul Abedin. Photograph courtesy Slade School of Fine Art, University College London.

exhibitions Abedin held in London during his stay, preferring to frame him as an apprentice rather than as a foundational postcolonial voice.[27] Indeed, if one examines the images Abedin provided to the magazine, a different story emerges. Rather than publishing the realist studies he produced in the context of his Slade lessons, Abedin submitted work that demonstrated his vision for modern (East) Pakistani art.[28] For example, a painting captioned "Pastoral Scene" uses ink brush methods and rapid brushwork executed with an economy of gesture to depict a large expanse of water punctuated by two figures in a schematically painted skiff pulled by two muscular oxen. The technique draws from an expressive language of ink developed at Santiniketan and its pan-Asian rejection of colonial academicism through a synthetic visual language developed by Rabindranath Tagore and Okakura Tenshin.[29] Abedin's use of ink painting was, however, much more expressionist in style, with an impetus toward social realism, as in his well-known *Famine* series.[30] The focus on subject matter in these works invokes rural life, particularly in the case of the circa 1951–52 painting of a bull twisting against its restraints (fig. 2.4). This was to become one of Abedin's more iconic images, and is identified as *Retreat* in this article despite the series being better known throughout his career as *Rebel Cow*, a pointed political allegory. Indeed, in this work we see what Iftikhar Dadi describes as "labouring bodies, as heroic figures who are frequently engaged in struggle," a rebuke to the colonial and postcolonial power structures that left East Pakistan impoverished and with little political power in the postcolonial Pakistani state.[31] In short, while the *Commonwealth Today* article may have portrayed Abedin as an eager student of British artistic practice, in reality he approached his studies with a critical eye, appropriating what was useful and rejecting the ideologies with which they were coded in order to build an anticolonial culture, language, and cultural infrastructure—one rooted in laboring bodies, folk traditions, and synthetic visual languages that refuted both British imperialism and Pakistani hegemony.

In contrast to what the article implies, Abedin's time at the Slade was less an apprenticeship and attempt to gain British patronage than a fact-finding mission for the newly independent nation of Pakistan (both East and West). This point is substantiated by the circumstances of his having been funded by the government of Pakistan to embark upon the research trip as the founding principal of the Government Institute of Fine Arts, Dhaka, just as it was being set up.[32] Furthermore, his itinerary for the trip, which lasted from 1951 to 1952, included not just London but also Brussels, Paris, Ankara, and Istanbul, as well as his attendance as the official representative of the government of Pakistan at the UNESCO International Conference of Artists at the Venice Biennale in September 1952.[33] In 1956–57, Abedin traveled on a Rockefeller Foundation–sponsored trip to the United States, Mexico, and Japan, and in 1961 he accepted an invitation to the Soviet Union, which awarded him a gold medal, demonstrating both how the Third World had become a battleground for influence during the Cold War and how this conflict opened up the possibility of multiple allegiances and a somewhat fluid space for nonaligned artists.

Like Enwonwu, Abedin was an influential government adviser and bureaucrat. He played a central role in the Pakistani cultural bureaucracy before Bangladesh's independence in 1971 and in the cultural leadership of Bangladesh afterward. Abedin served the Pakistani government in various capacities, such as chief designer of the information and publication director, and at the University of Peshawar, where he established the fine arts department. In East Pakistan/Bangladesh, Abedin took primary responsibility for the establishment and construction of the Government Institute of Fine Arts, Dhaka, where he continued to serve as principal until his retirement in 1967, after which he began working toward the establishment of the Sonargaon Folk Art and Craft Museum, which was inaugurated in 1975, a year before his death.

Artistically, Abedin's retirement from the Institute of Fine Arts provided him with time to devote to painting, which took a revolutionary direction in the 1970s. In 1969, Abedin joined the Bengali mass movement against Ayub Khan, the military ruler of Pakistan, and it was in this context that he created the monumental *Nabanna* (1970). This almost ten-meter-long paper scroll used a combination of ink, wax, and color to depict the Bengali struggle, drawing its grammar and materials from a multitude of sources: the ink and paper hand scroll from East Asian ink painting, realism from the streets of Calcutta, fluid wax resist from the British watercolor tradition, political voice from social realism, and emotional power from expressionism. This scroll sited the struggle in rural spaces, depicting agricultural labor, rural craft production, and the desperation of migrating populations. Reflecting the mixed parentage of his synthetic visual language, Abedin's nation-building was not, however, a provincial or essentialist nationalism but rather an anticolonial position that sought out solidarities. Indeed, as scholar Sanjukta Sunderason argues, Abedin developed what she calls a partisan aesthetics that participated in a visual language of struggle.[34] In 1970, for example, the Arab League invited Abedin to visit Palestinian refugees, and he produced a series of drawings, most of which were done in a loose realist hand heightened with passages of liquid expressivity where he used water to create wash in specific areas. In the 1970 *Palestine War, Jordan*, however, signed with his red signature seal, Abedin borrowed the angular, inky lines that he had used for his *Famine* paintings and *Retreat* (*Rebel Cow*) in order to convey trauma and to pull his aesthetic language away from Western epistemologies, creating a visual language of decolonization linked to struggle (fig. 2.5).

What is interesting about Enwonwu and Abedin is that their stories are not unusual, and one sees parallels, intersections, and variations in the stories of other students and visitors from the colonized world, such as Tseng Yu from Hong Kong (Slade, 1952–56); K. G. Subramanyan from India (Slade, 1955–56); Affandi from Indonesia (Slade, 1952); Shakir Ali (Slade, 1946–49), Khalid Iqbal (Slade, 1952–55), and Jamila Zaidi (née Zafar) (Slade, 1954–57) from Pakistan; Sam Ntiro (Slade, 1952–55) from Tanzania; and many others.[35] Indeed, this pattern, which combined metropolitan training and research with nation-building in the context of decolonization, was so common that when Indonesian artist Affandi visited the Slade in 1952, Slade professor William Townsend made the following remarks in his diary:

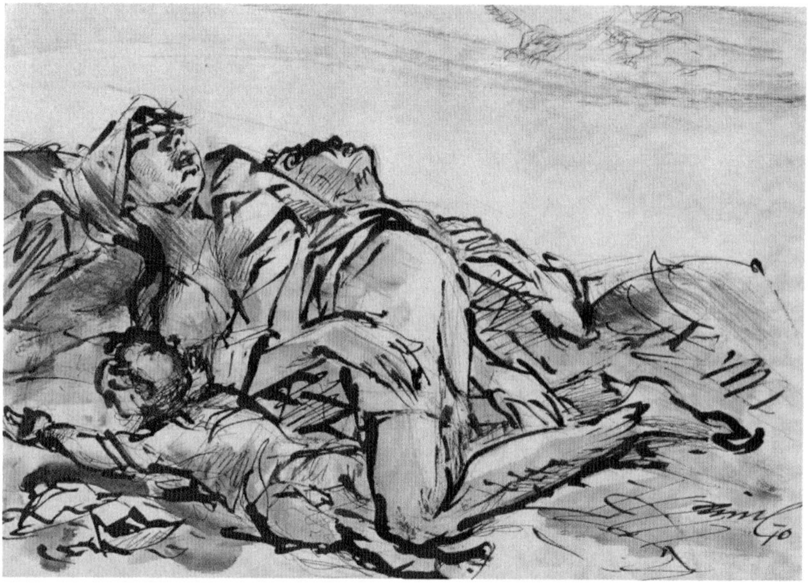

FIGURE 2.5. Zainul Abedin, *Palestine War, Jordan*, 1970. Black ink and wash on paper, 35.5 × 50.5 cm. Collection: Bangladesh National Museum. © The Estate of Zainul Abedin. Photograph courtesy Estate of Zainul Abedin.

> A visit from Mr. Affandi who is said to be the leading Indonesian artist and his very beautiful daughters. They are on a few months' visit; he hopes to return to Jakarta and open an art school. It is difficult to see how he will be helped by seeing the Slade. He has no knowledge of Western traditions, technical methods; has never been trained as an artist though he has been for a couple of years in India at various schools. In Indonesia there appear to be no teachers, but he believes it is possible now to have an "art school." I suppose this is a mystical need that goes with national independence. With its establishment he imagines funds, students and staff will appear; but he thinks of a centre, physically modest, with students working most of the time "in the native"![36]

What Townsend's remarks capture is the anticolonial ethos that was growing at the Slade among students from colonized and formerly colonized nations, "this mystical need that goes with national independence." Although they may have come for British training, what they developed out of their experiences at the Slade was something different, in friction with the official curriculum and in concert with students from other colonized territories. Indeed, a transversal comparison of Enwonwu's *Anyanwu* and Abedin's *Retreat* (*Rebel Cow*) reveals a poetics of nation-building in the context of decolonization that seeks expression through regional vocabularies that self-consciously set themselves apart from European epistemologies. Enwonwu's *Anyanwu* distances itself from his academic training at the Slade, where he mastered the vocabularies of realist draftsmanship at a high level, as well as the "primitivist" vocabularies that he experimented with as a student. The articulation of *Anyanwu* draws from the discourses of Négritude and the creation of elevating, pan-African visual vocabularies based on his studies of West African ethnography at UCL. Not just drawing upon historical sources from the distant past, *Anyanwu* also enters into dialogue with other Afrocentric modernisms such as that of Meta Warrick Fuller's bronze sculpture *Ethiopia* (1921), a renowned Harlem Renaissance work, to create a work that simultaneously leaves no doubt about its modernity.[37] In *Retreat* (*Rebel Cow*), Abedin chooses an image that self-consciously stages an Asian aesthetic language, undermining any claim that the *Commonwealth Today* article might make to cast him as a disciple of British artistic practices. Even in retreat, seeking independence for East Pakistan, Abedin as rebel cow asserts a Bengali poetics rooted in both the rural and the constructed pan-Asian aesthetics of Santiniketan.

Although employed in very different ways, the pan-Africanism and pan-Asianism invoked by Enwonwu and Abedin demonstrate a self-conscious distancing from Western visual vocabularies while employing the modern Western statecraft of cultural and infrastructural nation-building. Indeed, in their two-pronged approach, both men reveal a pattern of nation-building that is simultaneously aesthetic and infrastructural, negotiated through and against the colonial structures that they learned at the Slade, which enabled them to perceive, appropriate, and work in friction with colonial epistemologies in their efforts toward decolonizing modernism/s.

Decentering Modernism

For the students who arrived at the Slade in the late 1940s and early 1950s, on the cusp of independence and in the midst of national identity struggles, the project of staking out a national culture was tied to institution-building and was a fundamental aspect of birthing new nations. For the students who came afterward, of a slightly younger generation, the struggle was not to cast off the yoke of colonial culture but rather to participate in the rapidly forming community of nations as equals. Stuart Hall characterizes this moment as the first "wave" of Black British diaspora artists and writes, "The promise of decolonization fired their ambition, their sense of themselves as already 'modern persons.' It liberated them from any lingering sense of inferiority. Their aim was to engage the modern world as equals on its own terrain. . . . They came to see it [Britain] for themselves, to look it in the eye—and if possible, to conquer it."[38]

In 1957, the Slade brought together two artists who would each go on to define visual vocabularies that at once defied and co-constituted modernism as a global project, decentering European claims to universality: Ibrahim El-Salahi (Slade, 1954–57) from Sudan and Anwar Jalal Shemza (Slade, 1956–60) from Pakistan, both of whom eventually settled in the UK. Both El-Salahi and Shemza were artists who confronted their own epistemological impossibilities within the modern/colonial aesthetics taught at the Slade. Eventually, they defined new ways of situating their own critical positionalities with respect to a modernism that they sought to clarify as a global project, building worlds that included, yet decentered, Western visualities. By considering El-Salahi and Shemza together, we are, as Shih argues, "bringing into relation terms that have traditionally been pushed apart from each other due to . . . the European exceptionalism that undergirds Eurocentrism" and writing a transnational history of decolonization that sees these figures, who have generally been understood as relatively isolated in the history of art, as revelatory of larger art historical structures.[39]

El-Salahi and Shemza both studied at the Slade during the time of transition that came after William Coldstream had assumed leadership of the school in 1949. Under Coldstream, the pedagogical philosophy and approach to figural representation in the life room—the heart of a Slade education—shifted dramatically, changing from an emphasis on the mastery of an academic drawing method to an exploration of individual perception and representation.[40] Coldstream wrote:

> The difficulty about art schools in our time, which I imagine applied to art schools for a very long time before, was that one's programme was very unrealistic, based on an ideal of painting which had no existence anywhere, the mixture of trying to achieve a Renaissance drawing, which of course was an impossibility really, coupled with an almost surrealist juxtaposition of, say, [Walter] Sickert or [Philip] Wilson Steer. It produced a situation in which one was almost bound to postulate the kind of painting which didn't exist and which one couldn't imagine. One was trying to do something quite impossible as far as the academic side of it went.[41]

This impossibility of empirical practice within art historical models was further exaggerated for students coming from outside of Europe, who felt most strongly the constraints of the straitjacket of European art history. From 1949 to 1956, the history of art was taught in weekly lectures by Renaissance scholar Rudolf Wittkower and, after he left, by the polymath Ernst Gombrich. Although, as Shemza's comments later in this chapter demonstrate, Gombrich's teachings were Eurocentric, I argue—following the analysis of another Gombrich student, postcolonial art historian Partha Mitter—that Gombrich's lessons contained within them a provocation toward decolonization.[42] As Mitter points out, although Gombrich's knowledge only extended to the history and aesthetics of European art, his perspective on the modern system of the arts was not epistemologically closed, resulting in the famous opening statement of *The Story of Art* (1950): "There really is no such thing as Art. There are only artists."[43] More important, according to Mitter, was the possibility of epistemological pluralism afforded by Gombrich's work on cultural codes in his next project, *Art and Illusion: A Study in the Psychology of Pictorial Representation*, which he was working through in his lectures at the Slade before its publication in 1960.[44] As Mitter notes, this book prefigures the study of visual culture in its approach to visual forms beyond the classical canon, for him opening critical methodological pathways. He writes, "It was Gombrich's method that enabled me to challenge the unquestioned acceptance of the superiority of the classical canon."[45]

IBRAHIM EL-SALAHI ARRIVED at the Slade in 1954 on a grant from the colonial Ministry of Education in Sudan, after studying painting for two years at the School of Design at Gordon Memorial College in Khartoum, where he both mastered naturalist realism and was encouraged to think analytically about color in a postimpressionist idiom.[46] El-Salahi majored in painting and studied calligraphy at the Slade, where, in his words, "as taught by my new instructors . . . I had to confirm [*sic*] to the requirements of British art schools of the time, which stipulated that students master realist drawing and painting."[47] There, in addition to mastering figure-drawing and basic painting, El-Salahi studied art history with Gombrich and spent time at the British Museum, looking at old manuscripts in the library and studying ancient Egyptian hieroglyphics.[48]

El-Salahi describes how he assimilated his experiences at the Slade:

> Gradually, toward the end of my time at the Slade, I began to compose with coloured squares and triangles, which I used to establish the visual field and its masses according to their position in space, their colour, and vanishing point. At the same time, I had retained my childhood interest in calligraphy, and was trying to explore its abstract symbolism

> in hopes of deciphering its visual genesis. In painting two-dimensional realizations of calligraphic forms and figures, I was on the point of making my work completely abstract but for a passing comment from one of my teachers: "Here you are very much influenced by Mondrian." I had no knowledge of Mondrian, so I hurried over to the Tate Gallery to see his art for the first time. Looking at his work, I was quite sure there was no connection between Mondrian's total abstraction and my humble attempts to compose a painting liberated from the illusion of the third dimension. I was fascinated by that notion at the time, and it has continued to haunt me, together with the discoveries of the Renaissance era. I was hoping to develop a satisfactory representational substitute within a two-dimensional picture.[49]

Although his ultimate goal—to find a visual idiom that embraced his interest in calligraphy—already existed in seed form while he was at the Slade, it was only after he returned to Sudan that he transformed these early attempts at developing a "painting liberated from the illusion of the third dimension" into a satisfactory visual language. In an anecdote that El-Salahi was fond of repeating, he recounts that after his graduation from the Slade, he staged a few exhibitions of the work he had done in England at the Grand Hotel in Khartoum and was shocked by the total lack of audience interest. For El-Salahi, those critical failures laid bare the coloniality of the training that he had received at the Slade and the inoperability of using that language to address a newly postcolonial audience. El-Salahi subsequently stopped painting for two years and immersed himself in the visual cultures of Sudan, through which he began reimagining decolonizing modernism/s.[50]

Building on the work of Osman Waqialla, who had pioneered secular Arabic calligraphy in Sudan, El-Salahi became a leader, alongside Ahmed Shibrain, of what later became known as the Khartoum School. In the late 1950s and early 1960s, El-Salahi experimented with the calligraphic forms that he had learned as a child but broke them open, revealing what he describes as a "Pandora's box" of forms, where "in place of those broken-up letters I discovered animal and plant forms, sounds, human images, and what looked like skeletons with masked faces."[51] In the 1964 painting *The Last Sound*, a centrifugal composition anchored by a dark circle that resembles a trumpet or a mouth fans out into forms that evoke calligraphy, landscape, and mythical creatures in a reference to the passing of El-Salahi's father, a Muslim cleric, and his return to the eternal universe (fig. 2.6). In this iconic series, which emerged out of El-Salahi's period of searching, the artist created "a new visual alphabet" that combined

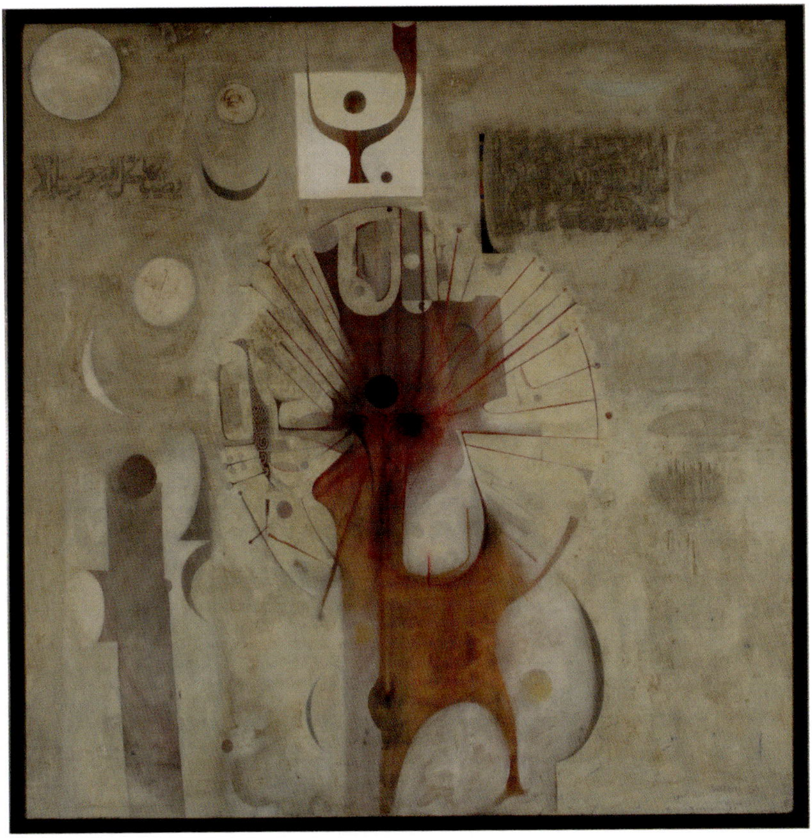

FIGURE 2.6. Ibrahim El-Salahi, *The Last Sound*, 1964. Oil on canvas, 121.5 × 121.5 cm. Collection: Barjeel Art Foundation. © Ibrahim El-Salahi, DACS, London/CARCC, Ottawa 2023.

"broken-up" Arabic calligraphy with oneiric visions that wove together a fabric of cultural allusions as diverse as Sudan's cultural topography.[52] The visual language he developed was a highly personal one, conceptualized through the idea of a self that was not only highly individualist but also aware of situating itself within a multiplicity of different discourses, contexts, and audiences.

Unlike Enwonwu and Abedin, who were chiefly concerned with nation-building through institutions and cultural articulations, El-Salahi, who initially returned to Sudan to participate in nation-building efforts, was also focused on what he called the "authentically creative individual."[53] He writes: "This individual can relate to all humans of all creeds and ethnicities on an equal footing. It goes without saying that [they are] . . . able to learn from the experiences and discoveries of others, and make use of what is learned, [which] is very different from both subordination of the other and a pitiful dependency on and fascination with the achievements of the other."[54] This is a crucial passage, in which El-Salahi critiques colonialism through the "subordination of the other," as well as colonized mentalities and primitivism, both of which he invokes simultaneously as a "pitiful dependency on and fascination with the achievements of the other." Ultimately, El-Salahi's ambition is for the individual to be able to relate to "humans of all creeds and ethnicities on an equal footing," decolonizing visual language within the decentered space of co-constituted global modernism/s.

ONE WONDERS HOW El-Salahi and Shemza (Slade, 1956–60) would have conversed on that sunny day in 1957 when they sat next to each other in front of the Slade for a formal photograph of the class of that year, El-Salahi thinking that Shemza was too clean cut and well dressed to be an artist, Shemza perhaps seeking the company of someone who shared a similar postcolonial experience in London.[55] For Shemza, arrival at the Slade was a brutal awakening, as he went from being an established painter to being a not particularly successful student: in the first months he failed his drawing test, and all the paintings that he submitted for the Young Contemporaries Exhibition were rejected.[56] Not unlike Enwonwu, who was required to register for two semesters of remedial training, or in Ogbechie's words, "ideological reorientation," Shemza found that his arrival at the Slade revealed his disjuncture from expected visual paradigms.[57]

Perhaps the most excruciating yet transformative experience followed a lecture given by Ernst Gombrich. Shemza wrote of this experience:

> One evening, when I was attending a Slade weekly lecture on the history of art, Prof. Gombrich came to the chapter on Islamic Art—an art which was "functional"—from his book, "The Story of Art." I remember leaving the room a few minutes before the lecture finished, and sitting on a bench outside. As the students came out, I looked at all their faces; they seemed so contented and self-satisfied. I went home and looked again in the mirror. This time I couldn't find any familiar face at all, neither the beginner at the Slade, nor the "celebrated artist." I couldn't talk; I just stared. After all, it wasn't a very pleasant sight.
>
> All evening I destroyed paintings, drawings, everything that could be called "art." All night I argued with somebody—as I was told next morning by my hostel neighbour. All day restlessness sent me from place to place, until I found myself in the Egyptian section at the British Museum. For the first time in England, I felt really at home.[58]

As with El-Salahi and Enwonwu, museums were an ambivalent sanctuary from the Eurocentrism of student life, a system whose claim to universality revealed itself to these students as false at various moments in their journeys. For Shemza, the realization came all at once that Islamic art did not partake of "universal" European epistemologies and could not be called "art" because it was functional. Upon this realization, Shemza went home and destroyed "everything that could be called 'art'"—that is to say, everything that uncritically embraced Western models and formats. Restless, he wandered until he found himself in the Egyptian wing of the British Museum, where, "for the first time in England, I felt really at home."

That moment of alienation allowed Shemza to see the operations of Western modernism and enabled him to launch an anticolonial critique, as well as the possibility of solidarity. Indeed, it is crucial to note that Shemza's response was not that of an essentialist assertion of national identity. In other words, he found himself at home not in the South Asian collections of the British Museum but rather in the Egyptian wing. Shemza continued, "No longer was the answer simply to begin again; the search was for my own identity. Who was I? The simple answer was: A Pakistani. But this wasn't enough. I could see Pakistan in my mind's eye: Lahore, where I came from, my friends, painters, their work—all little Picasso's, Cézanne's, Braque's, Van Gogh's [*sic*]. I could see a third rate 'Paris.' The 'celebrated artist' was lost at last, as was the beginner at the Slade. What's more, I had lost my home. I was an exile, homeless, without a name."[59] In this passage, Shemza describes an artistic journey in which he wrestles with the contours of his identity, realizing through his encounter with Gombrich's Eurocentrism that the modernist epistemes that he had embraced while in Pakistan were themselves colonized. The scales having fallen from his eyes, he understood that he was an exile in his own body and that the path forward would require him to create a new visual language that departed from the academic realism he was learning at the Slade, the language of European modernism, and overly simplified notions of Pakistani identity. Although his original intention was similar to Enwonwu's and Abedin's, in the sense that he was planning to return to Pakistan in order to contribute to postcolonial nation-building efforts, Shemza ultimately remained in the UK and created an artistic response that navigated the complexities of postcolonial identity through the creation of multistable figures that shift between epistemes and decenter European claims to modernism/s.[60]

In the 1958 work *The Wall*, Shemza created a painting that was at once abstract, representational, and decorative, piercing the heart of the problem posed by Gombrich's analysis of Islamic art as functional (fig. 2.7). The work

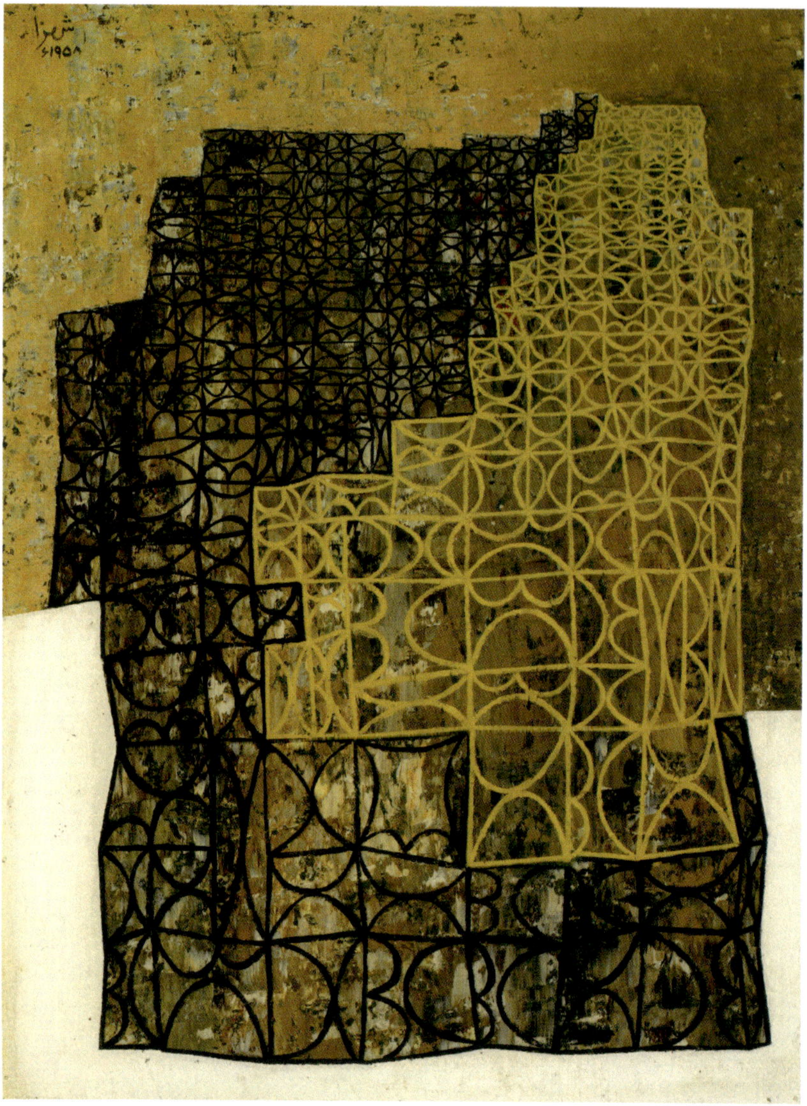

FIGURE 2.7. Anwar Jalal Shemza, *The Wall*, 1958. Oil on board, 60 × 44.5 cm. Collection: Birmingham Museums Trust. © Estate of Anwar Jalal Shemza.

appears at first entirely abstract, placing an abstract figure defined by graphic lines against a two-toned ground of thick, impasted paint in a manner that nods toward Paul Klee, an important reference point for Shemza. The title *The Wall* pulls the work back to a realm of representation, however, causing a shift in the viewer's perception of form, as the figure resolves into what in some of his other works of the same period is explicitly identified as a city wall, ornamented with Islamic patterns that in this context call into question the distinction made in Western modernism between abstraction and decoration in the non-Western world.[61]

The Wall functions like a multistable figure, or *Kippbild*, the classic example being the duck-rabbit discussed by Gombrich in *Art and Illusion*, whose beak transforms into long ears with a shift in the viewer's perception. This model, as theorist Christoph Holzhey argues, allows for the coexistence of contradictory claims "without dissolving differences between conflicting accounts or establishing a higher synthesis."[62] In Shemza's *Wall*, this multistable reading allows for the coexistence of multiple ways of seeing while maintaining their individual integrity and allowing each interpretation to critically engage with the other. It is as if, in this work, Shemza is taking Gombrich's thinking about the openness of art's epistemologies to its logical conclusion and using it to challenge his claims about Islamic art. By positing abstraction, realism, and decoration as three possible contradictory readings within the same work, Shemza creates a gestalt shift that questions their separability. Indeed, the conundrum posed by Shemza's multistable figure posits the inextricability of modernism and its presumed others in a visual statement on modernism/s as a global and co-constituted project that affirms the coexistence of multiple ways of seeing, decentering European claims to modernist universalism and asserting the possibility of decolonizing modernism/s.[63]

THE TRANSVERSAL ARTICULATIONS of decolonizing modernism/s at the Slade posited in this chapter enable us to connect histories that have previously been seen as disconnected, as "multiple modernisms" or "other modernisms," and which reified the notion of an unmarked modernism untouched by the addition of supplementary modernisms. This chapter proposed the notion of transversals as a model to understand how artists engaged in a transnational project of decolonizing modernism/s, and how this phenomenon co-constituted a larger cultural response to the universalist claims of European modernism. By relying on global microhistory and the poetics of comparison as relation, this transversal analysis enables us to make sense of decolonizing modernism/s at the earliest moments of its formation. This proposal theorizes it not as a series of parallel but disconnected modernisms, nor as a dissemination of modernism from center to periphery, but as entangled and transnational decolonizing modernism/s with their own internal logics, multistable figures, geometries, and rhythms.

Significantly, Shemza's *The Wall* became the cover image of Rasheed Araeen's 1989 *The Other Story: Afro-Asian Artists in Postwar Britain*.[64] The work thus takes on another life as an acknowledged foundational moment in the history of the Black Arts Movement in Britain, in addition to decolonizing modernism/s and asserting what Enrique Dussel calls "transmodernity," which imagines modernity as pluriversal and co-constituted.[65] Araeen's acknowledgment of *The Wall* speaks to the importance of the transversal histories that I have outlined here, as they form the foundations of what later became more explicitly articulated as solidarity movements. Weaving together the postcolonial histories of Afro-Asian artists in Britain and building solidarity through *The Other Story*, establishing the journal *Third Text*, and conducting other cultural activities, Rasheed Araeen was part of the next generation of artists and the next chapter in this story, which understands decolonizing modernism/s transversally and transnationally, cutting across national postcolonial histories as well as global and diasporic art histories.

NOTES

Research for this chapter was supported by the Paul Mellon Centre for British Art and Asia Art Archive's London, Asia research program, as well as by the Social Sciences and Humanities Research Council of Canada. Thanks to Iftikhar Dadi, Atreyee Gupta, and Sanjukta Sunderason, as well as the anonymous readers, for their comments and feedback. A later and expanded version of this chapter was published as Bruchet and Tiampo, "Slade, London, Asia." That essay is accompanied by the online archival exhibition *Slade, London, Asia: Animating the Archive (Part 1)*; https://www.britishartstudies.ac.uk/index/article-index/london-asia-and-the-slade-archives/article-category/animating-the-archive.

1. Keswick, *Thistle and the Jade*, 161.
2. Murata, "'*Choshu* Five' in Scotland," 284–88.
3. See "UCL celebrates 150th Anniversary of Japan's Choshu Five," University College London, July 3, 2013, https://www.ucl.ac.uk/news/2013/jul/ucl-celebrates-150th-anniversary-japans-choshu-five.
4. J. Lee, "Commonwealth Students in the United Kingdom, 1940–1960."
5. Llewellyn, "Histories and Contexts."
6. Khullar, "Parallel Tracks." Khullar uses the metaphor of parallel tracks to define a mode of comparison (between Pan Yuliang and Amrita Sher-Gil in Paris) that does not universalize but is attentive to connections and disjunctions.

7. My reference to the term *pluriverse* is informed by Mignolo, *Darker Side of Western Modernity*; and de la Cadena and Blaser, *World of Many Worlds*.

8. This method provides a third option beyond "connections" and "resonances" suggested by Reiko Tomii as a way of connecting art histories. Tomii, *Radicalism in the Wilderness*.

9. Global microhistory is a discourse that was first articulated through a series of three interconnected conferences, spearheaded by the University of Warwick. "Global Microhistory: AHRC Network," University of Warwick, accessed October 1, 2019, https://warwick.ac.uk/fac/arts/history/ghcc/research/globalmicrohistory.

10. Karin Zitzewitz proposes the notion of art infrastructure as a means of analyzing artistic worlds, using Brian Larkin's notion of infrastructure as an "architecture for circulation" and a built network that enables the "flow of goods, people, or ideas, and allow[s] for their exchange over space." Zitzewitz, "Infrastructure as Form," 343; Larkin, "Politics and Poetics of Infrastructure."

11. Shih, "Comparison as Relation," 82.

12. Mitter, "Decentering Modernism"; Tiampo, *Gutai*.

13. Ogbechie, *Ben Enwonwu*, 66.

14. Ogbechie, *Ben Enwonwu*, 67.

15. Enwonwu's postgraduate work was continued at the UCL under C. Daryll Forde.

16. Ogbechie, *Ben Enwonwu*, 4–84.

17. Ben Enwonwu, letter to William Coldstream, September 12, 1958, pencil note box 48, University College London Special Collections.

18. William Coldstream, letter to Ben Enwonwu, September 20, 1958, pencil note box 48, University College London Special Collections.

19. Enwonwu, "Problems of the African Artist Today," 177.

20. Ogbechie, *Ben Enwonwu*, 79.

21. Chika Okeke-Agulu, "On Ben Enwonwu's 'Anyanwu,'" *Ọfọdunka* (blog), August 8, 2016, https://chikaokeke-agulu.blogspot.com/search?q=anyanwu. Ogbechie's analysis of this work demonstrates the ways in which it weaves a decolonial narrative through multiple layers of reference to Edo royal portrait sculpture, Enwonwu's own *Song of the City* series, the Harlem Renaissance aesthetics of Meta Warrick Fuller, and a tradition of African American emancipation sculpture. Ogbechie, *Ben Enwonwu*, 128.

22. Enwonwu, quoted in Ogbechie, *Ben Enwonwu*, 128.

23. Ben Enwonwu, letter to William Coldstream, September 24, 1958, University College London archives, UCLCA/4/1/2/4/17.

24. Enwonwu was challenged by the Zaria Art Society and its advocacy for a "natural synthesis" after independence in 1960. Prominent Zaria Art Society members included Uche Okeke, Bruce Onobrakpeya, and Demas Nwoko. See Okeke-Agulu, *Postcolonial Modernism*; Gassmann de Sousa, "Decolonizing Nigerian Modernism"; and Lecznar, "Weathering the Storm."

25. Okeke-Agulu, *Postcolonial Modernism*, 131–82.

26. Newton, "Zainul Abedin," 15–17. *Commonwealth Today* magazines were undated, leaving the determination of year to contextual analysis. With thanks to Susan Collins and Liz Bruchet for sharing, and Helen Downes for clarifying the reference. The full essay is reproduced in Bruchet and Tiampo, "Slade, London, Asia."

27. The two exhibitions were organized by the Royal India, Pakistan and Ceylon Society at the Imperial Institute (which became the Commonwealth Institute in 1961) and at the Berkeley Galleries in London. The first occurred December 3–8, 1951, and the second January 14–26, 1952. For a fuller analysis of these exhibitions, see Hoek and Sunderason, "Journeying through Modernism."

28. E.g., *Rainy Day* (pen on paper, 1951, London), reproduced in Falvo, *Zainul Abedin*, 169. Abedin's positionality is fractured, as Iftikhar Dadi and Sanjukta Sunderason argue, between being an East Pakistani artist and an "artist-bureaucrat" working for the Pakistani government. See Dadi, *Modernism and the Art of Muslim South Asia*, 99–112; and Sunderason, "Shadow-Lines."

29. See Siva Kumar, *Santiniketan*. Although it is not present in these paintings, Abedin often used a red ink chop in his signature, referring to East Asian artistic languages through their signatory practices, as early as 1944. Thanks to Sanjukta Sunderason for discussing Abedin's handling of ink with me and to R. Siva Kumar for sharing his book and insights during his residency at Carleton University in 2018. The image can be consulted in Bruchet and Tiampo, "Slade, London, Asia."

30. Sunderason, "Shadow-Lines."

31. Dadi, *Modernism and the Art of Muslim South Asia*, 110.

32. The Institute of Fine Arts was founded in 1949 as the Dhaka Art School, and in 1963 became the East Pakistan College of Arts and Crafts. In 1972, its name changed again to the Bangladesh Government College of Arts and Crafts, and in 1983, it became known as the Institute of Fine Arts, the name by which it is known and cited in most publications. In 2008, it became the Faculty of Fine Arts of the University of Dhaka.

33. Hoek and Sunderason, "Journeying through Modernism"; UNESCO, *Artist in Modern Society*.

34. Sunderason, *Partisan Aesthetics*.

35. Bruchet and Tiampo, "Slade, London, Asia."

36. William Townsend journal, February 25, 1952, n.p., University College London Special Collections. For more on Affandi, see Claire Holt, *Art in Indonesia*.

37. Fuller's sculpture is also known as *Ethiopia Awakening*. See "Meta Vaux Warrick Fuller, Ethiopia, 1921," National Museum of African American History and Culture, accessed July 31, 2024, https://nmaahc.si.edu/meta-vaux-warrick-fuller-ethiopia-1921.

38. Hall, "Black Diaspora Artists in Britain," 5.

39. Shih, "Comparison as Relation," 79.

40. Chambers, "Prototype and Perception," 196.

41. William Coldstream, quoted in Chambers, "Prototype and Perception," 196.

42. Partha Mitter, interview with the author, July 13, 2019; Mitter, "Paradox of Ernst H. Gombrich," 315–29. Mitter studied under Gombrich from 1965 to 1970 and obtained his PhD from UCL in 1970.

43. Gombrich, *Story of Art*, 15.

44. Chambers, "Prototype and Perception," 197.

45. Mitter, "Paradox of Ernst H. Gombrich," 328.

46. El-Salahi, "Artist in His Own Words," 83.

47. El-Salahi, "Artist in His Own Words," 83.

48. On his academic experiences, see Holledge, "Myriad Aspects of Ibrahim El-Salahi"; and Amna Malik, "Transnational Slade: Ibrahim El-Salahi," Slade Archive Project, June 17, 2014, https://blogs.ucl.ac.uk/slade-archive-project/2014/06/17/transnational-slade-ibrahim-el-salahi. On visiting the British Museum, see Ibrahim El-Salahi, interview with Ulli Beier, in S. Hassan, *Ibrahim El-Salahi*, 106.

49. El-Salahi, "Artist in His Own Words," 83.

50. El-Salahi, "Artist in His Own Words," 87.

51. El-Salahi, quoted in Beier, "Right to Claim the World."

52. On "a new visual alphabet," see El-Salahi, "Artist in His Own Words," 88. Salah Hassan discusses the impact of the diversity in Sudan, where almost every major African ethnic and linguistic group is represented. He distinguishes between the two major cultural groups that have formed for political and ideological reasons: "In northern and central Sudan, highly Islamized and relatively Arabized cultures, fused with local pre-Islamic elements; and stretching south and into the peripheries of the northern region, strongly 'African' cultural elements, represented by traditional religions as well as by a visible presence of Christianity." Hassan situates El-Salahi's work and the Khartoum School within a search for a shared Sudanese identity. S. Hassan, *Ibrahim El-Salahi*, 15.

53. El-Salahi was arrested in September 1975 and imprisoned for six months without trial, following false accusations of antigovernment activities. He has since lived outside Sudan.

54. El-Salahi, "Artist in His Own Words," 91.

55. This anecdote was related to me by Iftikhar Dadi. Iftikhar Dadi, WhatsApp message to the author, September 28, 2019.

56. Shemza, "Artist's statement, July 1963."

57. Ogbechie, *Ben Enwonwu*, 66.

58. Shemza, quoted in Dadi, "Calligraphic Abstraction," 11.

59. Shemza, quoted in Dadi, "Calligraphic Abstraction," 11.

60. Shemza moved back to Pakistan in 1960 with the intention of joining the National College of Arts and contributing to the enterprise of nation-building, but the artist never found suitable employment and moved back to the UK permanently in 1961.

Multistable figures and the idea of complementarity—allowing for two contradictory figures to coexist in one image, such as the duck/rabbit—were the theoretical focus at the ICI Berlin Institute for Cultural Inquiry in 2011–12. "Complementarity ICI Focus 2011–12," ICI Berlin, accessed October 1, 2019, https://www.ici-berlin.org/projects/complementarity-2011-12/.

61. Iftikhar Dadi writes about how Shemza addresses Gombrich in the following analysis of Shemza's *Roots* series: "It should be noted that Islamic art has been characterized in art-historical scholarship precisely as ornamental, decorative, and applied—or 'functional' in the way Gombrich had described it in the lecture that had proved to be so shattering to Shemza earlier. For modern artists drawing inspiration from 'Islamic art' however, the relation between modernism and decoration cannot be so disavowed. In one sense, the *Roots* series brings the dangerous question of ornament and its relation to modernism to a point of crisis, especially with reference to modernism's intimate

yet unacknowledged relation to the 'decorative arts' of the non-Western world." Dadi, "Calligraphic Abstraction," 14.

62. Holzhey, introduction to Holzhey, *Multistable Figures*, 7.

63. Gombrich, *Art and Illusion*, 4. For a fuller inquiry into the theoretical potential of the *Kippbild*, or multistable figure, as a conceptual model, see Holzhey, *Multistable Figures*.

64. Araeen, *Other Story*.

65. Dussel, "World System and 'Transmodernity.'"

Part II

THE SOVIET BLOC AND COMMUNIST CHINA

3

Soviet Art before and after the Thaw

BORIS GROYS

The historical period after the Second World War was defined primarily by the Cold War, which took place between former allies the United States and the Soviet Union. In an art context, this conflict was represented by a cold war between realist art and abstract or, more generally speaking, modernist art. In both cases, art fulfilled a similar ideological function: to present each country's side of the conflict as the spiritual heir of Nazi Germany. In his 1939 essay "Avant-Garde and Kitsch," Clement Greenberg already drew parallels between Nazi and Soviet art.[1] Soviet and Nazi ideologies were, of course, very different and produced different kinds of art. Here it is enough to say that one cannot find in Soviet art the celebration of the naked Aryan (male or female) body that was at the center of Nazi art. But the propaganda art of both Stalinist Russia and Nazi Germany was based on the tradition of naturalist, figurative painting and sculpture and rejected modernist practices, especially abstract art, which Greenberg wanted to defend. At that time, Greenberg did not believe that American capitalism could become a reliable supporter of artistic modernity. He wrote that the American ruling class, like Soviet and Nazi regimes, sought to erase aesthetic differences between the bourgeoisie and the masses, which would ultimately lead to the proliferation of kitsch.[2]

However, after the Second World War, modernist art, and especially abstract art, began to enjoy political and economic support from the American ruling class as a symbol of individual freedom, as Serge Guilbaut has shown.[3] Soviet socialist realism, in contrast, was regarded in the West as a symbol of totalitarian oppression, similar to the oppression that took place in wartime Germany and Italy. It is this suppression of "true" modernist art that has attracted the attention of Western art criticism rather than the production of a different kind of art that deviated from the Western modernist canon. This interpretation of modernist art as the only art that deserves this name was influenced by European émigrés who fled National Socialism (or Nazism) and came to the United States before and during the Second World War. That is also why modernist art became an integral part of the program of reeducation that was practiced by Americans after the war in the Western part of Europe, especially in Germany and Italy. This program was simultaneously directed against the still lingering fascist and Nazi ideological past and against the ideological influence of the Soviet Union.

The ideological strategy of official Soviet art criticism followed a similar pattern. To understand this strategy, one has to remember the origins of socialist realism. In the 1930s, the artistic avant-garde was already being interpreted by official Soviet art critics as a manifestation of a new capitalist antihumanism. The gradual disappearance of the human figure, especially the human face, from modernist painting and sculpture was interpreted by Soviet theoreticians as a sign of submission of the human being to the inhuman forces of technology and collective unconscious, a submission characteristic of capitalism entering the stage of imperialism, in Vladimir Lenin's description.[4] The artists of the avant-garde were accused of celebrating and glorifying this new antihumanism. Soviet socialist realism was understood, in contrast, as a defense of humanism and an attempt to secure the humanist values betrayed by the Western bourgeoisie.

The turn from the avant-garde toward socialist realism and humanism that took place in the Soviet Union in the 1930s was theoretically influenced by Georg Lukács. In his famous 1934 essay on German expressionism, Lukács diagnosed expressionist "activism" to be a precursor of National Socialism.[5]

Lukács stressed "irrational" aspects of expressionism that later, according to his analysis, culminated in the National Socialist ideology. In a footnote to the text added in 1953, he stated that the persecution of expressionist artists during the Third Reich did not contradict his analysis.[6] In numerous essays published in the Soviet Union in the 1930s, Lukács continued to critique modernist art and writing as manifestations of "bourgeois" irrationalism and antihumanism—a critique that had already been formulated in the writings of Georgi Plekhanov and Lenin.[7] At the time, fascism was understood by the Soviet Marxist theoreticians as irrational and futile "revolutionarism" expressing the mentality of the European petite bourgeoisie and directed against the power of historical laws that, according to Marxism, inevitably led capitalist industrial civilization toward proletarian collectivism. But terminologies such as the "petit bourgeois revolt," "irrationality," and "extreme individualism" were also the standard characterizations of avant-garde art used by Marxist critics from Plekhanov to Leon Trotsky.[8]

Of course, the return to a realist tradition that took place in the Soviet Union in the 1930s had much to do with both the stabilization of state power and the abandoning of the revolutionary rhetoric inside the country. The Soviet Union was also confronted at this time with a new wave of fascist revolutions in Europe, especially in Italy and Germany. As a reaction to these revolutions, Soviet ideology and politics increasingly became more defensive and traditionalist. Thus, during the 1930s, socialist realism had almost completely dropped its revolutionary rhetoric and become culturally conservative, proclaiming as its main goal the defense of humanism and traditional cultural values. The slogan "Socialism or Barbarity" became central to the Soviet ideology of socialist humanism, directed against fascism but also against modernist art understood as a form propagating barbarity, irrationalism, and the cult of violence. Not accidentally, before the Second World War, the Soviets organized the International Congress for the Defense of Culture (1935) in Paris. Today, it is interesting to read André Breton's polemics against this congress: in the name of the surrealists, Breton rejected the congress's agenda as an attempt to impose a culturally conservative program on the political Left under the pretext of struggle against fascist barbarity.[9] However, in the eyes of communist ideologues, Breton's position appeared profascist, not dissimilar to the position of the Italian futurists. Accordingly, the struggle against Western modernism during the Cold War was interpreted by Soviet theoreticians as a continuation of the struggle against fascism and imperialism in the name of humanism.

The defense of humanism against antihuman modernism remained the central ideological position of socialist realism until the end of the Soviet Union in the second half of the 1980s. However, the official Soviet understanding of humanism changed during this period, which was also reflected in art. Right after the war, we find a few examples of a spectacular, triumphalist style that is often associated with socialist realism. But in general, Soviet art became much more intimate, even oriented toward private life. It propagated not so much the radiant future but rather a kind of petit bourgeois idyll. Such images of private happiness reflected the sensibility of a society that sought rest after the years of war.

But the real change in the concept of socialist humanism took place after the death of Joseph Stalin in 1953, and especially after the twentieth Congress of the Communist Party, where Nikita Khrushchev denounced the "cult of personality," allegedly installed by Stalin, and required the party to return to the so-called Leninist norms.[10] The period of de-Stalinization that followed took its name from the title of a 1954 novel by Ilya Ehrenburg, *The Thaw*. Ehrenburg was, incidentally, the main organizer of the 1935 International Congress for the Defense of Culture, and Breton describes his meeting with Ehrenburg and the heated polemics, accusations, and insults that they exchanged. The title of Ehrenburg's novel, however, suggests a return of human feeling and warmth after the long winter of Stalinism, a return to true humanism after the period of antihumanist, Stalinist rule. In other words, overcoming Stalinism operated within the same paradigm of socialist humanism as Stalinism itself. Accordingly, the opposition between Soviet humanism and Western modernism had not lost its relevance, as "decadent," "antihumanist" Western art remained an ideological taboo. However, the return to the pre-Stalinist 1920s ideology would not have been possible without a certain, albeit very restricted, rehabilitation of the Russian avant-garde of the same period. This partial rehabilitation was symbolized by the erection of the monument at one of the central Moscow squares to Vladimir Mayakovski, the revolutionary poet who had been close with the Russian futurists. The authorities also opened the Museum of Mayakovski, where exhibitions of work by Vladimir Tatlin, Kazimir Malevich, and other futurists were mounted and readings of futurist poetry took place.

The return to the pre-Stalinist 1920s aesthetics after Stalin's death also meant a return to revolutionary romanticism after decades of Stalinist bureaucratic rule, as well as a new internationalism after a long period of national isolation. The new Soviet government, under Khrushchev, began to align itself with national liberation movements, establishing contact with Yugoslavia's president, Josip Broz Tito, who had broken from Stalin, and with the nonaligned countries. The Cuban Revolution became a cult in the Soviet Union; images of Fidel Castro were everywhere. The same can be said of Gamal Abdel Nasser of Egypt, who got the title "The Hero of the Soviet Union." Patrice Lumumba University, named for the leading figure of liberation in the Congo, was founded in Moscow in 1960 specifically for students from African and Latin American countries.

But for young Soviet artists, one of the most decisive events of the time was the Festival of Young People and Students, which took place in the summer of 1957. The festival attracted young people from fifty-two countries and featured an art exhibition with 4,500 works made by artists from all over the world. In 1959, Soviet viewers had the opportunity to see an exhibition of American art, including works by Mark Rothko, Jackson Pollock, Willem de Kooning, and others.[11] Both exhibitions were important for the Soviet artists of the period, many of whom were for the first time directly confronted by art that their contemporaries had made outside Soviet borders. The sensation of living in a globalized, unified world was further enhanced by Yuri Gagarin's 1961 journey into outer space and around the earth's orbit. Now, the earth began to be experienced as a home for mankind as a whole; the lines of ideological divisions began to appear obsolete.

This new progressivist and internationalist mood found its most immediate manifestation in the architecture of Khrushchev's time. Stalinist architecture was historicist; it wanted to be grandiose and spectacular. This desire was subjected to harsh critique and rejected right at the beginning of the Khrushchev era. In its place was proposed a new architecture, which was in a way a continuation of Russian avant-garde and Bauhaus architecture and was simple, inexpensive, and easy to construct. Architects wanted to build not for visitors and tourists but, rather, for the masses, for the ordinary people, away from the palace architecture of Stalin's time. The so-called panel houses that emerged as a result were constructed from blocks produced at a panel factory. They suggested the point of origin of a tradition—a starting point for a new era—a kind of neo-avant-garde. The panel houses of the Khrushchev period aesthetically translated the egalitarian, communist promise; they offered an image of universal equality, shorn of any signs of privilege and aesthetic distinction. It is interesting that many critics characterized this architecture as "inhuman" because it was monotonous, standardized, and egalitarian.

The relationship between the artistic avant-garde, including Malevich, and the neo-avant-garde panel houses went deeper than the desire to establish a new geometrical canon and reduce architecture to level zero. The architects of the radical Russian avant-garde aimed to dissolve the concept of a house as an individual unit, typically understood as an "organic" architectural artwork, a manifestation of its creator's artistic individuality, and an embodiment of function and style's unity. Instead, they apprehended the house as a loose and potentially variable combination of standardized apartments. These architects used cars, trains, and airplanes as models for apartment buildings. They conceived of individual apartments as free-moving units that could be combined and recombined to build temporary, shifting, changing housing agglomerations instead of traditional houses. The famous Russian avant-garde poet Velimir Khlebnikov dreamed about the "boxes made out of bent glass walls or mobile staterooms outfitted with doors with rings, on wheels, with their own inhabitants within . . . so that these staterooms could be set up on a train (special tracks, platforms with places) or a steamship: inside each one inhabitants could take a trip without going outside."[12] This poetic vision inspired the architects of the so-called disurbanism, such as Moisei Ginzburg and Mikhail Okhitovich, who in 1929 designed individual apartments and houses as "transportable-dwelling units" that could reintegrate into another building complex if so desired. Malevich went even further and suggested that such apartment units should be made in a way that would allow them to be assembled into spaceships that could potentially fly into cosmic space to create "flying cities" over the surface of the earth.[13] Such projects show that the idea of a prefabricated, standardized apartment was intimately connected to the notion of the human being as a permanent traveler and the idea of the house as a site of a merely temporary interruption of the travel. The radical break with the historical past was thus understood as the beginning of travel that had no end because it brought one into the infinite cosmic space.

The Soviet art of the Thaw reflected this neoconstructivist and sci-fi disposition. And it also reflected a neo-avant-garde will for reduction, minimalism, and geometrical abstraction. In this respect, the group Dvizhenie (Movement) is exemplary. The art of this group was motivated by a faith in technical progress and a desire to enter infinite cosmic space, and thus visions of a communist future were substituted by science fiction. At the same time, the members of the group believed that they had a chance to be officially accepted by the Soviet authorities, and indeed, the state allowed them to organize some public events. This readiness to participate in public life reflected a more general attitude that was widespread among the Soviet creative intelligentsia of that time. Poets like Yevgeny Yevtushenko or Andrei Voznesensky attracted crowds with their public readings; similar crowds thronged theaters that staged ideologically and aesthetically risky performances, such as Sovremennik and Teatr na Taganke, where plays by Bertolt Brecht were performed alongside those of contemporary Soviet authors. Of course, the building of the Berlin Wall and, even earlier, the suppression of the Hungarian Revolution of 1956 were not overlooked. But these frustrating events could not completely extinguish the hope that Soviet society would move toward liberalization, even if this movement took a considerable amount of time.

However, the atmosphere drastically changed in December 1962, after Khrushchev visited an exhibition of new Soviet art. This visit became the decisive turning point for further Soviet art development. The exhibition presented a range of styles, including traditional socialist realism, a kind of neo-Cezannism, surrealism, symbolism, and pure abstraction. In a rage, Khrushchev insulted the artists and demanded a return to "normal," "healthy," "positive" art.[14] This very public scene of indignation dashed all hopes for official recognition of art committed to the heritage of the avant-garde or even a moderate modernism. Again, modernist art became the face of the ideological enemy, namely Western capitalism culminating in an art market that betrayed traditional humanist values. In the famous 1963 essay "Why Am I Not a Modernist?," Mikhail Lifshitz, a close friend and collaborator of Georg Lukács, reiterated the main points of the Soviet critique: modernism is cultural fascism because it celebrates irrationality and antihumanism. He wrote:

> So, why am I not a modernist? Why does the slightest hint of such ideas in art and philosophy provoke my innermost protest? Because in my eyes modernism is linked to the darkest psychological facts of our time. Among them are a cult of power, a joy at destruction, a love for brutality, a thirst for a thoughtless life and blind obedience.... The conventional collaborationism of academics and writers with the reactionary policies of imperialist states is nothing compared to the gospel of new barbarity implicit to even the most heartfelt and innocent modernist pursuits. The former is like an official church, based on the observance of traditional rites. The latter is a social movement of voluntary obscurantism and modern mysticism. There can be no two opinions as to which of the two poses a greater public danger.[15]

At the time, the power over the Soviet art institutions, including museums, exhibition spaces, and art publications, was concentrated in the hands of the official Union of Soviet Artists. In many ways, this union also controlled the everyday life of its members, who lived in apartments and used studios that belonged to the union, spent their vacations in the union's vacation houses, and went to the union's hospitals for treatment. Here, it is important to note that in the Soviet Union, only the members of the Union of Soviet Artists were considered to be artists. They were also obligated to be guided in their work by the principles of socialist realism. Thus, in the Soviet Union, to not be a socialist realist was tantamount to not being recognized as an artist.

In effect, not being recognized as an artist also meant not being able to have a studio, not being able to exhibit work, and not being able to get a review. The closely monitored circuits of the official art system were a closed club. Those who did not belong were not considered artists.

The antimodernist, anti-avant-garde ethos excluded artists who worked in the modernist tradition but could not completely suppress modernist and postmodernist art. Unofficial artists were ignored and excluded from official public spaces, but they were not systematically persecuted. Consequently, a split emerged between official and unofficial art, one that characterized the Soviet art world through to the end of the Soviet Union. One could say that the Cold War was internalized by the Soviet art system, for inside the Soviet Union, art became divided into official and unofficial ideological camps. Official art was identified as being truly "Soviet." Unofficial art was considered to aesthetically represent the West at a time when political representation of Western positions and attitudes was otherwise impossible. That is why Soviet unofficial art was "more than art." It was the West inside the East.

The situation further solidified after Khrushchev was removed from power in 1964. In official art, representations of communist leaders became less glorifying than they had been during Stalin's time. Instead, the official artists began to monumentalize workers and ordinary people to a degree to which Stalinist art had not. On the one hand, the intimate character that marked paintings of the 1950s became rare, as ordinary Soviet citizens came to be presented as heroes and masters of their country (figs. 3.1). On the other hand, unofficial art shifted toward themes drawn from everyday life and represented in a kind of pop art (fig. 3.2). In many instances, Russian artistic strategies reflected a certain familiarity with contemporaneous developments in Western art outside of the Soviet Union. In retrospect, one can say that the division of Soviet art into official and unofficial art that took place during and after the Thaw created the possibility for the emergence of a new and original artistic phenomenon: artistic analysis of the functioning of visual language in Soviet ideological propaganda and in everyday Soviet culture. Indeed, this division not only opened the possibility of practicing—albeit unofficially—a Western type of modernism inside the Soviet Union but also created the conditions to look at the Soviet Union from a quasi-external position, a position of "internal emigration." This external look from the inside produced, in the second half of 1960s, the art of Moscow conceptualism.[16]

In the 1960s and 1970s, the first generation of Moscow conceptualists, such as Ilya Kabakov, Erik Bulatov, Dmitri Prigov, and Lev Rubinstein, used the language of the "simple Soviet citizen," albeit in an ironic, neo-Dadaist

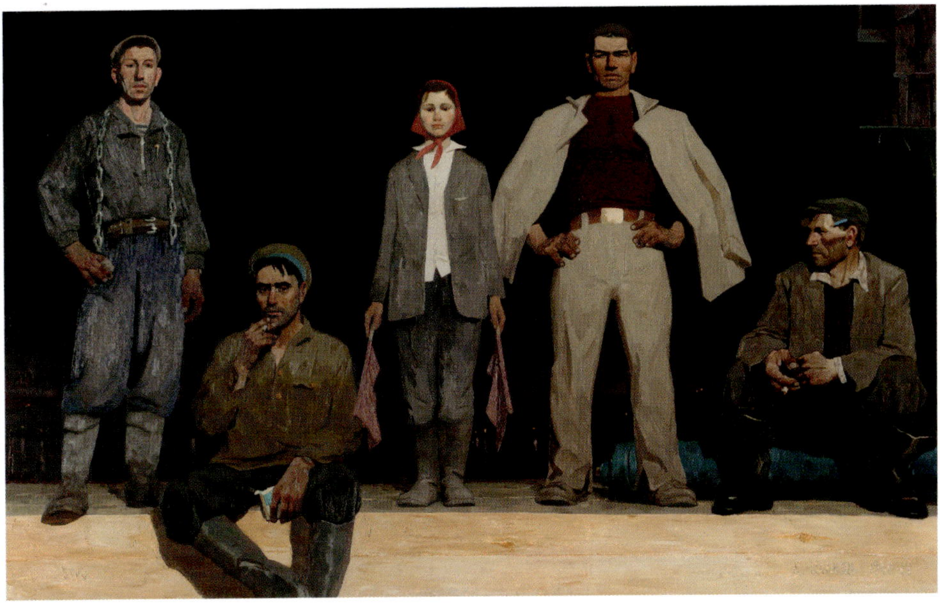

FIGURE 3.1. Victor Popkov, *Builders of Bratsk*, 1960–61. Oil on canvas, 183 × 302 cm. Collection: The State Tretyakov Gallery, Moscow.

way (figs. 3.3 and 3.4). The rigid formulations of official Soviet ideology were inevitably damaged and displaced through this "uncultivated" reuse. Kabakov and Prigov, in particular, frequently drew on the storehouse of everyday uncultivated theorizing for commentaries on their own art and that of others. The most diverse theoretical discourses and artistic practices thus suffered a linguistic catastrophe in a way that was highly entertaining to the informed viewer. Thus it may be said that Moscow conceptualism took the discursive mass culture of its time as its subject, the very same discursive culture that was then omnipresent in the Soviet Union. Moscow conceptualism was indeed a kind of discursive pop art.

Conceptual art, of course, has its origins in the West. But it underwent a transformation when it was adopted by Moscow artists, resulting from the specific circumstances in which art as a whole functioned in the Soviet Union. Conceptual art can be characterized briefly as the result of placing image and text on the same level. An image is replaced by a written commentary, by a description of a certain art project, or by a critical statement. This use of language can be seen as a dematerialization and hence decommercialization of art. In the capitalist West, an artwork is, above all, a commodity. Art is primarily defined by the art market. Every commodity, however, is first and foremost a material

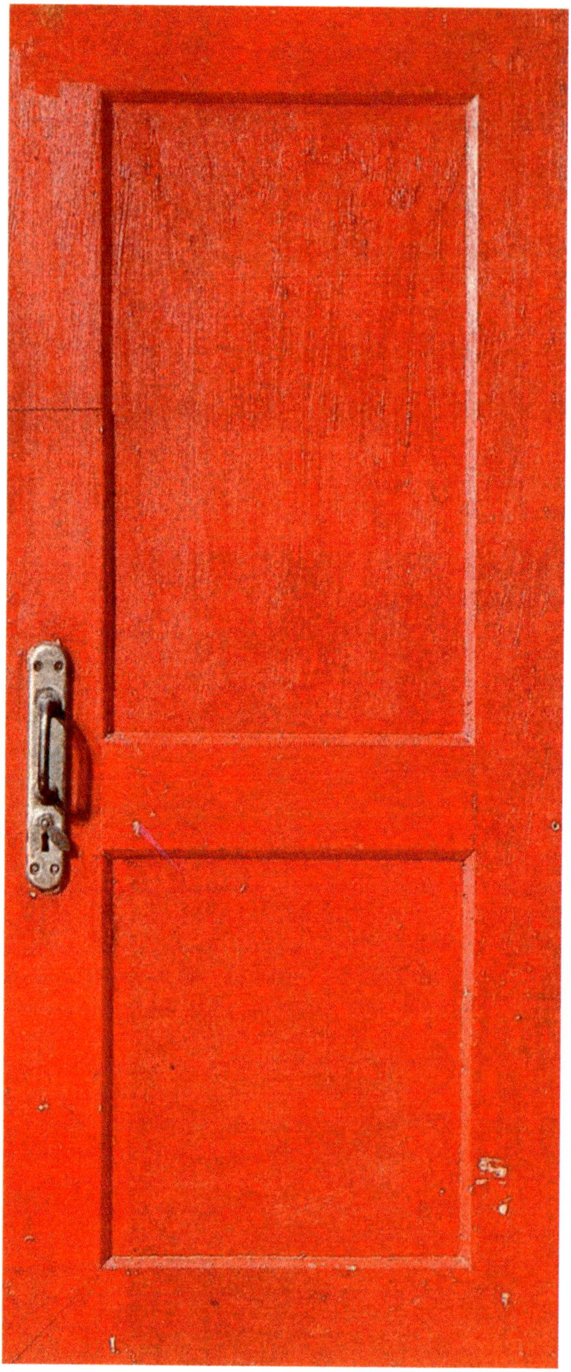

FIGURE 3.2. Mikhail Roginsky, *The Door*, 1965. Oil on wood, handle, 160 × 70 × 10 cm. Collection: State Tretyakov Gallery, Moscow.

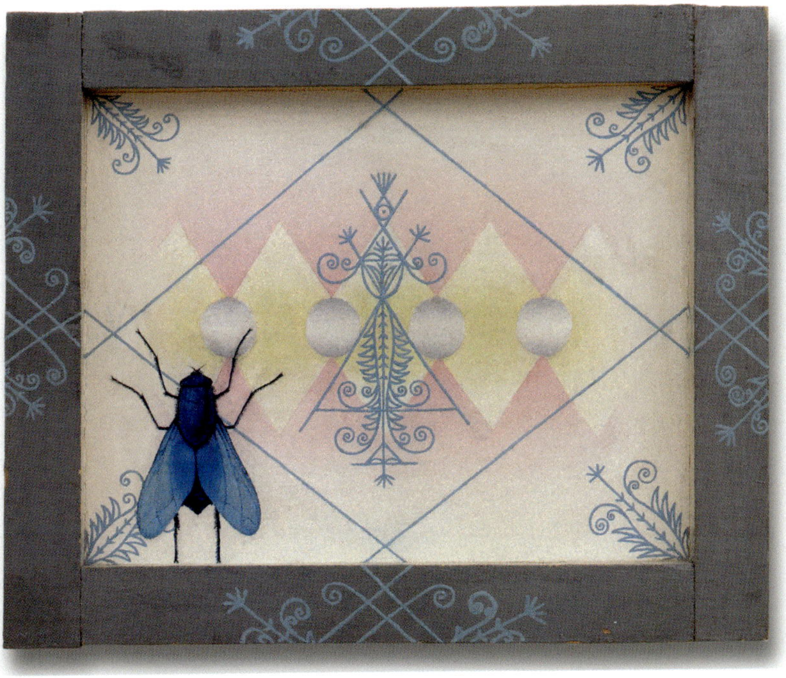

FIGURE 3.3. Ilya Kabakov, *The Queen Fly*, 1965. Oil and enamel on Masonite and wood, 48.5 × 60 × 6 cm. Collection: Department of Russian and Slavic Studies, New York University.

object, an object that is actually visually seductive. Hence, it is tempting to see the substitution of the artwork with the word as a path going from servitude to the "materialist" art market, toward the freedom of the immaterial—and hence the unsaleable, "unexchangeable" artistic word. Meanwhile, of course, it has become clear that text is also a kind of image, because language has its own materiality, and conceptual art can therefore neither lead the artwork all the way to immateriality nor liberate it fully from commerce. In retrospect, conceptual art can rather be seen as a crucial step toward objectifying and hence commercializing language. In any case, the relationship of art to the art market—and to the market in general—was and is a central theme for Western conceptualist theory and praxis.

In the Soviet Union, by contrast, there was no market and, hence, no art market. Official art was produced under the system of state patronage, and unofficial artworks could be bought only directly from the artist. Thus, the value of an artwork was determined not by the rules of the market economy but by the rules of the symbolic economy that governed life in the Soviet Union.

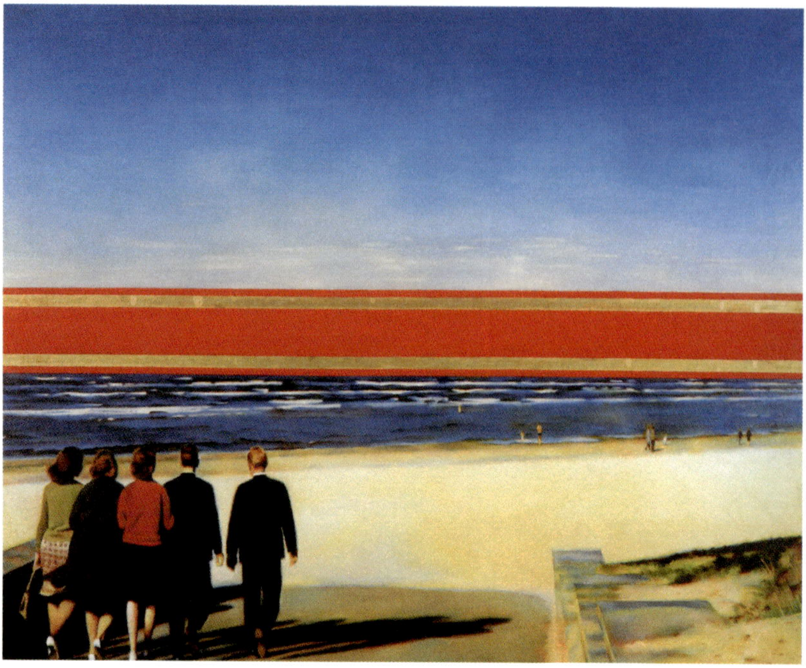

FIGURE 3.4. Erik Bulatov, *Red Horizon*, 1971–72. Oil on canvas, 140 × 180 cm. Private collection.

These were rules of social recognition and political relevance as laid down in certain texts—whether official statements or unofficial pamphlets—that determined the value of every single work of art. The theoretical, philosophical, ideological, or historical commentary on an artwork—and not its price—ultimately decided its fate. Ideological texts circulated in the Soviet symbolic economy just as money circulated in the Western market economy. It could thus be said that Soviet culture had always already been conceptual. When looking at a painting, normal Soviet viewers quite automatically, without ever having heard of the Art and Language group, for instance, would intuitively replace the visual with ideological-political-philosophical commentary, and they would take only this commentary into account when assessing the painting in question, thereby assigning it categories such as Soviet, half-Soviet, non-Soviet, anti-Soviet, and so on. From this, it followed that the explicit use of texts—of art commentary, philosophy, ideology, science, or literature—in artwork as practiced by Moscow conceptualists functioned primarily to reveal the symbolic economy that defined all of Soviet culture as such, rather than as an alternative to a Western-style market economy.

However, to be critical of a certain symbolic economy means also to be a part of it. Precisely for this reason, Moscow conceptualism was a provocation for both sides of the Soviet political spectrum. The negative official reaction was predictable. The blasphemous, irreverent, ironic use of the official Soviet language was perceived as anti-Soviet. But Moscow conceptualism was also a provocation for the unofficial art milieu, because Moscow conceptualists began to invade the supposedly pure, nonideological space of the independent, unofficial culture with signs of Sovietness. The majority of unofficial artists, writers, poets, and intellectuals believed that true protest against the oppressive power of the Soviet system consisted not in criticizing but in ignoring it. And thus they saw in the artistic use of Soviet symbols an advertisement for the Soviet ideological regime and its expansion into the territory of unofficial culture, rather than a critique of this regime. In this sense, their critique of Moscow conceptualism was not unlike the well-known critiques of pop art with which we are by now familiar. And, of course, this critique was, in its turn, criticized by Moscow conceptualists as exemplifying an elitist disregard for the real culture of the majority of the Soviet population.

But even in the West, the Moscow conceptualist strategy was hardly understood, even though the group was better known internationally than any other postwar Russian artistic movement. In the West, popular culture was understood primarily in terms of consumption and entertainment. This diminished interest in, and understanding of, the popular, collective dimension of religious and ideological practices. And one should not forget: under the conditions of the Cold War, Soviet culture remained for a majority of the Western public an unknown and ultimately uninteresting phenomenon. Paradoxically enough, the reason for that lay in the fact that communism was regarded in the West as something already very well known. In turn, Soviet culture also came to be mapped in relation to a Western understanding of Marxism. Looking at the Soviet Union, Western intellectuals became convinced that they interpreted Marxism better than the Russians did—and this insight was enough for them to see the whole of Soviet culture as simply a historical mistake. For intellectuals on the left, any further investigation of the Soviet culture made little sense, because it was clear from the beginning that this culture was based on a dogmatic interpretation of Marxism. While traditional Russian cultural creations (by Fyodor Dostoyevsky, Leo Tolstoy, etc.) may have appeared interesting, Soviet culture was of interest only to clarify why the Russians were so terribly wrong in their reading of Karl Marx. Thus, intellectuals on the left were interested in only one question: how to keep the promise of a better life, of the utopia, and of the transformation of society alive after this promise was so cruelly parodied and so deeply compromised by the Soviet reality. On the right of the Western political spectrum, intellectuals saw the communist regime simply as a machine of repression and were interested only in the cultural activities that were censored by the Soviet power, but never in the culture that was generated by Russian communism. And that means that almost nobody in the West was interested in the culture of Soviet communism itself; they were interested only in their own relationship to, and interpretation of, communist ideology. The same is true for our time—the only thing that the West is interested in is explaining once more how badly Russia has understood and implemented, this time, not communism but capitalism. It will take some time to see that Russian culture is different from Western culture and has its own logic. But in culture, unlike life, one has time.

NOTES

1. Greenberg, "Avant-Garde and Kitsch."
2. Greenberg, "Avant-Garde and Kitsch."
3. See Guilbaut, *How New York Stole the Idea of Modern Art.*
4. See Lenin, *Imperialism.* The title of the most important exhibition of Russian avant-garde art—*Art from the Age of Imperialism*—which was organized by the State Russian Museum in 1931, directly referred to the book. See Jolles, "Stalin's Talking Museums."
5. Lukács, "Expressionism."
6. Lukács, "Expressionism," 113.
7. In this respect, the most characteristic is Plekhanov's essay on Henrik Ibsen. See Plekhanov, "Ibsen, Petty Bourgeois Revolutionist." Lenin also writes in the draft of a resolution directed against the Proletkult movement: "Marxism has won its historic significance as the ideology of the revolutionary proletariat because, far from rejecting the most valuable achievements of the bourgeois epoch, it has, on the contrary, assimilated and refashioned everything of value in the more than two thousand years of the development of human thought and culture. Only further work on this basis and in this direction, inspired by the practical experience of the proletarian dictatorship as the final stage in the struggle against every form of exploitation, can be recognized as the development of a genuine proletarian culture." See Lenin, "On Proletarian Culture," 316–17.
8. See Trotsky's critique of futurism in his essay "Futurism."
9. Breton, "On the Time When the Surrealists Were Right," 243.
10. In other words, the pre-Stalinist understanding of socialism of the 1920s.
11. See Simms, "1959 American National Exhibition in Moscow."
12. Chan-Magomedov, *Pioniere der sowjetischen Architektur*, 63.
13. Chan-Magomedov, *Pioniere der sowjetischen Architektur*, 65.
14. Khrushchev's conflict with the artists, including Ernst Neizvestny, is described in Berger, *Art and Revolution.*
15. Lifshitz, "Why Am I Not a Modernist?"
16. See Groys, *History Becomes Form.*

4

Rent Collection Courtyard, the "Atomic Bomb of the Art World"

VIVIAN LI

In late August 1966, during the incipient stages of the Cultural Revolution (1966–76) in China, students and teachers of the prestigious Central Academy of Fine Arts in Beijing smashed the school's plaster cast collection of established sculptural masterpieces with axes and shovels.[1] Used as models for the school's students to make sketches as part of their basic training, the collection included plaster casts of Michelangelo's *David*, the Venus de Milo, and the Apollo Belvedere, as well as Buddhist sculptures from various renowned cave temples in China. With the destruction of the plaster casts of what were deemed canonical artworks, the scales for measuring artistic value in the still young communist nation were symbolically and definitively overturned. A month

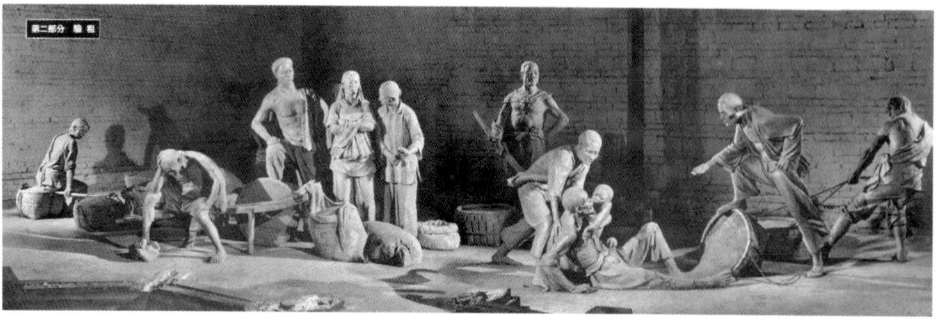

FIGURE 4.1. *Rent Collection Courtyard*, 1965. Detail of the second tableau. Clay. Dayi County, Sichuan Province.

later the large-scale exhibition of one of the most important works in Chinese modern art, *Rent Collection Courtyard*, opened in Beijing in the room once dedicated to ancestral veneration in the Forbidden City. Its placement in the former seat of imperial authority and culture intimated a crucial turning point in modern Chinese art and values.

Rent Collection Courtyard, a ninety-six-meter-long sculptural installation consisting of 114 life-sized clay figures, depicts scenes of downtrodden farmers bringing their harvest as rent to the landlord Liu Wencai during pre–communist revolution China (fig. 4.1). Built in 1965 in rural Dayi County of Sichuan Province, it is installed along the perimeter of a courtyard in Liu's countryside manor where rent was once collected. The figures are arranged in six successive tableaux portraying each stage in the collection of rent: rent submission, grain inspection, chaff removal and grain measurement, settlement of accounts, forcing of rent payment, and the final revolt showing a gathering of a few disgruntled young male farmers.[2]

Soon after its creation, *Rent Collection Courtyard* was pronounced an official model artwork by the rising cultural impresario and Mao Zedong's wife, Jiang Qing, in February 1966.[3] *Rent Collection Courtyard* was also reproduced in whole and in part and exhibited in other major cities, such as Shanghai and Wuhan, and in the allied countries Albania and Vietnam as socialist art par excellence.[4] Within the Chinese art world, Wang Zhaowen, a sculptor turned influential art critic and editor in chief of the national fine arts journal *Meishu* (Art), praised *Rent Collection Courtyard* as the "atomic bomb of the art world," worthy of study by all artists.[5]

Describing a phenomenon as analogous to an atomic bomb was a common practice during the 1960s. China was actively developing nuclear weapons in order to protect itself from the Soviet Union and the United States as well as to enhance its international standing and prestige. In October 1964, China tested its first atomic bomb, and two years later, in October 1966, it launched its first nuclear missile. In June 1967 China detonated its first hydrogen bomb. Although the description of *Rent Collection Courtyard* as an artistic "atomic bomb" links the work to broader postwar concerns, the concept of "postwar art" as a discrete period in art and art history has limited critical purchase in China's art historiography. Rather, in China the significant departure point in postwar art history is the 1949 Chinese communist revolution. After the Second World War, the Nationalist Party and Chinese Communist Party resumed a bitter civil war that concluded with the communist revolution, which serves as the critical turning point in China's art history as well as its modern political chronology. Consequently, the term *art after the revolution* (*jiefang hou de yishu*) is often used instead of *postwar art* to describe the art period of the 1950s and 1960s. The significance of *Rent Collection Courtyard* and its legacy powerfully underscores the important relationship between revolution and modernization in postwar, postrevolutionary China. Like with many other socialist and communist postwar countries, and at the same time unlike the North Atlantic and its modernism, mixed feelings exist today about China's postwar art because the path of modernization in its postwar years was inextricably intertwined with revolution.

Rent Collection Courtyard represented many major changes in China's post-1949 reconsideration of art and culture, making it worthy of its epithet as an "atomic bomb."[6] Here, I focus on the leading issue artists and art administrators grappled with in the Chinese postwar period that culminated in the creation of the sculpture group, an issue that also, through *Rent Collection Courtyard*'s wide circulation, permeated a variety of art and cultural discourses abroad: What is the proper relationship of modern art to the masses? In China, the concept of the masses was intimately tied to the countryside. The countryside was where the majority of the country's population resided and it served as the historic site of the revolution. The city and rural binary instituted by the policies of the young Chinese communist administration, with the intent to introduce more social and economic parity between the two, inadvertently deepened the urban and rural divide. The later heated denunciation of the corrupt city and the championing of the virtuous countryside during the Cultural Revolution, when *Rent Collection Courtyard* debuted, references this heightened divide. The desire for both modernization and revolution, or what social historian Jeremy Brown calls "revolutionary modernization," in bringing the city and countryside closer together dramatically impacted the context for artmaking.[7]

The success of a work of art in postwar, postrevolutionary China was thus judged by how convincingly the artist addressed the new audience of the now politically awakened masses. Artists' interactions with the countryside in turn became key. *Rent Collection Courtyard*'s collective creation with the artists and community directly in the countryside, the sculpted figures' and rural viewers' mutual activation, and the material construction from the abundant locally sourced clay were acclaimed as solving the prominent debate in China's postwar art of how to reconcile the conceptual as well as physical distance between art and the masses. Rather than proposing a solution, though, this chapter demonstrates how *Rent Collection Courtyard* underscored the complex tensions between the modernizing and revolutionary tendencies that existed in late postwar art in China, and how a group of artists worked within and without these social and political trends.

Rural Modernity

Although the Chinese communist government institutionalized artists' relationship with the countryside, the belief in the country's uneducated rural majority as the keystone to modern Chinese art and culture actually predated the establishment of the Chinese Communist Party. The May Fourth Movement in 1919, a large political and cultural event, witnessed a major shift in intellectuals' regard of the masses and their popular culture from one of derision to one of respect.[8] The subsequent folklore movement of the 1920s saw scholars going to the countryside to collect and preserve folk literature, while leftist writers and artists in the 1930s traveled to the countryside to learn about folk art and culture. These activities embody the ambitions of the new generation of post–May Fourth Movement cultural intellectuals to broaden the defined field of culture to include the popular forms and content of the masses. By the early 1930s, their ambitions also extended to broadening the range of recipients of this reconstituted culture to include the uneducated masses. Therefore, the new communist government's call for an active artistic and cultural engagement with the countryside was symptomatic of a larger push to depict, define, and legitimize the experiences of the masses and, hence, the new nation.

By the time *Rent Collection Courtyard* was produced in 1965, the prerequisite activity of working for an extended period of time in the countryside had already become a normative part of artistic praxis. The activity of "experiencing life" (*tiyan shenghuo*) was a basic part of the academic curriculum in the People's Republic in the mid-to-late 1950s in an attempt to bridge the perceived gulf between intellectuals and the life of the masses. Students and teachers, including those from art schools, would regularly go to the countryside or sometimes urban factories to labor with farmers and workers. For example, by 1965, the Sichuan Fine Arts Institute (SFAI) required students to spend eighteen months on socialist education, which entailed working outside of the school, effectively decreasing classroom time.[9]

During the time spent laboring outside, artists as well as art students were encouraged to make sketches of people they encountered, which they then took back to their studios in the city and developed into finished works. Due to the nationwide adoption in the early People's Republic of artists sketching while working in the countryside, sketching became established as an independent art form by the late 1950s. Within the sought-after equivalence of artists' social experiences with the masses and artistic realism in postwar China, realism exceeded its connotation as a modern mode of representation to become synonymous with firsthand experience with the masses.

The widespread adoption of sketching in the countryside in the 1950s also presented an increasingly corporeal demand on the artist. At the Second Cultural Congress Meeting (*wenhua hui*) in 1953, the premier, Zhou Enlai, specifically called upon artists and writers to travel to the countryside and factories and to enter these spaces not merely as spectators but to "become one with the life of the masses" (*he renmin qunzhong de shenghuo dacheng yipian*).[10] A year after Zhou Enlai's invocation, in the April 1954 issue of *Meishu* the celebrated cartoonist Hua Junwu published a cartoon to accompany his satirical short story of an artist who spends decades toiling with a model in his studio rather than improving his technique by leaving the studio to live and sketch among the masses.

The events leading up to the 1965 making of *Rent Collection Courtyard*, however, indicate that the institutional definition of art's relationship with the countryside and the masses remained unresolved. For instance, when the SFAI, located in the city of Chongqing, first received the unusual invitation from the rural county of Dayi to help create the clay sculpture group *Rent Collection Courtyard* for exhibition in the countryside, several members of the school were ambivalent. Some argued that the project would simply be an illustration, so "it is not worth it" (*meiyou gaotou*), while others remarked that since the sculpture was to be made with clay, a fragile and base material, the sculptors would not be making sculpture but "making models" (*gao moxing*) with no artistic value. Moreover, since the sculpture would be made in the countryside, "no matter how good it is nobody would know of it" (*zai nongcun gao zai hao ye meiyou ren zhidao*).[11]

The prospect of going to the countryside also posed a real hindrance to the rising young sculpture faculty at SFAI. Wang Guanyi, for example, had already participated in two prestigious national art exhibitions in Beijing but had to turn down an invitation to participate in the next one in order to accept the assignment of leading the graduating sculpture class to Dayi.[12] The making of *Rent Collection Courtyard*, though, was opportune for the participating students. Before the invitation from Dayi arrived, the five graduating students had been laboring for months in the countryside rather than receiving instruction and making works in the classroom. In the absence of substantive studio time, their participation in the *Rent Collection Courtyard* project served as their collective graduation project.[13] The countryside, and, in particular, urban artists' and intellectuals' relationship to it, was thus a pervasive yet ever-evolving presence in the artistic life of postwar China.

Vernacular Approaches to Modern Sculpture

Aside from the graduating sculpture students, the *Rent Collection Courtyard* team comprised a uniquely diverse mix of roughly twenty people, including a scriptwriter; a photographer; the two academically trained sculptors from SFAI, Zhao Shutong and Wang Guanyi; and the venue's art staff, which consisted of the two painters Zhang Fulun and Tang Shun'an, the sculptor Li Qisheng, and the third-generation folk sculptor Jiang Quangui, as well as volunteer assistants who taught at the local elementary school. The elaborate orchestration of this unique collaboration across many disciplines and work units was made possible by the vision and official authority of Ma Li, the head of the Wenjiang District Propaganda Department, who oversaw the activities of Liu Wencai's former manor cum class-education museum.

Ma Li's interest in sculpture stemmed from his view of the vernacular and folk arts as potential sources of inspiration for a new visual culture that could engage the masses. Observing the ubiquity of Buddhist sculpture in the city, countryside, mountains, and roadsides "poisoning the working people's thinking," he proposed: "Why can't we use these forms to denounce the evil crimes of the landlord class?"[14] In 1960, with the reinstallation of the galleries at the Dayi Landlord Class-Education Exhibition Hall in response to visitor evaluations over its first year of operation, Ma Li had already begun to encourage sculpture exhibits.

After the Sino-Soviet split in the early 1960s, Chinese sculptors were also shifting their focus away from foreign paradigms and toward domestic models, in search of a uniquely "Chinese" form of modern sculpture. For instance, at

Beijing's Central Academy of Fine Arts, sculptors Wang Linyi and Hua Tianyou studied Han dynasty (206 BCE–220 CE) and Tang dynasty (618–907 CE) sculpture, respectively. Other sculptors chose to travel the country to study vernacular and Buddhist sculpture—for example, at Mount Wutai in Shanxi, at locations in Yunnan, and at the recently excavated Dazu caves in Sichuan.[15] During their preparation, the *Rent Collection Courtyard* art team also traveled to several historic temple sites to study various sculptural approaches. They visited the twelfth-century Dazu cave grottoes in the countryside to study their narrative strategy and the composition of multiple sculptural tableaux, each depicting different Buddhist parables; they also studied sculptural strategies for diversifying facial expressions in a large group of figures, such as in the group of five hundred lohan sculptures in the ninth-century Baoguang Temple in the neighboring city of Chengdu.

Ma Li, though, not only encouraged the art team to study existing sculptural techniques to reach a new art audience but also exhorted the team to combine their talents and variety of expertise. For example, the notable folk sculptor Jiang Quangui, who was hired in 1964 for the purpose of readying *Rent Collection Courtyard* and making other clay sculptures for exhibition, was responsible for shaping several of the figures' clothing. Consequently, the figures' attire is often reminiscent of the fluid, scroll-like treatment of drapery in late Buddhist sculpture, as in the several flourishing curves of fabric around the sleeves, front fold, and sash in the figure of a mother (fig. 4.2). Since Jiang's sculpted faces also appeared stylized like Buddhist temple bodhisattvas, the SFAI academic sculptor Zhao Shutong would alter the faces with greater attention to anatomy so that they were "modern peasant face[s]."[16] Jiang also taught the rest of the art team the time-saving folk sculpture techniques used to make lasting clay sculptures like those built for temples. Such vernacular techniques usually involve a wooden armature and readily available, inexpensive materials for shaping and modeling such as hemp, wheat stalks, rice husks, wire, clay, and sandy soil. In the case of *Rent Collection Courtyard*, a wooden armature and wire were fixed to the ground where the figure would stand (fig. 4.3).

The combination of vernacular and academic techniques, however, exposed reservations and assumptions about the vernacular approach to sculpture, compared with the academic approach practiced in the city. There were, for instance, disagreements from the outset between Jiang Quangui and the sculptors from SFAI. During one group meeting, one of the school's sculpture students told Jiang, "I have not yet found anything worth learning from you."[17] The academically trained sculptors on the team were also uncomfortable using black round glass for the eyes, as was common in temple and folk sculptures, because they

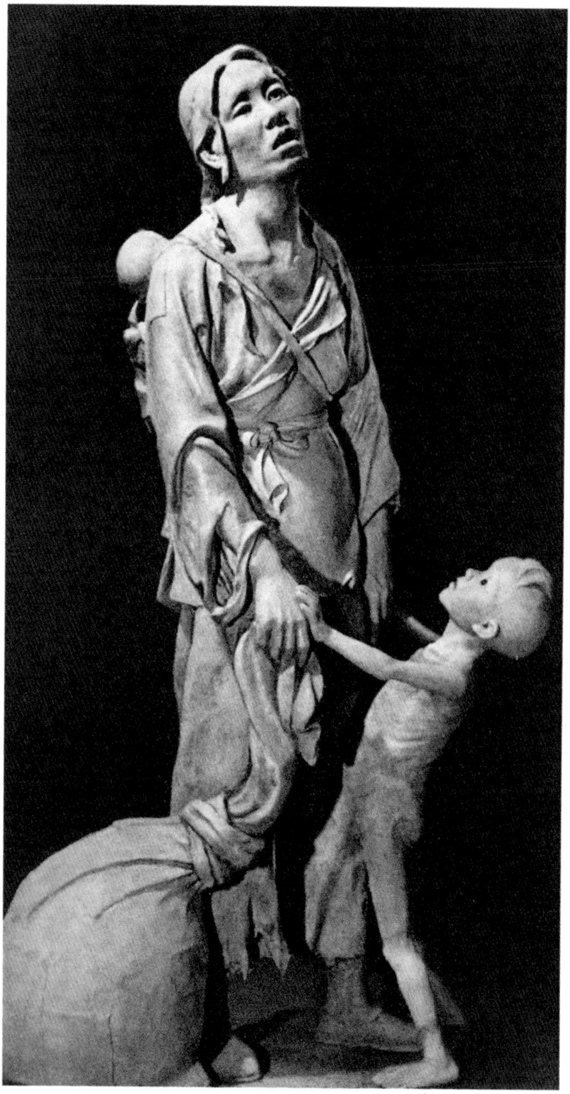

FIGURE 4.2. *Rent Collection Courtyard*, 1965. Detail of widow and child. Clay. Dayi County, Sichuan Province.

feared it would look "fake" (*jia*), although they capitulated when the intended audience, the farmers, responded to them favorably.[18]

During the preparatory work, the local party unit arranged for the sculptors to visit former tenant farmers, who would recount their history of victimhood under the landlord. Locals also described the landlord and his men to the sculptors, and some even served as models for *Rent Collection Courtyard*. The artists similarly emphasized their "open-door production" (*kaimen chuangzuo*) approach, which entailed leaving the doors to the courtyard open while

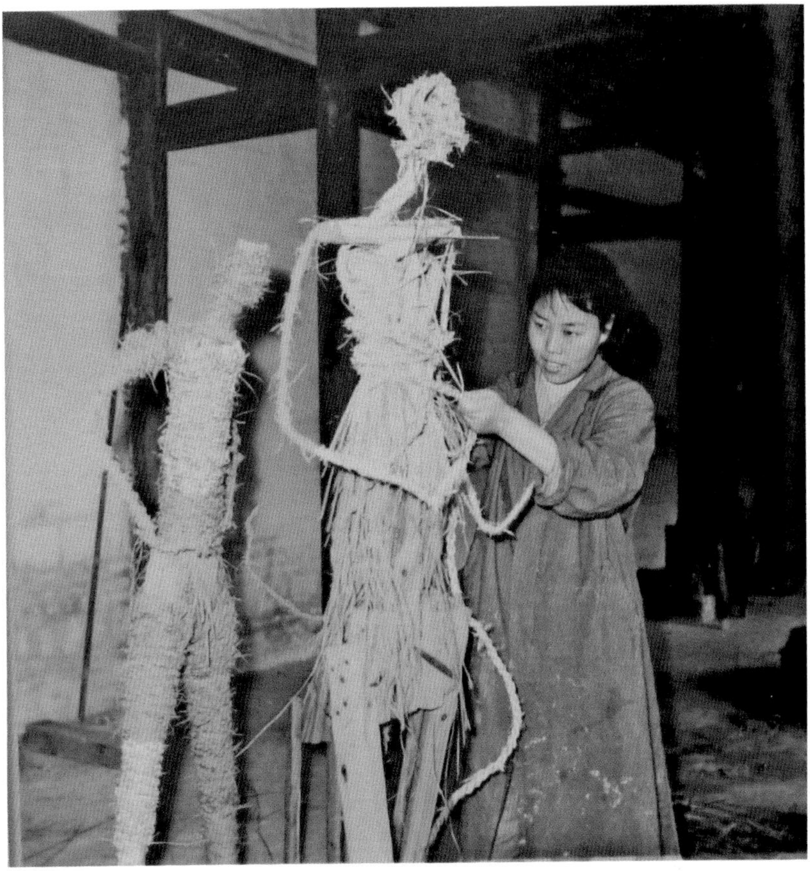

FIGURE 4.3. Zhang Fulun wrapping wooden armature in straw ropes for *Rent Collection Courtyard* sculptures, 1965. Dayi Landlord Class-Education Exhibition Hall, Dayi County, Sichuan Province.

working so that curious locals could stop by to see the work in progress and offer feedback.[19] During their free time, the art team described often going to local market fairs and the grain collection depot to make sketches and photograph faces and bodies engaged in different actions and poses (fig. 4.4).[20] The prominence given to reimagining the relationship between modern art and the masses encouraged the makers of *Rent Collection Courtyard* to synthesize the rich diversity of sculptural practices that coexisted in 1960s China. The efficient material and stylized techniques of Jiang Quangui combined with the SFAI sculptors' academic practices of sketching and anatomical study produced an original and syncretic monumental work.

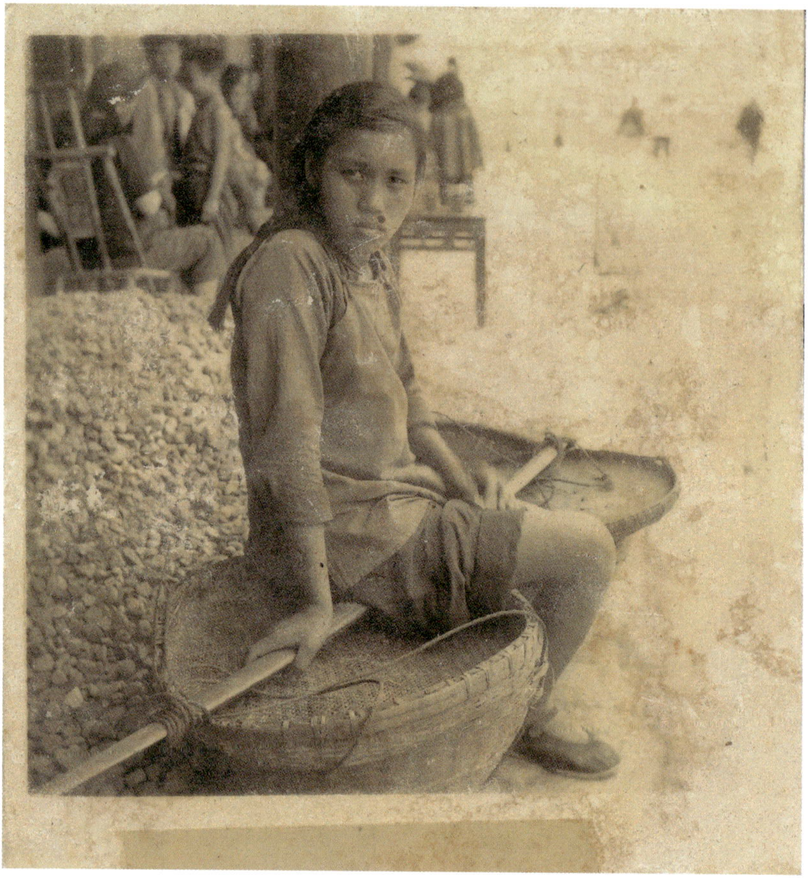

FIGURE 4.4. Market scene, Dayi County, Sichuan Province, 1965. Photograph by the *Rent Collection Courtyard* art team, made during fieldwork.

In the actual modeling of the expressive sculptures, the sculptors focused on gestures rather than bodily poses to enliven the clay figures and "to make the viewers feel the same as the sculptures."[21] This was achieved through a cast of extras, or "middle characters" (*zhongjian renwu*), representing ordinary people. In *Rent Collection Courtyard*, such figures fill the transitional spaces and corners and most often are represented in mundane postures such as sitting, watching, and waiting. Whereas the melodramatic gestures of the main characters may be deemed "kitsch" in their conspicuously dramatic depictions of class struggle, such as a young boy's left arm raised in anticipation of the blow of a henchman's whip, the gestures of the middle characters appear "true" or convincingly self-aware and natural in the ambiguity of their reason and

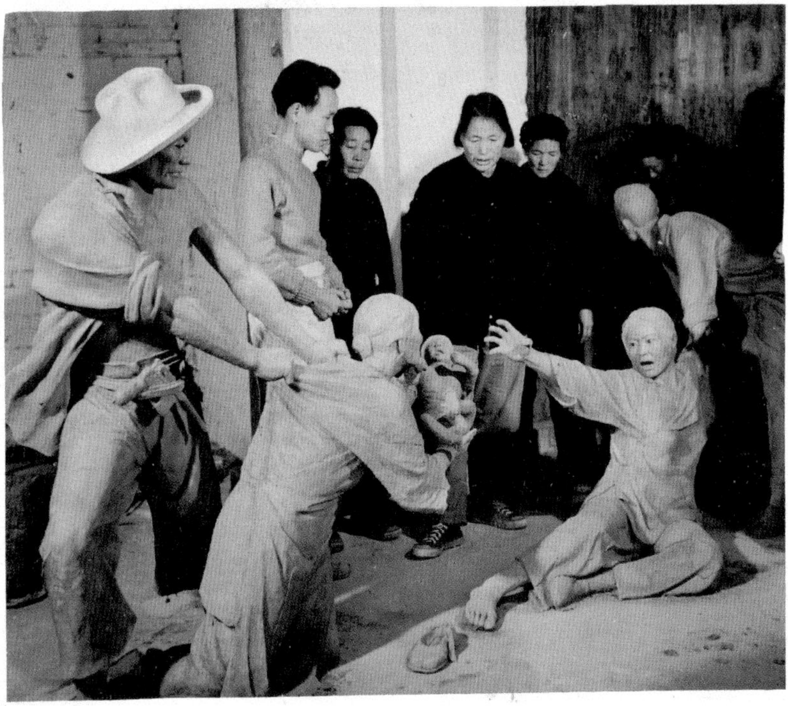

FIGURE 4.5. Sculptor Wang Guanyi (*far left*) showing alleged victims Luo Erniang (*left*) and Leng Yueying (*center*) the figures in *Rent Collection Courtyard* depicting their stories. Dayi County, Sichuan Province, 1965.

meaning. Art critic Wang Zhaowen especially marveled at the expressive nature of these characters' hands, such as those of the girl gripping the basket pole between tableaux 1 and 2 (see fig. 4.1) and those of the mother and daughter pulling a basket of grain together between tableaux 2 and 3.[22] Herein lay the "success" of *Rent Collection Courtyard* in the context of the roiling radical and revolutionary currents of the times. The emotive and sentient life-size sculptures activated the rural courtyard space into a stage on which local visitors could perform acts of empathy with, or violent acts of retribution on behalf of, the sculpted figures (fig. 4.5).

Needless to say, the success of the sculpture was ultimately measured by the local rural viewers' response to the sculptured figures. According to Wang Guanyi, the artists who created *Rent Collection Courtyard* were elated at the exhibition opening when a group of six elderly female farmers "instantly understood the piece."[23] As was widely retold in the media, Wang had to restrain one of the women, who upon entering the courtyard installation prepared to hit the henchman in the first tableau with her walking stick. Instead of admonishing these former tenant farmers of Liu Wencai, the sculptors invited them to walk around the courtyard and explain the piece. Although they had never seen *Rent Collection Courtyard* before, Wang claimed that the former tenants were able to explain each depicted story "very clearly" without any assistance. The artists', and subsequently the media's, frequent retelling of this event shows how *Rent Collection Courtyard* was deemed praiseworthy in its ability to communicate empathetically with both the masses and rural viewers. Despite the differences between rural and academic sculptural conventions that indeed existed, the composite of the various sculptural practices shared by the art team, and endorsed by Ma Li to appeal to the masses, contributed to the collective making of a new visual culture that endeavored to be both modern and revolutionary.

Clay Politics

Destined for wide dissemination by the state media, *Rent Collection Courtyard* began its long trajectory from its permanent courtyard site in Dayi County in the then remote Sichuan Province into national and international visual culture. The remarkable ability of *Rent Collection Courtyard* to inspire more sculptural works in spite of its obdurate material permanence can be attributed primarily to clay. Clay appealed to the masses as a material not only because it is sourced from the countryside but also because it can be shaped simply and directly with the fingers.

Rent Collection Courtyard's use of clay to make sculpture in the countryside was interpreted politically in the press as creating art that was accessible to and representative of the masses. In a 1966 essay, "A Revolution in Sculpture," published shortly after *Rent Collection Courtyard* opened in Sichuan, an anonymous writer criticized the use of bronze, stone, marble, and granite in sculptures that portrayed the theme of class struggle and oppression. Hailing *Rent Collection Courtyard* as the new touchstone in sculpture, the author argued that "art must be brought to their [the working people's] doorstep."[24] Hua Junwu, the arts editor of the *Renmin ribao* (*People's Daily*), also lauded *Rent Collection Courtyard* as a *yangban*, or model, for "mak[ing] our new socialist sculptors from the city walk into the vast countryside."[25] Hua's and the anonymous writer's discussions of *Rent Collection Courtyard* reveal the imbricated values of power latent in clay. As in many other societies, clay in China has been historically associated with the non-elite and everyday life, in contrast to the more permanent materials that have been employed to create lasting sculptural symbols of authority, such as ritual bronze vessels and stone steles as well as the modern granite and marble *Monument to the People's Heroes* (1952–58) in Tiananmen Square. *Rent Collection Courtyard*, it would appear, significantly transformed the general view that sculpture was necessarily urban, expensive, and thus inaccessible to the masses.

The choice of material used in *Rent Collection Courtyard* also complemented Mao's charge to exterminate the so-called counterrevolutionary bureaucrats in urban institutions of power. Selecting clay for such a famous sculptural installation as *Rent Collection Courtyard* served to both outright reject the corrupt authorities in the city and honor the "artless" peasants and workers in the countryside. Hence, on the eve of the Cultural Revolution, *Rent Collection Courtyard*'s widely celebrated and heavily politicized use of clay effectively reversed art's hierarchy by prioritizing this basic material and the medium of sculpture. The use of clay was now deemed most suitable for constructing works commemorating workers' and peasants' subjugated past as well as their role as leaders in the present.

The art world's focus on the economy of making *Rent Collection Courtyard*—such as Hua Junwu's praise of the fact that the massive ensemble had been made at just three yuan a figure and in only four and a half months—also positioned *Rent Collection Courtyard* as a celebratory overcoming of the physical and financial obstructions that were usually associated with producing and installing sculpture.[26] Subsequently, at the height of the Cultural Revolution, the use of clay and its supposedly straightforward technical and manual approach spurred a nationwide movement to reproduce *Rent Collection Courtyard* in large cities such as Wuhan, Chongqing, Shanghai, and Beijing. Effectively, *Rent Collection Courtyard* allowed the narrative of the countryside to enter the major urban centers of postwar China.

Emphasizing sculpture as a narrative vehicle, other cities chose instead to create sculptures of local stories of oppression following the production model of *Rent Collection Courtyard*. Based on stories from oral histories gathered by the artists, sculptors used clay to collectively create grand multifigured series of life-size tableaux, which were then installed on actual sites of alleged crimes. For instance, Guangdong's 208-figure *Holy Infant Orphanage* (1966–68), made by the sculpture department of the Guangzhou Academy of Fine Arts, portrayed the suffering of orphans under the orphanage's Catholic administration; the thirty-three-figure, life-size *Old Foolish Man of Dashu* in Sichuan, created by SFAI in 1966, was installed in the rural Dashu commune; and the 106-figure *Wrath of the Serfs* in Lhasa, completed in 1976, was exhibited in the Lhasa Revolutionary Museum and created by sculptors from the Central Academy of

Fine Arts in Beijing and the Lu Xun Art College in Shenyang. Similarly, they lived with and researched the community in the Tibetan countryside to create the highly dramatic sculptural production. Although such works inspired by *Rent Collection Courtyard* lacked the original's unique collaboration of distinctly different artistic approaches, countless re-creations and reproductions of *Rent Collection Courtyard* nonetheless continued to set the stage for visitors nationwide in major urban settings to respond empathetically to the inequality and class exploitation of their rural compatriots during the tumultuous Cultural Revolution in China.[27] In the late 1960s, at the height of the Cultural Revolution, *Rent Collection Courtyard* also physically brought the urban population into the countryside. Several buses and trainloads of urban work units across China, from as far away as the Palace Museum in Beijing, flooded rural Dayi daily and overwhelmed the local resources and infrastructure. Work units were mandated to visit the sculpture group as part of their political education.

In the late 1960s and 1970s, the dissemination of *Rent Collection Courtyard* in the form of reproductions additionally brought the sculpture to international attention. A radically revised re-creation of *Rent Collection Courtyard* made for exhibition in Albania in 1968 became the physical version of *Rent Collection Courtyard* that traveled internationally.[28] Constructed in Beijing, in the former Hall of Literary Brilliance (Wenhua Dian) of the Forbidden City, the version sent to Albania consisted of ninety-nine plaster figures produced by a team of sculptors, some of whom were from the original art team in Dayi, such as Zhao Shutong and Wang Guanyi.[29] Unlike the original Dayi version, the Albanian version was revised to accentuate the important leadership role of the Chinese Communist Party. Particularly in the last two newly added tableaux, the revolt and seizing of power showed figures from the Chinese People's Liberation Army leading farmers to take up weapons and together struggle against the landlord, even though in reality Liu Wencai died before the communists arrived in Sichuan. In the last tableau, a People's Liberation Army officer and a farm girl hold up a placard reading "The People's Government" (*renmin zhengfu*), while a People's Liberation Army soldier and an armed farmer together hold up a volume of Mao's writings in front of an enormous backdrop, with Mao's picture framed by sunrays. The distinctions between the original Dayi installation and its re-creations, however, were not lost on contemporaneous viewers. As one foreign visitor to the exhibition of the *Rent Collection Courtyard* re-creation at the Forbidden City in Beijing noted, the sculpture had transformed into a rote spectacle with a glowing portrait of Mao Zedong lit by flashing neon lights, whereas in the Dayi installation the sculptures had elicited sympathy and empathy.[30]

Arguably, the work that *Rent Collection Courtyard* was expected to perform had changed substantially since the Sino-Soviet split, as China endeavored to succeed the Soviet Union on the global stage. Coinciding with the interest in Maoism in Europe and North America during the late 1960s and early 1970s, the version of the sculpture made for Albania thus attempted to persuade international audiences to follow Maoist thought by emphasizing the people's reliance on the leadership and guidance of the army and Mao Zedong. Consequently, when the illustrated book *Rent Collection Courtyard: Sculptures of Oppression and Revolt* was produced in 1968, the Foreign Languages Press in Beijing decided to feature images of the Dayi version of *Rent Collection Courtyard* as well as the revised last tableau from the Albanian version.[31] Reproductions of some of the pieces made in the Albanian version as well as large-format photographs of the original Dayi installation were sent to Vietnam, too, and exhibited in Hanoi from January 20 to February 16, 1968. Thus, *Rent Collection Courtyard*'s journey from the arguably culturally disconnected countryside to the international stage further upended the urban-centric hierarchy of modern art.

Just as *Rent Collection Courtyard* was becoming an intrinsic part of a larger network of cultural exchange between socialist and communist governments, the 1968 photo book reached the celebrated Swiss curator Harald Szeemann. Fascinated by the sculpture group's collective production, Szeemann attempted without success to have the tableaux included in the 1972 Documenta exhibition, *Questioning Reality—Image Worlds Today*.[32] Adrian Henri also featured the sculpture group in his seminal 1974 book *Total Art: Environments, Happenings, and Performance*, which exposed even more artists and intellectuals in Europe and North America to *Rent Collection Courtyard*. Presented by Henri alongside well-known European and American artists such as Niki de Saint Phalle and Ed Kienholz, the sculpture was juxtaposed with Duane Hanson's *Race Riot* (1969–71) as two examples of a seemingly analogous combination of sculptural realism and social protest within the emerging discourse of postmodernism in global art.[33]

Coda

It would appear that *Rent Collection Courtyard*—the "atomic bomb of the art world"—actualized not only postwar China's but also the postwar European avant-garde's desire to meld art with everyday life. At the same time, the sculpture group was created in the postrevolutionary Chinese countryside in support of the Maoist state's critique of the past. *Rent Collection Courtyard* raises important questions for a global art history of the postwar: How might we approach the relationship between art and revolution under disparate postwar conditions? How might we understand the dialectic between artistic revolution and political revolution, and indeed between modernism and art for the masses? Paradoxes abound insofar as *Rent Collection Courtyard* is concerned: Although *Rent Collection Courtyard* successfully reversed the modern urban-centric values of postwar art and culture for a time, its collective production and site-specific presentation in the countryside nonetheless transformed it into a discursive symbol quickly incorporated into the very same urban institutional frameworks it sought to subvert. In turn, *Rent Collection Courtyard*'s creation and display in rural China, as well as the unprecedented collaboration between academically trained artists and folk sculptors, came to be uncritically celebrated as an official project of mass art and symptomatic of the politics of its time. Notably, the version of *Rent Collection Courtyard* installed in Beijing's Palace Museum was destroyed and discarded ten years later, after the conclusion of the Cultural Revolution in 1976. Although the nation and the world that *Rent Collection Courtyard* helped define in the 1960s and 1970s inexorably changed, the original 114-figure clay sculpture group remains on view today, in situ, in rural Dayi. In 1996, the site was given official designation as a Major Historical and Cultural Site Protected at the National Level (*quanguo zhongdian wenwu baohu*). Now lauded in China, as well as internationally, more as a powerful testament to the successful realization of mass art than as a depiction of class struggle and Maoist leadership, *Rent Collection Courtyard* continues to exemplify revolutionary modernization in postwar art. We conventionally think of the atomic bomb as a weapon of destruction. Yet the enduring story of *Rent Collection Courtyard* indicates that the atomic bomb can sometimes become a metaphor for the generation of something new, something novel, out of the ravages of the old.

NOTES

1. During the Cultural Revolution, a period from 1966 to 1976, Mao Zedong, the leader of the Chinese Communist Party, attempted to regain central control over the direction of the party. He called on the masses, particularly the youth who became known as the Red Guard, to rebel against those people in the party and other social institutions deemed reactionary or counterrevolutionary.

2. Variations of the total number of tableaux include four for the original and a multiple number of variants in *Rent Collection Courtyard*'s later, revised versions. See Zhao Shutong, "Speech by Comrade Zhao Shutong," in *'Shouzu yuan' nisu qunxiang guangmo zuotan hui shang de fayan* [Rent Collection Courtyard clay sculpture group work experience study symposium], published by the Chinese Artists Association for Internal Study, 1966, 3; "Shouzu yuan" folder, Sichuan Cultural Bureau, PRC Sichuan dossier no. 124, Sichuan Provincial Archives, Chengdu, China.

3. The designation of "model," or *yangban*, status for works of art in Mao's China began in early 1965, when the opera *The Red Lantern* was lauded in the *Theater Journal* as being an "outstanding model." Later that year, the same journal praised *The Red Lantern* along with the opera *Shajiabang* as "models of the revolutionizing of Peking opera." Subsequently Jiang Qing enthusiastically appropriated the term in her reviews of art. See Paul Clark, *Chinese Cultural Revolution*, 57, 59.

4. A fiberglass re-creation of *Rent Collection Courtyard* was also exhibited in the city hall of Toronto in 1987 and in Japan before returning to China. Ye Yushan, interview with the author, May 22, 2013.

5. "Meishu jie de yuanzidan," *Sichuan Dayi dizhu zhuangyuan chenlieguan "Shouzu yuan" caisu—zuotanhui jilu'* [Sichuan Dayi Landlord Manor Exhibition Hall's color sculpture 'Rent Collection Courtyard'—Discussion proceedings], n.d., 3; "Shouzu yuan" folder, Sichuan Cultural Bureau, PRC Sichuan dossier no. 124, Sichuan Provincial Archives, 3, Chengdu, China. Unless otherwise noted, all translations by the author.

6. See V. Li, "Redefining Artistic Value in Communist China."

7. J. Brown, *City versus Countryside*, 2.

8. The May Fourth Movement was spurred by student protests in Beijing on May 4, 1919, against the Chinese government's acceptance of the Treaty of Versailles, which transferred the northeast province of Shandong from Germany to Japan. The protest inspired a rise in nationalism as well as contempt for traditional elite intellectual and political systems. The May Fourth Movement affected a new generation of thought leaders, stimulating, e.g., the reorganization of the young Nationalist Party as well as the birth of the Chinese Communist Party. See H. Li, "Making a Name."

9. See Liu, *Sichuan meishu xueyuan xiaoshi*, 91–92.

10. Zhou, "Wei zongluxian er fendou," 50.

11. Rent Collection Courtyard Collective Sculpture Team, "Xian ge sixiang de ming."

12. Büttner, "Transformations of a Work of Art," 26. Wang Guanyi, interview with the author, November 21, 2013.

13. Zhang Shaoxi, interview with the author, November 15, 2013. The team from the SFAI sculpture department comprised the two teachers Zhao Shutong and Wang Guanyi and graduating students Li Shaoduan, Long Xuli, Zhang Shaoxi, and Fan Degao. Student Liao Dehu also participated but due to illness had to leave midway through the project.

14. "Women weishenme bu keyi yunyong zhe yi xingshi lai kongsu dizhu jieji de zui'e!" in *Dayi xian dizhu zhuangyuan chenlieguan yingyong caisu wei jieji jiaoyu fuwu* [Dayi Landlord Manor Exhibition Hall uses color sculpture to serve class education] November 3, 1965, 78; "Shouzu yuan" folder, Sichuan Cultural Bureau, PRC Sichuan dossier, no. 124, Sichuan Provincial Archives.

15. Sullivan, *Art and Artists of Twentieth-Century China*, 163.

16. Wang Zhi'an, *Hongtian juechang*, 240–46.

17. Zhao, "Speech by Comrade Zhao Shutong."

18. Wang Guanyi, "Speech by Comrade Wang Guanyi," in *'Shouzu yuan' nisu qunxiang guangmo zuotan hui shang de fayan* [Rent Collection Courtyard clay sculpture group work experience study symposium], published by the Chinese Artists Association for

Internal Study, 1966; "Shouzu yuan" folder, Sichuan Cultural Bureau, PRC Sichuan dossier no. 124, Sichuan Provincial Archives, Chengdu, China.

19. Rent Collection Courtyard Collective Sculpture Team, "Shouzuyuan nisu chuangzuo de gousi sheji," 4.

20. Wang Zhi'an, *Hongtian juechang*, 240–46.

21. Zhao, "Speech by Comrade Zhao Shutong."

22. Y. Li, "Lun Wang Zhaowen," 86.

23. Wang Guanyi, interview with the author, April 13, 2013.

24. "Revolution in Sculpture," 31.

25. See Hua, "Zhide xuexi de diaosu hao yanbang," 4.

26. See, e.g., Hua, "Zhide xuexi de diaosu hao yanbang."

27. Visitors to a re-created sculpture installation of *Rent Collection Courtyard* in Shanghai reportedly sang "The East Is Red" and shouted slogans such as "Never forget class struggle! Remember blood-and-tears hatred." Ho and Li, "From Landlord Manor to Red Memorabilia," 22.

28. Albania was the only Eastern European nation to side with China after the Sino-Soviet split in the early 1960s. Not only were revised sculptures for *Rent Collection Courtyard* made and shipped to Albania, but so were the painted scenery and props used in the exhibition. The Tirana exhibition opened on April 28, 1968, and Enver Hoxha, the leader of Albania, liked the sculpture group so much that the Chinese authorities agreed to give it to Albania after the show. See V. Li, "*Rent Collection Courtyard*, 1968, Palace of Culture."

29. Wang Guanyi, interview with the author, July 28, 2011.

30. See Laing, *Winking Owl*, 62.

31. *Rent Collection Courtyard*. The book was translated into Esperanto (*Rentkolekta korto argila statuaro*), Portuguese (*O pátio da cobrança das rendas esculturas de barro*), German (*Hof für die Pachteinnahme*), Spanish (*El patio de los arriendos*), French (*La cour des fermages*), and English.

32. In a letter to Feng Bin, Szeemann described his fascination with *Rent Collection Courtyard* as not politically motivated, stating, "There must be a misunderstanding: the Redness was never a problem for me concerning Chinese Art. But the Courtyard is a fantastic cooperative art work that's it." Harold Szeemann, letter to Feng Bin, August 4, 2002; box 2011.17.30, Szeemann 2000–2002 folder, "Cai Story" subfolder; box 662, folder 3, Getty Research Library, Los Angeles. *Rent Collection Courtyard* internationally publicized the mode of collective art production that actually has a long history in modern China. For an overview, see Ho, "People Eat for Free."

33. Out of the more than eighty artists and art collectives Henri featured, the four other non-Euro-American artists and their works, besides *Rent Collection Courtyard*, are Kazuo Shiraga's *Challenging Mud* (1955), Atsuko Tanaka's *Electric Dress* (1956), Ay-O's *Rainbow Room* (1964), and Yayoi Kusama's *Phalli's Field* (1965–66).

Part III

PACIFIC PASSAGES, ATLANTIC OSCILLATIONS

5

Godzilla's Schizophrenia

Americanization and Amnesia in Postwar Japan

ALEXANDRA MUNROE

For Okwui

The atomic bombs over Hiroshima and Nagasaki in August 1945 compelled the unconditional surrender and defeat of the Empire of Japan to the Allied forces, effectively ending the Second World War. Driven by militarist ideology and the dream of a unified Asia under the Yamato race, wartime Japan had ruled over nearly three million square miles of the Asia Pacific region, making it one of the largest maritime empires in history. It was also one of the most brutal. But with the US-led occupation and its quick adoption of Japan as a principal ally in the rising Pacific front of the Cold War, Japan's history and

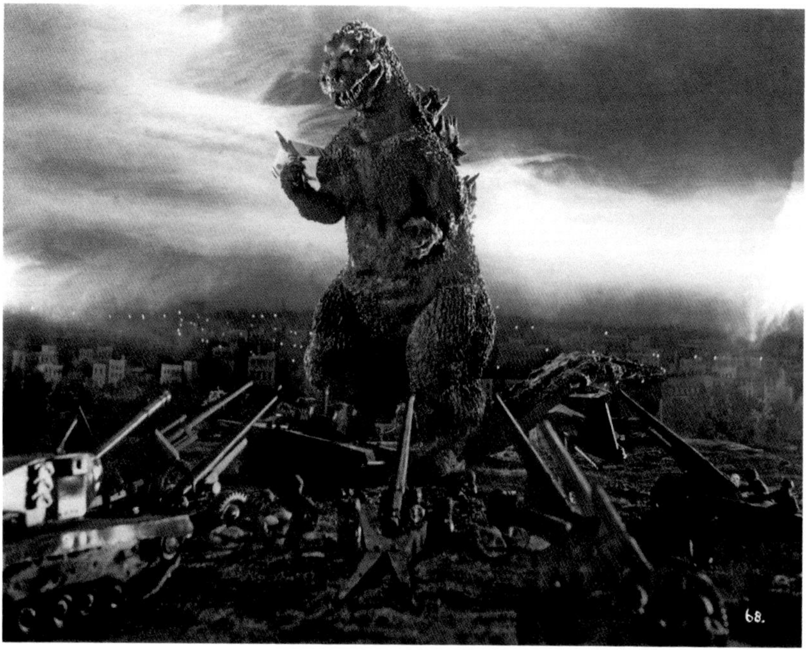

FIGURE 5.1. Still from *Godzilla*, 1954, directed by Honda Ishirō. *Tokusatsu* (special-effects) film, 97 minutes. ©1954 Toho Co. Ltd.

memory of the war were officially erased. American elite academies, working closely with the Department of State, successfully recast the image of Japan from an aggressor to a victim nation. Demilitarized and in the throes of rapid reconstruction, post-war Japanese society also did an about-face and embraced America's influence. This chapter explores the complexity of Japan's "culture of defeat" by looking at the ways certain artists, including *Godzilla* director Honda Ishirō, responded to this acute state of political and ideological ambiguity (fig. 5.1). On the one hand, they rejected America's inventions of (and policy prescriptions for) a pacified, effeminized, and contemplative Japan. On the other hand, they deliberately internalized what Gutai founder Yoshihara Jirō called "the psychological realism" of American humanism expressed in avant-garde art.[1] This polarity is what I call "Godzilla's schizophrenia." It is no coincidence that this great monster movie picturing catastrophic violence, material destruction, and atomic-bomb aberration on a truly giant scale was released in 1954, the year the Gutai group was founded. Whose war shapes the post-war?

Postwar Revisited offers a long-overdue opportunity to rethink the post-war era, and to redraw its histories from less familiar perspectives.[2] Curiously, few essays deal with the *war* that conditions the *post-war*. The periodization of postwar is enduring. Both the geopolitics and the culture that followed the putative end of the Second World War were related to the war itself; understanding this relationship should be at the heart of our project. In fact, there was no single war and no single postwar experience. There were tens if not hundreds of wars, most originating in the late nineteenth century, when colonial empires from the Pacific to the Atlantic were using military force to gain territories on land and sea literally all around the globe. By 1931, when the Japanese invaded Manchuria, allegedly for resources to fuel their rapid industrialization, conditions were ripe for wars of independence from the British, for the Nazi rise in Germany, and for civil war in China between Mao Zedong's Chinese Communist Party and Chiang Kai-shek's Kuomintang.

But if we have multiple wars that conditioned multiple post-wars, we also have multiple histories that nations have produced to glorify, justify, or display guilt for the carnage. These official histories, narrated in textbooks, museum exhibitions, war memorials, and political speeches, communicated the message of what was lost and what was gained. Yet, as my chapter demonstrates, often these post-war histories of the war were not really histories at all; rather, they were discursive constructions created by governments to serve political and ideological ends in the advancing Cold War between the United States with its NATO allies and the newly expanded communist world encompassing the Soviet Union, its Eastern Bloc, "Red China," and the postwar communist states in the Northeast and Southeast Asia sphere.

The case of Japan is extraordinary in this regard. The atomic bombs of August 6 and 9, 1945, forced Japan's final concession to surrender, effectively ending the Second World War and Japan's decades-long aggression across Pacific Asia. But Japan's end came long after its Axis allies Italy and Germany had given up battle.[3] Preoccupied by the fate of the imperial house and defending the theocratic premises of state Shinto that ensured the sovereign's divine status, Emperor Hirohito and his Supreme War Leadership Council stalled the peace talks for several critical months. They saw they had been militarily defeated but remained indifferent to the catastrophic suffering that the ongoing war was causing to their own people and to millions of others across Asia, the Pacific, and the West.[4] Even after the first atomic bomb exploded, Japan's government did not surrender but instead gathered to plan how long it would take to develop a similar weapon of mass destruction.

The iconic image of the atomic bomb blast over Hiroshima (Nagasaki is rarely imagined) achieved one of the greatest perversions of war history ever: virtually overnight, it cast the Japanese people as victims of unspeakable horror perpetrated by the dual evils of modern Western science and US imperialism over the inferior "yellow race." This view obliterated the inconvenient facts that Japan itself was an advanced war machine. In Emperor Hirohito's name, the totalitarian state promoting Japan's racial superiority in its militarist march across Asia was responsible for the deaths of twenty million Asians, including some fifteen million Chinese, 3.1 million Japanese, and more than sixty thousand soldiers of the Western Allied forces.[5] The story of post-war Japan is thus the story of how Japan's history and memory of the war were officially erased and how some found their own psychological expression at the fringes of official culture.

Significantly, this total reimagining of Japan was deliberately produced in large part by the US government. The United States entered the Second World War only on December 8, 1941, after the Japanese launched a surprise attack on its Pacific fleet in Pearl Harbor. America's defeat of Japan meant the reestablishment of the United States as a Pacific power. The occupation government (1945–52) under US supreme commander of Allied powers Douglas MacArthur lost no time in co-opting Japan as America's principal ally and military post in the rising Pacific front of the Cold War: China fell to Mao in 1949, and the Korean War of 1950–53 led to the division of the Korean peninsula, with the North falling to Soviet influence. From the immediate postsurrender period and through the 1960s, American elite academies, working closely with the US Department of State and its newly sanctioned partner, Japan's ruling Liberal Democratic Party, successfully recast the image of Japan from an aggressor to a victim nation, and from an anti-Western ultranationalist state to a liberal democracy marked by a pro-American orientation. In order to appreciate the extent of this discursive reversal, and to understand the effects such a strange betrayal had on some Japanese artists, it is useful to review the ideological construction that permitted Japan's Pacific War.

Japan's Total War

In 2000, the historian Herbert P. Bix published the book *Hirohito and the Making of Modern Japan*. Drawing on long-taboo material that had come to light after Hirohito's death in 1989, *Hirohito* was the first biography of the modern emperor to ascribe war responsibility to this curious man who had been the center of fanatical national worship since his enthronement as a living deity in 1928. The *Economist* called the book a "historical bombshell."[6] It won the Pulitzer Prize and the National Book Critics Circle Award and was a bestseller in Japan. As Bix wrote, "Above all, the new materials make it possible for us to appreciate how Hirohito embodied—as no other Japanese did—the contradictory logic of Japan's entire modern political development."[7]

Hirohito, known posthumously as Emperor Showa for the name of his sixty-three-year reign (1926–89), inherited the mandate from his grandfather Emperor Meiji, "the Great." With the 1867 overthrow of the military shogunate, whose rule since 1192 had diminished the power, if not the symbol, of the imperial house, the pro-modernization oligarchs "restored" the court and made Emperor Meiji the polestar of the nation's modern transformation. The imperial court was separated from the government according to contemporary models of European monarchy. And yet, in an effort to instill the emperor with an inviolable status that could serve a nationalist cause, the Meiji constitution asserted the emperor was the successor in a sacred blood lineage with divine rights dating to the mythological origins of the archipelago. The emperor of the Chrysanthemum Throne was cast as monarch and supreme commander of the armed forces ("head of empire") and venerated as a living god, an embodiment of Shinto in human form.[8]

A second legacy of the Meiji Restoration was Japan's new colonial empire and status as a formidable regional power. The oligarchs understood the economic and political importance of colonial expansion to Japan's advance as an industrial power on a par with the West. As early as 1895, when Meiji forces defeated Qing China in the first Sino-Japanese War, Japan set forth building its Pacific empire. As countries across Asia, Africa, and the Middle East fell under the control of Western powers in the late nineteenth century, Japan boldly matched them, competing for and winning Asian colonies. Joining the feast known as "slicing the Chinese melon," Japan gained the island of Formosa as its first colony in 1895 as well as international concessionary territories, leaving China badly broken. Triumph over czarist Russia in 1905, after a sensational victory at sea, established imperial Japan as a global force to be reckoned with. The empire's regional hegemony was further assured in 1910, when it overthrew the Joseon dynasty and "annexed" the Korean peninsula as its second colony. Aided by effective government propaganda, these gains stimulated the rise of nationalist fervor at home and a growing sense of racial and cultural superiority over the peoples of China and Korea. The bitter relations between Japan and its neighbors today are the inheritance of these colonial attitudes.

During the First World War, Japan joined the Allied side, fighting against German territories in northeast China. The transfer of these rights to Japan after the war sparked riots in the newly founded Republic of China, where emotions of betrayal and humiliation ran high. As historian John W. Dower has written, "[Japan] was rewarded by being seated as one of the 'Big Five' nations at the Versailles peace conference, where the victors met to punish Germany and rearrange the world. No other non-White, non-Christian people at that time could have imagined playing the great game of global power and influence at this level; nor could anyone anticipate the disastrous breakdown of security that lay ahead."[9] As colonial expansion continued with Japan's takeover of Manchuria in 1931 and its increasing aggression across China, culminating in the Rape of Nanjing in 1937, Japanese political ideology developed around a new spiritual nationalism called the Imperial Way (*kodo*). Sanctioned by Emperor Hirohito, who had inherited the throne in 1928, *kodo* denoted a kind of "holy war" against the "demonic Anglo-Americans" and all Western doctrines of democracy, liberalism, and individualism. It promoted Shinto principles to purify Asia from the influences of Western political culture and to eliminate those who resisted Japan's divine mandate to unify "the eight corners of the world" under the benevolent morality of the emperor-deity.

The territorial expanse of Japan's Greater East Asia Co-prosperity Sphere peaked in 1942. Its reach extended from the mid-Pacific to the deep interior of China and from the Aleutian Islands in the north to the Western colonial enclaves of Southeast Asia, including the Dutch East Indies, French Indochina, the British colonial possessions of Burma, Malaya, and Hong Kong, and the American colony of the Philippines. At home, once-modernist painters like Fujita Tsuguharu (Léonard Foujita) lent their talents to the propagandists, creating war paintings that praised martyrdom for the Imperial Way. But by 1943, it was clear the mission was doomed. Younger and younger Japanese troops were recruited, only to die on battlefields oceans away from home, and greater and greater numbers of them died in futile kamikaze suicide attacks or perished of starvation and disease in Pacific island jungles. In 1944, the United States began a firebombing and napalm campaign targeting Japanese cities and their populations. Under the command of Curtis LeMay, US B-29 planes firebombed scores of Japanese cities, destroying entire metropolises and striking hundreds of thousands of civilians. The bombing of Tokyo on March 9–10, 1945, razed sixteen square miles and was the most devastating inferno in the history of human warfare at the time. Still denying the threat of defeat, Hirohito and his war cabinet vowed to fight on until his "hundred million" subjects all died "like shattered jewels."

American occupation policy allowed Hirohito to remain on the throne for forty-two more years. He was the only Axis leader to have survived the Second World War and perhaps the only commander who was spared trial at a war tribunal. The perpetuation of Emperor Showa's monarchy was part of US strategy to retell Japan's wartime past as simply a misguided folly; purged of a few bad agents, the nation could return to its peaceful course toward modernization and rejoin the international (read: Western) league of advanced nations. Hirohito's continuity would symbolize that narrative, as announced in the official portrait of the first postsurrender meeting between US occupation commander General MacArthur and the emperor he insisted remain. The emperor's presence and his silence sanctioned the nation's repression of its wartime past. As long as the Japanese could not and did not pursue Hirohito's central role in the war, they could and did deny their own.

Postsurrender Japan and Americanization

Writing on the theme "Japan under occupation," the photographer Tōmatsu Shōmei commented: "If I were to characterize postwar Japanese history in one word I would answer without hesitation: 'Americanization.'"[10] Indeed, the US occupation promoted Americanization across every variety of political, ideological, and cultural institution, embedding its mores into the lived experience of ordinary Japanese. Throughout the postsurrender period (1945–52), splits between Japan's reception of and resistance against the occupying culture created, euphemistically speaking, a kind of schizophrenia within the national psyche. Writing in his revisionist history *Embracing Defeat: Japan in the Wake of World War II*, John W. Dower observes: "It would be difficult to find another cross-cultural moment more intense, unpredictable, ambiguous, confusing, and *eclectic* than this one."[11]

On the one hand, Dower argues, postsurrender Japan emerges as a culture "in sensuous embrace" with its occupying victor, America.[12] Among liberal Japanese who had suffered during the war, the United States was the object of their sheer gratitude for liberating Japan from totalitarianism and the system of "emperor worship" and for forcing the nation's renunciation of militarism. The occupation also enabled a cult of all things "new," from lipstick colors and jazz bars to reformist organizations seeking to establish a modern order of liberal values. Sexual mores loosened. In the arts, expressionism flourished. In this reading, the United States was "embraced" as an empowering agent of free expression after years of totalitarian rule. The popular cartoonist Katō Etsurō, who had been a wartime propagandist, captured the jubilation brought about by the "democratic revolution." In one cartoon, giant scissors branded with an American star cut the chains of a despairing man marked "the people," while a banker type and military man flee in the background (fig. 5.2). Here, the occupier is the people's liberator.

In the arts, the occupation mission to institutionalize "democratization" led to the establishment of the Yomiuri Indépendant Exhibitions. Sponsored by Japan's leading liberal newspaper and held annually at the Tokyo Metropolitan Art Museum from 1949 until 1963, the Yomiuri Indépendant was an unjuried exhibition open to artists unaffiliated with the *dantai* salons that had dominated the prewar art establishment. Initially, it sponsored important loan exhibitions introducing contemporary international art to the Japanese public, inciting a sense of participation in overseas trends after a long period of isolation. It was also here, at the third Yomiuri Indépendant Exhibition, which traveled to Tokyo and Osaka in 1951, that the Gutai founder Yoshihara Jirō first encountered Jackson Pollock's drip paintings. The pure, direct, and tactile dynamism of Pollock's gestural abstractions catalyzed Yoshihara to envision a new era of art for Japan. "It might be called psychological realism," Yoshihara said in a roundtable discussion published in the art journal *Kansai Bijutsu*. "I think contemporary American painting has spontaneously resolved the problem of humanism today, because it relates at a deep level to the psychological experience of the human being."[13] By the mid-1950s, the Yomiuri Indépendant had become the central venue for younger, unknown artists to exhibit their experimental work, often flouting cultural orthodoxies while promoting "humanist" values of individual creativity, internationalism, and freedom of expression.

The 1955 Yomiuri Indépendant included works by twelve Gutai artists, marking the group's first exhibition. Coming of age during the heyday of Japan's Americanization, these Gutai artists reveled in bodily violence and material destruction as a means of making art. Shimamoto Shōzō's paintings, made by shattering glass bottles of house paint, and Shiraga Kazuo's *Wrestling with Mud* performance (fig. 5.3) were acts of personal catharsis as much as they were Dadaist antics staged for the press. Shiraga's "psychic individualism" calls upon a selfhood strong enough to strike against the tame configurations of postwar society and polity. In his essay "The Establishment of the Individual," which appeared in the *Gutai* journal in 1956, he writes:

> In politics, totalitarianism fails; in culture, that which is unfree and akin to totalitarianism must be purged. If you believe that your art has a spiritual meaning and it helps you develop yourself, such art will truly be on the cutting edge of world culture.... The stronger your will, the more resilient you will be when faced with all nonhuman forces. Today's intelligence must be neither escapist nor content with limited freedom.... Without establishing psychic individualism, we cannot establish any worthwhile culture for the whole.[14]

Other counterculture expressions in postsurrender Japan were less optimistic. Existentialism and nihilism were popular among writers and intellectu-

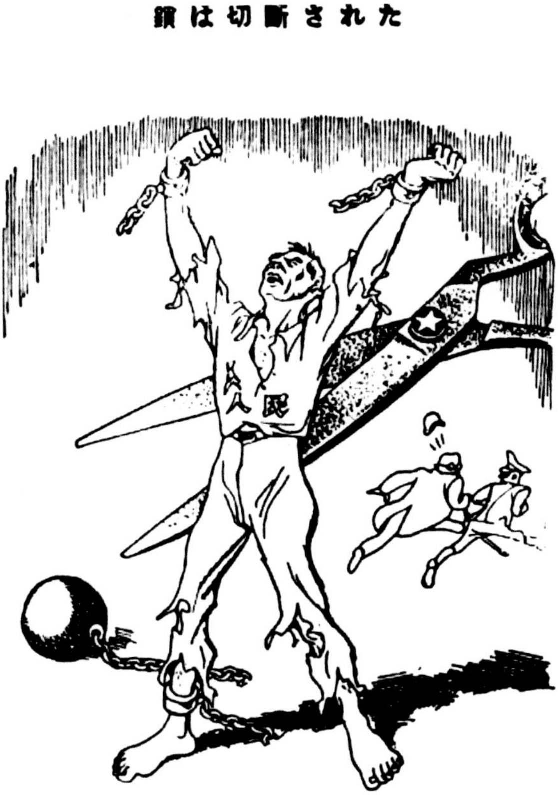

FIGURE 5.2. Katō Etsurō, "The Chain Has Been Broken," from Katō Etsurō, *Okurareta kakumei* [The revolution we have been given] (Tokyo: Shōwa 21, 1946).

als, who argued that the recent war had not only wrecked civilization; it had wrecked the absolute value of all systems of truth. But for the writer Sakaguchi Ango, the spectacle of decadence in the wake of Japan's appalling defeat held out the possibility for a genuine humanity to emerge. In his influential 1946 essay "On Decadence," he wrote, "Could we not say that the kamikaze hero was a mere delusion, and that human history begins from the point where he takes to black marketeering? . . . And perhaps that the emperor too is no more than an illusion, and the emperor's true history begins from the point where he becomes an ordinary human? Japan was defeated, and the samurai ethic has perished, but humanity has been born from the womb of decadence's truth."[15] Another aspect of decadence was the cult of *nikutai*, or "the carnal body." The writer Tamura Taijirō was explicit in praising the authenticity of raw sexuality over the deforming wartime spirituality of "national polity" (*kokutai*, literally "body of the nation"). In his sensational 1947 novel, *Nikutai no mon* (Gate of flesh), Tamura equated the postwar promise of individual freedom with

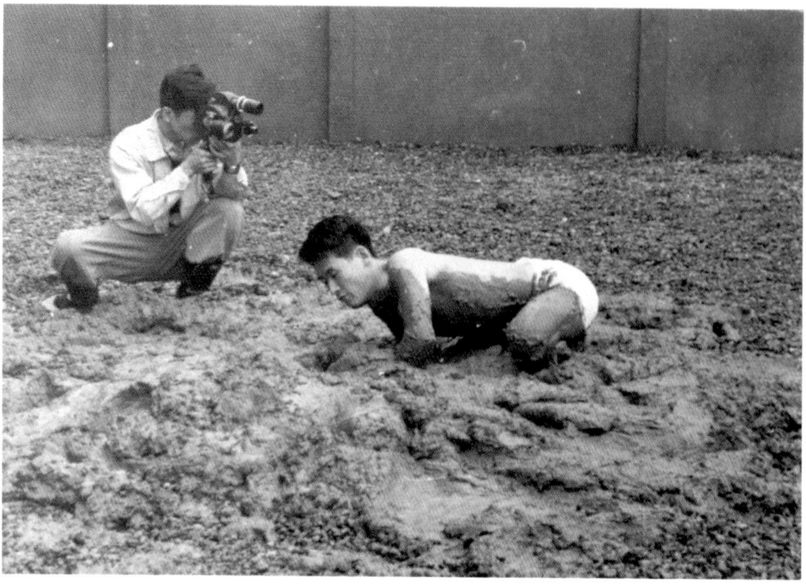

FIGURE 5.3. Shiraga Kazuo, *Wrestling with Mud*, 1955. Performance view, third execution, First Gutai Art Exhibition. Courtesy Amagasaki Cultural Foundation. © Shiraga Fujiko, Hisao and the former members of the Gutai Art Association. Photograph: Ōtsuji Kiyoji.

the quest for a "modern self" alert to individual subjectivity, authenticity, and physical reality: the "gate of flesh," he writes at one point, is the "gate to modernity."[16]

One of the unforeseen developments in the postsurrender period was the enormous popularity of the newly restituted Japanese Communist Party. As the only group that could claim to have resisted ultranationalism in the 1930s, Marxists had special status among the postwar intelligentsia and its deepening "community of remorse." Ironically for the occupation forces, it was the communists who first embraced the American agenda and promoted, along with them, the values of secular universal principles over Shintoist wartime ideologies. Increasingly, members of the dominant intellectual class called upon their American liberators to deliver more radical liberalization, pushing them to go beyond the limited promises of bourgeois democracy.

Though American policy in the early occupation era fostered social liberalization and the military's dismantling, China's fall to communism in 1949 and the Korean War outbreak in 1950 led to a "reverse course" policy that enforced an antilabor, anticommunist, and remilitarization agenda in line with emerging Cold War mobilization. Exploiting the menace of communist Chinese and North Korean aggression, the conservative government of prime minister Yoshida Shigeru instigated a widespread "Red Purge" in collaboration with the American occupation authorities. Further, in apparent violation of the 1947 constitution, wherein Japan renounced war and its right to possess military potential, General MacArthur authorized the Japanese government in 1950 to form the National Police Reserve (now the Self-Defense Force), whose stated aim was the maintenance of internal security. Increasing government control over individual civil rights culminated in 1952 with the passing of the controversial Subversive Activities Prevention Law, which liberal intellectuals vehemently opposed as an infringement of artistic freedom of expression.

Artists, intellectuals, and political agitators who had earlier supported American reforms in Japan now joined in opposition to the conservative shift, protesting what they perceived as newly entrenched statism. The central event for this opposition was the leftist struggle against the US-Japan Security Treaty, known as Anpo. The treaty, ratified in 1952, gave the United States the right to develop Japan as a military base in the expanding Pacific Cold War arena. From the mid-1950s, labor unions, women's groups, cultural organizations, and members of the Japanese Communist Party and socialist parties organized a succession of massive strikes and violent demonstrations against the treaty's renewal, culminating in a national crisis in 1960. The so-called Anpo movement stimulated an unprecedented outburst of radical political action by ordinary citizens, including avant-garde artists.[17]

At the center of the Anpo crisis was the conflicting response of the Japanese people to the cultural and political Americanization of Japan. Japanese who had supported US policy felt betrayed. Others who had embraced the promise of peace were once again threatened by the specter of world war. They recoiled from the horrors of Hiroshima and Nagasaki yet were drawn in their state of fragile recuperation to the world of plenty that the occupation culture proffered; the US policy to resocialize Japan into the world of American middle-class values, promising inclusion in the new "free world" order, included access to Hollywood films, washing machines, and Cadillacs. Tōmatsu Shōmei, who emerged as one of the leading figures in the postwar school of Japanese photography, chronicled the images of Americanization in the series *11:02 Nagasaki*, which recorded the freakish keloid burns and physical deformities caused by A-bomb radiation in Nagasaki's Catholic communities, and in *Chewing Gum and Chocolate*, a portrait of the American bases in Japan (fig. 5.4). In these photographs, Tōmatsu captured the confused era of postwar Japan, including its wartime past that was silenced but not gone. As the artist reflected, "In Nagasaki, I witnessed not only the vestiges of war, but a postwar

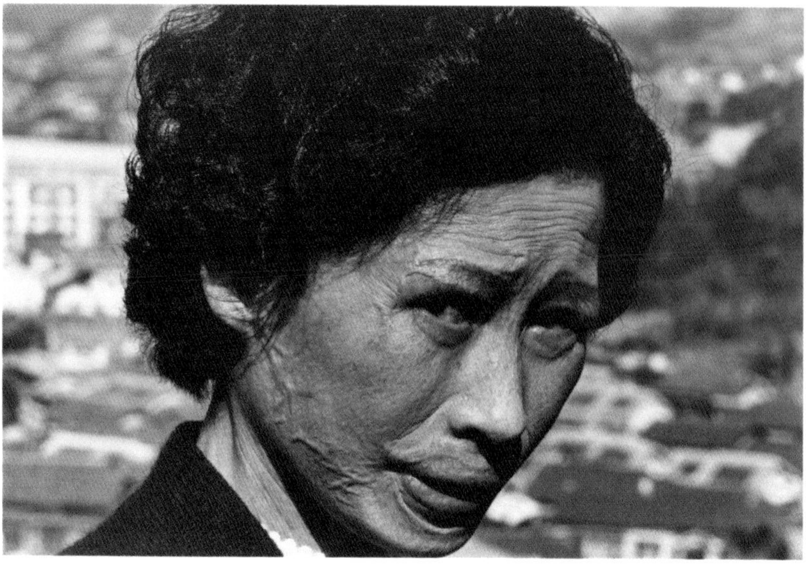

FIGURE 5.4. Tōmatsu Shōmei, *Hibakusha Tsuyo Kataoka, Nagasaki*, 1961 (printed 2000). Gelatin silver print, 27 × 40 cm. Collection: San Francisco Museum of Modern Art, Gift of the Kurenboh Collection. © Shomei Tomatsu—INTERFACE. Photograph: Don Ross.

without end. I once believed that ruins were cities reduced to ashes. Nagasaki taught me that ruins can also be found in the human soul."[18]

Fabricating America's Japan

In 1946, the American anthropologist and folklorist Ruth Benedict published *The Chrysanthemum and the Sword*. Commissioned by the Office of War Information, this study presenting Benedict's research on the cultural patterns of "the enemy" was designed to aid the US military to successfully administer the Allied occupation. A pioneer of "the culture and personality school" within social science, Benedict argued that typologies of national characteristics were enduring and transhistorical determinations of collective behavior. Famously, she used this method to cast the Japanese as victims of a "shame culture" that emphasized members' performance within the social group, as opposed to the West's culture of guilt and its privileging of individual conscience.[19] The implications of this holistic theory were vast: it posited Japan as unique and passed the buck on war accountability to "national characteristics of social harmony and conformity."[20]

In his essay "Disciplining the Enemy: Area Studies and the Relocation of Japan," intellectual historian Harry Harootunian demonstrates how Benedict's use of social science to define Japanese behavior became the foundation for the postwar creation of Japanese "area studies" as a "field of knowledge" within the American academy.[21] Significantly, area studies departments at Yale, Harvard, Princeton, and Stanford were closely tied to US geopolitical, economic, and sociocultural interests. Promoting fixed-cultural values of "consensuality, uninterrupted continuity and an endless present derived from an exceptionalist experience," the academy served the state's agenda to produce a narrative of postwar Japan characterized by its very own administration of national reform, reconstruction, and democratic renovation.[22] As Harootunian argues:

> Few fields of study have been initially organized as a response to wartime circumstances demanding a holistic knowledge of the enemy in order to facilitate its destruction. The closest parallel has been the recent recognition within colonial studies that knowledge about the colonized was a necessary instrument of effective control. . . . With Japan, knowledge of the enemy was extended into the postwar period to become the basis of Occupation policy, and resembled a kind of neo-colonialism that has left its mark on Japan's own efforts to represent itself. But if the war supplied the inaugural moment for the study of Japan by Americans, the Occupation and Cold War constituted the two principal props for the organization of a knowledge field and its dissemination.[23]

The coordination of government, business, and academy in the formation and dissemination of Japan as a subject of knowledge was made possible by what Harootunian calls "the wartime cohort": men who had served in the American occupation as translators, interrogators, or gatherers of military intelligence, and others, like Edwin O. Reischauer, who became Japan specialists by virtue of their missionary origins. Raised in Japan, Reischauer, for instance, was an academic at Harvard and worked for the government during and after the war. He became the US ambassador to Japan from 1961 to 1966 and was one of the architects of the group's "modernization theory." Other members of the "cohort" were academics Robert N. Bellah, Ronald Dore, Marius Jansen, John Hall, Jim Morely, and Robert E. Ward.

In this narrative, Japan's rapid development since the Meiji Restoration fulfilled a universal aspiration for nation-states to become modern capitalist democracies along the western "modernization" model. In order to reclaim Japan from its anti-Western bellicosity, however, the modernization theorists cast the Pacific War as an aberration. Reischauer posed his famous "derailment theory" to explain how Japan had been briefly diverted from its peaceful development course by a few rogue militants such as General Tojo, who had accidentally risen to power in the 1930s and led Japan to war. This image of Japan's prewar modernization as a train "derailed" from its industrial progress was powerfully enduring. It shaped Japan's postwar narrative of the empire's advanced fascist and imperialist war machine by virtually denying the state's strategic agency in any of it. From 1958 to the early 1970s, leading American academics, including members of the "cohort," convened the annual Conference on Modern Japan. The conference produced six volumes of papers on topics dealing with Japan's modernization and "generated countless studies in dissertations, articles, monographs and books which still seek regularly to demonstrate the singularity of meaning illuminated by the narrative of Japan's modernization."[24]

This discursive construction imposing a set of essentialist characteristics on Japanese society, culture, and historical trajectory also impacted the study of Japanese art history and the reception of Japanese art in American museums. In this version, Japanese culture was idealized as contemplative and impoverished. The most influential authority on Japanese art and culture in America was D. T. Suzuki, the prolific author, translator, and advocate of Zen Buddhism who taught at Columbia University in the 1950s and counted several Beat and Fluxus artists, most notably John Cage, among his adherents. "As a personality," enthused the music critic Winthrop Sargeant in the *New Yorker* in 1957, "he radiates not only the general glamour that attaches to aging Oriental men of wisdom but a special serenity that makes him a magnificent living example of the doctrine he preaches."[25] Suzuki's popular Zen promoted solitary or rustic artistic practices and minimalist forms of Japanese art such as ink-wash landscape painting and tea ceremony, often overlooking how these very arts flourished under the sect's military shogunate patronage. New York's Asia House Gallery, founded by John D. Rockefeller III in 1957 with an aim to promote Asia in America, opened with an exhibition of pan-Asian Buddhist sculpture; its first show dedicated to Japan was held in 1961, titled *Tea Taste in Japanese Art*.

These efforts privileged a specific set of aesthetics and promoted them as Japan's national style. Across American museums and university art history departments, Japan's bawdy subculture and history of grotesque images like the Buddhist Hell Scroll and Hungry Ghost genres were devalued within the canon along with the fabulously ornate aesthetics of *kazari* and *hade*.[26] The occupation narrative also confined the academic and curatorial study of Japanese art within America strictly to the premodern era; advanced art was tolerated to the extent that it conformed to the desired aesthetic program. Modernist calligraphic abstraction was encouraged; contemporary social realism was not.

Within Japan, the occupation narrative served as a balm. It anesthetized the Japanese from dealing with the critical projects of coming to terms with their wartime history and of processing the psychological impact the war had on both individual and national identity. Unlike in Germany, there was no official reckoning in Japan of the nation's wartime experience or accountability. Thus, with Hirohito installed as an emblem of Japan's passivity, the trauma of war could not be publicly exorcised. Yet ironically, the influence of American popular culture enabled a subculture of violent imagination to emerge, unleashing the paradoxical urge to escape from history and to relive it. As Japanese neo-pop critic Sawaragi Noi observes:

> In the imaginary reality of postwar Japan—in which the Self-Defense Forces cannot explicitly be called "military forces"—such memories and fears have never been channeled into legitimate political consciousness. Instead, they have been transformed into the monstrous catastrophes and apocalyptic delusions depicted in the bizarre world of manga and anime. These images bespeak a profound psychological repression.... When we reexamine the massive number of images of war, carnage, destruction, nuclear irradiation, and ruins stored in such subculture genres as manga, anime and *tokusatsu* [special-effects film], we begin to understand that the Superflat space of postwar Japan constitutes a reflection of the nation's paradoxical history—a reflection engendered by the suppression of memories of the twofold violence Japan experienced as both victimizer and victimized, as well as its fear of the Cold War.[27]

Enter Godzilla

In the inaugural 1954 film, a prehistoric reptile is awakened from ancient slumber when a US-detonated hydrogen bomb explodes in the depths of the South Pacific Ocean. Monsterized through radiation exposure, the giant Godzilla (Gojira) lashes his way to the shores of Japan and wreaks spectacular destruction on its cities and populations; scenes of crowds screaming as they perish in horrific ways animate the film's enduring terror. While originally inspired by the American monster-film genre, especially *King Kong* (1933) and *The Beast from 20,000 Fathoms* (1953), *Godzilla* arose from Japan's particular unease with its own history as the world's first nation to have experienced the atomic bomb. The *tokusatsu* special-effects film, released by the Japanese studio

Toho just nine years after the atomic bombing of Hiroshima and Nagasaki, triggered a mass reliving of suppressed war trauma. The need was rapacious. As *Godzilla* went on to become Japan's most popular monster film, with an extensive franchise, its iconic status within the Japanese creative subculture grew. The contemporary artist Murakami Takashi has done as much as any public intellectual to illuminate Godzilla's meaning in the context of postwar Japan. He writes:

> Godzilla's terrifying size, ferocity and scale of destruction reveal the enormity of fear experienced by the Japanese in the wake of the atomic bombings, and the movie has a strong antinuclear and antiwar message. . . . It is impossible to separate the shocking destruction of the flame-spewing Godzilla—who burned the city of Tokyo to ashes overnight—from the trauma felt by Japanese in memory of the massive fire-bombings of Tokyo, and of the A-bomb dropped on Hiroshima and Nagasaki. With Godzilla, the dread of nuclear holocaust left an indelible mark on Japanese creativity, and this disquieting undercurrent would persist in popular culture for decades.[28]

To Murakami, Godzilla also emblemizes a narrative of national humiliation. Japanese people have suffered from the culture and politics of "infantilization," he argues, whereby their forced dependency on the United States as "protector" and "superpower" has produced a willful negation of both adulthood and nationhood. That is, the Japanese have refused—or rather, *have been refused*—to grow up. The problem, Murakami suggests, is that Japan is mired in a state of disempowerment. "A pervasive impotence defines the culture of postwar Japan," he remarks, "where everything is peaceful, tranquil, lukewarm. Our general removal from world politics and distorted dependence on the U.S. leaves us in a circumscribed, closed-in system, inhabiting an Orwellian, science-fiction realm."[29] Think, for instance, of the artist's 2005 exhibition *Little Boy: The Arts of Japan's Exploding Subculture*, which explored how cartoons and animation, elsewhere conceived for children, have been appropriated by artists as a means to resolve the trauma of atomic war, the devastation of defeat, and the unmoored, apolitical state that has emerged since (fig. 5.5). Focused often on apocalyptic imagery, with frequent references to atomic explosion and futuristic annihilation/salvation, the cartoons that dominate Japan's adult media and entertainment industries provide a screen that both exaggerates and diminishes the real history that they function to suppress.[30] The immensely popular children's TV anime series *Time Bokan* (1975–76), for

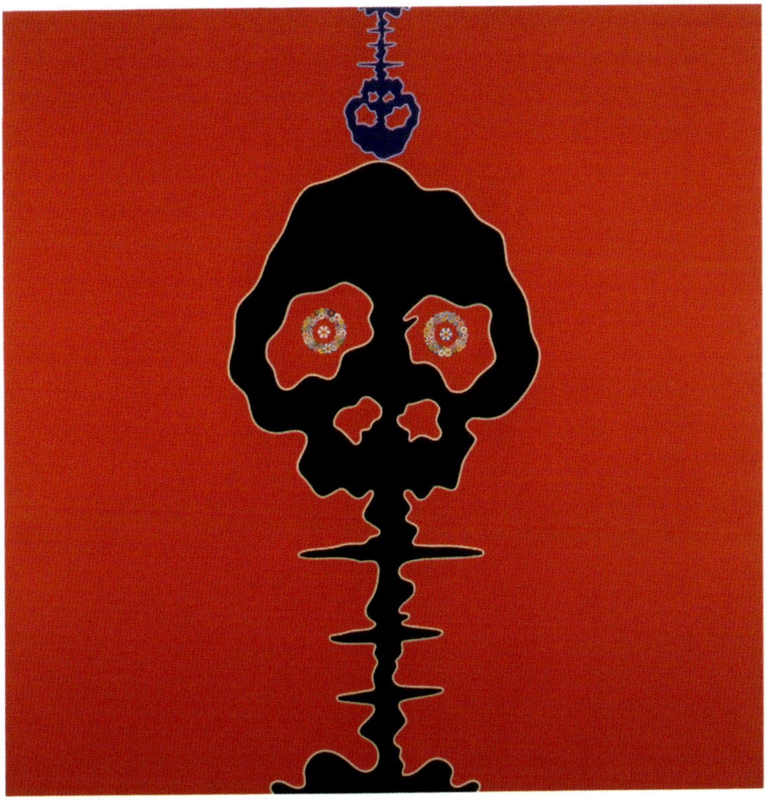

FIGURE 5.5. Takashi Murakami, *Time Bokan—Red*, 2001. Acrylic on canvas mounted on board, 180 × 180 cm.

example, features a mushroom cloud explosion at the end of each episode. But like real life in postatomic Japan, the goofy protagonists reappear in the next installment as if nothing had ever happened.

In 1954, *Godzilla*'s references to America were not subtle, beginning with the monster's birthplace at the site of the recent US atomic testing in the Bikini Atoll. But when the first American version of *Gojira* was released in 1956 as *Godzilla, King of the Monsters!*, the implicit and explicit criticisms of the United States in Honda Ishirō's original film were cut out. This effort to "Americanize *Godzilla*" has continued for more than sixty years, as exemplified by Hollywood's 2014 version of *Godzilla*, directed by Gareth Edwards. In this version of the creation story, the United States is absolved of any responsibility for giving rise to the radioactive monster that scourges the planet after the Second World War. Rather than present the Bikini Atoll blasts as Cold War brinksmanship, Edwards presents them as the US government's last-ditch attempt to kill the beast.[31] Even in fiction, America's insistence on negating Japan's war experience and casting itself as savior remains stubborn.

The question behind the diagnosis "Godzilla's schizophrenia" is this: For the Japanese, does the monster represent psychic rage or passivity toward the American victors? Or do both states paradoxically coexist in the nation's postwar identity? The totalizing ideologies produced by the United States and reproduced within Japan itself eventually became unsustainable. Leftist intellectuals, student movements, and avant-garde artists coalesced around resistance to this quasi-fictional, disempowering culture. In this reading, Gutai founder Yoshihara Jirō's emphasis on aberration might be interpreted in a new light. Perhaps his famous battle cry, "Do what nobody has done before!," reflects more than the avant-garde edict to break away from past orthodoxies; it may also arise from the polarizing seduction of—and repulsion toward—America and the war.

NOTES

1. Yoshihara and Nakamura, "America no kindai kaiga," 12; translated and quoted in Munroe, "All the Landscapes," 25.

2. In this chapter, I intentionally use both *post-war* and *postwar*. The reason for the hyphenated spelling is that it highlights my narrative on the war. Japanese names are given in Japanese order, with surname first and given name second.

3. Benito Mussolini was deposed, and Italy surrendered to Allied powers on September 8, 1943; Adolf Hitler's suicide on April 30, 1945, prompted Germany's immediate unconditional surrender.

4. For an analysis of how the Japanese imperial government delayed surrender, see Bix, *Hirohito and the Making of Modern Japan*.

5. Estimates of Pacific War fatalities vary according to source. The numbers cited here are based on those provided in Bix, *Hirohito and the Making of Modern Japan*.

6. *Economist*, "God Dethroned."

7. *Economist*, "God Dethroned," 6.

8. For a history of the Meiji construction of monarchy, see Tanaka, *Japan's Orient*.

9. Dower, *Embracing Defeat*, 21.

10. Tōmatsu, quoted in Munroe, "Postwar Japanese Photography," 62.

11. Dower, *Embracing Defeat*, 23.

12. Dower, *Embracing Defeat*, 23.

13. Yoshihara and Nakamura, "America no kindai kaiga," 12; translated and quoted in Oyobe, "Human Subjectivity and Confrontation," 93; translation adapted by the author in Munroe, "All the Landscapes," 25.

14. Shiraga, "Establishment of the Individual," 279.

15. Sakaguchi, "Discourse on Decadence"; cited in Dower, *Embracing Defeat*, 156.

16. Tamura, quoted in Dower, *Embracing Defeat*, 158.

17. For the political and cultural impact of Anpo on the Japanese avant-garde, see Munroe, *Japanese Art after 1945*.

18. Tōmatsu, "Christ in the Nuclear Age."

19. Benedict, *Chrysanthemum and the Sword*, 1.

20. See Bix, *Hirohito and the Making of Modern Japan*.

21. Harootunian, "Disciplining the Enemy," 3.

22. Harootunian, "Disciplining the Enemy," 23.

23. Harootunian, "Disciplining the Enemy," 4.

24. Harootunian, "Disciplining the Enemy," 26.

25. Sargeant, "Great Simplicity"; quoted in Winther-Tamaki, "Asian Dimensions of Postwar Abstract Art," 146.

26. The concept of *kazari*, "the will to decorate," is an aesthetic style of dynamic display prevalent in the Momoyama and Tokugawa shogunate cultures. *Hade*, meaning gaudiness or ostentation, animates such art forms as Noh and Kabuki theater and the tradition of samurai military pageantry. See Rousmaniere, *Kazari*.

27. Sawaragi, "On the Battlefield of 'Superflat,'" 204–5.

28. Murakami, *Little Boy*, 20.

29. Murakami Takashi, discussion at Japan Society, New York, November 10, 2004 (notes by the author).

30. See Munroe, "Introducing Little Boy," 240–62.

31. Tsutsui, "For Godzilla and Country."

6

The Work of Salvage

Jess, Allegory, and the Atomic Bomb

TARA MCDOWELL

Science has realized and affirmed what men anticipated in dreams neither wild nor idle.—HANNAH ARENDT

Scientists love Dada too: they grow mushrooms ten miles tall.—JESS

Madmen

If *postwar* necessarily remains a slippery term, entirely dependent upon the context in which it is deployed, one definitive, planetary "post" of postwar is that it occurs after the atomic bomb was detonated. In the United States the atomic age was a psychic condition reinforced daily, however abstract it remained for most Americans. While climate change differs both physically and conditionally, the postwar era of the atomic bomb shares with our current moment its imminent threat of a catastrophe that is of our making but seems beyond our control. American artists grappled with this condition both directly and indirectly, often with other aspects of life in the 1950s and 1960s with which it seemed so entangled. The artist Jess, whose career unfolded almost entirely in San Francisco and whose interlocutors included artists like Wallace Berman, Bruce Conner, George Herms, and Jay DeFeo and poets like his partner Robert Duncan, Helen Adam, Michael McClure, and Jack Spicer, developed a practice spanning five decades and including painting, collage, drawing, film, book illustration, and poetry. Drawn entirely from appropriated sources, Jess's artworks veer from woozy Romanticism to something weirder and more impacted and unsettling, collages and paintings both menacing and overloaded. A few of them conjure—allegorize, I would argue—especially vividly the desperation, madness, and horror vacui of the new world order of the atomic age. This chapter begins with a reading of one particular example and moves on to argue that Jess's attempt to piece together an image of the world from its wreckage and debris—a process he called salvage—is bound up with his personal experience with atomic energy as a nuclear chemist in the 1940s.

But much later, in the summer of 1974 in San Francisco, long after he had abandoned science for art, Jess made a midsize collage that he titled *The 5th Never of Old Lear* (fig. 6.1). The collage's paper elements are glued onto two wooden slabs, so that the imagery spills over the picture plane's first edge, down all four sides about an inch, and continues across a second tier, hugging this three-dimensional support like an expertly wrapped gift. The image flow has a peculiar, soothing consistency and an affinity for pattern and decoration. It is the opposite of the agitprop Dadaist tactics of Richard Huelsenbeck and Raoul Hausmann, or even the atomized spin cycle of Hannah Höch's *Cut with the Kitchen Knife*. That the collage is lacking in iconoclastic fervor, that its visual idiom is more like a lullaby than a scream, is part of what makes it peculiar, proof of just how dominant the Dada collage aesthetic has been for a century. But the balm of the image's homogeneity mitigates a scene as monstrous as any Dada or surrealist nightmare.

The work's visual cohesion results from a consistency of medium: most of the cut-up and pasted-on scraps are reproductions of engravings. The choice of engraving, a technology for mechanical reproduction before photography, makes the collage seem older than it is, which is not uncommon in Jess's work. Jess employs a modern visuality—collage—but his materials belong to an earlier visual culture, and an obsolete technology. The reparative process

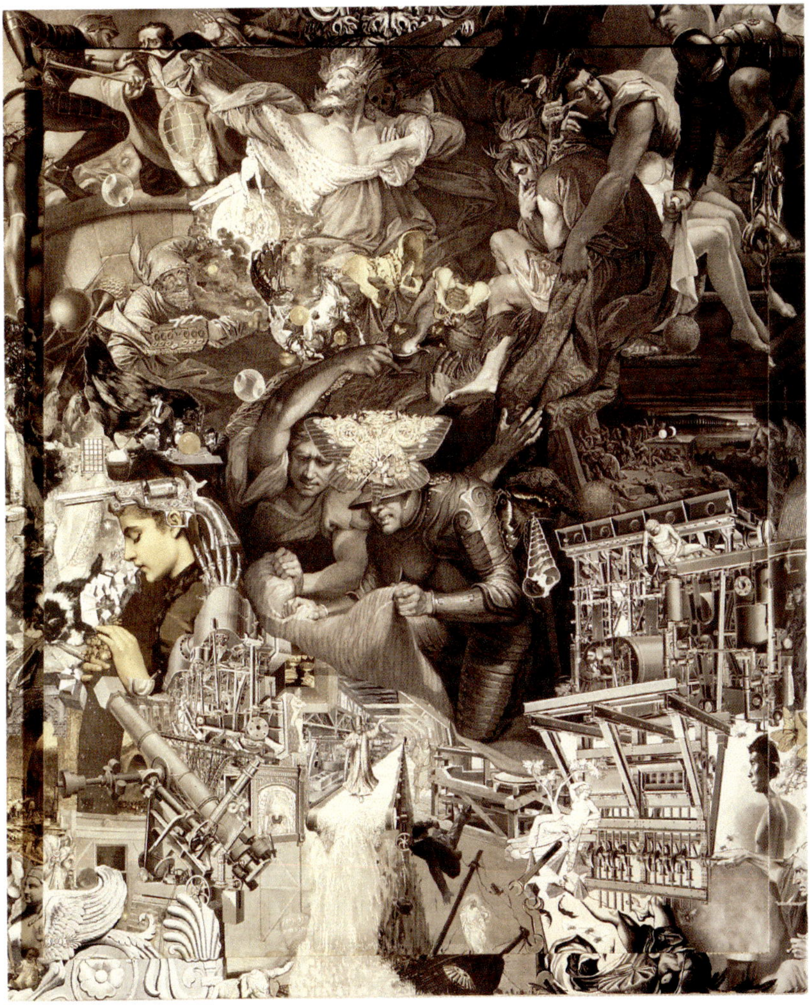

FIGURE 6.1. Jess, *The 5th Never of Old Lear*, 1974. Paper collage elements on three-dimensional support, 83.8 × 71.1 cm. Collection: Mary Patricia Anderson Pence.

and ethos of reuse, recycling, and even rescue is made plain by the collage's insistence on its pastness. "All my work . . . comes from salvaging," Jess once explained. "It is all about rescuing or resurrecting images."[1]

Visual consistency may smooth out or conceal this nightmarish scene, but in time its pictorial logic comes into view. The collage is divided into two halves, the upper half governed by bodies in motion and the lower dominated by machines. Bodies and especially limbs—sinewy arms and legs extended and curved—counter the geometry and cold steel of the machinery below.

Butterflies flit across the whole. They undo any clean divide between the two halves and punctuate the dark mood with a touch of lightness. Bubbles drift up from the glassblower at center left, indicating fragility, even breakability. By this point, more than twenty years into his collage practice, Jess is clearly a master of the medium. He makes the picture appear effortless, as if it could be no other way, but this degree of seamlessness and dynamism is achieved with tremendous skill and patience.

Two men at center, a soldier and servant holding an oil lamp overhead, serve as the fulcrum for the picture's two worlds. Their centrality is emphasized by the seal that marks the true center of the picture, a point of stillness in an otherwise thoroughly writhing image. The men clutch the covering that separates the lower portion from the upper, although it is unclear whether they reveal or hide what lies beneath. Their cohort above remain oblivious, so deeply absorbed are they in their own agonized dramas. And dramas they are: these men are all excised from an early nineteenth-century folio illustrating William Shakespeare's dramatic works.[2] At the turn of the century John and Josiah Boydell had commissioned Britain's leading painters to illustrate Shakespearean scenes and employed dozens of engravers to translate the paintings into engravings, which were reproduced in this volume.[3] Some were considered successful—Benjamin West approved of William Sharpe's engraving of his *King Lear*—but many are mediocre, mottled from overuse of stippling and composed with stock figures in canned arrangements. The challenge of working with such material was certainly pleasurable for Jess. This confidence in one's abilities to recognize the neglected potential of an undervalued image—to save the image, to put it bluntly—is another facet of the project of salvage, of a lifelong labor of "rescuing or resurrecting images."

In choosing this compendium of prints, Jess had found the consummate manifestation of his own artistic practice, a practice entirely predicated on acts of appropriation and translation. Consider the sheer number of transformations that resulted in the Shakespeare volume Jess held in his hands: the prints are copies of paintings, which are illustrations of literary scenes, which describe events that were historical even in Shakespeare's time and often themselves deeply speculative. Take, for example, the disappearance of the two young princes from the Tower of London around 1483, which Shakespeare amplifies in *Richard III* into their assassination on Richard's order.[4] The engraving depicts the moment just before the assassination and becomes the pivot of Jess's collage. Jess removes the princes from the scene, so the two assassins now gaze upon the phantasmagoria of machinery below.[5] This gargantuan composite engine room is lifted from nineteenth-century issues of *Scientific American*—a forum for science enthusiasts and a primary source document of the industrial revolution, one whose focus on new inventions fostered a heady atmosphere of progress. In the center Jess places a grain belt, now transformed into a waterfall. On the left is a pair of "improved triple expansion engines," the *Scientific American* caption tells us, that Jess turns on their sides.[6] And on the right are more engines, all flipped upside down. Jess made his own improvements to this new industrial machinery, fusing them into a powerful and elaborate machine, a Frankensteinian creation.

Of the Shakespearean murderers and madmen populating the upper realm, all of whom are caught in moments of violence or torment, the most dramatic is King Lear, taken from Sharpe's engraving. Lear, veering into madness, is caught with his companions in a brutal storm. The collage's title, *The 5th Never of Old Lear*, derives from a later passage in the play, in which Lear grieves the death of his daughter Cordelia: "Thou'lt come no more, never, never, never, never, never!" Lear's repetition of *never* is feverish and progressively unhinged, but the fifth *never* has a certain finality to it, a realization both tragic and clear. A catastrophe has occurred. Jess does not name this catastrophe, since the elements of his works, in his words, "must all remain in flux so that no single story dominates."[7] This is why the blanket both covers and reveals the grotesque engine room below. It is why references to the most devastating moments in Shakespeare coexist with butterflies that fly across the same surface.

The 5th Never of Old Lear presents a scene at the moment of its greatest intensity, its dramatic peak. The imagery tells us so, but the title does too. Such theatricality is signaled on the level of both sources and composition. The collage is an allegory, a theatrical staging of a catastrophic encounter between upper and lower registers.[8] The upper register is in turmoil, perhaps prompted by the revelation below, which must be smothered at once. Above we witness a chaotic disintegration of humanity, a breakdown of even the most basic social contract: another human being's right to live. The material culture of the eighteenth and nineteenth centuries gives form to this catastrophe, but it belongs firmly to the twentieth century. In what follows, I argue that Jess's confrontation with nuclear power and the atomic bomb was translated here into the high theatricality of madness, murder, and machines.

Heavy Water

Jess was born Burgess Franklin Collins in 1923 in Long Beach, California. He studied chemistry at the California Institute of Technology, in Pasadena, and, along with many others, was drafted into the army during the Second World

War. But here his formation (for postwar art history, at least) takes a singular turn: Jess spent twenty-two months in Oak Ridge, Tennessee, as a chemist working on the Manhattan Project.[9] Though it was top secret at the time, we well know what the effort produced: an atomic bomb, which annihilated Hiroshima and Nagasaki in the summer of 1945 and, to quote Leo Szilard, the Hungarian émigré physicist who initiated the Manhattan Project, ushered in "an era of devastation on an unimaginable scale."[10]

The history of the development of the atomic bomb is one of scale. An "unimaginable scale," in Szilard's words. A colossal, stupendous scale of resources marshaled and consumed to produce the bomb, of enrichment facilities half a mile long that produced mere grams of weapons-grade uranium and plutonium, of copious amounts of water needed to cool spent fuel slugs, and ultimately of the death and destruction caused in Hiroshima and Nagasaki. In Hiroshima, 100,000 were killed instantly; of these, 95,000 were civilians.[11] It is no wonder that something so unfathomable would soon be linked with the mushroom cloud, an image with such a clearly delineated form, an image that can be comprehended, managed, and even aestheticized. But before this image was formalized, the rhetoric surrounding the bomb reinforced its vastness of scale. "We face the prospect either of destruction on a scale which dwarfs anything thus far reported," declared a *New York Times* editorial the day following Hiroshima that now seems utterly bizarre, "or of a golden era of social change which would satisfy the most romantic utopian."[12] What the *Times* failed to predict was the future of the bomb as the centerpiece of a Cold War structure dominated by two superpowers, each of which had the capability to destroy the other as catastrophically as the violence unleashed on Hiroshima and Nagasaki.

The Manhattan Project aimed to develop a weapon that would harness the power of a split atom before the Nazis did, but it only became formalized, and urgent to the US government, after the attack on Pearl Harbor in 1942. The scope of the endeavor quickly became national, with the construction of three primary facilities spread out across the nation: uranium was enriched in Oak Ridge; Los Alamos, New Mexico, became the centralized research laboratory and, later, testing facility under J. Robert Oppenheimer; and a massive plutonium production factory was erected in Hanford, Washington. Edward Teller recalled fellow physicist Niels Bohr telling him, "You see, I told you it couldn't be done without turning the whole country into a factory. You have done just that."[13] The transformation of Oak Ridge—a ninety-two-square-mile parcel of "impoverished hill country" on the Clinch River near the Great Smoky Mountains National Park in eastern Tennessee—into a company town of 75,000 in a scant three years is a testament to the resources put at the disposal of the Manhattan Project, which at its height employed 130,000 people and was equivalent in size to the US automobile industry (fig. 6.2).[14] At Oak Ridge, the most massive structures were those that enriched uranium, such as the K-25 plant, a U-shaped facility that covered over two million square feet, or the Y-12 complex, which used an electromagnetic separation process and eventually comprised 286 buildings. Jess arrived at this sprawling construction site in April 1943, just days after the entire area was fenced in with barbed wire, public access was closed off, and its borders began to be monitored by seven guarded checkpoints.[15] Once inside he would have seen staggering pieces of visual propaganda, such as billboards reminding workers, "What you see here / What you do here / What you hear here / When you leave here / Let it stay here."

One of the most significant transformations in twentieth-century science is scale, and no other endeavor dramatizes this transformation like the Manhattan Project.[16] Nuclear fission is a process that occurs at the level of the atom's component parts, or on the smallest scale imaginable. Yet, in an acute reversal, very large machinery, and much of it, is needed in order to generate atomic fission. This scale shift is absurd, as Jess intuits when he writes, "Scientists love Dada too: they grow mushrooms ten miles tall."[17] A Dadaist response to this dialectic of scale and the similarly unfathomable gulf between daily life at Oak Ridge and the horror of the bomb seems appropriate (and here it is worth recalling that Dada emerged as a response to the First World War).[18] In the face of such maddening vastness, some artists tried to fill space—Jess is in this camp, as is Robert Rauschenberg, who famously declared that his greatest fear was running out of world. Others went the opposite route and reveled in the emptiness of an atomic detonation—conceptualist Yutaka Matsuzawa's celebration of nothing, of invisibility and vanishing, is especially weighted when seen against the background of a Japanese postwar world view.[19]

Eventually Jess realized that he was participating in something very wrong. Such "evil methods [were] not conducive to self-esteem," he explained to the writer Rebecca Solnit. "I remember the army had secret films in color [of Hiroshima, immediately after it happened, showing horrible burns and sickness]. People were passing out, and so was I."[20] Bay Area filmmaker Lawrence Jordan remembers Jess telling him, "When they dropped the bomb, I knew science was made by black magicians."[21] This is the nightmare of *The 5th Never of Old Lear*, the revelation beneath the blanket that leads to murderous anguish above.[22] Jess's treatment of the large-scale devastation that was the wartime endgame of atomic chemistry is indirect and allegorical. His is a world come undone. Jess used the very same issue of *Scientific American*—Jess, the ex-chemist, is

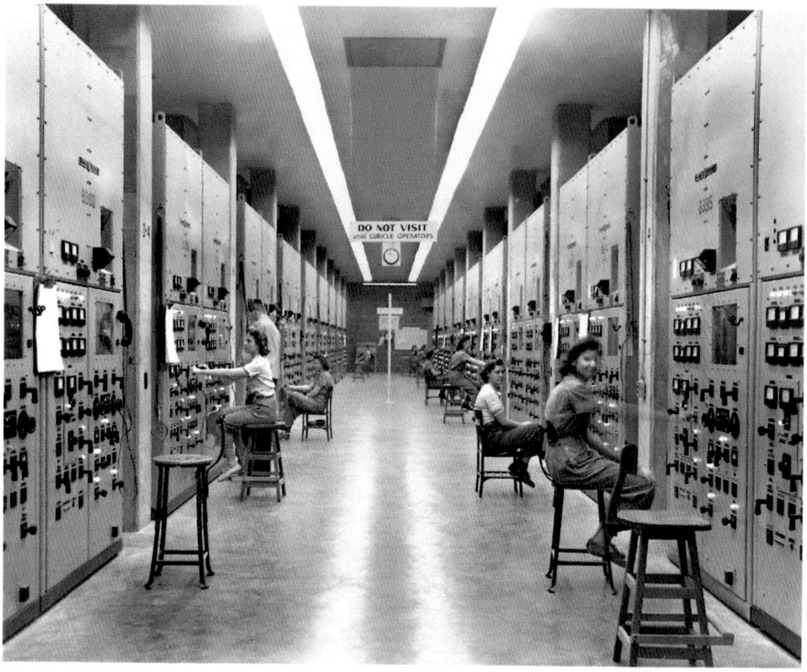

FIGURE 6.2. *The Calutron Girls*, Y-12, Oak Ridge, Tennessee, 1944.

the scientific American—to source both the collage's monstrous engine room and an astonishing, deeply strange series of paintings called the *Translations* (fig. 6.3). The devices depicted in the publication represent the science that appealed to Jess, the science of the tinkerer, small-scale and alchemical, often without predetermined application. A prelapsarian science. This is the science he wants to rescue and preserve in paint. It could not be further from the industrial-scale big science that would produce the most destructive weapon the world had then seen. *The 5th Never of Old Lear*, by contrast, is nightmarish, not unlike the ways paintings by Hieronymus Bosch are nightmarish. Bosch and Jess pose a shared question: How does one represent the monstrous?

Jess reacted slowly to what he had experienced at Oak Ridge. "People are all very different," he explained. "I held it off until Hanford."[23] After the war Jess worked as a chemist for the Hanford Engineering Works, the nation's plutonium factory in Washington state.[24] While reluctant to discuss this period of his life, he has described the dream that constituted his break from it: "At one point, around 1948 while I was working with atomic chemistry, I had a very strong and convincing dream that the world was going to completely destruct

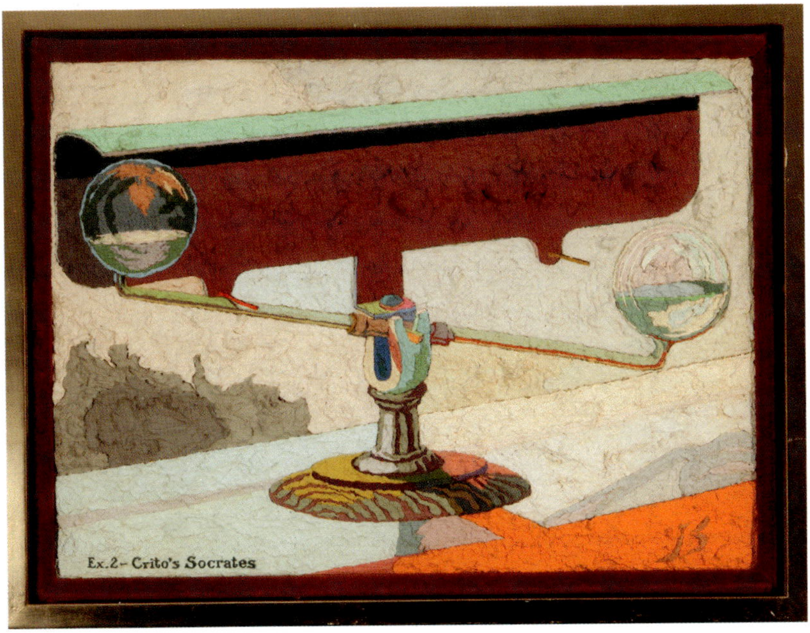

FIGURE 6.3. Jess, *Ex. 2—Crito's Socrates: Translation #3*, 1964. Oil on canvas on wood, 45.7 × 63.5 cm. © The Jess Collins Trust.

by the year 1975. I'm sure the kind of work I was doing had some effect on my state of mind at the time."[25] And again, "I had a dream—what Jungians call the Big Dream—in which the world is being incinerated. It was stated very clearly that the world had only 25 years."[26] Soon after, Jess quit his job, dropped his last name (Collins), and moved to San Francisco. He enrolled at the San Francisco Art Institute and met the preeminent American poet Robert Duncan, with whom he exchanged marriage vows on New Year's Day, 1951. Within two years, his life had changed dramatically, though it remained structurally the same until Duncan's death in 1988.

When asked about Oak Ridge and Hanford, Jess claimed that the period prompted a break or schism and with effort became psychically and mnemonically inaccessible. Declining an interview request from his alma mater, the California Institute of Technology, Jess writes, "I made the break almost 50 years ago, and willfully workt [*sic*] at erasing continuity with my life before devoting myself to art. I would be put in turmoil to rake it over."[27] Surely we can empathize with Jess's reluctance to dwell on years spent in the service of producing weapons of mass destruction.[28] And as that period receded into history and was supplanted for Jess by a consistent practice as an artist and a life with Duncan in San Francisco, it may well have grown hazy and inconsequential, an error of youth.

But science is frequently in his work. It is variously experimental, alchemical, industrial, or nuclear. Nuclear science makes an appearance in the series *Heavy Water or the 40 & 1 Nights or Jess's Didactic Nickelodeon*, forty-one collages full of rich jewel tones and warm, golden metals that Jess made in 1955 in Majorca from *Life* magazine issues. The first part of their title, *Heavy Water*, refers to modified water used in nuclear reactors to encourage fission. Even the image of the mushroom cloud appears on occasion. *If All the World Were Paper and All the Water Sink* (1962) is an homage to Gustav Klimt, but while Klimt stitches the picture plane together like so many textiles, Jess scatters pattern in the wind like bits of paper, as if the yellow mushroom cloud in the center of the painting ripped apart the fabric of the picture and its world (fig. 6.4).[29] Surely the painting conjures Jess's apocalyptic dream: the presence of a "self-portrait" in profile, watching from the side with tarot deck in hand, makes this point.[30]

Jess's dream is an origin myth, a *fable convenue*. It calls to mind another notorious artistic origin myth from the same war, Joseph Beuys's plane crash in the Crimea. The Tatars discovered Beuys in the snow and, so the story goes, wrapped his body in fat and felt, which become foundational, alchemical materials in his sculptural practice.[31] Beuys's origin myth enacts a psychic survivalism (to paraphrase Benjamin H. D. Buchloh), not to mention a materialist salvage. This postwar negotiation of self in relation to events lived and subsequently historicized has affinities with Jess's struggle to come to terms with the development and deployment of the atomic bomb by the United States, and his own involvement with that project. The dream was one way of bracketing and disavowing this event. Dropping his last name was another.

Just as Beuys would confront the aftermath of German fascism despite the war's end, so too did Jess live in the atomic age, his break with nuclear science notwithstanding. If we take *Life* magazine, which Jess read voraciously and cut up with similar energy, as a barometer of the cultural mood in the 1950s, the repercussions of a nuclear detonation on American soil were a constant and palpable concern.[32] Atomic testing continued in the Nevada desert throughout the Cold War, and on one occasion Jess wrote of feeling the blast of a nuclear detonation as far away as San Francisco.[33] This was the new world order, and its threats and traces were everywhere.

Jess was not the only artist to depict the mushroom cloud during the Cold War. Unsurprisingly, Andy Warhol, Roy Lichtenstein, and James Rosenquist all painted one of the most charged icons of the age. Echoing the rhetoric of

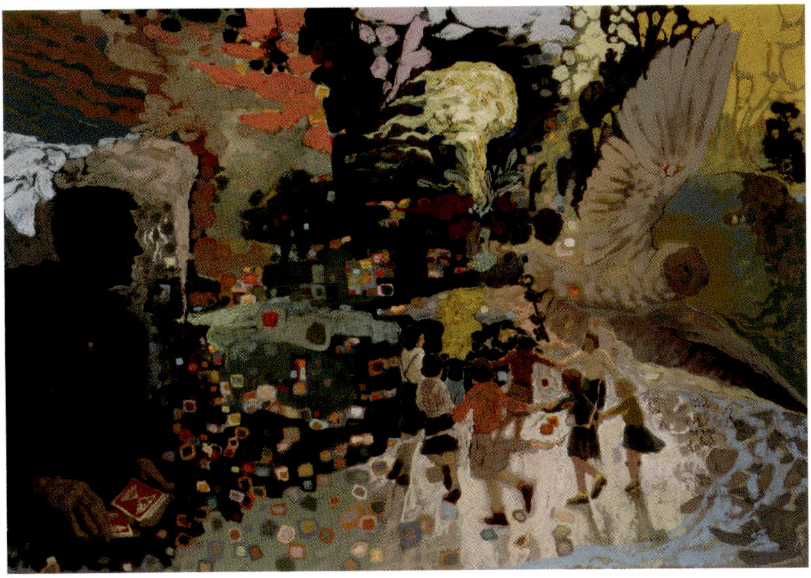

FIGURE 6.4. Jess, *If All the World Were Paper and All the Water Sink*, 1962. Oil on canvas, 96.5 × 142.2 cm. Collection: Fine Arts Museums of San Francisco, museum purchase, Roscoe and Margaret Oakes Income Fund, Museum Society Auxiliary, Mr. and Mrs. John N. Rosekrans, Jr., Walter H. and Phyllis J. Shorenstein Foundation Fund, Mrs. Paul L. Wattis Fund, Bobbie and Michael Wilsey, Mr. and Mrs. Steven McGregor Read, Mr. and Mrs. Gorham B. Knowles, Mrs. Edward T. Harrison, Mrs. Nan Tucker McEvoy, Harry and Ellen Parker in honor of Steven Nash, Katherine Doyle Spann, Mr. and Mrs. William E. Steen, Mr. and Mrs. Leonard E. Kingsley, George Hopper Fitch, Princess Rainieri di San Faustino, Mr. and Mrs. Richard Madden, 1994.31. Photograph courtesy Fine Arts Museums of San Francisco. © The Jess Collins Trust.

unimaginable scale cited above, Lawrence Jordan explains that the mushroom cloud "was by that time both an icon and an emotionally charged image, almost too much for the mind to comprehend."[34] In 1965, Warhol applied his signature repetitive silkscreen technique to his canvas *Atomic Bomb*.[35] Also in 1965 Lichtenstein painted *Atom Burst* and Rosenquist included a mushroom cloud overlaid with an umbrella (a symbol of fallout) in his mural-sized, wraparound painting *F-111*. And in that same year Rauschenberg included an image of the mushroom cloud in one of the panels in his *Dante's Inferno: Drawings for Dante's 700th Birthday*. Jess's insistence on storytelling is part of what sets his work apart from the pop treatments of the mushroom cloud, which focus instead on the image's iconicity. In the hands of Warhol, Lichtenstein, and Rosenquist the mushroom cloud is an icon, a pure sign, and it receives the same artistic treatment as any other pop icon: the mushroom cloud picture is made with the same silkscreen painting technique Warhol used for Marilyn Monroe or Elizabeth Taylor, and the same dot matrix Lichtenstein used for Mickey Mouse or Donald Duck. As a pure sign it occupies with ease the same visual field as an apple-cheeked blond toddler or a bowl of spaghetti.

But the mushroom cloud was a subject of art more than a decade earlier, appearing in works as disparate as San Francisco Beat poet and filmmaker Christopher Maclaine's surreal *The End* (1953), which follows six people the day before a nuclear apocalypse, and Robert Frank's photograph of a postcard rack at a souvenir shop, *Hoover Dam, Nevada, 1955*. Frank's photograph shows three postcards from which the tourist, browsing the rack after pulling over for a pit stop or scenic view, may choose: the Grand Canyon, the Hoover Dam, or the mushroom cloud. These are the main roadside attractions in Nevada, and such a display proposes the three images as interchangeably epic, spectacular, and impressive to their would-be purchasers. Frank's inscription to his son Pablo at the bottom of the photograph, "For Pablo—Remembering the trip to California 1956—Hoover Dam Nev.," underscores the photograph's status as a souvenir from the Frank family's trip across the United States in 1955–56, which resulted in Frank's *The Americans*. The shared characteristic of all photographs is remembrance of what is past, but this particular postcard clearly shows that by this time the mushroom cloud had been successfully pried apart from its destructive effects on Japan; abstracted into a sublime event in a sublime location, the Nevada desert; aestheticized into a form with clear, recognizable shape; and marketed as a tourist attraction.[36]

It is precisely this aestheticization that Jess's friend and fellow San Franciscan Bruce Conner lays bare in his 1976 film *Crossroads*.[37] Conner used recently declassified footage of the atomic test detonations, code-named Operation Crossroads, at Bikini Atoll in 1946. With half the world's available film on-site to take some one million images at the moment of detonation, the explosion was the most photographed event in history.[38] Conner edits the footage to repeat the event, so that the film's viewer seems to watch this spectacle over and over from different viewpoints, and adds sound effects by Patrick Gleeson and a hypnotic electronic score by Terry Riley to reinforce the debilitating visual seduction induced by the explosion. Like *Crossroads*, Jess's *The 5th Never of Old Lear* understands the deep contradiction of its subject, its representational double bind, but for Jess allegory and theatricality suited the absurdity, the unrepresentability, of the subject at hand. And picturing the moment of the world's wreckage through salvaged fragments of that world maintained a vivid and excruciating ambivalence.

Jess's worldview does not derive only from the iconicity of the mushroom cloud or its threat of annihilation, as his origin myth might seem to insist. Instead his work as an artist and his model of self are founded on the principle of salvage, which developed from his encounter with nuclear waste in Hanford, Washington. For Jess, as for most Americans, the atomic bomb was experienced only indirectly. It remained an abstraction: an imminent threat or deterrent, an aestheticized sublime, and a pop cultural icon. Even fallout, a regular presence in the pages of *Life*, was invisible, an absurdity pointed to by Rosenquist's appropriation of the umbrella in *F-111* as "protection" against what is essentially deadly air. But nuclear waste was part of Jess's daily life at Hanford in 1948 and 1949, several years after the bombs were dropped and the war had ended. And this, he later admitted, was why he abandoned science for art: "More and more I came to contemplate that utter impasse that confronts all production of nuclear materials: namely, the impossibility of safe (for the planet earth) disposal of radioactive long-lived wastes. So I turnd [*sic*] to the playing field that had beckoned to me since childhood, and there I've been engaged for going on 50 years. I can hardly explain it more clearly."[39]

Jess's fears were well founded. The Hanford Site, 500,000 acres of scrubland in eastern Washington state, is now one of the most contaminated places on earth and the most contaminated in North America.[40] Hanford, the world's first plutonium production facility, was a massive industrial complex with multiple reactors, processing plants, and hundreds of support buildings. It was difficult to find men and women willing to come to Hanford, a dismal frontier town plagued by sandstorms and threatened by contamination.[41] As the "workhorse" of the nuclear industry, Hanford produced seventy-five tons of weapons-grade plutonium, with each gram of this plutonium generating eight thousand gallons of radioactive waste.[42]

When Jess was at Hanford, in the early years of the Cold War, the brief was simply to produce as much plutonium as possible, regardless of the consequences, which have been dire. The greatest threat was from gaseous radioactive wastes emitted into the atmosphere. And of these airborne emissions, iodine 131 was the most toxic and released in the greatest quantities from the stacks of Hanford's processing plants. Iodine 131 seeks the thyroid when it enters the body, which leads to cancer. Workers at Hanford had more than seventy times the recommended iodine levels in the thyroid.[43] At Hanford, Jess worked to scrub excess iodine 131 from airborne emissions. His job, then, was to attempt to mitigate the most toxic aspect of the most toxic process at what is now the most toxic site in the nation. This was what he did, every day, for months. It is striking that in the face of this invisible toxicity, he would spend a lifetime filling empty surfaces to counter its horror vacui.

Even more important, salvage became a vital condition of production for this artist over the next fifty years. Recall Jess's words from earlier in this chapter: "All my work . . . comes from salvaging," he tells us. "It is all about rescuing or resurrecting images."[44] Jess's commitment to salvage not only was a reaction to his wartime experience but must be understood in a larger frame, as a form of world-building. In the shattered world of modernity, the collector, Hannah Arendt tells us, "only needed to bend down . . . to select his precious fragments from the pile of debris."[45] And so Jess sifts from the wreckage of a world shattered by the atomic bomb and reverberating with the constant threat of annihilation, a world in which madmen have cast reason aside. After participating in this world-shattering, Jess staged a break from that event and wrapped that break in the protective blanket of an origin myth, and then spent a lifetime salvaging a world from its discarded, neglected fragments, finding a place within his self-made constellation in which they belong.

NOTES

Epigraphs: Arendt, *Human Condition*, 2; Jess, handwritten entry in a notebook given the title page "A Skeptic Milieu Medallion," 1954–75, Jess Papers, Bancroft Library, University of California, Berkeley (hereafter cited as Jess Papers).

1. Auping, "Interview with Jess," 25–26. Additionally, Jess made a series of eight paintings called the *Salvages* in the 1970s and 1980s (the same period in which *The 5th Never of Old Lear* originates) by reworking older canvases. Though from a very different point of view, like Asger Jorn's modifications these paintings are deliberately unaggressive, reparative, and wishing to preserve and even to treasure the absurd and the "worthless" cast upon the shores of everyday life.

2. In May 1974, Jess signaled his intention to begin this work, "a large engraving paste-up, using the old lovely eighteenth century engravings culld [*sic*] from a vandalized Shakespeare folio." Jess, letter to Federico Quadrani, May 24, 1974, Jess Papers.

3. First published in 1803, uncle and nephew John and Josiah Boydell's ambitious, but ultimately ruinous, undertaking was titled, with helpful expository flair, *A Collection of Prints from Pictures painted for the purpose of illustrating the dramatic works of Shakespeare by the Artists of Great Britain*. See W. Friedman, *Boydell's Shakespeare Gallery*.

4. Shakespeare, *Tragedy of King Richard III*, 294.

5. The two men peering into the abyss of the machine room are something of an inversion of the unveiling of the Wizard of Oz. L. Frank Baum's Oz books were favorites of Jess and his partner, the poet Robert Duncan.

6. *Scientific American*, "Improved Triple Expansion Engines," 262.

7. Auping, "Interview with Jess," 26.

8. Auping, "Interview with Jess," 24. Jess considered all pictures to be allegorical.

9. Jess was assigned to the Special Engineer Detachment in Oak Ridge. His "Summary of Military Occupations" states in staccato, bureaucratic language that he "worked in a chemical laboratory, conducting investigations and research in the 'Manhattan Engineers District.' Did analytical control on processes of a secret nature." Certificate of honorable discharge, Jess Papers.

10. Rhodes, *Making of the Atomic Bomb*, 749.

11. Lindqvist, *History of Bombing*, 112. Herbert P. Bix puts the estimate at 100,000–140,000, with 100,000 people dying in the next five days. He argues that the Japanese emperor ideology made surrender nearly impossible, such that only the combination of the atomic bombs and the Soviet declaration of war on Japan made surrender possible. This is echoed in admiral Mitsumasa Yonai's remarkable statement: "I think the term is perhaps inappropriate, but the atomic bombs and the Soviet entry into the war are, in a sense, gifts from the gods." Bix, *Hirohito and the Making of Modern Japan*, 509.

12. Some scientists involved in the bomb's production, however, were devastated by what had occurred. As the German chemist Otto Hahn put it, "I was shocked and depressed beyond measure." Rhodes, *Making of the Atomic Bomb*, 735–36.

13. Rhodes, *Making of the Atomic Bomb*, 500.

14. Rhodes, *Making of the Atomic Bomb*, 486; Hughes, *Manhattan Project*, 56.

15. Rhodes, *Making of the Atomic Bomb*, 487.

16. Jeff Hughes argues that this shift culminates with the Large Hadron Collider. Hughes, *Manhattan Project*, 13.

17. Jess, "Skeptic Milieu Medallion."

18. In an interview with Rebecca Solnit, conducted for her publication *Secret Exhibition*, Jess explained, "I was a private in the lines sitting at a bench to monitor production of the product." Jess, interview by Rebecca Solnit, May 24, 1988, transcript, Jess Papers. See also Solnit, *Secret Exhibition*.

19. As is his well-known 1970 instructional work *My Own Death*, which declares: "When you go calmly across this room, go my own death goes across your mind like a flash of lightning, that is my future genuine death and is similar not only to your future death but to past hundred millions of human beings' deaths and also to future thousand trillions of human beings." See "Yutaka Matsuzawa, My Own Death, 1970," Nonaka-Hill, accessed August 1, 2024, https://www.nonaka-hill.com/artists/116-yutaka-matsuzawa/works/728-yutaka-matsuzawa-my-own-death-1970/.

20. Jess, interview by Solnit.

21. Lawrence Jordan, interview by the author, March 21, 2011.

22. Jess described nuclear energy as nightmarish: "At the time I was involved with nuclear energy, the direction it was going seemed questionable, nightmarish in some ways." Auping, *Jess*, 10.

23. Jess, interview by Solnit.

24. Auping, "Interview with Jess," 19.

25. Auping, "Interview with Jess," 19.

26. Jess, interview by Solnit.

27. Jess, letter to Michael Rogers, n.d., Jess Papers.

28. Elaine Scarry, in comparing nuclear weapons to torture, argues that these phenomena annul any shared sense of humanity: "Both torture and nuclear weapons inflict their injuries without permitting any form of self-defense, both inflict their injuries without obtaining any authorization from their own legislatures or populations; both starkly nullify even the most minimal requirements of a contractual society; both destroy the foundational concept of law." Scarry, *Thinking in an Emergency*, xv.

29. Jess, letter to Federico Quadrani, February 10, 1972, Jess Papers.

30. It is not Jess, but a stand-in, a photograph of the Olympic track star Bob Mathias taken from *Life* magazine.

31. Buchloh, "Beuys," 47.

32. A selection of *Life* feature headlines from a six-month period in 1955, when Jess was actively making many collages from these pages, affirms this point: "Facing the Fallout Problem: The AEC [Atomic Energy Commission] Reports and Scientist Advises What to Do about Radiation," February 28, 1955; "As the Bomb Goes Off and the Cloud Heads East . . . Science Tackles Radiation Peril," March 21, 1955; "Atomic Entombment: Hanford Buries 'Hot' Masses in the Cold Ground," May 9, 1955; "H-Bomb Hideaway: Completely Equipped Family Shelter to Bury in Backyard Costs $3,000," May 23, 1955; "The H-Bomb Builder's Atom Show: Dr. Edward Teller Puts On a One-Man Television Program to Help Popularize His Favorite Subject," June 6, 1955.

33. He wrote to Duncan, "Felt an earthquake jolt yesterday up in studio, but turnd [*sic*] out that it was an H-blast from Nevada!" Jess, letter to Robert Duncan, April 26, 1968, Robert Duncan Collection, Poetry Collection of the University Libraries, University at Buffalo, State University of New York.

34. Lawrence Jordan, email message to the author, April 2, 2012.

35. Laurie Anderson has a cottage theory as to why Warhol chose fifteen minutes of fame in his well-known quote, as opposed to five or ten or twelve: "Fifteen was a very famous Cold War number. I remember seeing it in the headlines of papers like the *New York Post*. Fifteen minutes was the time it took for an ICBM to reach New York from Moscow." Anderson, "Time and Beauty," 116.

36. See also Hales, "Atomic Sublime," 8.

37. Conner had also used images of atomic explosions in *A Movie* (1958), *Cosmic Ray* (1961), and *Report* (1963–67). In *Report*, which includes footage of the John F. Kennedy assassination that Conner filmed on his television set, the final image is an atomic bomb exploding while a radio report from the morning of the assassination announces, "We have a brilliant sun today."

38. Weisgall, *Operation Crossroads*, 121.

39. Jess, letter to Jonathan Weisman, August 25, 1994, Jess Papers.

40. For Hanford's history, see also Gerber, *On the Home Front*; Findlay and Hevly, *Atomic Frontier Days*; and Grossman, "Hanford and Its Early Radioactive Atmospheric Releases."

41. Findlay and Hevly, *Atomic Frontier Days*, 21–22.

42. Findlay and Hevly, *Atomic Frontier Days*, 43, 34.

43. Grossman, "Hanford and Its Early Radioactive Atmospheric Releases," 6.

44. Auping, "Interview with Jess," 25–26.

45. Arendt, introduction to *Illuminations*, by Walter Benjamin, 45.

7

"The Eternal Modernity of the Church"

Art in the Sugar Mill and the University in the Philippines

PATRICK FLORES

In the 1950s in the Philippines, two Catholic churches were built: the Church of St. Joseph the Worker, at the Victorias Milling complex in Negros Occidental, in the central islands of the Visayas; and the Chapel of the Holy Sacrifice at the University of the Philippines, an educational institution founded by Americans in 1908 in Manila and moved north to Quezon City in 1948. The first was located in the countryside, right at the heart of vast sugar plantations; the other in an emergent city, itself planned earlier by Americans, who had heavily pummeled the capital during the Pacific War (1941–45): "A brutal one-month battle to take Manila cost the lives of thousands of Americans, sixteen thousand Japanese, and tens of thousands of Filipinos. Eighty percent of

Manila was destroyed, making it the second most damaged city in the war after Warsaw."[1] Meanwhile, in Negros, as the Americans began to close in, the Japanese gutted the mills. "No large-scale industry in the country suffered as much from the effects of the war as the sugar industry."[2] Negros and Manila represented different facets of the postwar condition in a postcolony that had just gone through three successive colonialisms and was now being thrust into the whirl of rebuilding.

Both institutions, the sugar mill and the university, aspired to modern integration with the world economy through the export of sugar, on the one hand, and the production of supposedly universal, secular knowledge, on the other. The sugar enterprise initiated the country into industrialization and enabled the native elite to diversify the sources of their wealth in other industries, and "their need to secure overseas markets strengthened the ties of dependency and neocolonialism that have characterized modern Philippine-American relations."[3] In fact, that same elite had supported the Americans in the Philippine-American War and had wanted to secede altogether from the precocious Philippine democratic republic, the first in Asia. According to one account: "The introduction of iron mills into sugar processing in the 1860s marked the initial industrialization of the country.... In 1850, Negros produced only a total of 3,000 piculs of sugar; in 1893, the production level jumped to 1.8 million piculs."[4] Secular education at the University of the Philippines, on the other hand, placed its faith firmly in the "truth, unfettered by social, political, and sectarian limitations."[5]

The first president of the university, American theologian Murray Bartlett, stressed the "moral value of work" and believed that "the surest and quickest way of bringing about the Filipinization of government is through the university." His emphasis on "character" and his call to "breed" not "aristocrats, but unselfish workers for the common good" cohered with his vision for a Filipino university.[6] Thus he was invested in the discourse of the national: "There can be no greatness without nationality. The world-centers of knowledge are essentially national. With students from all parts of the world, Berlin is essentially German and Oxford essentially English. This university should not be a reproduction of the American university.... It must grow in Philippine soil, it must not be transplanted from foreign shores."[7]

The sugar mill, a capital-intensive facility, and the plantation were the loci of accumulation, unimaginable inequity, and profound feudalism and therefore became the grounds for social movements led by messianic religious figures and armed revolutionaries. For its part, the university pretended to the relative autonomy of critical thought and became a hothouse of activism and youth radicalization in the 1960s and 1970s, at which point the Philippine state was eventually captured by military rule.

The Church of St. Joseph the Worker, in Negros was part of a project to reconstruct Victorias Milling, considered one the largest integrated sugar mills in the country and in Asia (fig. 7.1). The mill had been built in 1919 by the Ossorio family, led by the couple Miguel Jose Ossorio and Maria Paz Yanco; the family later commissioned the architectural firm Raymond and Rado, based in New York and Tokyo, to design a church for the community of around three thousand in 1947 as part of the scheme to consolidate refineries in one area in the aftermath of the war. The nave and the sanctuary of the church were built on separate foundations and linked by movable beams. The architects conceived of a simple, earthquake-proof structure that "employed concrete blocks, made by the mill, laid as hollow piers which then served as formwork for the reinforced concrete beams and roof."[8] The materials used were confined to reinforced concrete and concrete block masonry, and the building was designed to withstand natural calamities and the demands of a tropical climate; these requirements were similarly made to respond to local labor capabilities.[9] The attention to the tropical context was emphasized by the "thirteen sets of doors [that] allowed the church to be completely opened on three sides. Deeply overhanging roofs provided shade and a rain screen above protecting worshippers from monsoon rains" (fig. 7.2).[10]

The facade was decorated by Ade (Adélaïde de) Bethune with a mosaic made of shards of Coke, whiskey, beer, and milk of magnesia bottles sourced in situ. Sculptures of religious figures bore local traits, and the *Stations of the Cross*, all made by Benjamin Valenciano, took risks with divergent iconography like Pontius Pilate and centurions morphing into the constabulary of the day (fig 7.3). Arcadio Anore did the brass work on the pulpit engravings. The most prominent detail in the sanctuary is Alfonso Ossorio's painting of the Catholic Last Judgment, a work which, over time, came be known as "The Angry Christ" (fig 7.4). It swarms the altar and infests the ceiling and the beams. According to Ossorio: "The subject was worked out in terms of the main action that takes place in the sanctuary, which is the sacrifice of the mass. I had a large seated figure of Christ with hands open, supported by the hands of God the Father that came out of the blue. . . . It is the Last Judgment, it's a continual last judgment with the sacrifice of the mass that is the continual reincarnation of God coming into this world."[11] One of the architects, Antonin Raymond, thought this ornamentation to be unfortunate, having obscured the natural concrete work and the entire architectural expression. For the Philippine art critic Emmanuel Torres, though, it was a tour de force: "Using cluster-images that destroy all

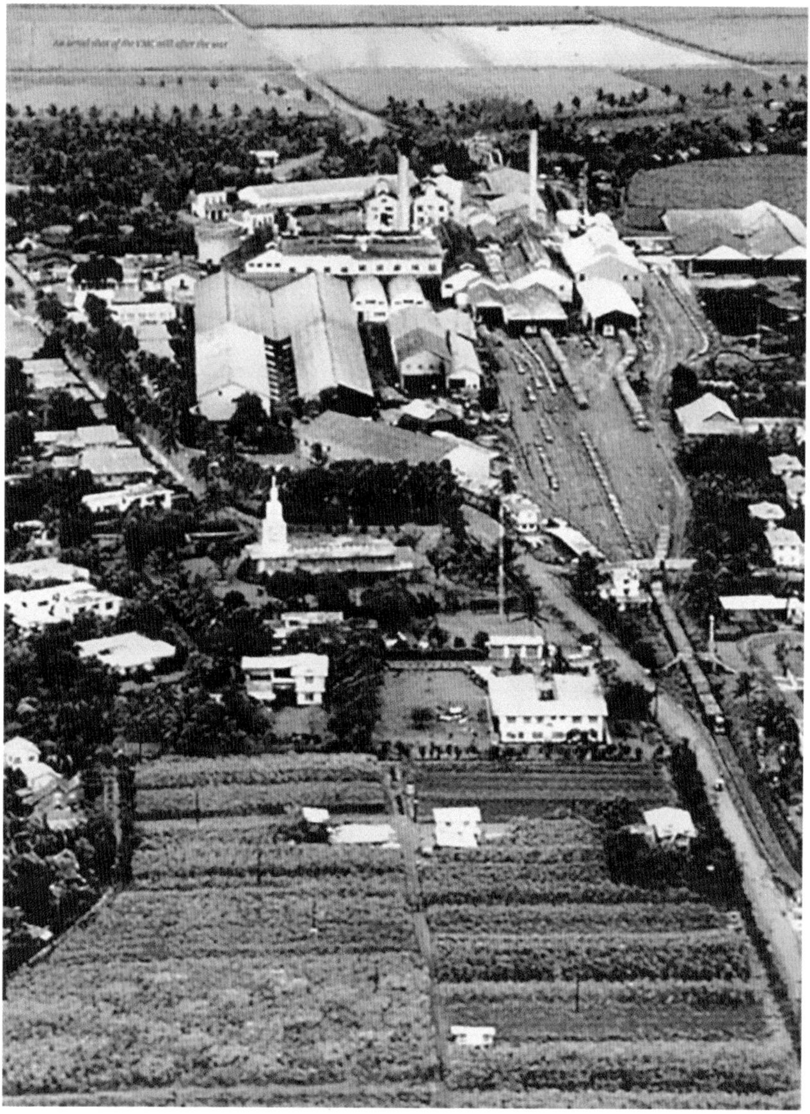

FIGURE 7.1. Antonin Raymond and Ladislav L. Rado, architects, Church of St. Joseph the Worker, Victorias Milling Complex, Negros, Philippines, 1947–51. Photograph courtesy Victorias Milling Company Inc. Museum Library.

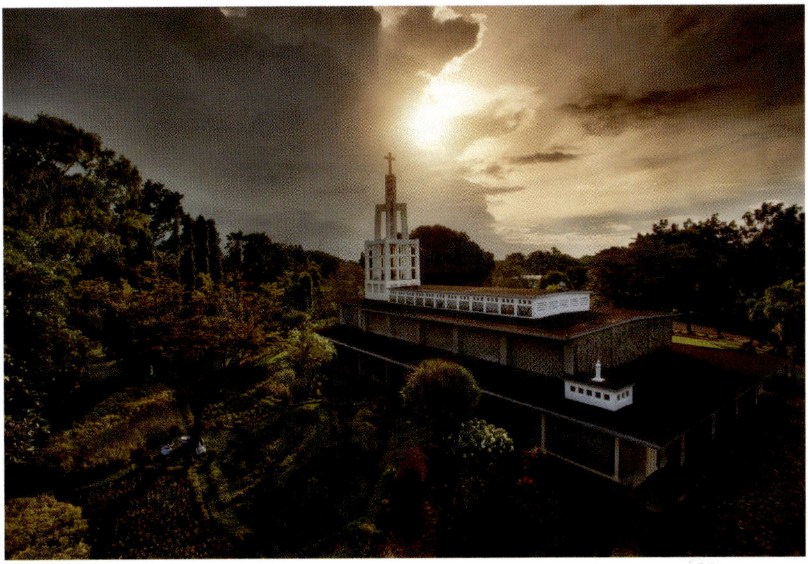

FIGURE 7.2. Antonin Raymond and Ladislav L. Rado, architects, Church of St. Joseph the Worker, Negros, Philippines 1947–51. Photograph courtesy Victorias Milling Company Inc. Museum Library.

notion of three-dimensional (naturalistic) space; fantastic, hopped-up, 'psychedelic' colors; severe distortions of faces and other parts of the anatomy; ambiguous shapes that suggest several things at once—flames, tears, waters, ovaries, sperms, lashes, mouths—in combinations that make the viewer feel he is beholding something that is not of this world, a spiritual frenzy, or a profoundly mystical moment." It is in this light that Torres insists on the auspice of the structure: "Contemporary, universal . . . and aesthetically satisfying . . . in some ways, Filipino."[12]

Alfonso Ossorio, the son of the founder of the mill, was an interlocutor of Jackson Pollock and Jean Dubuffet. In fact, he was a patron of both artists, collecting Pollock's early work and installing Dubuffet's Art Brut collection in his estate in the Hamptons, fabled for its conifer arboretum. He was born in 1916 in the Philippines, attended Harvard to study art, became a naturalized American citizen in 1933, was a medical illustrator during the war, and came back in 1950 to Negros for ten months to create the large painting of Christ. His father was a "Spanish sugar processor who pioneered centrifugal milling" during the First World War.[13] As one writer has noted, the fact that Ossorio was "born in the Philippines, wealthy, urbane, multilingual, religious, gay, an articulate writer-critic, a formidable collector . . . might script him

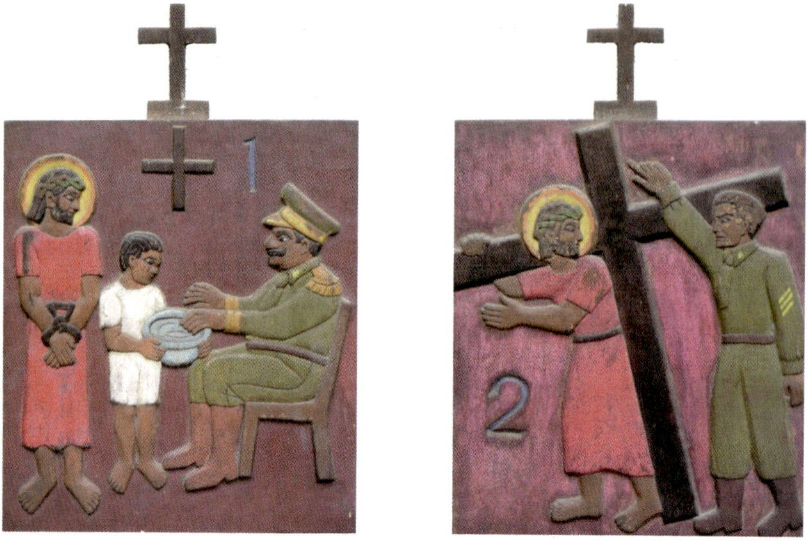

FIGURE 7.3. Benjamin Valenciano, two panels from the series *Stations of the Cross*, ca. 1951, in the Church of St. Joseph the Worker. Carved wood. Photograph courtesy Victorias Milling Company Inc. Museum Library.

outside the muscular all-American postwar art history that was the engine of critical appraisal in the 1940s and '50s."[14] One of the intentions of this chapter is to broaden this appraisal of the history of postwar modern art by positing Ossorio's eccentric practice and the place of the Philippines in that eccentricity.

At the University of the Philippines, the Chapel of the Holy Sacrifice was built in 1955. It was designed by the architect Leandro Locsin (fig. 7.5). He was born in 1928 to an elite family in Silay, Negros Occidental, that had ties to the sugar industry and local politics. He studied music first before pursuing architecture in Manila. In his senior year, he worked at the Ayala company, where the artist-connoisseur Fernando Zóbel took notice and recommended him to his relative Frederic Ossorio, one of the scions of the founders of Victorias Milling, who wanted to build a church in the mill. Locsin worked on the innovative design of a "circular chapel." The project fell through, but the mill's loss was the university's gain.[15]

The edifice was hailed as an achievement because "it was the Philippines's first chapel in the round with an altar in the middle, it was the first thin-shell concrete dome in the Philippines, and it was the architect's first building commission."[16] It radically defied the transept as the key idiom of church architecture in the predominantly Catholic Philippines. The church consisted of a spherical

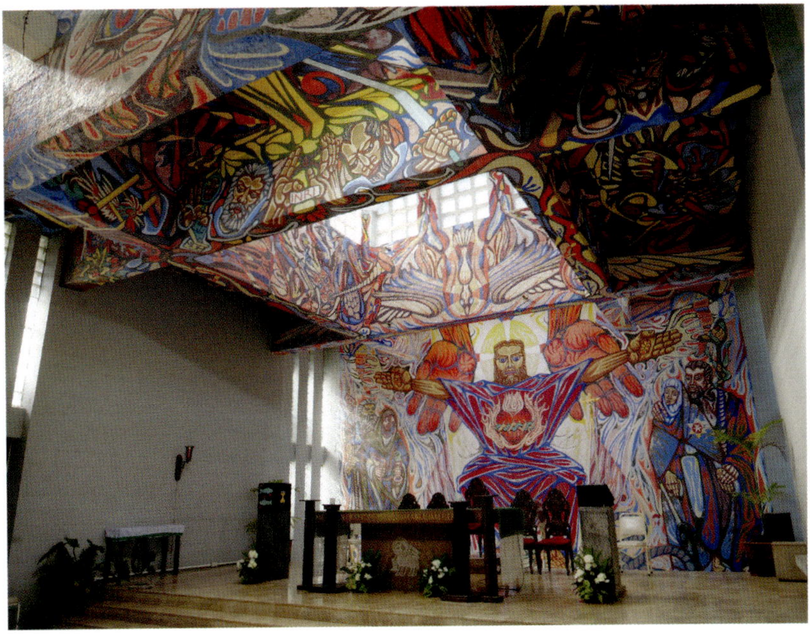

FIGURE 7.4. Alfonso Ossorio, mural, Church of St. Joseph the Worker, ca. 1950. Photograph, 2014, courtesy Victorias Milling Company Inc. Museum Library.

dome, with the main concrete shell supported by reinforced columns, and was open on all sides. It was adorned by modern art of its time: the crucifixion with the dead and risen Christ on both sides of the cross; an abstract terrazzo floor piece; and cubist *Stations of the Cross*.

The church was commissioned by the Jesuit chaplain of the university, John Delaney. At the time of construction, he was involved in debates about the role of religious life in the secular environment of the university; he challenged the dominance of Greek-letter fraternities in student politics. The city of Quezon, where the university stood, had been envisioned by the government as a new city, developed by Philippine architects, led by Juan Arellano, who were sent to the United States and South America to observe the evolving architectural scene and who implemented the initial plans of American architect William Parsons. Founded in 1939 and declared the country's capital in 1948, it was named after the president of the Philippines, Manuel Quezon, who had served from 1935 to 1944 during the American Commonwealth period. The ruin of the war had been so overwhelming that the postwar president Manuel Roxas earnestly embarked on a plan to replace Manila as the capital. According

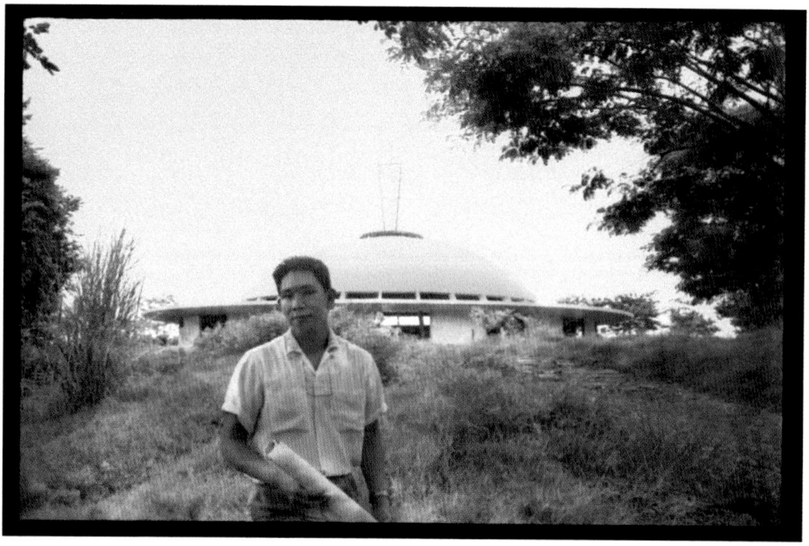

FIGURE 7.5. Leandro Locsin, architect, standing in front of Parish of the Holy Sacrifice, University of the Philippines, Quezon City, 1955. Photograph by Nap Jamir. Photograph courtesy Nap Jamir Collection.

to the architectural historian Gerard Lico, "The final choice [for the new capital] was the old Quezon City, including the underdeveloped and plateau territory up to the Novaliches watershed."[17] In a document drafted by the Capital City Planning Commission for this project in 1948, the capital city was to be seen "politically, as a seat of national government; aesthetically, as the showplace of the nation, a place that thousands of people will come to visit as an epitome of the culture and the spirit of the country; socially, as a dignified concentration of human life, aspirations, endeavor and achievement; and economically as a productive self-contained community."[18] This master plan envisaged a "new Capital City where our constitutional offices will function in an atmosphere of dignity, freedom and human happiness will rise as the citadel of democracy in the Orient" (fig. 7.6).[19] At the heart of this plan was Constitution Hill, a testament to the American democratic legacy. While posturing as modernist, the master plan hewed to the allegories of empire when it proposed names for edifices (fig. 7.7):

> It is imperative that symbolic and dignified names be given to each one of them. These could be called Palaces or Houses. We have the Palace of Justice in Paris, and the Buckingham Palace in London. We have the House of Parliament [*sic*] in Washington. Being a democracy and a Republic,

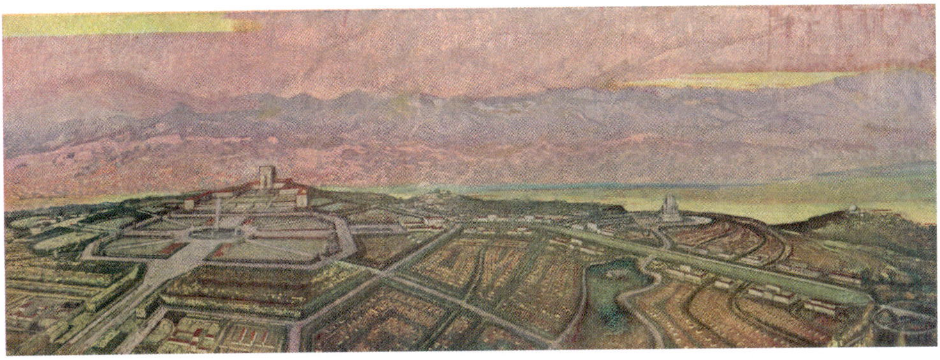

FIGURE 7.6. Juan Arellano, View of Summit, Proposed Plan for the Capital City, 1949. Photograph courtesy HTC Laboratory Digital Archives, University of the Philippines Diliman College of Architecture.

> we favor the designation of the Houses to our main buildings, and the House of Congress could be very appropriately and symbolically called the House of Wisdom, the Palace of the President, the House of Prudence, and the Offices of the Supreme Court and other moderating bodies, the House of Justice.
>
> Wisdom, Prudence and Justice, the three main virtues so often mentioned and extolled in the Proverbs, would become the distinguishing qualities of the three main departments of our government. A name that can add prestige to the place and it can inspire great deeds and restrain improper use of power.[20]

It was also in 1948 that much of the University of the Philippines moved from Manila to its present site in Quezon City. Modifications of the plan for the capital city came and went, up to the point when a legislative complex was nearly ready to be erected. But the plan became too grandiose, too reminiscent of Brasilia, and just too impractical. The grand design was ultimately abandoned in 1960.

After completing the plan for the university, Locsin moved on to become the main architect of the central business district in Manila, developed by relatives of the Ossorios, designing its first buildings and the gated enclave of the elite called Forbes Park. First Lady Imelda Marcos then asked him to design the Cultural Center of the Philippines, which opened in 1969, and other buildings on land on Manila Bay reclaimed from the sea, for a cultural complex to host events by the International Monetary Fund–World Bank and Miss Universe, among others.

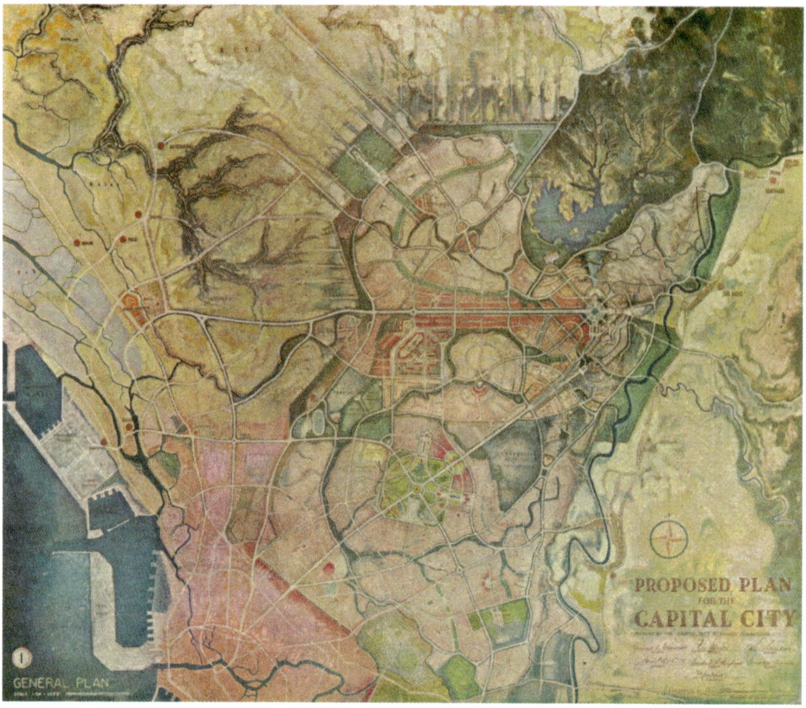

FIGURE 7.7. Juan Arellano, Proposed Plan for the Capital City, 1949. Photograph courtesy HTC Laboratory Digital Archives, University of the Philippines Diliman College of Architecture.

These two instantiations in the Philippines offer ways to critically reflect on the postwar as a formative condition because of the rupture of the war and the desire for sovereignty. In the Philippines, this was a particularly fraught process in the sense that independence had already been achieved in 1898, but American imperial incursion in the Pacific usurped it. The Philippine-American War was carnage, killing one out of every seven Filipinos.[21] When the Japanese invaded in 1941, the country was subjected again to four years of Japanese rule and equivalent atrocities. It was therefore thrilling for the country to cobble together its birthright after the Second World War. The postwar in this context was an inchoate moment in which the rubble of war offered the language of colonial critique and became the ground on which a finally free nation could stand. That said, the elites of the country who pursued self-government looked elsewhere in the same vein. The thrill also encompassed a sense of belonging to the world, through the institutions of the sugar mill and the university, from whose premises two churches rose to serve as a defense against communism and an affirmation of the resilience of the church. This modernity endeavored to produce a spiritual and ethical subject whose religious experience was aestheticized through architecture. The sugar barons in the Philippines, for instance, styled themselves as cosmopolitan and cultured, parlaying their affluence into patterns of consumption that crystallized modernity through "up-to-date agricultural methods, the technologically sophisticated 'centrals' (i.e., mills), and the entrepreneurial genius of the industry's founders and leaders."[22]

The first instantiation of the postwar was reconstruction in light of the breathtaking devastation and loss of lives the Philippines had suffered during the war, which was one of the most horrible in history. The aesthetic of this reconstruction may have been exemplified by the use of reinforced concrete as the mutating material par excellence. Antonin Raymond expressed confidence in concrete and its plastic potential. As one critic of his practice said, "Concrete is a truly international material used worldwide. From another perspective, it is a regional material through the use of locally found aggregate and the techniques and ideals of its builders. Concrete, as a liquid that becomes a solid, can be further considered 'more a process than a building material.'"[23] Raymond had apprenticed for Frank Lloyd Wright and worked with him to design the Imperial Hotel in Tokyo. Ladislav L. Rado, who, like Raymond, was from the former Czechoslovakia, was a student of Walter Gropius and a peer of Josef Albers. Raymond is esteemed in Japan as its "first modern architect," and he did a seminal project for a spiritual guru in Puducherry, India, in the 1930s. He was the ideal architect between worlds who could shuttle between Asia and Europe, a "go-between" who transferred the "latest concrete technology from one area to the next."[24] Raymond was also commissioned to design American embassies and military bases, as well as test structures of Japanese houses in 1943 for prospective operations as commissioned by the US Engineer Office in Utah.[25]

Modern church architecture in different parts of the world looked to reinforced concrete as its main construction material, in fact its key access to being contemporary, as it was at once light and strong, as opposed to the traditional heft of domes and vaults. As Locsin would himself assert, "Forget steel and glass, concrete is our material" (fig. 7.8).[26] Concrete, indeed, was an index of modernity, internationalism, industrialization, and labor-demanding plasticity. This fascination with and perhaps fixation on plasticity prominently figured in the discourse of Philippine modern art; it was the language needed to disengage from, though not totally refuse, realism. It was this virtue of plasticity that paved the path for abstraction to take root and flourish in the 1950s in Manila, culminating in the exaltation of the nonobjective in painting. According to Raymond: "Concrete is plastic and should be treated as such, but because it

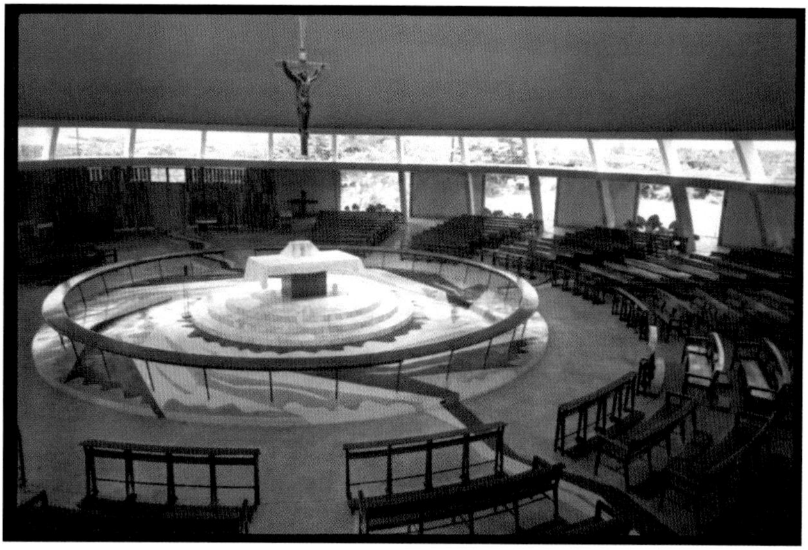

FIGURE 7.8. Leandro Locsin, architect, Parish of the Holy Sacrifice (interior), University of the Philippines, Quezon City, 1955. Photograph by Nap Jamir. Photograph courtesy Nap Jamir Collection.

is plastic it is quite different from stone and brick, which are heavy masses. Its main quality is its amazing strength and flexibility even when light. Nervi in Italy and Candela in Mexico and myself believe in that."[27]

Moreover, concrete was prized for its fluidity and lightness in spite of its exceptional tectonic integrity. Such an aleatory aesthetic related well to Ossorio's own protean sensibility. Dubuffet evocatively described the easel paintings that Ossorio did almost feverishly in the evenings in Negros while he was painting the mural during the day: "Grimacing or screaming faces; hands with fingers forming strange signs; excrescences, digitations, umbilical depressions, viscera sprouting filthy tufts of hair; hideous sexual organs—all seething with varicosities, leprosies, abscesses."[28] His work involved the "process-intensive wax-resist technique, building up a rich vocabulary in layers of wax, black ink, water-based paints, and other drawing materials."[29]

Second, this reconstruction procedure was a coincident of liturgical reform that manifested itself quite strongly in church architecture. Such reform entailed efforts "to bring the congregation into more active participation in the Mass. Its architectural effect is to bring priest and congregation physically closer together around the focal point of the altar."[30] Paramount for Locsin was the "urge toward community life" of the "people of our times" and that the interior of the church should be focused on the Eucharistic sacrifice and not mainly devotion.[31] This reform could only be animated by the art of the time; exemplary in this regard were churches of the period in France, at Plateau d'Assy, Vence, Villefranche-sur-Mer, and Ronchamp, which were decorated by artists like Henri Matisse, Georges Rouault, and Jean Cocteau. Here the artworks in the two Philippine churches resonate. Ossorio was conscious of this stimulus. According to him, as he conjured the Last Judgment in his massive altar work that suffuses the architecture and engulfs the worshipper: "It worked out beautifully because the services take place usually very early because of the heat and the church had been oriented so that the sun would come in and strike the celebrant as he stood at the altar with this enormous figure behind him. It worked, if I do say so myself. And although they loathed it at the time it was done it is almost now a place of pilgrimage."[32] The relationship between liturgical reform and contemporary art was intimate. According to M. A. Couturier, "Where there is no natural life, there can be no supernatural life; and where there is no living art, no sacred art can be possible either, for actually there is no art at all."[33]

Third, this reconstruction may have touched a nerve of mysticism, a search for unity amid the fragmentation in the wake of the war. The man at the helm of the sugar mill, Frederic Ossorio, also a son of the founders, wrote that "there was then, in 1946 . . . the imperative to sow a seed whose incremental growth could heal not only the Victorias community, but to show a function, born out of weakness, of the greater power which is liberated by humility, for the reconciliation of Asia itself."[34] His brother Alfonso would further elucidate this desire for wholeness through mediation of the human, who is "the link between God and the material world. Which is the whole idea of the sacrifice of the mass. It's all one kettle of fish. . . . It is simply that it is all one unity. Even a little waste piece of plastic or a bone is just as much alive as the abstract concept of God, which is meaningless unless it is incarnated."[35] For Alfonso, his return to the Philippines was also a coming to terms with his troubled childhood and his sexuality, as he read on the island the Freudian book by Nandor Fodor about trauma and prenatal conditioning.[36] The Philippines had also condensed for him an "intolerant religious culture" that had "insulted and injured" him and for which he was painting his relentless Christ. However this mystical quality was characterized, the church in Negros evinced a Catholic animus that was part of the atmosphere of postwar reconstruction, signifying "that Christianity is a living thing, able to revitalize itself, and heighten one's awareness of the Faith as a continually growing, changing, organic reality that is intrinsically bound to a particular time and place."[37]

This particularity is surely romanticized. Ade Bethune, who did the mosaic work on the facade of the church, would sketch out the orientalist "adventure" in the Philippines. A Belgian liturgical artist whose family migrated to the United States and contributed to various endeavors of the Catholic Church as an artist, she was asked by Ossorio to help him complete the decorations of the church in Negros. She confessed that she had had no "idea about the Philippines" and had merely read *Reader's Digest* to find out more; the publication reported that "the Philippine industries had been entirely destroyed by World War II and that every article of commerce, down to the plainest kitchen plate was still being imported from the States." In Negros, she would describe this scene: "For the sea shore to the blue, mahogany-covered mountains on the eastern horizon, there is nothing but fields of sugar cane waxing strong and sweet under the sun." Such a scene was one of feudal toil and industrialization that Bethune conflated as the sensorium and the scent of the province: "Three thousand souls . . . are attached . . . to the mill at Victorias. Some of them even work a concrete block machine, thus adding the smell of fresh cement to the prevailing fragrance of molasses and steam emanating from the boiler room close by."[38]

This incarnation of the spirit takes place as a performance within a church that is carefully crafted to stage it. Locsin's design for his church, for instance, harnessed the element of light. There are "five shades of light in the cove at the interior base of the dome: white, green, red, yellow, and blue," with the intensity calibrated according to the time of day and part of the mass. Father Delaney was said to have instructed Locsin to design a "completely open building that would provide a dramatic setting for the Mass while symbolizing the eternal modernity of the church."[39] This setting created the possibility of multiple dialogues across a congregation that faced one another, seeing their fellow churchgoers in a circular formation, a view uninterrupted by columns. The priest, while central, performs the mass in the round, as it were, and projects an illusion of participation among those who hear it. In 1968, the avant-garde Philippine composer Jose Maceda, exponent of musique concrète in Asia, premiered his Pagsamba (Music for a Religious Ritual) in the church, consisting of a hundred performers, a hundred voices, and two gong groups to create at once stereophony, music, and malleable sound. The fact that an avant-garde musician chose this space for the event is a tribute to the modernity of its architecture.[40]

The theoretician of Christian architecture Rudolf Schwarz identifies the "dome of light" as one of the formal templates of a church. He conceptualizes this setting as evocative of infinity: "All the land and all the nations spread out without end within the universe. The vault of the world is a pellucid infinitude, clear and transparent like an evening sky high in the mountains, ethereal and incorporeal, a golden effulgence where the heavenly beings are hovering motionless in bliss. Heaven is everywhere, earth everywhere, the one melting into the other."[41] The church at the university echoes this paradigm, which stresses the primacy of emotion. The Negros church, though retaining the proscenium format, can also address this emotional imperative: "The whole structural system, dictated by materials, results in a down-to-earth character and lower proportions. Into this technically conceived composition the contrast between deep, thin overhangs, massive piers, and pierced clerestories, as well as the overall fresco of the sanctuary wall, introduce essential emotional elements."[42]

Fourth, the postwar may have encouraged the creative formation of a humanist and cosmopolitan artist of broad sympathies. Alfonso Ossorio possessed a robust intellectual disposition. Raymond painted; did pottery, textile design, furniture, furnishings, lighting fixtures, and garden design; and even played the cello to "achieve true integration."[43] Locsin was a painter, pianist, tastemaker, collector of antiquities, and set designer for Martha Graham in Manila and New York.

More challenging to acknowledge in this chapter is the tangent of church and state. In a paternalistic and patrimonial state like the Philippines, in which the economy is yoked around an oligarchy, and in a society so deeply tied to the colonial faith of Catholicism and its folk translations, the church and the state are difficult to decouple. Delaney, the priest who commissioned the Chapel of the Holy Sacrifice, had "sought to put a stop to the brutalities in fraternities and sororities, and cleanse student politics . . . and bring Christ and his principles into . . . political life."[44] Raymond stated in his autobiography that the sugar tycoons had told him that one way "to prevent the spread of communism on the island of Negros . . . would be to imbue the people with an ardent religious spirit by reviving their interest in Catholicism"—the reason the church had to be built.[45] This would be confirmed by Frederic Ossorio, who spoke of the church as a "deep Christian commitment to the Christian faith" and a "means of buttressing Philippine democracy against an emerging communist insurgency."[46]

It is often imagined that church and state, religion and nation, are antinomies. But the colonial government in the Philippines under Spain was for the most part an assemblage of church and state, and at times when there was conflict, the clergy did not deem it impossible to assassinate the governor-general, for example, as happened in 1719. The discussion of the two Philippine churches tends to surmount the said antinomies. In the context of the industrialization of the economy through sugar and the Filipinization of government through university education, the modern form may have been carved out from the interests of a political theology to encourage more collectivity in liturgy. The latter was foreseen to take place within an architecture that is attentive to a local and theatrical environment. Moreover, it sought to convene a group of the faithful who are bound in some kind of mystified unity perceived to have been torn apart by the war and subsequently threatened by forces like communism and secularization.

It is at this point that the notion of political theology productively replaces "religion" and prompts us to reflect on the relationship between the erstwhile binary "church and state" and to understand how "the modern age redefines and rebinds politics and theology in an attempt to manage its deepest tendencies toward chaos and dissolution."[47] Talal Asad thus has gestured toward the need for the "anthropology of the secular," and Carl Schmitt has argued that "many theological and political concepts share a common structure."[48] The modernity of church architecture indexes the formative nature of this postwar political theology: "Out of this convergence of reinforced concrete, the spectacle and the collective, Catholic church architects developed a program for church architecture that was both liturgically and architecturally innovative."[49] This progressive architectural aesthetic fleshed out a practice that unmoored religious doctrine from its colonial origins in the Philippines, flattened its catechism and iconography, and foregrounded the neutrality and putative universality of the modern form. Within this modernist structure, a particular kind of religious agency was being honed, one that needed to be revitalized after the war and had to renew the faith in religion that was posing and hailing itself as of its time, a timeliness that could only be dramatized by the contemporary medium of concrete and the contemporaneity of the church. As the historian Adrian Forty asserts: "If concrete offends, it is not so much for being 'unnatural,' but rather because it threatens the convention of the division between nature and the non-natural."[50]

This problematic of political theology, therefore, tries to surmount the dialectical elaboration of church and state, the religious and the secular, and instead animates a more polyphonic conversation on modernity at different registers. The modern could be regarded as a purely progressivist project, advancing toward the future and altogether forsaking the past. It could be self-consciously citing the past as an origin from which it transforms into something else. It could be a way to mediate colonial trauma, either to elide or to absorb it through the internationalist language of abstraction or styles like cubism or fauvism, which were integrated into the churches. The discrepant practices of Ossorio in Negros and Locsin in Quezon City in relation to the modern implies the range of ways in which modernism could be invoked as a symptom of either trauma or transcendence, thus meshing both church and state in a dynamic. As Marcel Gauchet puts it: "Religion was historically the state's condition of possibility. The state could not have been established had it not reflected the earlier division between society and its foundation. . . . It put a new face on a very old faith in externality: the feeling that we owe society something other than ourselves."[51]

Finally, it might be fitting to frame the discussion of the two 1950s churches in the Philippines within a precursor and a possible future. In 1914, the Filipino Felix Manalo founded Iglesia ni Cristo, or the Church of Christ, a homegrown global religion considered by one scholar to be "the most successful form of indigenous Christianity to have arisen in the Third World in the twentieth century."[52] A mark of its presence all over the country and overseas is its highly original and hybrid architecture of spires, arches, canopies, and palatial interiors; its church's typical structure, following the template of Carlos Santos-Viola, includes an "exuberant use of fanciful forms and ornaments . . . [and a] brilliant white facade whose silhouette is a cusped Gothic arch or a flattened Saracenic arch."[53] Its followers' zeal partly rests on the prophesy of Christ's church rising in the Far East in the Philippines and radiating outward to the far West of the Americas and Europe, beginning in Hawaii. The religion's first Gothic-like concrete church was built in Manila in 1948; the building, designed by Alfredo Luz, then evolved to have a more elaborate design in the 1960s. This religious organization lies beyond the authority of the Church of Rome and votes in elections as a formidable collective. It celebrated its centenary in 2014, and its grandest project to date takes us to another instance of architecture as a kind of political theology: when it opened, the Philippine Arena was the biggest multipurpose indoor facility of its kind in the world. In this epilogue, the church, wherever and however it assembles its people, redeems the promise of modernity by reconstituting the mass of its faithful and placing them within the ample embrace of its concrete refuge.

NOTES

1. Abinales and Amoroso, *State and Society in the Philippines*, 163.
2. Quirino, *History of the Philippine Sugar Industry*, 81.
3. J. Larkin, *Sugar and the Origins of Modern Philippine Society*, 6.
4. Lachica, *Ayala, the Philippines Oldest Business House*, 19.
5. Taylo, "Bartlett as First President," 18.
6. Taylo, "Bartlett as First President," 18.

7. Taylo, "Bartlett as First President," 19.
8. Oshima and Whitaker, "Portfolio," 190.
9. Raymond, Rado, and Weidlinger, "Alternate Designs for a Church," 48.
10. Oshima and Whitaker, "Portfolio," 190.
11. Alfonso Ossorio, quoted in Ottmann and Kosinski, *Angels, Demons, and Savages*, 11.
12. Emmanuel Torres, "Chapel of Saint Joseph the Worker in Victorias," 1967, 4, Papers of Alfonso Ossorio and Edward Dragon Young, 1902–2000, Harvard Art Museums Archives, Harvard University. See also Manahan, "This Is Not an Angry Christ."
13. B. Friedman, *Alfonso Ossorio*, 13.
14. Ottmann and Kosinski, *Angels, Demons, and Savages*, ix.
15. Klassen, *Architecture in the Philippines*.
16. Polites, *Architecture of Leandro V. Locsin*, 203.
17. Lico, *Arkitekturang Filipino*, 383.
18. Lico, *Arkitekturang Filipino*, 383.
19. Lico, *Arkitekturang Filipino*, 384.
20. Lico, *Arkitekturang Filipino*, 385–86.
21. Isaac, introduction to *American Tropics*, xv.
22. Billig, *Barons, Brokers, and Buyers*, 1.
23. Oshima, "Characters of Concrete," 66.
24. Oshima, "Characters of Concrete," 75.
25. See Loeffler, "Architecture of Diplomacy"; Čapková, "Influence of Spirit and Not of Form."
26. Polites, *Architecture of Leandro V. Locsin*, 10.
27. Raymond, "Antonin Raymond: Interview with Tange Kenzō (1960)," 310.
28. Dubuffet, "Initiatory Paintings of Alfonso Ossorio," 117.
29. Steele, Albro, Homolka, et al., "Materials and Techniques," 134.
30. Christ-Janer and Foley, *Modern Church Architecture*, 9.
31. Locsin, "Directions for the Building of a Church," 16.
32. Quoted in Ottmann and Kosinski, *Angels, Demons, and Savages*, 11.
33. Couturier, "Religious Art and the Modern Artist," 270.
34. Torres, "Chapel of Saint Joseph the Worker in Victorias," 5.
35. Quoted in Ottmann and Kosinski, *Angels, Demons, and Savages*, 11.
36. Fodor, *Search for the Beloved*.
37. Torres, "Chapel of Saint Joseph the Worker in Victorias," 3.
38. Bethune, "Philippine Adventure," 110–13.
39. Polites, *Architecture of Leandro V. Locsin*, 203.
40. Dioquino, "Kumintang."
41. Kieckhefer, *Theology in Stone*, 236.
42. Raymond, Rado, and Weidlinger, "Alternate Designs for a Church," 48.
43. Raymond, *Antonin Raymond*, 318.
44. Cortes, "Tan's Devoted Presidency," 325.
45. Raymond, *Antonin Raymond*, 256.
46. Oshima and Whitaker, "Portfolio."

47. Hammill and Lupton, introduction to *Political Theology and Early Modernity*, 3.
48. Asad, "Religion, Nation-State, Secularism," 193; Schmitt, *Political Theology*, 14.
49. Forty, *Concrete and Culture*, 175.
50. Forty, *Concrete and Culture*, 59.
51. Gauchet, "Primitive Religion and the Origins of the State," 120.
52. Reed, "Iglesia ni Cristo, 1914–2000," 564.
53. Reed, "Iglesia ni Cristo, 1914–2000," 582.

8

Antipodean Vision

Postwar Arts in Australia and the South Pacific

TERRY SMITH

Experiences during the Second World War shaped postwar consciousness in countries throughout the South Pacific region, as did the emerging realignment of global power along Cold War lines. These two factors figure profoundly in art during the 1945–65 period, although they do so, as we might expect, in distinctively different ways in each country. To my mind, the depth of these differences in each art center, the considered refusals of total commitment to modernization, and the persistence of cultural continuities raise considerable doubt about the overriding emphasis on "the modern" in art historical enquiries into art made outside of the West during the twentieth century. Such an emphasis, especially when it excludes all other motivations, implies that achieving modernity was the primary concern of every artist and of everyone else involved. Revisionary research is occurring all over the world today as historians and curators, and many artists, search for local—as distinct from Euro-American—groundings for contemporary art practices. They are reaching back over the immediate past (the already early years of contemporary art), over the transformative moments of the 1960s and 1970s (with all their local differences), to the "multiple modernities" of the early and mid-twentieth century. This amounts to a massive, and entirely necessary, enterprise of art historical revision. Yet if we revise the histories of nineteenth- and twentieth-century art everywhere on the planet in terms that presume that every artist always aspired to modernize—and either succeeded, tried but failed, or refused to do so (and was therefore reactionary)—we risk overlooking the resonances within art practice and institutional formation of the fact that ideas concerning modernity, modernization, and modernism were historical constructions and Western, or more precisely North Atlantic, fictions. While there is no doubt that these conceptual deformations had measurably significant impacts on all aspects of life in actual social, economic, and political formations throughout the world, they nonetheless also served (and still serve) to obscure the persistence in those places of traditionalism, cultural continuity, appropriations from adjacent cultures or from colonizing ones, deliberatively partial modernizations, countermodern tendencies, and Indigenous art production. Art made during modern times was always more complex, and made for different reasons, than art prioritized by the high-achieving but relatively narrow concentrations that we rightly label "modernist." The entire array of these interacting forces needs to be taken into account, and their relativities plotted, if we are to develop an art historical approach that, while acknowledging the historical impact of the Westernist model, supersedes it.[1] Let me show this to be the case in the South Pacific region, a major theater of conflict during the Second World War.

The Experience of War

The resonances of colonialism were everywhere. Maps showing the reach of what were known as "the imperial powers" in 1939 indicate British possessions as stretching from India, "acquired" in 1819, through the Gilbert Islands in 1919 (actually an Australian protectorate, as was New Guinea). US possessions stretched from Alaska (1867) down to the Philippines (1898), right into the heart of the South China Sea. The Dutch controlled Java and Papua, and the French controlled Indo-China. The Japanese were the latest imperial power to

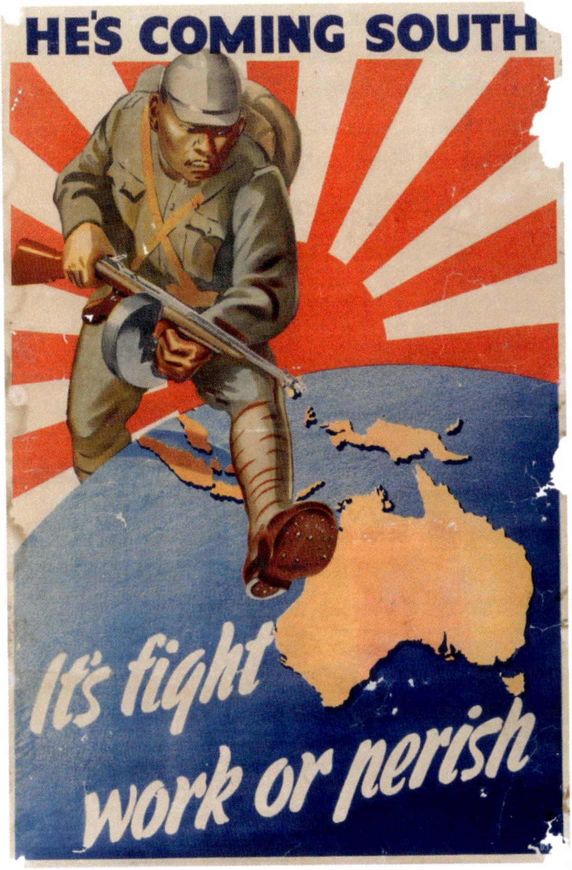

FIGURE 8.1. Australian Government Printing Office, *He's Coming South*, 1942. Offset lithographic poster, 75 × 50 cm. Collection: Australian War Memorial, Canberra, ARTV09225.

seek dominion in the region, having mandates on many Pacific islands and being in the course of a long, bloody, and ultimately futile attempt to conquer China.[2]

For countries such as Australia—with its small, overwhelmingly European settler population clinging to the edges of a massive landmass, a "torn continent," as we say, a page detached from the book of Europe that drifted into southern Asia—this volatility was perceived as a highly threatening situation. A poster entitled *He's Coming South* showed a predatory Japanese soldier leaping across the globe, fiercely determined to bayonet our southern continent. Prepared in 1942 as propaganda by the Australian government, it was deemed too upsetting to be distributed in Queensland and Melbourne (fig. 8.1).

Wartime experience was registered in a variety of ways. For example, an advertisement for Pond's lipstick and face powder in the April 21, 1945, issue of the *Australian Women's Weekly* shows a young woman doing war work ("packing food for the boys") but prioritizing greeting her lover when he comes home on leave. Official war artists—those commissioned to record life on the frontlines—produced celebratory battle pictures, but some had an eye for more intimate moments. Among them was Donald Friend, whose 1945 watercolor *Showers in a Ruin* hints at homosocial camaraderie among the soldiers.[3] In the main Australian cities, the arrival of US soldiers on leave had noticeable social impacts, as profiled by Sydney artist Weaver Hawkins in his 1945 vorticist painting *Jitterbugs*.[4]

Postwar Begins

By early 1945, the war in Europe and the Pacific was nearing its end, although it took, as we know, an act of unprecedented violence—the nuclear bombing of Hiroshima and Nagasaki—to bring about the surrender of the Japanese forces. The Australian War Memorial, a commemorative site and museum in the capital city, Canberra, holds many artworks showing various aspects of the experience, including the aftermath, of wars involving Australians. The beginnings of postwar are figured in paintings such as Stella Bowen's 1945 *Repatriated Prisoner of War Is Processed*, which tracks, in an idealized form, the stages of healing a returned soldier.[5] In contrast, evidence of the impact of the war in Europe was circulated, mainly through photographs and newsreels but also by artists, such as in Alan Moore's 1945 painting *Blind Man at Belsen*. Moore was a war artist stationed with the Welsh brigade that liberated the camp.[6]

Most Australian artists of consequence processed the war by absorbing its effects as resonances within the mythologizing of Australian experience that had become their main enterprise. Some did so allegorically, as in Arthur Boyd's 1946–47 *Melbourne Burning* (fig. 8.2). This is an apocalyptic image, one of projected fear, because, with the exception of Darwin, no Australian cities were bombed by enemy forces. Nevertheless, paintings such as this do register the greatest impact of postwar years in Australian art: it deepened the sense of alienation within the Australian imaginary, within its conception of its nationhood, and in the figuring of an Antipodean vision. The nation's sense of the tyranny of distance, its geographical and cultural isolation, increased. The colonial founder, Britain, was too far away, and too preoccupied with its own defense, to defend its "dominion" when it was threatened with Japanese invasion. Its reign as an empire was at an end. Sensing this, Australian polity pivoted toward dependence on the United States, the emergent empire. At the same time, fear of the interior of the continent grew among the white settlers: "Don't those Asian hordes know that the center is uninhabitable (except by a few natives)?" For

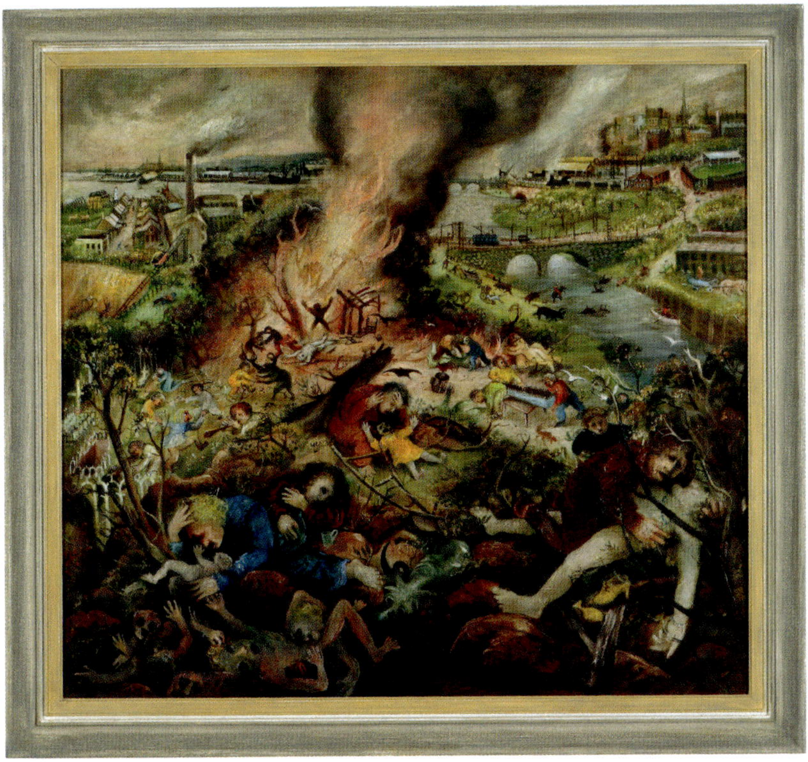

FIGURE 8.2. Arthur Boyd, *Melbourne Burning*, 1946–47. Oil and tempera on canvas, 90 × 100 cm . Collection: Museum of Old and New Art, Hobart. Reproduced with permission of Bundanon Trust.

the first time, Australians realized that their situation could become impossible for brethren allies to redeem; the battle might become ours alone.

The suddenly uncanny fragility of the ordinary was also laced with awareness of the everyday heroism of those who inhabited it, notably in Russell Drysdale's empathetic studies of the rural proletariat, such as 1945's *The Drover's Wife*.[7] Irony and indirection attended Sidney Nolan's treatments of similar subjects. In his 1946–47 *Ned Kelly* series, he drew on his experiences as a wartime deserter, his family memories of the already legendary Victorian outlaw and Irish recidivist (Nolan was related to one of the constables who hunted Kelly), his desire to transform the dominant Australian School of landscape painting, and his love of early twentieth-century European avant-garde art (fig. 8.3).[8] He once told me: "I wanted to see how Malevich's Black Square would look in the middle of our desert." This is modernist, this intention and this

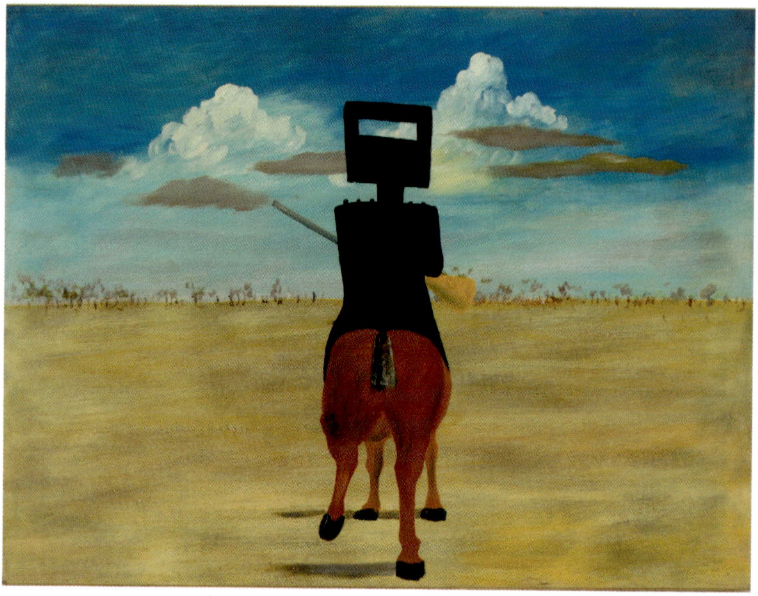

FIGURE 8.3. Sidney Nolan, *Ned Kelly*, 1946. Enamel paint on composition board, 90.8 × 121.5 cm. Collection: National Gallery of Australia, Canberra, Gift of Sunday Reed, 1977. 1976.277.

outcome. Very little else in Australian art of this period can be so described, with precision.

Testing the Atomic Age

For many Australian artists, the end of the war meant that the opportunity to visit Europe had returned. Albert Tucker, who like Nolan was one of the Angry Penguin group of expressionist-surrealist artists based in Melbourne for the duration, took the unusual decision to travel via Japan, where he made a number of watercolors at Hiroshima. We arrive at the second major impact of postwar in the South Pacific region, its transformation into a theater for the testing of atomic weapons, the deep arsenal of the Cold War, the machinery of "mutually assured destruction" that underscored the atomic age. In Weaver Hawkins's 1947 painting *Atomic Power*, a pilot stands shaken by the devastation that this new form of power has wrought (fig. 8.4). His shadow falls across the vaporized remains of victims, pale ghosts imprinted on the ground. Nothing by Australian artists, however, matched *The Hiroshima Panels*, painted by the husband-and-wife team Maruki Iri and Maruki Toshi between 1950 and

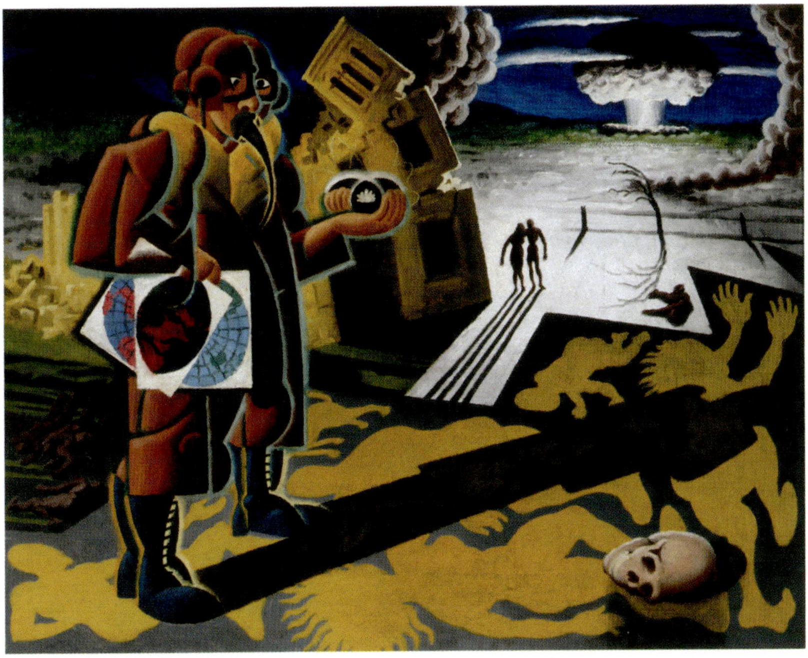

FIGURE 8.4. Weaver Hawkins, *Atomic Power*, 1947. Oil on hardboard, 61 × 78.5 cm. Collection: Art Gallery of New South Wales, purchased 1976. Photograph courtesy Art Gallery of New South Wales. © Estate of HF Weaver Hawkins. Photo: AGNSW. 92.1976.

1982.[9] These paintings toured the region as part of campaigns against the Cold War arms race. I recall seeing them as a schoolboy and remember how they shaped the nightmares shared by all of us during those years, when we regularly practiced running to underground shelters at the sound of sirens.

The response of New Zealand artists during the postwar period paralleled that in Australia. The work of the official war artists is evident in Russell Clark's 1945 *Japanese Planes, Rekata, Santa Isabella*.[10] Modernist responses also meant seeing one's environment as freshly strange, a site of alienation, inducing restless movement, a mood captured in Colin McCahon's 1950 *Six Days in Nelson and Canterbury* (fig. 8.5). The intensely religious artist is driven to imagine an environment prior to Christian revelation: "I saw something logical, orderly and beautiful belonging to the land and not yet to its people. Not yet understood or communicated, not even really invented. My work has largely been to communicate this vision and invent a way to see it."[11]

Thinking more broadly around the Pacific Rim, Rex Butler and A. D. S. Donaldson, an art historian and a painter who regularly collaborate, have

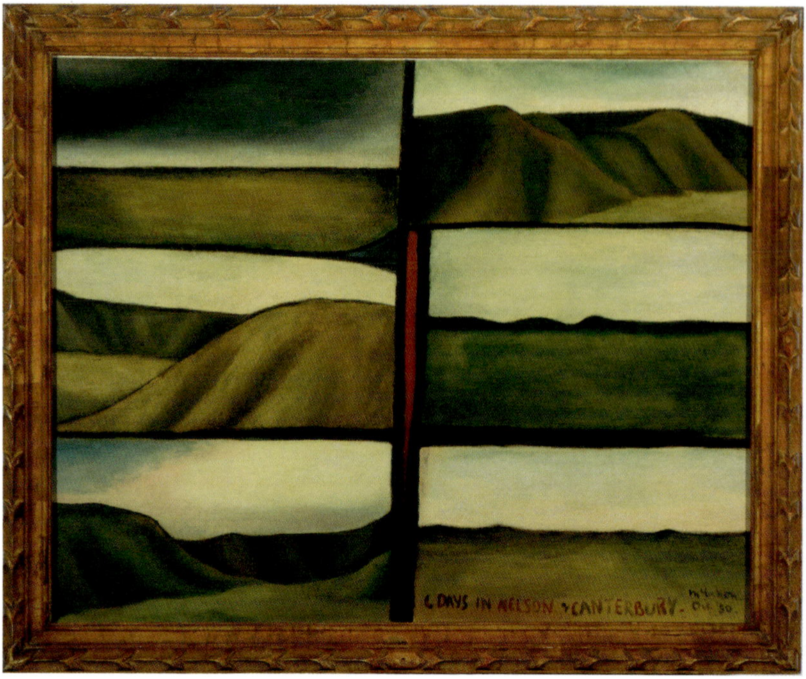

FIGURE 8.5. Colin McCahon, *Six Days in Nelson and Canterbury*, 1950. Oil on canvas on hardboard, 88.5 × 116.5 cm. Collection: Auckland Art Gallery Toi o Tāmaki, gift of Colin McCahon through the Friends of the Auckland Art Gallery, 1978.

recently pursued a line of thought that very much parallels the aims of this book.[12] Their insight is that the quasi utopianism—or, better, the transcendental, optimistically universalizing dreams—of the early twentieth-century abstract painters prior to the First World War, notably Wassily Kandinsky, Piet Mondrian, and Kazimir Malevich, survived the horrors of the mid-twentieth century, at least in the hearts of a number of abstract painters living and working around the Pacific Rim. This aspiration for a utopian art resurfaced in the 1950s and remained important during the 1960s as an element in abstract painting in Japan, the West Coast of the United States, Australia, and New Zealand. In their argument, Butler and Donaldson juxtapose works by Grace Crowley, born in Sydney and trained in Paris under André Lhote, who painted in Sydney from the 1930s; Frank Hinder, who studied in the United States and likewise painted in Sydney during the same decades as Crowley; and John McLaughlin, who was educated in Hawaii and worked in Los Angeles during the same years, arriving at his "hard edge" style in the 1950s.[13] This wider perspective enables us to see continuity, in terms of a continual refinement of abstraction, and coincidence, in terms of artists unknown to each other working on parallel tracks, mining the same sources. This, too, is modernist—that is to say, modernist in a broad, art historical sense.

Yet the belief that the global spread of social modernization meant the inevitability of abstraction in any art with claims to be modern was met with resistance, not only from those committed to earlier forms but also from those with alternative visions of the art most needed by the times. In Melbourne in 1959, a number of figurative expressionist artists—Charles Blackman, Arthur Boyd, David Boyd, John Brack, Bob Dickerson, John Perceval, and Clifton Pugh—signed on to *The Antipodean Manifesto*, written by art historian Bernard Smith. In their "defense of the image," they attacked the "Tachistes, Action Painters, Geometric Abstractionists, Abstract Expressionists and their innumerable bands of camp followers" for reducing "the living speech of art to the silence of decoration."[14] Denying that they sought to create a national style, they nevertheless demanded the right to "draw inspiration from our own lives and the lives of those about us," from "a young society still making its myths."[15] Charles Blackman's 1953 *The Shadow*, with its cowed schoolgirl metaphorizing innocence shaded by anxiety, exemplifies this stance (fig. 8.6). These artists, along with Drysdale, Nolan, and Tucker (and, in Sydney, John Olsen), were chief among those whose compelling imagery gave painting a leading role in shaping the Australian imaginary in the postwar period.

Decolonization Gathers Force

These considerations alert us to the third major element of postwar experience in the region, its decolonization. The imperialist model of empire, one that depended on distant control through local agents, had reached its limits. The British Empire imploded; the Dutch withdrew from the region in 1949; the French were expelled from Indochina in 1954; and Japanese expansion was pushed back to its main islands, which were occupied by the United States until 1952. Indeed, the United States exercised significant economic and political control over the whole region, being regularly drawn into wars, the resonances of which remain strong today. Indeed, the recent resurgence of China as a major regional and global power has revived talk of a new cold war in the area. Back in the 1950s, however, a counterforce was building. Working against the spreading confrontation between the First and Second Worlds, the newly independent nations made a major contribution to reshaping the postwar Cold War geopolitical order by establishing a set of "Third World" perspectives.

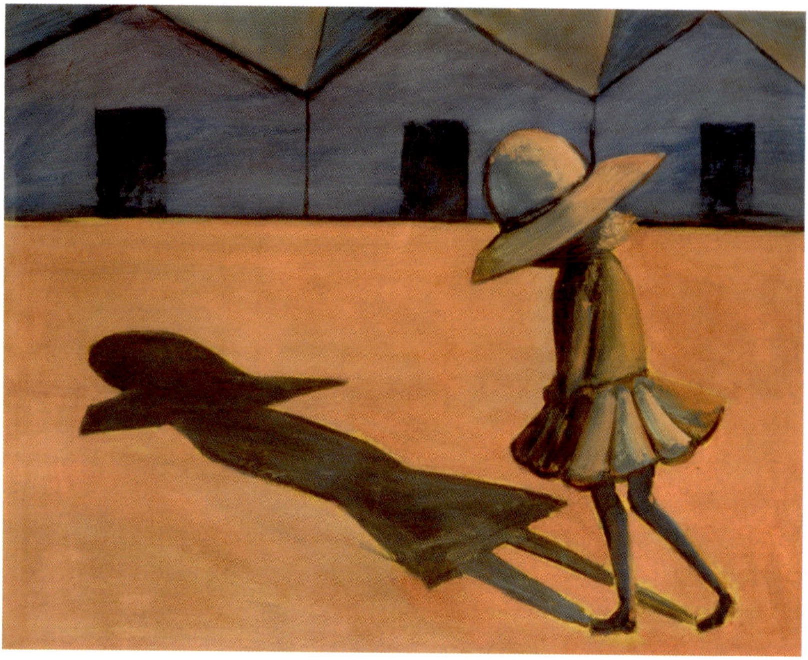

FIGURE 8.6. Charles Blackman, *The Shadow*, 1953. Enamel paint and tempera on cardboard, 59.2 × 75.4 cm. Collection: Heide Museum of Modern Art, Melbourne. Purchased from John and Sunday Reed, 1980.

The Bandung Conference, a meeting of Asian and African states, was organized by Indonesia, Myanmar (Burma), Ceylon (Sri Lanka), India, and Pakistan and took place April 18–24, 1955, in Bandung, Indonesia.[16] In Indonesia itself, however, these were the "years of living dangerously," mainly because of major clashes over the future direction of the recently independent country (1949, from the Dutch) between communist, Islamic, and other forces.[17] Artists such as Affandi painted subjects from everyday life. Others joined art groups affiliated with the Indonesian Communist Party, especially LEKRA, the People's Cultural Organization, which argued that artists should concern themselves with political struggle. In contrast, liberal artists in their "Cultural Manifesto" argued that art should not be the property of any political party. Still others were affiliated with Muslim parties and developed a kind of spiritual abstraction (after the postwar period). When a failed uprising in September 1965 was brutally suppressed by General Suharto, many of the LEKRA artists were killed or imprisoned. Among the latter was Djoko Pekik, who was imprisoned without trial in Yogyakarta in 1966. In 1972, he was released only to become an outcast. Several of his paintings are recollections of those years. During the Suharto years, which lasted until 1998, Indonesian artists favored techniques and approaches to subject matter mostly derived from Western art, although always adapted to local purposes. Jim Supangkat, a leading critic and one of Indonesia's best installation artists, calls this "multimodernism," arguing that it constitutes a mix quite specific to Indonesia, best described as "modernism seen through pluralistic principles."[18]

Indigenization Begins

In Aotearoa/New Zealand, Māori art has for centuries been grounded in the continuation and variation of themes relating to ancestral figures and narratives. They were often concentrated in ceremonial compounds, known as marae, which feature elaborate carvings and paintings of architectural detail and ceremonial objects. From the late 1950s, encouraged (and, indeed, in many cases, employed) by the innovative educator Gordon Tovey, working with Māori elders such as Pine Taiapa, several Māori artists used European modernist forms as vehicles for traditional iconography, as they developed individual responses to the rapid urbanization of their agricultural lands and their experience within a rapidly modernizing society. Arnold Wilson, Ralph Hotere, Paratene Matchitt, Selwyn Muru, Kāterina Mataira, Buster Black (John Pihema), and others have become known as the "Māori modernists."[19] In his 1965 *Kohatu*, Selwyn Muru deployed formats derived from Paul Klee and Mark Tobey to register the layered, embedded intensity of Māori rock art on the walls of caves near North Otago and Canterbury (fig. 8.7). Acquired in 1965, *Kohatu* was the first painting by a Māori artist to enter the national collection.

This artistic strategy, which was widely adopted by both Indigenous and settler artists during the postwar period, might merit the name *transcultural iconomorphism*. Always an awkward accommodation, it was usually contested from within the home culture as a kind of contamination. Nevertheless, it recurs constantly because it promises a shared space of cultural exchange that occurs in the process of making works of art when two or more artistic traditions come into conjunction and one of them no longer has the power to override and absorb the other. Among the Māori modernists, this hope is best embodied in Ralph Hotere's series of severely and sometimes serenely minimalist black paintings, which he began in the late 1960s and pursued throughout his subsequent career until his death in 2013. His 1984 painting *No Ordinary Sun* was inspired by an anti-nuclear-testing poem with this title by Hone Tuwhare.[20] In a parallel manner, pakeha (white) artist Gordon Walters adopted and varied the

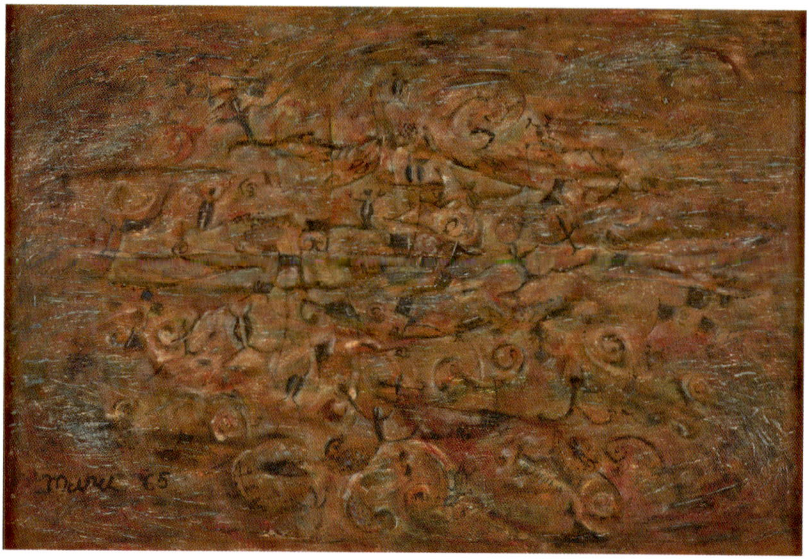

FIGURE 8.7. Selwyn Muru, *Kohatu*, 1965. Oil on hardboard, 120 × 79.5 cm. Collection: Museum of New Zealand Te Papa Tongarewa, Wellington. © Te Papa (1965–0020–1).

involuted motif known as *koru* (Māori for "loop"), derived from fern fronds and symbolizing new life, growth, strength, and peace, in a compelling series of op art paintings, beginning with the 1965 *Painting No. 1* (fig. 8.8).[21]

These exchanges register the fourth major postwar development in the region: the political struggle by Indigenous peoples for recognition and a degree of freedom. The visual arts were an essential weapon within their symbolic armory. Some beginnings may be found in the postwar period. I will conclude with three works by Australian Aboriginal artists. At a time when Aboriginal people had yet to achieve citizenship (which was not granted until a referendum in 1967), the ability of a few among their number to make art in modern mediums and styles astounded the general public. Albert Namatjira, a Western Arrernte man who adopted the techniques of watercolorist Rex Battarbee, became the most popular Australian painter of the postwar period. Among his followers was Otto Pareroultja, whose circa 1967–69 *Untitled (Central Australian Landscape with Ghost Gums)* animates a highly conventional European landscape format with the energy of the ancestral beings who created mountains and trees (fig. 8.9). These paintings come closest to what might be seen as an Indigenous modernism.[22]

Painted in 1963 by elders from the Yolngu people, the Aboriginal Bark Petitions sought recognition from the parliament of the Commonwealth of

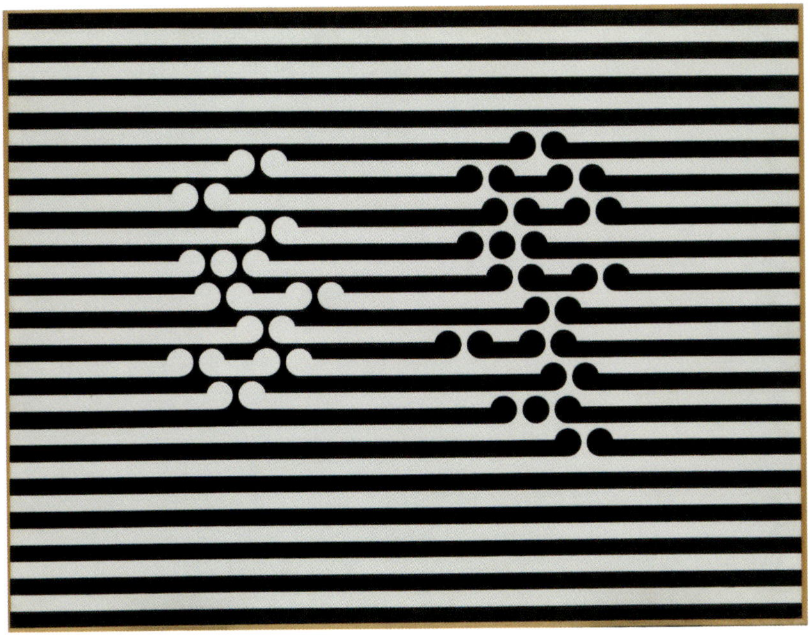

FIGURE 8.8. Gordon Walters, *Painting No. 1*, 1965. PVA on hardboard, 122 × 91 cm. Collection: Auckland Art Gallery Toi o Tāmaki, purchased 1966.

Australia of their rights to ownership of their lands, threatened by a bauxite-mining venture. Their hope was that when the politicians saw the ancestor figures, as painted in the borders around the document, the justice of their case would be instantly acknowledged. The politicians remained unmoved. The land rights struggle had a long way to go—indeed, limited rights began to be granted only in the 1990s and remain rare.[23]

One of the signatories of the petitions was Mawalan Marika, an elder of the Rirratjingu clan, from Yirrkala, in North East Arnhem Land. As part of his responsibilities, he traveled from his remote community to the major settler cities. His 1963 painting known as *Sydney from the Air* (fig. 8.10) uses natural ochers on bark to suggest (at right) the outlines of Sydney Harbor, but it concentrates on an array of brown and mustard-orange rectangular shapes, the lines that connect them, and the hatching (his clan design) between them. The painting was collected by Karel Kupka, son of František Kupka, the great Czech modernist, and spent some years in the Musée des Colonies (Palais de la Porte Dorée) in Paris. Kupka's enthusiasm for this art was inspired by his seeing it as "an encounter with another age," as being from the "dawn of art,"

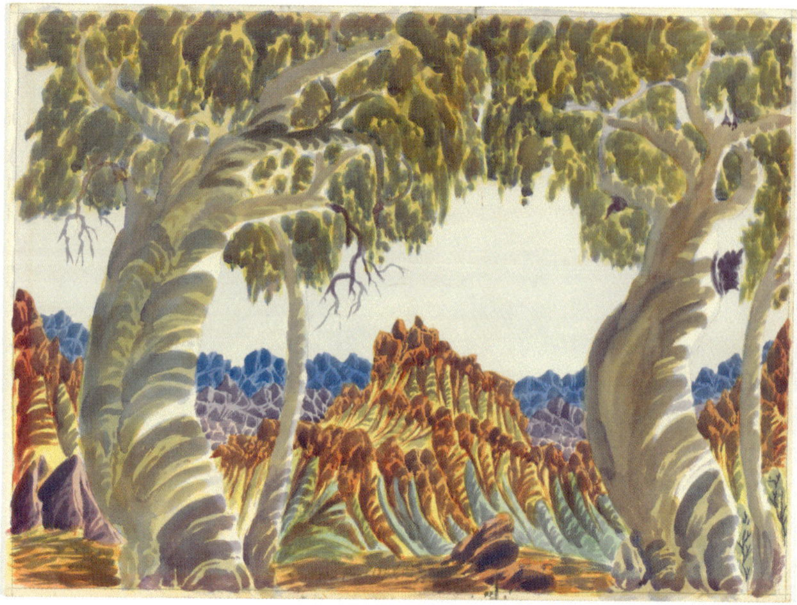

FIGURE 8.9. Otto Pareroultja, *Untitled (Central Australian Landscape with Ghost Gums)*, 1967–69. Watercolor with black pencil, 38 × 53 cm. Collection: National Gallery of Australia, Canberra, Purchased 2005. © The Estate of Otto Pareroultja, licensed by Aboriginal Artists Agency Ltd., 2005.1202.

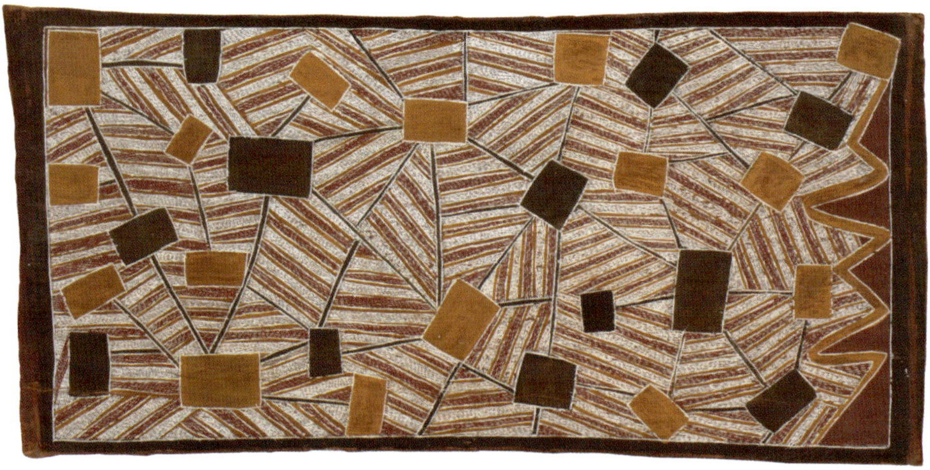

FIGURE 8.10. Mawalan Marika, *Map of painter's travell [sic] by plane from Yirrkala to Sydney* (or, *Sydney from the Air*), 1963. Ochers on bark, 43.3 × 91.3 cm. Photograph courtesy National Museum of Australia. Photograph by Jason McCarthy. Licensed by Aboriginal Artists Agency Ltd.

as the title of his book on the subject states. But *Sydney from the Air* is not a static image, a landscape literally seen from above, as in Margaret Preston's appropriation of bark paintings from the region, for example, in her *Flying over the Shoalhaven River* (1942).[24] Marika was an elder much practiced in demonstrating Yolngu law to the outsiders who had the power to impact the lives of his people. *Sydney from the Air* has been mistitled. Henry Skerritt notes that

> for many years, it went by the title *Map of the Artist's Travel by Plane from Yirrkala to Sydney*; but Marika's work is not a "map" in any conventional cartographic sense. Rather, it is a painting about relationships: the path of the aeroplane is pictured as creating a series of connections, which unite disparate people and places. By overlaying this journey onto a bed of cross-hatching, Marika suggests an analogy between this journey and the path of the ancestors, the residue of which remain in the Dreaming paths that unite all points in space and time. There is an elegant simplicity to this allegory, designed to explain the complexities of Yolngu cosmology to an uninitiated audience.[25]

By showing the embedment of the *balanda* (white people's) mode of moving across the country *within* his own, and thus within those of his ancestors, Marika pictures the contemporaneity of incommensurable cultural difference while at the same time, and in the same spaces, showing us the ground plan of coevality. This was the kind of world-picturing necessary for postcoloniality to succeed and for all of us to become truly postwar.

NOTES

1. For a developed version of this argument, see T. Smith, "Rethinking Modernism and Modernity Now"; and T. Smith, "Art History's Work-in-Pro(re)gress."

2. See Iriye, *Origins of the Second World War in Asia and the Pacific*; Twomey and Koh, *Pacific War*.

3. For Donald Friend's work, see "Showers in a Ruin," Australian War Memorial, accessed August 2, 2024, https://www.awm.gov.au/collection/ART22907.

4. For Weaver Hawkins's work, see "Jitterbugs, 1945," Art Gallery of NSW, accessed August 2, 2024, https://www.artgallery.nsw.gov.au/collection/works/91.1976/.

5. For a discussion of Stella Bowen's work, see Wilkins, *Stella Bowen: Art, Love and War*.

6. For Alan Moore's *Blind Man at Belsen*, see "Exhibition Theme—Captivity," Canadian War Museum, accessed August 12, 2024, https://www.warmuseum.ca/cwm/exhibitions/artwar/artworks/art27620_blind-man-in-belsen_e.html.

7. For Drysdale's painting, see "Russell Drysdale 'The Drover's Wife,'" National Gallery of Australia, December 16, 2010, https://nga.gov.au/on-demand/russell-drysdale-the-drovers-wife/.

8. See J. Clark, *Sidney Nolan*, 58–88.

9. For Maruki Iri and Maruki Toshi's *The Hiroshima Panels*, see Maruki Gallery for the Hiroshima Panels, accessed August 12, 2024, https://marukigallery.jp/en/hiroshimapanels/.

10. For Russell Clark's *Japanese Planes, Rekata, Santa Isabella*, see Christchurch Art Gallery Te Puna o Waiwhetū, accessed August 12, 2024, https://christchurchartgallery.org.nz/blog/collection/2013/07/japanese-planes-rekata-bay-santa-isabel-by-russell.

11. McCahon, "Beginnings," 363–64.

12. Butler and Donaldson, "Against Provincialism."

13. The term *hard edge* was coined by the *Los Angeles Times* art critic Jules Langsner and curator Peter Selz in 1959. See Los Angeles County Museum of Art, *Four Abstract Classicists*.

14. B. Smith, *Antipodean Manifesto*, 165–67. For context, see Heathcote, *Quiet Revolution*.

15. B. Smith, *Antipodean Manifesto*, 165–67.

16. Twenty-nine countries, representing more than half the world's population, sent delegates. According to the *Encyclopaedia Britannica* (Albert, Nirala, and Sinha, "Bandung Conference"):

> The conference reflected the five sponsors' dissatisfaction with what they regarded as a reluctance by the Western powers to consult with them on decisions affecting Asia; their concern over tension between the People's Republic of China and the United States; their desire to lay firmer foundations for China's peaceful relations with themselves and the West; their opposition to colonialism, especially French influence in North Africa; and Indonesia's desire to promote its case in the dispute with the Netherlands over western New Guinea (Irian Jaya). Major debate centered upon the question of whether Soviet policies in Eastern Europe and Central Asia should be censured along with Western colonialism. A consensus was reached in which "colonialism in all of its manifestations" was condemned, implicitly censuring the Soviet Union, as well as the West. The Chinese prime minister, Zhou Enlai, displayed a moderate and conciliatory attitude that tended to quiet fears of some anticommunist delegates concerning China's intentions. A 10-point "declaration on the promotion of world peace and cooperation," incorporating the principles of the United Nations charter and Indian Prime Minister Jawaharlal Nehru's Five Principles ("mutual respect" for other nations' "territorial integrity and sovereignty," nonaggression, noninterference in "internal affairs," equality and mutual benefit, and "peaceful coexistence"), was adopted unanimously.

17. See Day and Liem, *Cultures at War*; Lindsay and Liem, *Heirs to World Culture*.

18. Supangkat, *Indonesian Modern Art and Beyond*, 10.

19. See D. Skinner, "Indigenous Primitivists"; Mane-Wheoki, "Class of '66"; and D. Brown, "Mana Modernism." More generally, see D. Skinner, *Carver and the Artist*.

20. For Ralph Hotere's *No Ordinary Sun*, see Auckland Art Gallery Toi o Tāmaki, accessed August 12, 2024, https://www.aucklandartgallery.com/explore-art-and-ideas/artwork/20141/no-ordinary-sun.

21. For an account of Walters's artistic evolution, see Dunn, "Enigma of Gordon Walters' Art."

22. Caution should be exercised when using such terms, as Ian McLean warns in "Aboriginal Modernism in Australia."

23. See J. Clark, *Aborigines and Activism*, 93–121.

24. For Margaret Preston's painting, see "Margaret Preston 'Flying over the Shoalhaven River,'" National Gallery of Australia, December 16, 2010, https://nga.gov.au/on-demand/margaret-preston-flying-over-the-shoalhaven-river/.

25. Skerritt, "New Lines of Flight."

9

Integración plástica

The Postwar Synthesis of the Arts as Seen from Mexico in 1952

JENNIFER JOSTEN

On the left side of a photograph from 1985, a ritual procession of eight-foot-tall, abstract, low-relief figures climbs a stairway to the sky (fig. 9.1).[1] On the right side is a shocking sight: the collapsed floors of the building to which this stairway once provided access. Exposed steel cables and tubes stream down, some still attached to chunks of concrete or poking out from pastel-painted plaster. Amid the wreckage dangle a pair of kitchen cupboards, some torn yellow wallpaper, a water heater: reminders that several hundred people lived in this structure, one of the twenty-two buildings that made up Mexico City's 1952 Centro Urbano Presidente Juárez (President Juárez Urban Center)

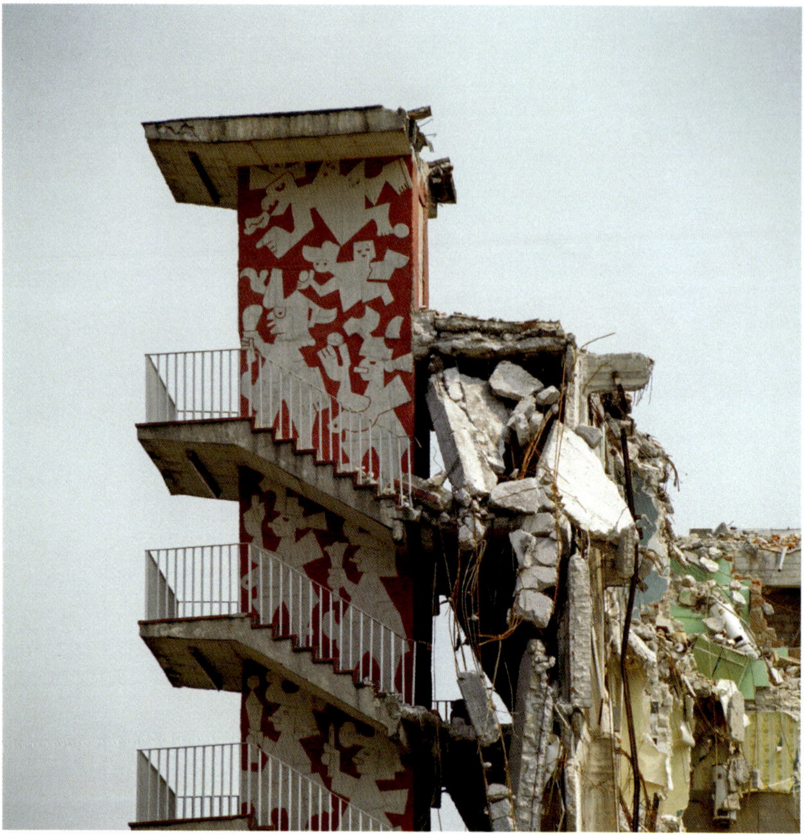

FIGURE 9.1. Centro Urbano Presidente Juárez (Multifamiliar Juárez), Mexico City, after the earthquake on September 19, 1985. Photograph by Bob Schalkwijk.

(fig. 9.2). Built by the Mexican government on a swath of land in the capital's *colonia* Roma, the complex, known as the Multifamiliar (multifamily) Juárez, provided much-needed modern housing for five thousand to six thousand residents—bureaucrats and their families—near the historic center, where many of them worked and studied. The figures carved into its stairways and other structural components, which evoke ancient Mesoamerican legends, were designed by artist Carlos Mérida as part of the complex's *integración plástica* (plastic integration, or the integration of sculpted and relief forms into architecture). The harmonious synthesis between Mario Pani's midcentury modernist architecture and Mérida's decorative program, with its local resonances, made the development emblematic of the art and architecture of Mexico's postwar "economic miracle."[2]

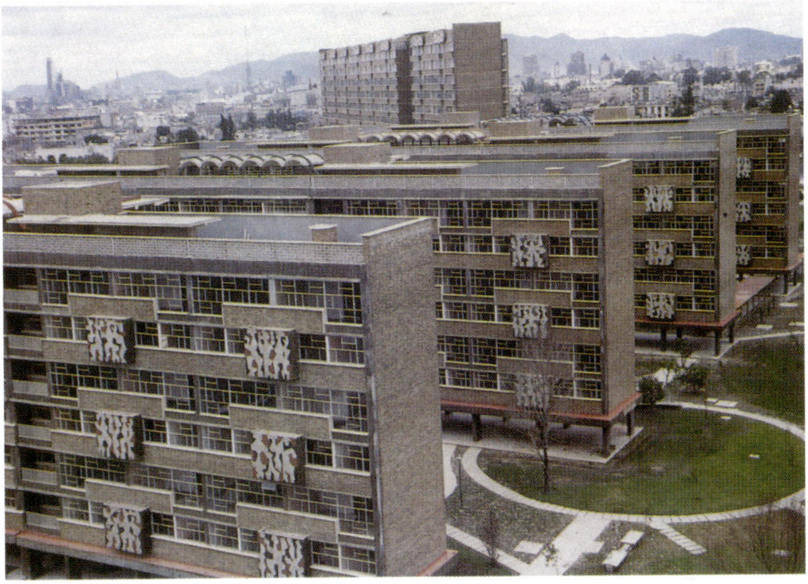

FIGURE 9.2. Multifamiliar Juárez, Mexico City, 1952. Designed by Mario Pani and Salvador Ortega, with concrete reliefs by Carlos Mérida.

On September 19, 1985, a devastating earthquake destroyed several of the Multifamiliar Juárez's towers and hundreds like them, leaving as many as ten thousand residents of Mexico's capital dead, fifty thousand injured, and two million homeless. Scientists later ascertained that five- to fifteen-story buildings had been particularly susceptible to the shock waves that resonated through the loose soil on which they sat, which was part of the former lake bed at Mexico City's heart.[3] The complex was also subject to fiscal instability, particularly after Mexico's 1982 debt crisis. These circumstances led to its total demolishment, including structures that could have been salvaged.[4] Photographer Bob Schalkwijk's dramatic image captures the chasm separating the economic and cultural advances and governmental promises of the postwar era in Mexico, represented by the solid staircase with Mérida's steadfast, upwardly mobile modernist Mesoamerican figures, and the wholesale abandonment of social welfare policies in the 1980s, figured here as the literal collapse of state-sponsored housing due to its unstable foundations (see fig. 9.1).[5]

While collaborating with Mérida at the Multifamiliar Juárez, Pani was also working with Enrique del Moral to plan the new Ciudad Universitaria (University City) of the Universidad Nacional Autónoma de México (National Autonomous University of Mexico, or UNAM) and contending with the artists selected to produce *integración plástica* for its key buildings. The campus, a sprawling complex of steel-and-glass structures on pilotis (Le Corbusier's term for columns that raise a building above the ground), was sponsored by the regime of Miguel Alemán, Mexico's first president of the postwar era and of the Partido Revolucionario Institucional (Institutional Revolutionary Party, or PRI). The aim of the new campus was to shift an estimated 25,000 students and professors from the center of the capital to its southern fringe. In contrast to the Multifamiliar Juárez, the Ciudad Universitaria's structures, built on an ancient lava field south of the city, have so far been impervious to destruction by natural or other forces. As a result, these International Style buildings, adorned with exterior figurative mosaics by David Alfaro Siqueiros, Juan O'Gorman, Diego Rivera, and other artists associated with the so-called Mexican School of Painting, continue to dominate public perceptions of a hegemonic figurative approach to *integración plástica* in postwar Mexico (fig. 9.3).

This is a testament to the relative success of the campaign Siqueiros led in the early 1950s to achieve postrevolutionary Mexican muralism's "second stage," in the form of large-scale, realist, exterior mosaic reliefs. But opportunities to challenge this perception have arisen in recent years. In 2007, it became possible to experience a contrasting approach that likewise arose in 1952 Mexico City: artist Mathias Goeritz's Museo Experimental "El Eco" ("The Echo" Experimental Museum, 1953) (fig. 9.4). Goeritz, a German artist and art historian who had arrived in Mexico only three years earlier, used a private commission for a commercial art gallery, bar, and restaurant to devise a reinforced-concrete structure that is essentially a habitable abstract sculpture, within which integrated abstract artworks were wholly synthesized. El Eco's restoration and inauguration as a noncollecting museum has played a key role within a broader reconsideration of the diverse, multivalent forms of aesthetic engagement that arose in Mexico in the first decades of the Cold War.[6]

The aesthetic and political debate waged by architects, artists, and critics who advocated for distinct approaches to *integración plástica* in early 1950s Mexico has been understood almost exclusively in terms of national issues. This is fitting, given that Mexico City has long dominated culture as well as politics within a highly centralized nation that was governed from 1928 to 2000 by a single party, the PRI. But this national emphasis has obscured the extent to which Mérida, Pani, Siqueiros, and Goeritz actively participated in an international Cold War battle concerning the appropriate aesthetic language for large-scale public art, in which figuration was aligned with communism and abstraction was aligned with capitalism. A key battleground was the postwar Congrès Internationaux d'Architecture Moderne (International Congresses of Modern Architecture, or CIAM),

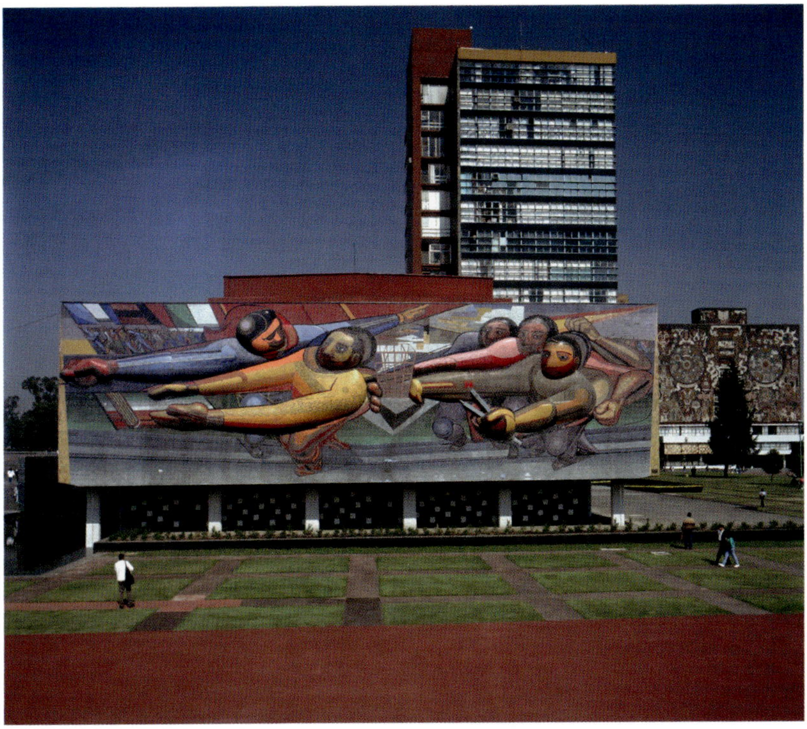

FIGURE 9.3. Ciudad Universitaria, Universidad Nacional Autónoma de México, Mexico City, 1952. Lead planners Mario Pani and Enrique del Moral. Mosaics: (*near*) David Alfaro Siqueiros, *El pueblo a la universidad, la universidad al pueblo . . .* , 1952–56; (*far, right*) Juan O'Gorman, *Representación histórica de la cultura*, 1952. Photograph by Bob Schalkwijk.

where Le Corbusier and his associates, most notably Sigfried Giedion and Fernand Léger, called for an abstract *synthèse des arts majeurs* (synthesis of the major arts) as a counter to Soviet socialist realism.[7] While Mexico-based architects and artists did not participate directly in CIAM, the key points of the debate resonated in the forms and discourses for which they advocated in 1952 Mexico City. In contrast to the narrow set of aesthetic interventions tolerated by Le Corbusier (essentially polychromed walls and the occasional abstract mural by his hand), each of the artist-spokesmen driving Mexico's midcentury *integración plástica* promoted distinct aesthetic and economic positions: realism and communism, in the case of Siqueiros; abstraction and private ownership, in the case of Goeritz; and abstraction and anticommunism, in the case of Mérida. Their public art projects harbored significant political stakes and implications that resonated far beyond the local and national contexts on which scholarship on the *integración plástica* debates of the early 1950s has focused.

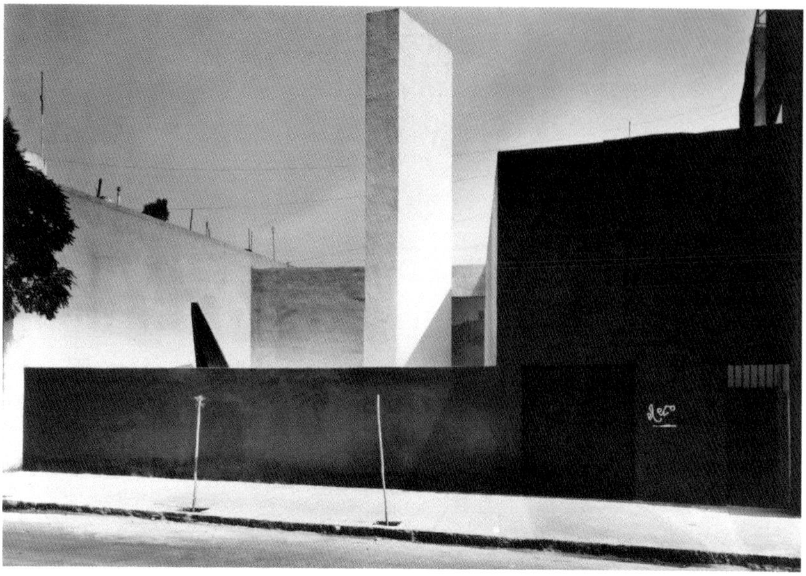

FIGURE 9.4. Mathias Goeritz, architect, Museo Experimental "El Eco," Mexico City, 1953. Photograph by Marianne Goeritz.

Forging *Integración plástica*

Mexican *integración plástica* arose in the context of a single-party state that drew on the nation's rich legacy of preconquest and viceregal sculpture and reliefs integrated into architecture to assert an enduring, cohesive identity.[8] After more than two decades of efforts to nationalize resources and industries following the Revolution of 1910–17, Mexico's ruling party shifted course during the Second World War, aligning to an unprecedented degree with the political and capitalist interests of the United States. This fueled dramatic increases in industrialization, population, and rural-to-urban migration in Mexico, all of which were felt most strongly in Mexico City. With existing buildings bursting at their seams, president Miguel Alemán (1946–52) prioritized the construction of modern residential and institutional complexes where the Mexicans of the future would live, study, and work. These developments remain the most tangible aesthetic manifestations of Mexico's uneasy integration into the capitalist "West" under the PRI. The international prestige accorded to the avant-garde realist murals that José Clemente Orozco, Rivera, and other artists had produced for the federal government in the postrevolutionary 1920s ensured that public artworks would continue to play a key role in the new constructions of Mexico's postwar building boom. It did not, however, dictate the content or style of postwar integrated artworks, which by the late 1940s were being described in the Mexican press as *integración plástica*: a term that denotes the fusing of plastic (that is, sculpted or molded) artistic elements into architecture to produce long-lasting exterior designs, as distinct from flat mural painting.[9]

As the lead planner for several of the megaprojects built by the PRI under Alemán, including the Multifamiliar Juárez and Ciudad Universitaria, Pani channeled design principles advocated by Le Corbusier and the CIAM's 1933 Charter of Athens: most notably the elimination of the multiuse street in favor of concentrated nuclei of superblocks of reinforced concrete and steel, raised on pilotis to allow pedestrians to move underneath (see fig. 9.2). Curved roads and underpasses maximized parklike green spaces and kept traffic flowing. Pani and his associates were likewise familiar with the postwar synthesis of the arts promoted by Le Corbusier and André Bloc, who called on architects and designers to work with muralists and sculptors at the outset of the large-scale building projects of France's postwar reconstruction. The aim of that effort, according to Nicola Pezolet, was "to make the built environment more humane and to give everyday spaces a sense of harmony, joyful ornateness and visual consistency. The goal was to renew the place of art in civic life and to temper the perceived negative side effects of Americanization."[10] Circumstances were different in Mexico in many ways. There, the physical landscape was untouched by war, and the single-party state was committed to channeling gains made in literacy during the postrevolutionary decades into the expansion of higher education, bureaucracy, and industry—all of which demanded new infrastructure adorned with nationalist emblems. Yet there, too, commercialism was on the rise as a result of increased US influence and investment, leading to calls to (re)center national culture within new civic and community centers and monuments. Whereas, in practice, Le Corbusier only tolerated limited artistic interventions, *integración plástica* efforts in Mexico were created along a broad aesthetic spectrum: from the nationalist content rendered in figurative mosaics at the Ciudad Universitaria, to Mérida's abstract concrete reliefs of ancient Mesoamerican myths at the Multifamiliar Juárez, and the international abstract and nonobjective designs Goeritz commissioned for and produced at El Eco.

Siqueiros's and O'Gorman's contrasting approaches to figuration sit in close juxtaposition to each other at the UNAM. Siqueiros's *El pueblo a la universidad, la universidad al pueblo: Por una cultura nacional neohumanista de profundidad universal* (The people to the university, the university to the people: For a national neohumanist culture of universal profundity; 1952–56), pictured in the foreground of figure 9.3, is a cement relief covered in glass mosaic. It features five monumental male figures (four students and a gray-haired professor) who extend the tools of their labors—a pencil, a book, a structural model, and a compass—outward: a visual argument that public support of higher education would be repaid tenfold in public benefits. The mural occupies a broad surface of the Central Administration Building, designed by Pani and Enrique del Moral. As a result of the lack of cooperation between architects and artist, it is positioned relatively close to the ground, where it neither harmonizes with the building's steel-and-glass tower nor is visible to the automotive traffic Siqueiros sought to engage. Visible behind it in figure 9.3 is the distinctive mosaic-covered book tower of the Central Library, whose architecture and *integración plástica* were both designed by O'Gorman. All four sides of this ten-story reinforced concrete box are covered with *Representación histórica de la cultura* (Historic representation of culture, 1952): a complex set of symbols related to Mexico's history and cosmology, realized in a mosaic of colored stones from across the nation. In the wake of its completion, Siqueiros issued public criticisms of the library's lack of synthesis, describing it as imported architecture clad in a traditional Mexican costume.[11]

While Siqueiros, O'Gorman, and Rivera were embroiled in controversies and feuds concerning their *integración plástica* efforts at the Ciudad Universitaria, Mérida's collaboration with Pani at the Multifamiliar Juárez—the largest decorative project ever carried out by a single artist in Mexico in terms of area—was receiving accolades in the national and international press for its harmonious integration of abstract Mesoamerican motifs into the buildings' reinforced concrete surfaces. This positive reception had in no way been assured, given the challenges Mérida had previously faced as a result of his foreign citizenship and commitment to abstraction. The artist, born in Guatemala in 1891, had moved to Mexico City in 1919 and quickly became incorporated into the burgeoning postrevolutionary art scene. In 1923, he joined Rivera, Siqueiros, and a handful of their peers in signing the "Manifiesto del Sindicato de Obreros Técnicos, Pintores, y Escultores de México" (Manifesto of the Technical Workers, Painters, and Sculptors Union of Mexico), a founding document of the postrevolutionary mural movement. Unlike them, however, Mérida never participated in Mexico's Communist Party. By the 1930s he had broken definitively with the Mexican School's leaders and the figurative approach they advocated, instead pursuing stronger ties to commercial networks for abstract art in the United States and Europe. The works he made during and after the Second World War, some of which fuse surrealist formal approaches with ancient

Mesoamerican motifs, attracted the attention of José Gómez Sicre, then head of the Visual Arts Section at the Pan American Union in Washington, DC, who was seeking to promote modern artists of the Americas who were distanced from communist agendas.[12] Mérida suited this project in several ways, with his ties to Guatemala, Mexico, and the US market and his commitments to Maya cultural expressions and international abstraction—all of which challenged the formal and ideological dominance of social and socialist realism in Latin America. When opportunities to execute *integración plástica* projects began to arise in Mexico in the context of Alemán's postwar, developmentalist regime, Gómez Sicre aided Mérida in promoting his abstract approach to integrating art into architecture—not only in Mexico but in his native Guatemala and elsewhere in Latin America.[13] Gómez Sicre's advocacy contributed to Mérida's embrace by other "Cold Warriors" during the 1950s, including Stefan Baciu, representative of the Brazilian Congress for Cultural Freedom. Following the CIA-sponsored coup of Guatemala's democratically elected government in 1954 (a watershed event of the Cold War), Mérida would become the dictatorial regime's public artist of choice.[14]

Whereas Mérida sought and obtained commissions from the Mexican and Guatemalan governments, Goeritz's interests lay in the private sector. The German émigré had arrived in Mexico in 1949 to teach art history at Guadalajara's recently founded Escuela de Arquitectura (Architecture School). He immediately forged a connection with prominent architect Luis Barragán and began designing abstract sculptures for the latter's modernist designs. In 1952, Goeritz gained a commission to design a for-profit art gallery, restaurant, and bar for a small, rented lot in Mexico City's central *colonia* San Rafael. Far exceeding the ambitions of his commercial investors, Goeritz took this opportunity to design and construct El Eco, his experimental museum. Although it never opened to the public under his direction, its architecture provided a locus for Mexico's Cold War aesthetic and political debates by uniting abstract sculptures, reliefs, and murals by Goeritz, Mérida, internationally recognized painter Rufino Tamayo, and veteran abstract sculptor Germán Cueto, alongside examples of avant-garde music and dance, within a reinforced-concrete structure formed from sloping black and gray walls that never meet at a right angle. Soon after its completion, Goeritz joined the faculty of the UNAM's Facultad de Arquitectura as the director of its foundational Educación Visual (Visual Education) program. Through this and his editorship of an art section for Pani's journal *Arquitectura México*, Goeritz was a crucial conduit for international concepts and debates in postwar Mexico. Concurrently, he had a profound impact on Mexico's built environment through the nonobjective murals, sculptures, and structures he integrated into designs by Pani, Ricardo Legorreta, Pedro Ramírez Vázquez, and other key figures in postwar Mexican architecture.[15]

Goeritz and Mérida consciously circulated their public projects and declarations within distinct international circuits. Goeritz focused on groups of artists and critics in Europe and the United States who sought to transcend national, and avowedly political, affiliations. Mérida, meanwhile, embraced the decidedly Latin America–focused anticommunist agenda of the Pan American Union (later the Organization for American States) and the Congress for Cultural Freedom. Mérida's and Goeritz's cachet among Mexico's architects and critics made them threats to Rivera and Siqueiros, who published xenophobically charged vitriol against their *integración plástica* efforts in their occasional broadside, *Arte Público*. Goeritz courted their attacks and benefited from the championing of clearly identified anticommunist writers, including Anita Brenner and Mauricio Gómez Mayorga, while avoiding joining any group or side himself. Mérida, meanwhile, openly critiqued the Mexican School in terms of form, content, and ideology and gave his support to anticommunist agendas in Guatemala and beyond.

Mérida's New Muralism, Melted into Architecture

Mérida's frustration with governments wary of embracing abstract art was rooted in his experiences with regimes in both Guatemala and Mexico. In October 1944, Juan José Arévalo's election ended decades of dictatorial rule in Guatemala and initiated the nation's "Ten Years of Spring," in which measures were instituted to restrict the economic control historically wielded by the United Fruit Company. A few years later, Guatemala's revolutionary government invited Mérida to exhibit there for the first time in decades. Some journalists praised his recent paintings, which incorporated vague references to Maya subjects into abstract compositions, as a breath of fresh air. Others, however, criticized what they saw as the absence of social value in these works that differed sharply from the impressionist and social realist tendencies then prevalent in Guatemalan painting. Gómez Sicre defended Mérida in the international press, claiming that the artist's engagement with abstraction was legitimized by his Maya heritage. While Brenner had made similar claims in the late 1920s, it was only after joining forces with Gómez Sicre in the postwar era that Mérida avowed his identity as a "mixture . . . of Maya-Quiché Indian and Spaniard" in print in an autobiographical essay that first appeared in the Pan American Union's magazine and has circulated widely since then.[16] Mérida's active claiming of a mestizo identity was in line with the practice of Mexican artist Rufino

Tamayo, whose Indigenous Zapotec heritage played an important role in his self- and public perception as a representative of postrevolutionary Mexican culture. It was a novel strategy in Guatemala, where a clear separation between Indigenous and Ladino (European-identified) populations remained in force well into the twentieth century. Mérida's hopes that Guatemala's democratic government would promote him as its representative artist were dashed when governmental authorities rejected a proposal from Gómez Sicre to send a solo show of Mérida's recent works, focused on *integración plástica* projects, as its contribution to the 1952 Venice Biennale.[17]

Mérida took offense at what he considered Guatemalan bureaucrats' incomprehension of and indifference to his breakthrough practice. He had already faced this phenomenon in Mexico, most publicly in 1949, when Pani and del Moral commissioned him to design an abstract decorative program for the exterior of a steel-frame building they were constructing for an insurance company on Mexico City's Paseo de la Reforma. Mérida devised a series of exterior plates covered in geometric patterns in multicolored enamel, which would separate the floors. But while it was still under construction, the building was sold to the government; the minister in charge ordered that Mérida's designs be stripped from the building because of their appearance. Artists including Rivera and Siqueiros came to the defense of Mérida's works, petitioning that they be protected under the national patrimony law President Alemán had recently instituted. After a protracted battle in which Mérida's Guatemalan citizenship figured prominently, his works were removed from the exterior and refitted to the building's bathroom stalls.[18]

Pani arguably made up for this frustration and humiliation with the commission he offered Mérida in 1951, to execute the *integración plástica* for the twenty thousand square feet of exposed concrete on the staircases and protrusions of the Multifamiliar Juárez (see fig. 9.2). For this vast project, which needed to be inaugurated before Alemán's presidential term concluded in November 1952, Pani sought a single, well-established artist who avoided participating in Mexican politics. In contrast to his experience with Siqueiros at Ciudad Universitaria, Pani worked closely with Mérida from an early point in the design process to develop an integrated decorative program, on which they received no bureaucratic interference. Mérida based his designs on studies of pre-Columbian and sixteenth-century codices, most notably archaeologist Alfonso Caso's 1953 *El pueblo del sol*, which is illustrated by artist Miguel Covarrubias's line drawings of figures from preconquest and sixteenth-century Mesoamerican codices. Each of the five "type B" buildings had seventy-two apartments, spread over ten stories and with a protruding emergency staircase running down its central spine. Mérida decorated these with iconographic programs based on key Mesoamerican legends, including the Maya Popol Vuh and four drawn from Aztec traditions. The staircase in Schalkwijk's photograph (see fig. 9.1) is decorated with abstract, two-dimensional representations of the key attributes of Aztec deities Quetzalcoatl and Tezcatlipoca, along with the sun and moon, based on the Aztec Leyenda del Quinto Sol (Legend of the Fifth Sun), as described in Angel María Garibay's 1945 *Epica náhuatl* (fig. 9.5).[19]

Over several months in 1952, Mérida's designs were incorporated into the complex in the form of painted concrete reliefs carved into the balconies, stairways, and automotive underpasses of the buildings. After his assistant, Alfonso Soto Soria, transferred Mérida's designs to the poured concrete surfaces, a group of expert stone carvers chiseled out the negative areas around the designs (fig. 9.6). Special plastic paints were then used to coat this carved-out negative space in a coordinated palette of brown, red, green, and blue (see fig. 9.2)—the same four-color scheme that Le Corbusier employed for the brise-soleils of his iconic Unité d'Habitation (1947–52) in Marseilles, France. The relief figures were left as rough, exposed concrete: a hallmark of postwar European modernist architecture (fig. 9.7). In less than two years, Mérida and his assistants had completed modern Mexico's largest *integración plástica* program.[20]

Although Mérida's designs presented discrete Mesoamerican myths in coherent ways, his program was not a didactic one. No labels were provided, and no specific social or political aims were proposed. Instead, Mérida's carved and painted reliefs suggested a sense of continuity or association between Mexico's pre-Columbian and modern citizens and asserted that the abstract designs of the pre-Columbian era, which had themselves been integrated into monumental ancient architecture as sculptural and relief forms, were uniquely relevant to Mexico's postwar modernist agenda. *Integración plástica* at the Multifamiliar Juárez was thus aligned with the ideology of cultural *mestizaje*—the blending of Indigenous American and European tendencies—just as Mérida had begun describing his own identity. Though it never functioned as a tourist attraction, Mérida and Pani's monumental effort was praised by local and international critics alike as a sensitive synthesis of art and architecture that was well suited to its specific postwar context: infused with local and national meaning, yet free of didacticism; unifying rather than divisive.[21] In its public patronage, sheer scale, and total integration, it represented the most monumental achievement of Mérida's career.

As work at the Multifamiliar Juárez progressed, Mérida campaigned to gain more mural-scale commissions. Gómez Sicre enthusiastically partnered with him, hosting an exhibition of recent paintings and mural projects at the Pan

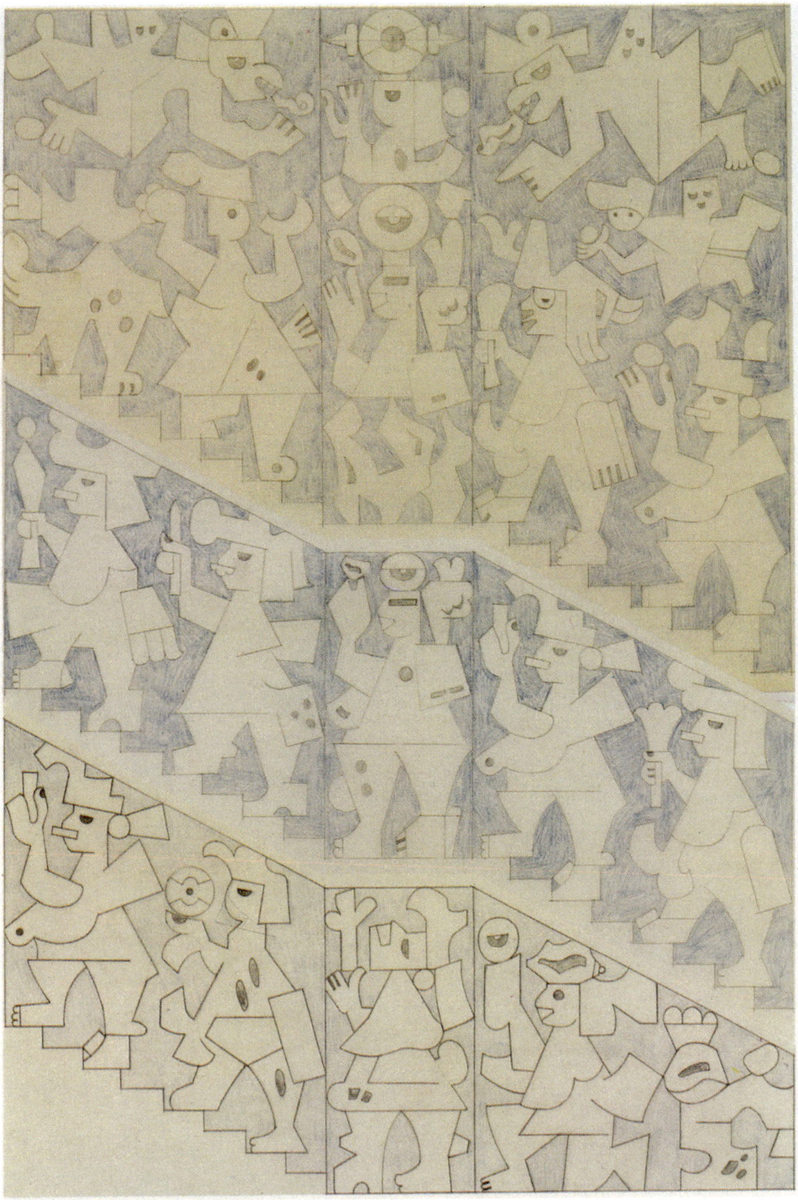

FIGURE 9.5. Carlos Mérida, Drawing for Building B staircase, Multifamiliar Juárez, Mexico City, 1952. Pencil on paper.

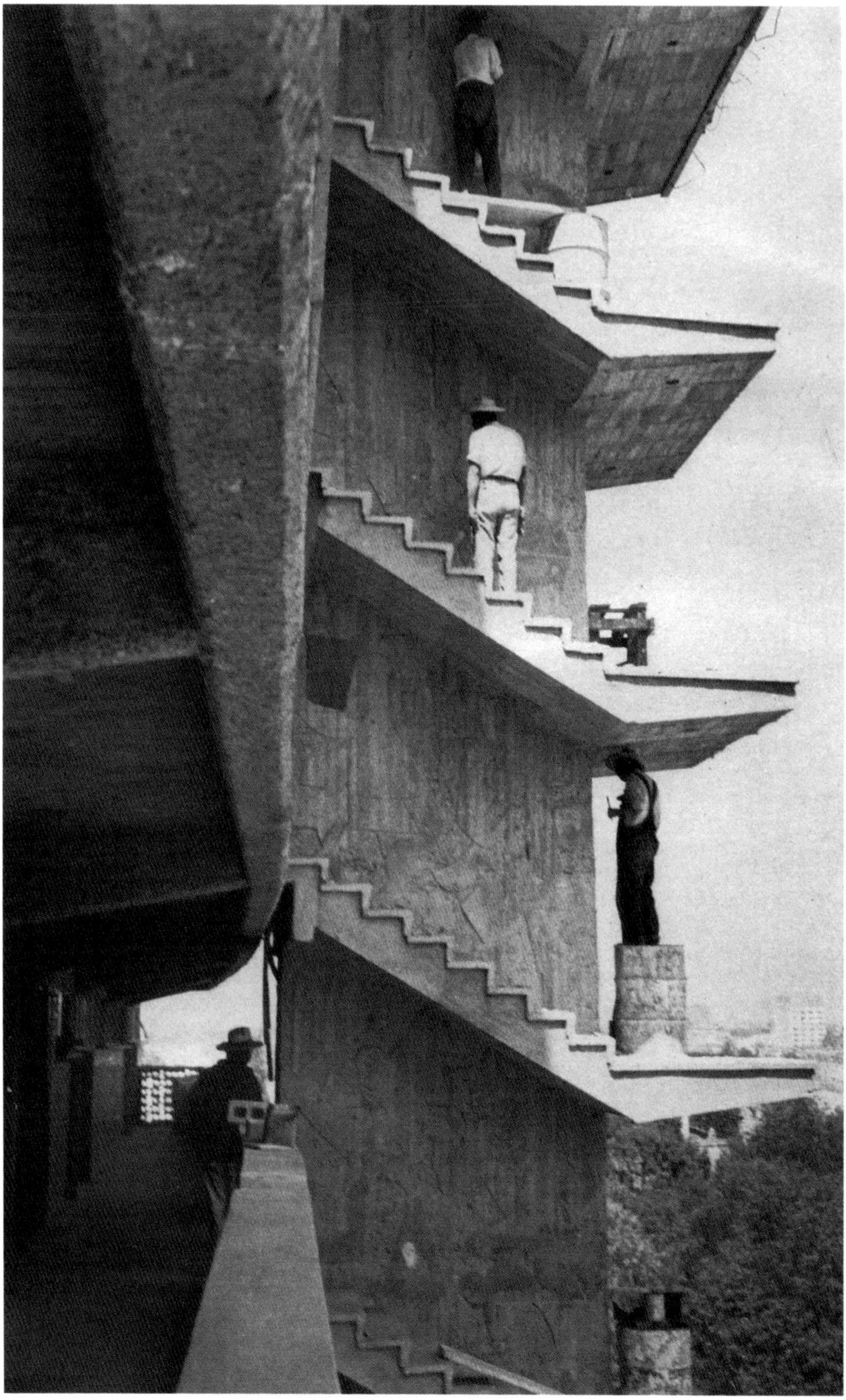

FIGURE 9.6. Carving the reliefs at the Multifamiliar Juárez, 1952.

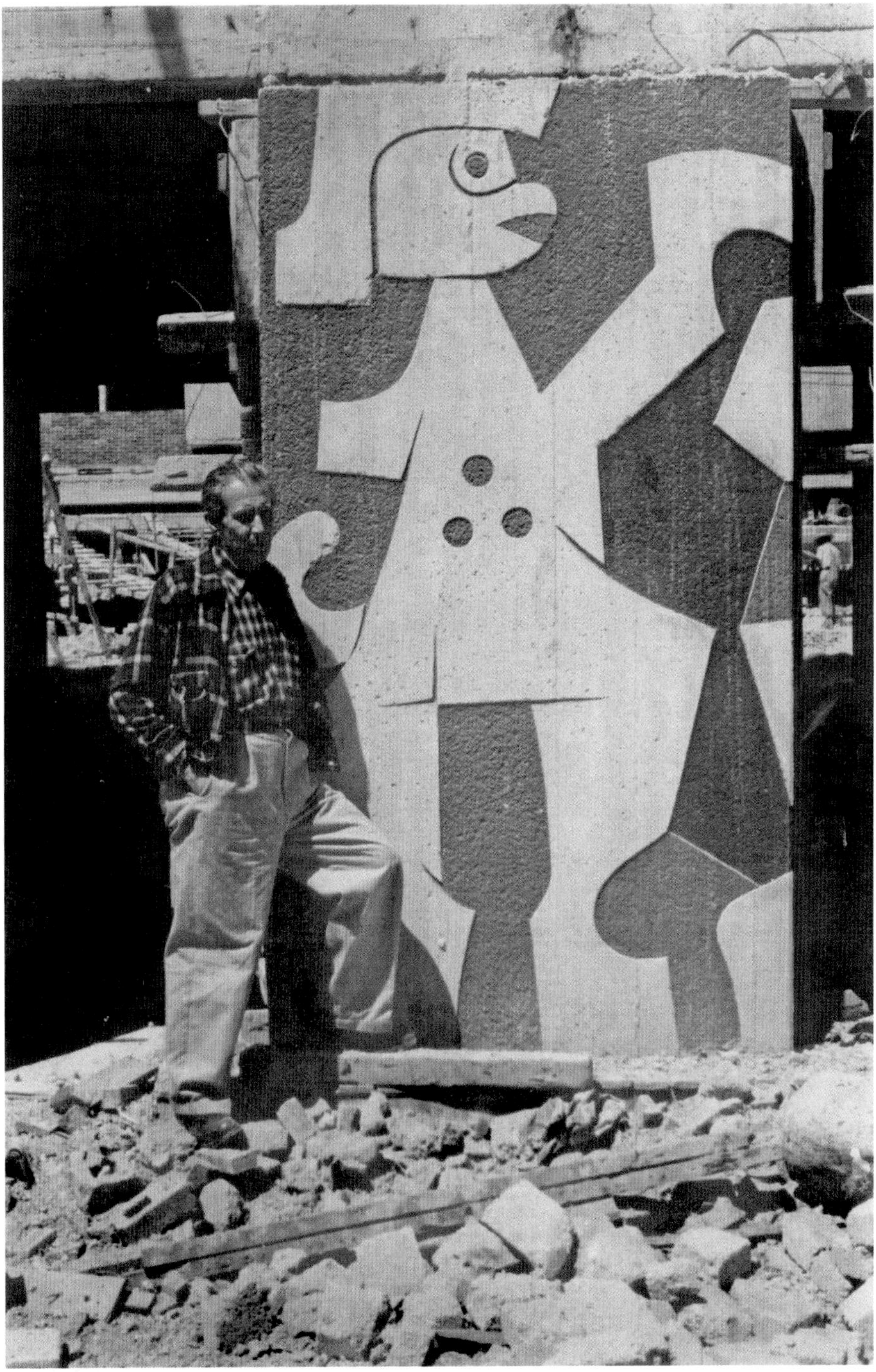

FIGURE 9.7. Carlos Mérida with a completed relief at the Multifamiliar Juárez, 1952.

American Union in 1951. When the same exhibition traveled to New York's New Gallery in February 1952, its catalog included a set of brief statements issued by Mérida. These bear a striking parallel with the "Nine Points on Monumentality" drafted by Léger, Josep Lluís Sert, and Giedion in 1943, which set the terms for the integration of abstract art into architecture in the postwar West.[22] "Painting has to be melted with the architectonic unit," Mérida declared. Emboldened by the support of Gómez Sicre and others, he wrote that "a new muralism must be born.... Art of the future, without demagogism, without rhetoric, without political calligraphy, eminently universal. Art for the masses, for the eyes of everyone, for the emotional enjoyment of the world."[23] In the Mexican context, Mérida's invocation of demagogism would have been understood as a reference to Rivera and Siqueiros—a fact of which Goeritz was well aware when he quoted it in an article about the Multifamiliar Juárez for *Arquitectura México* a few months later.

That Goeritz was captivated by Mérida's *integración plástica* for the Multifamiliar Juárez is no surprise: here was a form of postwar primitivism not unlike his own in character, supported by Mexico's government on a monumental scale and with a daily audience of thousands of residents. Goeritz described Pani and Mérida's collaboration as having reached a level of "integration only very rarely achieved in reality, in which both the architect and the plastic artist realized that in order to create in true harmony, one does not impose oneself, but rather submits."[24] From this same urge, he wrote, sprung "that fraternal feeling of cooperation capable of giving the world the most important works of humanity."[25] This fraternalism, which echoed the conclusion several CIAM participants had reached in 1947 regarding the synthesis of the arts, directly contrasted with the contentious scene unfolding at Ciudad Universitaria at the same moment, when the state temporarily stopped payments on the production of the Mexican School artists' mosaics.[26] By providing the first detailed analysis of Mérida and Pani's collaboration, Goeritz positioned himself as a like-minded cosmopolitan whose embrace of ancient Mesoamerican forms within the context of global abstraction could suit both the nationalist interests of those in power and the tastes of modernist architects and their private clients.

The Echoes of Goeritz's El Eco

Goeritz's 1952 article on Mérida coincided with the construction of his own experiment in melting sculpture into architecture: El Eco, his for-profit gallery, bar, and restaurant in central Mexico City. This private commission signified a remarkable opportunity for the artist. Goeritz was able to design the building with complete liberty and to incorporate his own, and others', works of art into the site. An unprecedented experiment in architecture and *integración plástica,* El Eco quickly became the eye of the storm regarding the Mexican School's continued monopoly on official culture. Arguably, one of the echoes that Goeritz most avidly sought to resonate in his museum was that of CIAM's postwar discourse. In his 1953 "Manifiesto de la Arquitectura Emocional" (Emotional Architecture manifesto), he critiqued the architecture of the modern movement for having lost touch with "the community," writing that modern man felt "crushed by the exaggerated 'functionalism,' logic and usefulness of modern architecture. . . . He asks—or will one day ask—that architecture with its modern means and materials give him a spiritual lift or—said in a simpler way—move him, as did in its time, the architecture of the Pyramid, the Greek temple, the Romanesque or Gothic cathedral, or even that of the Baroque palace."[27] El Eco, he would later write, was intended to be "a poetic structure whose arrangement of passageways, walls, ceilings, openings, and enclosures took one repeatedly by surprise."[28] Within this context, the patio was "the culmination of the series of 'emotions' that the spectator was expected to experience while strolling through the building."[29] Like Le Corbusier, however, Goeritz remained vague concerning which emotions could or should be stimulated by this architecture.

Referring perhaps to the rise of postwar existentialism, Goeritz wrote that "emerging from the conviction that our time is filled with high spiritual uncertainty, El Eco wants only to be an expression of these, aspiring—not so consciously, but almost automatically—to *integración plástica* to cause a maximum of emotion in modern man."[30] Its integrated artworks were to include a mural by Tamayo in the main interior space, two murals by Mérida in the bar, and a metal relief sculpture by Cueto. Several articles appeared in the press celebrating El Eco, including a manifesto by Mauricio Gómez Mayorga, a noted liberal anticommunist architect and writer, entitled "Sobre la libertad de creación" (On creative liberty). His support for Goeritz and El Eco, he wrote, was a means of demonstrating his opposition to "the direction that a clique is attempting to take art in Mexico, from public architecture to lyric poetry." Gómez Mayorga was, of course, referring to Siqueiros and Rivera, as well as to Carlos Lazo's hold on governmental architectural policy and commissions. He wrote that El Eco was what was greatly needed "not only to bring together and exhibit the new, but to keep creative liberty alive, enflamed and visible; to seed rebellion, a spirit of combat and disobedience in the youth, and in all who are capable of certainty and artistic passion, and also to deflate, burn, and break before them the idols, Judases, empty piñatas, and false values that have attempted to convert themselves into the prophets and ministers of art in Mexico."[31]

Goeritz's efforts caught the attention not only of Mexico's architectural community but of other powerful figures as well. Once it became apparent that El Eco would never actually open as an experimental museum following the unexpected death of its patron, Daniel Mont, Goeritz was nominated by the rector of the UNAM to serve as the university's first official "museographer," or director of fine arts.[32] The nomination sparked vehement attacks by Rivera and Siqueiros, who published a public letter stating, "We cannot allow him to be in charge of showing the work of Mexican artists in exhibitions, museums or libraries, as he couldn't touch the works without dirtying them, which would not happen if it were a Mexican who was given this post at the University."[33] Rivera and Siqueiros's xenophobic attack on Goeritz's character and works indicates the extent of the threat he posed to their grip on official culture following the stir created by El Eco. Ultimately Goeritz took another position at the UNAM, joining the Facultad de Arquitectura as the developer and instructor of a basic design course modeled on the foundation courses of the Bauhaus. This new position confirmed his abiding allegiance to Mexico's architects and gave Goeritz a platform from which he indelibly influenced the character of architectural education at Mexico's largest and most prestigious program.

Mérida as Cold Warrior

In October 1953, a month after El Eco's pre-inauguration, Mérida's traveling exhibition of his *integración plástica* works went on view at Mexico City's venerable Galería de Arte Mexicano. For it, Mérida translated and expanded his brochure statement, now stating directly that the "old concept of Mexican muralism (Montenegro, Rivera, Siqueiros, Orozco) now no longer exists" and claiming that Siqueiros's call for a "new realism" was "a disguised academy, only suited for political calligraphy, for immediate use."[34] In response, Siqueiros declared that Mérida's politics were reactionary—something that he claimed was adequately represented by what he termed the "formal hybridization" of Mérida's Multifamiliar Juárez reliefs.[35] Spurred on by Siqueiros, Mérida made clear the hemispheric political stakes of his position in the statements he published in Buenos Aires, Caracas, and Rio de Janeiro in the following years, decrying the Mexican School and advocating for a new muralism, rooted in the abstract forms of Indigenous American art.[36]

As Mérida wrote to Gómez Sicre, he particularly hoped this message could take root in his native Guatemala. Ultimately, he succeeded in gaining several high-profile commissions there. These came not, however, from the government of democratically elected president Jacobo Arbenz but from the military junta of Carlos Castillo Armas, who deposed Arbenz in a CIA-sponsored coup in June 1954. In a later, undated autobiographical statement, Mérida wrote that he felt a "profound sympathy" and an "admiring friendship" for Castillo Armas, believing that he would "redeem" the Guatemalan Indian and make him "a total citizen."[37] The first of these commissions for the regime was a glass mosaic for the interior of the Municipal Palace, which Mérida titled *Un canto lírico a nuestra raza* (A lyrical song to our race)—yet another declaration of cultural *mestizaje*. The second was a monumental glass mosaic wall for the exterior of the Instituto Guatemalteco de Seguridad Social (Guatemalan Social Security Institute), built in the capital's new Centro Cívico (Civic Center) in 1958. For it he designed an allegory of social security in the form of planar human figures in stances that evoke ancient Maya representation, rendered in bright colors against a backdrop of modern buildings and volcanoes. Finally, in 1963, Mérida realized an extensive program of abstract enamel on copper murals, which he described as an allegory of Maya ritual dances, for the interior of the new Banco de Guatemala (Bank of Guatemala). For the building's exterior, younger sculptor Roberto González Goyri designed a program of unpainted concrete reliefs that, like Mérida's earlier reliefs for the Multifamiliar Juárez, clad the forms and materials of brutalist postwar international architecture with an indigenist sensibility. In carrying out these commissions, Mérida deepened his commitment to the Cold War discourse Gómez Sicre had developed in the 1940s, which celebrated indigenist American abstraction as a weapon in the battle against Soviet-inspired socialist realism. Ultimately, Mérida's approach to *integración plástica* provided a modernist facade for a state whose policies led, in the early 1980s, to the genocide of the very Maya people whose cultural forms he sought to channel. This discomfiting fact has gone uncommented on in the largely hagiographic Mexican and Guatemalan literature on the artist.[38] Indeed, Mérida's Guatemalan *integración plástica* projects have gone undiscussed in scholarship published in Mexico, and vice versa. This gives an indication of the lack of integration of these nations' cultural institutions, which may be understood within the broader context of the antagonisms that arise when states of disparate economic and political power share a border.[39]

Coda

Whereas Siqueiros died in 1974, Mérida lived long enough to witness the Guatemalan government's mass extermination of the Maya to whose heritage he laid claim. He died just nine months before the September 1985 earthquake that initiated the destruction of his most significant work, the Multifamiliar Juárez. Only Goeritz, who died in 1990, remained to see Mérida's painted reliefs demolished by the government that had commissioned them. In their stead, he saw the emergence of a new social power in Mexico: the mutual aid organizations that formed in response to the state's inability to mount a rescue effort for the tens of thousands trapped in wreckage.[40] Despite their manifestoes and radical claims for the salutary role of art in public life, artists working for the state in postwar Mexico, as in Guatemala, remained largely consigned to the role of court painters, producing symbolic forms that could only temporarily paper over the absence of democratic processes at their heart.

NOTES

1. The title of this chapter invokes *History as Seen from Mexico in 1936*, the original title of Isamu Noguchi's 1936 relief mural for Mexico City's Mercado Abelardo Rodríguez. As James Oles writes, with it, Noguchi emphasized his choice to represent not a "single place or event, but a vantage point." Oles, "Noguchi in Mexico," 12.

2. The Mexican "economic miracle" was a period of stable growth from the 1940s to the early 1970s, when the ruling Partido Revolucionario Institucional embraced import-substitution industrialization.

3. "Mexico City Earthquake of 1985," in *Britannica Academic*, accessed March 16, 2022, https://academic-eb-com.pitt.idm.oclc.org/levels/collegiate/article/Mexico-City-earthquake-of-1985/438094.

4. Paltridge, "Carlos Mérida's Integration of Art, Architecture and Ideology in the Multifamiliar Juarez," 130 (hereafter "Carlos Mérida's Intergration of Art").

5. Artist Gabriel Kuri has deployed Schalkwijk's photographs of the damaged Multifamiliar Juárez, and its demolition process, as part of international contemporary art exhibitions in recent years. See, e.g., Biesenbach, *Mexico City*. In these contexts, they suggest a decisive and devastating end to Mexico's period of postwar modernist optimism, paralleling Charles Jencks's infamous declaration that the demolishment of the Pruitt-Igoe housing complex in Saint Louis, Missouri, signaled the end of modernism.

6. Revisionist studies of art, architecture, and cultural infrastructures in Mexico between 1946 and 1968 include Eder, *Desafío a la estabilidad*; Cruz Porchini, Garay Molina, and Velázquez Torres, *Diplomacia cultural*; and Josten, *Mathias Goeritz*.

7. Giedion, *Architecture, You and Me*, 71–90.

8. For a thorough analysis of the relationship of historicism to national identity in twentieth-century Mexican architecture, see O'Rourke, *Modern Architecture in Mexico City*.

9. *Integración plástica* was a pressing concern of the journal *Espacios: Revista integral de arquitectura y artes plásticas* (1948–57), founded by Guillermo Rossell and Lorenzo Carrasco, directors of the Escuela Nacional de Arquitectura, which represented a broad spectrum of aesthetic and political positions in its pages, from Rivera and Siqueiros to Goeritz and Luis Barragán. *Integración plástica* was also discussed in Pani's journal *Arquitectura México* (1938–78) and in the cultural pages of major Mexico City dailies *Excélsior* and *Novedades*. Historiographic treatments of the concept include Goldman, "Imagining a City of Plastic Integration"; Torres, *Integración plástica*; and Noelle, "La integración plástica."

10. Pezolet, *Reconstruction and the Synthesis of the Arts in France*, 2.

11. O'Rourke, *Modern Architecture in Mexico City*, 266.

12. The key study of Gómez Sicre's activities and positions is Fox, *Making Art Panamerican*.

13. I am grateful to Adriana Ospina for providing access to Gómez Sicre and Mérida's correspondence, held in the archives of the Art Museum of the Americas, Organization of American States, Washington, DC, which details Gómez Sicre's efforts on Mérida's behalf.

14. See Baciu, *Carlos Mérida*; Paltridge, "Carlos Mérida's Integration of Art," 114–15.

15. See Josten, *Mathias Goeritz*, chaps. 3, 4, 7.

16. Mérida, "Self Portrait," 24.

17. Carlos Mérida, letter to José Gómez Sicre, March 16, 1952, Carlos Mérida correspondence, Art Museum of the Americas, Organization of American States, Washington, DC.

18. Paltridge, "Carlos Mérida's Integration of Art," 13–17.

19. Soto Soria, *Carlos Mérida*, 28; Paltridge, "Carlos Mérida's Integration of Art," 87.

20. Soto Soria, "Sus aportaciones técnicas," 64.

21. Paltridge discusses the responses of Mexico City critics Jorge Crespo de la Serna and Margarita Nelken in "Carlos Mérida's Integration of Art," 104–7. Museum of Modern Art curator Henry-Russell Hitchcock wrote of the Multifamiliar Juárez: "The colored concrete panels are better scaled to the exposed concrete structural elements and brown brick infilling than most Mexican external murals executed in mosaic. . . . The very positive architectural interest achieved in this project . . . indicates well how high are Latin American ambitions in the field of public building." Hitchcock, *Latin American Architecture since 1945*, 123.

22. The "Nine Points on Monumentality" first appeared in print in Giedion, *Architecture, You and Me*, 40–51. Regarding the circulation of the ideas contained therein beginning in the mid-1940s, see Ockman, "War Years in America," 28.

23. New Gallery, *Carlos Mérida*.

24. Goeritz, "La integración plástica," 421–22. Unless otherwise noted, all translations by the author.

25. Goeritz, "La integración plástica," 419.

26. As Giedion writes, "For cooperation to succeed a certain humility was demanded from all participants." Giedion, *Architecture, You and Me*, 71.

27. Zúñiga, *Mathias Goeritz*, trans. Sonia Levy-Spira, 30–31.

28. Goeritz, "Sculpture 'the Serpent of El Eco,'" 63.

29. Goeritz, "Sculpture 'the Serpent of El Eco,'" 63.

30. Goeritz, "Manifiesto de la Arquitectura Emocional," 28.

31. Gómez Mayorga, "Sobre la libertad de creación," 38.

32. See *El Popular*, "Siqueiros y Diego apelan al buen criterio del rector." See also Vargas, "Multicosas."

33. *El Popular*, "Siqueiros y Diego apelan al buen criterio del rector."

34. Mérida, "La pintura funcional," 133.

35. Paltridge, "Carlos Mérida's Integration of Art," 112.

36. Clippings of these publications are held in the Carlos Mérida artist file, Art Museum of the Americas, Organization of American States, Washington, DC; some are also included in Mérida, *Escritos de Carlos Mérida sobre el arte*.

37. Paltridge, "Carlos Mérida's Integration of Art," 115. The basis for Mérida's belief, and the extent to which he maintained it, are subjects for further research.

38. The one exception I have identified is the late Blair Paltridge; see Paltridge, "Carlos Merida's Integration of Art," 114–15.

39. See Buchenau, "Ambivalent Neighbor."

40. See Monsiváis, *No sin nosotros*.

10

Ancient Modernisms

Illegibility, Women, and 1950s Weaving

JENNI SORKIN

As both an undergraduate and a graduate student at Yale during the 1950s, studying painting with Josef Albers and Rico LeBrun, the artist Sheila Hicks circumvented the traditional discipline-specific lineage of modern art and developed a less formal relationship with two people who were to become her most influential mentors, art historian George Kubler and archaeologist Junius Bouton Bird. In a 1977 interview, Hicks recalled, "One day, George Kubler, the art historian, flashed on the screen a series of slides of pre-Columbian textiles. I remember thinking they were the closest thing to my dream world. One of them literally vibrated to me."[1]

An eminent Mesoamericanist, Kubler became a widely read theorist in the history of art after the publication of the book *The Shape of Time: Remarks on the History of Things* (1962). His popularity epitomizes the modernist search for new idea streams and links to the European sifting of the ancient past.[2] Moreover, it represents the break from European source material, throwing a wrench in the traditional circuitry of the transatlantic movement of prewar ideas, in this case, the transference of Bauhaus weaving from Germany to the United States. During the 1950s, Kubler's relationship to textiles was challenged, and arguably enriched, by his encounters with two weavers, Anni Albers and Sheila Hicks.

Kubler often mined textiles for their metaphoric potential in his writing, comparing history to a fabric "whose weave we know to be unbroken,"[3] and writing in *The Shape of Time*: "Instead, we can imagine the flow of time as assuming the shapes of fibrous bundles with each fiber corresponding to a need upon a particular theater of action, and the lengths of the fibers varying as to the duration of each need and the solution to its problems. The cultural bundles therefore consist of variegated fibrous lengths of happening, mostly long, and many brief. They are juxtaposed largely by chance, and rarely by conscious forethought or rigorous planning."[4] However evocative Kubler's metaphorical conceit, weaving is not a chance endeavor. It is a process that requires both "conscious forethought" and "rigorous planning." His notion of time can be conceived of using warp/weft terminologies. The warp is diachronic time (historical development through time) and the weft is synchronic (a particular, given time), splicing across the linear continuum depending upon need or chance occurrence. Referring to the marks or patches of different color sometimes found or created in thread, Kubler's use of the term *variegated* is particularly interesting in that it introduces many moments of potential diversification.

While it could be said that Kubler thought deeply about the tangible structure of weaving as a means of articulating highly abstract notions of historical time and discontinuity, he was not actively engaged in textile scholarship or research. The most straightforward explanation for this is that there were no surviving textiles from the Valley of Mexico, the eventual region of his expertise. However, Kubler was also a generalist, and his enduring work of scholarship, *The Art and Architecture of Ancient America*, also published in 1962, covers all the known Mesoamerican and South American civilizations, including those on the south coast of Peru, where textiles did survive. While Kubler was devoted to the recovery of pattern recognition in the ancient world, he rejected the important social and cultural associations that were embedded in textile fragments, preferring to read them as thematic cultural iconographies that reflected decorative sensibilities, rather than as the cornerstone of technological innovation, wealth, and commerce in pre-Incan regions.[5]

Recognizing his own limitations, Kubler referred both Albers and Hicks to Junius Bouton Bird, curator at the Department of Anthropology at the American Museum of Natural History in New York (fig. 10.1). A textile specialist, Bird had excavated sites in Chile and Peru, and he considered fabric to be a primary document of cultural development. While women were able to enroll in Yale's bachelor of fine arts program throughout the 1950s, they were not permitted to teach in Yale's art department or any other department. After teaching weaving and textile design at Black Mountain College intermittently for sixteen years, Anni Albers found herself cast in the unlikely role of faculty wife, as the spouse of Josef Albers, professor of art in Yale's art department, a post for which the couple left Black Mountain in 1949.

As an aside that reveals much about the insularity of Yale's male separatist culture, the literary scholar and English professor Cleanth Brooks once rather candidly extended his apologies to Mary Jarrell, wife of the poet Randall Jarrell, writing, "I surely hope you can both come and that the above letter hasn't made Yale seem altogether unfeeling about wives. The angle is that if Randall comes they will want him to stay on the campus where the boys can get at him . . . but if you could stand the separation we'd love to have you here."[6] Already serious collectors of pre-Columbian textiles and art objects, the Alberses made trips to Mexico beginning in 1936 and continued to do so throughout the ensuing decades.[7] In 1952, as neither Yale professor nor Yale student, Anni enrolled in Kubler's pre-Columbian art history course. During this time, she began a brief but productive correspondence with Junius Bird, in which she sought and received feedback on the paper she wrote for Kubler's class.

Titled "A Structural Process in Weaving: A Suggestion Applied to a Weaving Problem of a Remote Past and Applicable Today," Albers sought to resolve the disconnect between the preindustrial and twentieth-century weaving of pre-Inca wide fabrics, which seemed to contradict the physical evidence of extremely narrow loom technologies. *Pre-Inca* refers to the ancient civilizations of Paracas and Nazca that inhabited the south coast of modern day Peru. Albers praised the stunning feat of making such wide fabrics—wider than was thought possible—as "almost unbelievably high standards of achievement," theorizing that Nazca weavers doubled, tripled, and even quadrupled their warps.[8] On an upright loom, the warp tension comes from a strap that encircles the weaver's waist. Albers believed that the wide fabrics necessitated great strength, and her foregone conclusion was that men also were weavers. While

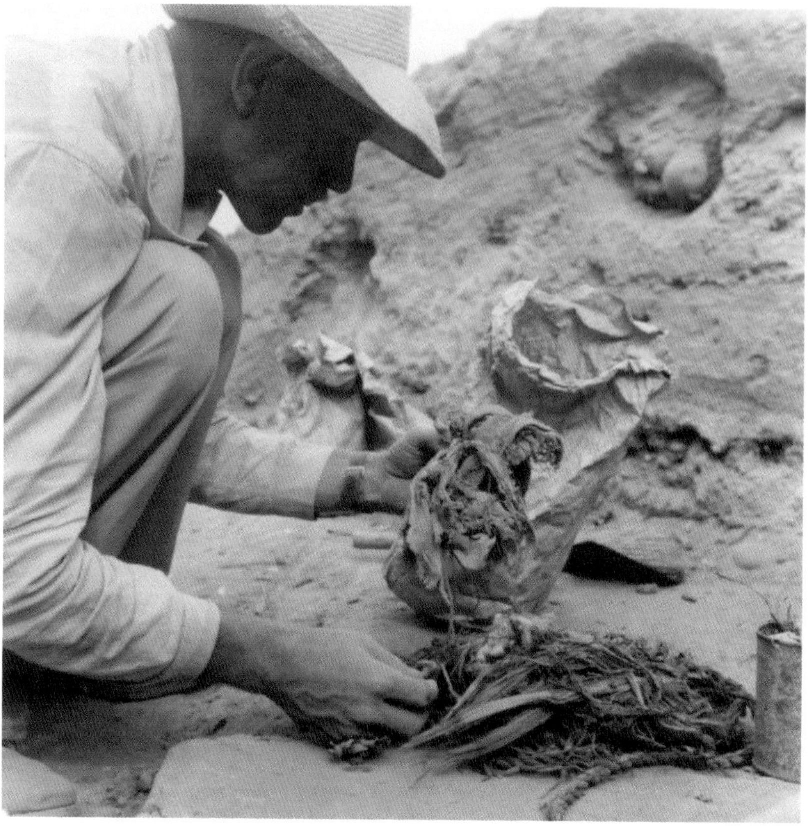

FIGURE 10.1. Junius Bird examining textile, botanical, and cordage specimens, Huaca Prieta, Peru, 1946–47. Photography by John Collier, courtesy Department of Anthropology, American Museum of Natural History, New York.

radical-sounding, her logic for this presumption is far from sound, amounting to a kind of internalized sexism. She writes, "My reason for believing that men, too, were weavers is that an outstanding trait of Peruvian fabrics lies in their structural intricacy and their highly organized formal position, both qualities for which men generally seem to have a greater affinity, judging by today's tendency."[9] The essay had already garnered high praise from Kubler, who recommended it for publication, offering to write the editors of *American Antiquity* and *Art Bulletin* on Albers's behalf.[10] As Kubler noted in his comments, "What you have written is splendid, and it shows all of the qualities of structural insight which you attribute to the weavers of the wide fabrics."[11] This praise unwittingly reinforces Albers's essay as sound in its "masculine" structural assertions, in possession of the same characteristics it sought to explain. Desiring more expertise, or a second opinion, Albers solicited additional feedback from Bird, sending him the paper a month after receiving Kubler's comments.[12] Bird offered helpful commentary, which Albers incorporated, and the article later appeared in her first book of collected essays, *On Designing*, published in 1959. *On Weaving* followed several years later, in 1965.

Classified as craft rather than as fine art, weaving has historically been marginalized as women's work. In the United States, this bias had its roots in the pervasive institutional sexism of the Bauhaus, which offered enrollment to women in only one of three workshops: textiles, ceramics, or bookbinding. While such a model was not directly replicated, the attitude was transferred to US art academies largely through the influx of European refugees funneled into the nation's art departments. Among the most influential was Josef Albers, who left the Bauhaus to teach at Black Mountain College, in North Carolina, arriving before the war in 1933. Josef taught painting and drawing, while Anni taught weaving and textile design.

With the insurgent interest in Black Mountain College and its Bauhaus origins, Anni Albers has been easily recovered as a protofeminist over the last decade, seen as a fierce and accomplished artist-intellectual who performed at a level equal to or greater than that of her male peers (her husband, Josef, the most crucial foil) but was never properly rewarded or acknowledged in her own lifetime. But the reality is more complex. Albers's professional life after Black Mountain was circumscribed by the particularity of Yale's intensely gendered circumstances. But her personal belief system remains a crucial obstacle. Hers was a protofeminist generation, invested in professional identities dependent upon what Anne Wagner calls "a gender-blind modernism," that is, the insistent separation between artistic identity and social identity.[13] If she upheld this distinction, a woman artist could not concede that the trajectory of her career was challenged or stymied by her gender. Both artist *and* wife, working in a craft medium secondary, or even tertiary, to painting, Anni Albers navigated the current of multiple, and mutable, identities. At Yale, she was forced to adapt, and adapt she did. In today's parlance, we would refer to her as a "nontraditional student," an assumption of the respect that that role garners: an adult making a sure-footed decision to brave a classroom full of college students in the late stages of adolescence. However, in Kubler's classroom, Albers would have not only been the only adult student; more than likely, she was also the only woman, and certainly the only middle-aged woman in the class, thirteen years Kubler's senior. It makes perfect sense that Albers, surrounded by men at Yale, would have inevitably seen the pre-Hispanic weavers as male: there were no potential resources to read her material differently or question the absolutism of Kubler's expertise. Though she was a weaver herself, she was embarking upon nascent material in a medium—writing—that was also still new but raises the question: Had the Alberses stayed at Black Mountain, and had Anni continued teaching, would she have written as seriously, intent on finding an audience?

It is only in very recent decades that archaeology has reconceived of ancient weaving as pointedly gendered. The archaeologist and textile expert Elizabeth Wayland Barber has conjectured that loom-based cloth production required not one weaver but two, and that two women weaving together across the millennia produced not only structured cloth but, in particular, the social conditions for intimacy, securing the bonds of a kind of prehistoric sisterhood, in which women bore the laborious nature of their task through verbal exchange: the transmission of stories, language, kinship, and other sorts of abstract ideas that coincided with cultural developments in ancient architecture, urbanity, collective child-rearing, and the like.[14] In this way, weaving itself can be seen as a form of gendered fealty, arguably one of the earliest structuring devices of female subjectivity.

UNABLE TO LEARN weaving through Yale's art department, Sheila Hicks recounts that Josef Albers would drive her to his home for sessions with Anni.[15] As Hicks recalls:

> I took "Art of Latin America," with Dr. George Kubler, and I chose to write about textiles because he had given a lecture showing beautiful old Peruvian mummy bundles. The textiles in them made a strong impression on me. And when I tried to write about them, I thought I'd have to learn how they were made—not just how they looked. At that point, Albers—Josef Albers—saw me struggling in my painting booth on improvised looms that were not looms; they were just stretchers—painting stretchers that I used to tie yarns into tension, and he said he would take me home and introduce me to his wife.[16]

Presumably, Anni helped Hicks fashion her own backstrap loom as early as 1955, which she tied to a bedpost to create her first weavings. At Black Mountain, backstrap looms had been popular as portable alternatives to traditional frame looms. Providing a further alternative to traditional institutional structure, Kubler introduced Hicks to Bird and arranged and approved of her choice of Bird as a thesis adviser.

The reigning expert on pre-Columbian textiles, Bird had undertaken the first excavations at the Huaca Prieta site, on the south coast of Peru, beginning in 1946. This was one of the most significant Andean excavations of the twentieth century, and Bird is credited with the discovery of more than four thousand textiles recovered from mummy bundles that had been well-preserved by the arid region. He was also the first anthropologist to hypothesize a "preceramic" civilization in Peru, in which cloth production preceded ceramics as the building block of ancient civilization.

Bird revered textile fragments as a fundamental record of technological and social development. Sensitive to the nuances of what he perceived to be "the evidence of skill or carelessness," or what British craft theorist David Pye would come to call "the workmanship of risk" in the late 1960s, Bird's 1954 catalog *Paracas Fabrics and Nazca Needlework* is a compulsive study that measures, tallies, and diagrams the decorative details, colors, and precise numbers of warp and weft threads in ancient textile fragments in an effort to establish "personal contact with the past."[17]

Throughout his extended introduction to the catalog, Bird refers to "the textile student," as though he could have predicted that Hicks would come to him not as an academic but as a weaver. Nurturing her interest in preindustrial forms of weaving, Bird's methodology perhaps found its true audience with artists rather than fellow archaeologists or art historians. It was precisely the quality of spontaneity that became prized throughout the 1960s by curators and critics who wished to elevate woven forms to the status of three-dimensional sculpture rather than two-dimensional tapestry. As Gilles Deleuze and Félix Guattari write, "In a striated space-time, one counts to occupy."[18] Through direct contact with cloth fragments, Bird endeavored to inhabit an otherwise unreachable space-time, incurring a kind of transhistorical intimacy with ancient weavers through the analysis of their conventional techniques, but more important, their improvisations. This slippage offered potential insight into the mind of the individual weaver: "Design and decorative details may tell us even more, and, if we seek with understanding, even something of the personality of the weaver may be revealed."[19]

Prefiguring Roland Barthes's theoretical correlation of writing and weaving, Bird's methodology regards the textile as a text, in which the distinct characteristics of the writer/weaver can be read or translated. For a culture that never developed a written language, such an idea must have seemed irresistible, allowing for the possibility of a secret self-awareness embedded into the fibers of the cloth by an anonymous laborer. In a chronologically and culturally distant society with no written record, Bird unearths the mute inscription of stifled individuality. Both tactile and dematerialized, Bird's fragments occupy the space of private subjectivity before the philosophical advent of individual consciousness. Through the specimens' perceived integration within their historical situation (anonymous labor combined with lack of free will), the fragment risks the possibility of complete disappearance or illegibility, rather than revelation. Thus, Bird's arrival at error—and its subsequent reclassification as artful impulsiveness—demonstrates his humanistic quest for the authentic subject.

Illegibility also permeated Bird's contemporary situation. In the late capitalist mid-twentieth-century United States, a very small number of people were fluent in the language of textile structures, of which a disproportionate number were women. Both of Bird's closest associates were women, Louisa Bellinger and Milica Dimitrijevic Skinner, textile specialists who were the actual hands-on researchers, compiling the hard data of his findings using thousands of grids and charts.[20] As weavers themselves, both Anni Albers and Sheila Hicks could read textiles. Josef Albers and George Kubler could not. This was due more to willful disinterest than to the inability to perceive intricate patterns of change. As late as the 1960s, such attitudes were largely still intact, as women were routinely redirected toward art education and crafts and actively discouraged from pursuing painting, sculpture, and architecture.

For his part, Josef Albers is best known as a painter whose rigorous teaching exercises were predicated on the creation of new visual forms. Albers was opposed to disorder and chance and sought to instill new habits of vision through the articulation and recognition of pattern. Likewise, Kubler wrote about linguistic change, but he never would have categorized the textile as a catalyst for altering either cultural, linguistic, or economic conditions over time.[21] Kubler did, however, concede that in Peru, "pottery, painting, and textile decoration therefore carried the burden of recorded communication." This statement is still not a full recognition of the textile as fully lingual, a source language itself, but rather as a vehicle of dissemination of the symbolic or the decorative.[22] For Kubler, the recognition of pattern was the recovery of process as opposed to the recovery of history. For Bird, however, pattern was a kind of speech, a deep structural recognition of linguistic progress.

This differentiation between Kubler's process and Bird's progress is an important one, as it incurs the differentiation between the art historical and the archaeological pursuit. Midcentury archaeology was a teleological discipline, invested in the recognition of technological progress through linear time, as validation of human achievement. Part of Kubler's contribution to art history was a template for resisting such historicist notions of time as a succession of developmental phases, as well as countering anthropology's treatment of history as a narrative project.

In *The Shape of Time*, Kubler sought to dislodge the art object from both the biological and the anthropological models, both organizing principles that rely heavily on evolutionary thinking. Instead, he committed himself to diagnosing the consistencies of form as a means of registering continuity without regard to chronology. The term *life* notwithstanding, Kubler believed that form had a life of its own, distinct from its relation to society, culture, or commerce, envisioning it as a force that replicates and resurfaces in distant cultures and circumstances. This amounts to an animistic portrayal of form, something closer to William Burroughs's self-replicating "word-virus" than to any notion of form rooted in a stable system of iconology, as mapped by Kubler's art historical predecessor, Erwin Panofsky.[23] Further complicating Bird's legacy of legibility is the crisis of faith. As Bird's female assistant Skinner wrote, "It is important to note that one cannot 'see' most of the designs in these textiles, since they have lost all of their dyes or pigments. Even when some color still remains, the designs can be fully comprehended only by a complex and time-consuming analysis by microscope."[24]

With the contemporary usage of high-beam lasers, scanners, MRIs, and computer algorithms, Bird's method of data collection is long outmoded and seems itself primitive from the standpoint of our digitized era. Bellinger and Skinner used a microscope to glean structural data and then plotted threads upon a graph to deduce the structure of the weave. If one could not really *see* the pattern in question, one could not begin to read the textile. This allowed Bird to assume sole authorship of the text, with his female assistants performing the interpretation, translating the invisible, illegible code into the known, but dying, language of pattern. Viewers of these findings, composed both of specialists and of the lay museum-going public, would have no choice but to *believe the weave* in its transmission. Often, that meant taking the leap of faith that the cotton specimen, a frayed, dingy mess of half-missing cordage, was actually imbued with a definitive structural form, a series of figures or stripes, for example, that was embedded in the textile's initial construction. For this reason, a diagram or drawing of the pattern usually accompanied the textile in both its photographic reproduction and physical display. The structural certainty of the symbolic form (the manifest patterns of cats, deities, or abstract designs) or "truth" might have compelled the viewer to move continuously between the drawn pattern and its authentic but illegible woven form.

There is no biographical record for Milica Dimitrijevic Skinner, but much information exists on Louisa Bellinger (1900–68), based on her publication record. Bellinger was a curator-analyst at the Textile Museum in Washington, DC, beginning in 1946. Previously, she had worked on the Dura Europos excavation project at Yale, authoring the final report on its textiles for the University Art Gallery. Bellinger was also a proficient weaver and embroiderer, and her large tapestry hangs on the south dining hall wall of Saybrook College. Josef Albers was actually a faculty fellow at the college. Created circa 1946, the work is an homage to the college, a document of its formative history, as the border is made of the names of the college's first master (who served 1933–46) and its initial twenty-three fellows, one of whom was her older brother, the Latin professor and poet Alfred Bellinger.[25] It seems highly likely that she might have known Kubler in some capacity through her work with the Yale University Art Gallery.

The strong bias against women was an acculturated one, prevalent in academic culture. This is underscored by a 1954 letter from Bird to Kubler: "I recently saw Elena Touceda in Washington. Her dropping out at Yale, as you might expect, involves a man and plans to get married. She called to see you before she left to explain the situation, but you were away. That is the trouble with girl students; you get a good one and invariably this happens."[26] In her single-minded devotion to the pursuit of her studies, Hicks would have been considered an exceptional "girl student." By 1957, Hicks was in Chile on a Fulbright fellowship to study pre-Inca textile production, following the maps that Bird had given her.[27] In a 1958 recommendation to Yale's Foreign Grant Office, Bird testified, "At the request of the University, I examined and passed on her thesis based on her textile experiments. This I found imaginative, original and indicative of ability. Recently she completed a trip to South America. Reports from various friends of mine in different countries were all enthusiastic. She apparently makes friends easily and was accepted, appreciated, and her departure regretted."[28] While perhaps indicative of the 1950s, Bird's commendation seems overly focused on Hicks's popularity rather than the intellectual merit of her endeavor. It is worth asking whether the same criteria for academic success would indeed have been applicable to "boy students." Upon graduating with an MFA in 1959, Hicks moved to Mexico, where she lived on her first husband's ranch among the Indigenous population in the valley of Taxco el Viejo, outside of Mexico City. She regularly sought out contact with the Mexican avant-garde, including Luis Barragán, Leonora Carrington, and Mathias Goeritz, with whom she taught design and color composition at the University of Mexico.[29]

Much more so than Kubler, Bird remained an important mentor to Hicks, and the extensive correspondence between them in the period from 1957 to 1964 attests to their mutual affection and reciprocity. Hicks credits Bird as having given her "reasons for going to see the weaving, the Indians, the villages, the architecture, and the archeology in Peru, Ecuador, Bolivia, and Chile. Basically he gave me a more focused way of traveling."[30] Traveling extensively, Hicks became an important conduit for Bird, promoting his work in Latin America by selling his books "en route," as well as sending him specimens and valuable information from abroad.[31] In 1959, she gifted an ancient specimen, a patterned, looped bag from Argentina, to the American Natural History Museum's collection and in 1964 sent Bird a loom she had purchased from an Indigenous man.[32] Clearly devoted to Bird, her allegiances are made apparent in a letter from 1958: "Among the things I brought back with me a PRIZE sculptured rock from Teohaunaco (maybe from their new excavations). Kubler has offered to buy it for the Yale Gallery Collection—with Yale money, too. However, I want you to see it before. It is wonderful to be back. Please relay *un abraza* a Peggy."[33] Ultimately, Kubler did buy the work for the Yale University Art Gallery, where it remains Yale's only example of art from this particular ancient site.

Between 1960 and 1965, Hicks produced two bodies of loom-based weavings. The first were miniatures, approximating both the size and the techniques of Bird's ancient specimens, while the second were monochromes, titled "hieroglyphs" and continued according to the techniques that Bird had postulated. These included double-sided weavings, four-sided selvages (a finishing technique), and weaving without heddles (a series of parallel wires or slats within the harness of the loom, used for separating the warp threads), a technology that Bird determined was absent from the fragments.

Mildred Constantine, a design curator at the Museum of Modern Art in New York, who was one of the great champions of Hicks's work, observed, "In the early 1960s Sheila Hicks was working on a weaving frame without heddles. Through this slow process she was able to compose patterns freely without the restraints imposed by a loom. The order of the interlacing could be improvised: whether over one, under one, or over six, under four or some other variant could be determined as the weaving progressed. Out of the groupings of warps and wefts she developed in relief a free imagery responsive to the play of light."[34] In a 1974 catalog, writer and textile specialist Monique Lévi-Strauss described Hicks's "hieroglyphs" as "developing the work on the basis of visual accumulation of textures, composing a system of signs that can be compared to handwriting."[35] Her evocation of handwriting returns to the issue of authorship problematized by Bird. Hicks's title itself references the pictographs of ancient cultures, where the woven pattern becomes a signifier of language, transforming the artwork into a quasi text. By combining such a term with the schema of monochromatic patterning popularized by color-field painters such as Barnett Newman and Ad Reinhardt, Hicks positions her production as illegible but singular, neither a pure replication of the past nor a complete merge with modernity.

Hicks's work is the nexus at which the art historical and anthropological discourses entwine. Cordage specimens were found during Bird's excavations on the north coast of Peru in 1946. Twining and netting were found to be the predominant forms of production, producing hammocks, baskets for storage and transport, and fishing nets. Bird amassed copious field notes on fishing nets in particular, analyzing 373 specimens and cataloging them according to such variables as mesh size, materials, repair sections, and usage, or as Bird put it, their "water-worn appearance," as well as through the observation of modern-day fishermen who utilized the nets from the shore during low tide.[36] According to anthropologist John Hyslop, who, along with Skinner, analyzed Bird's findings during the 1980s, "Part of Bird's interests in netting came from his interest in knots, gained from his extensive sailing experience."[37]

One of Bird's most exciting finds was a fishnet with eight gourd floats and a stone sinker still attached, where cords passed around and through each gourd and were knotted at its bottom. Even when he found eighteen stones wrapped with cotton cords, Bird does not propose a discussion of ritual, instead speculating they may have been sinkers used for fishing. While Bird cautiously speculated on the meaning of error in woven fragments, his analysis of binding is confined to its proof of usage. This was a strength praised in a glowing review of his voluminous 1954 catalog.[38] In his unpublished field notes, Bird notes mistakes in various warps, and concludes, "One naturally wonders what, if any, heddling device might have been used."[39] In 1952, Bird published an article titled "Before Heddles Were Invented," which, according to Hyslop, "expresses the clear opinion that heddles were not used."[40]

From Bird, Hicks absorbed a strong notion of reading textiles, but her devotion to structure was accrued from her work with Anni Albers. The combination proved extremely fruitful. This is exemplified by a letter Hicks wrote in 1969:

> Dear Anni,
>
> The recent exhibition at the Museum of Modern Art in New York brought me closer to you and your thought systems than ever before. It made clear to me the past I have been carefully and tediously threading since the encounters I had with you in New Haven in 1956 and 57. The concepts and clear manner of structuring ideas you introduced me to have lead [*sic*] me through many chaotic impasses while attempting to treat thread in a meaningful and poetic way.

Her closing statement, written in her own handwriting as a gesture of warmth, is perhaps the most compelling:

> Thank you again for opening up my mood, and supplying me with a legible map,
>
> Sheila[41]

Hicks's gratitude is evident; however, regarding the literacy of the discipline of weaving, it is her own notion of legibility that remains emblematic of her quest for forms. She has repeatedly returned to themes of reading and writing. This is visible even in Hicks's first mature, monochromatic works, *Blue Letter* (1959) and *White Letter* (1962), which were commissioned by curator Greta Daniels of the Museum of Modern Art and are Hicks's earliest institutional purchases (figs. 10.2 and 10.3).

Taken together, both letters function as an early manifesto, a treatise on the artist's own belief in visuality as a form of tactility, promoting touch as a more provocative way of seeing and sensing. As tactility was very much out of favor during the period of the late 1950s and early 1960s, Hicks's embrace of the haptic was really quite a radical statement to make by an all-but-unknown female artist. Second-generation abstract expressionism dominated New York's artistic climate, when color-field painters such as Morris Louis, Helen Frankenthaler, and Mark Rothko and their critical champion, Clement Greenberg, extolled the virtues of veiled layers of emergent color over wide swaths of canvas. In their works, the painter's hand is absent in favor of granting the paint a fluidity, or a mind of its own, to pool, stain, and eventually fade out.

By contrast, weaving is a laborious medium, and Hicks's weavings are self-consciously hand-constructed. She employs blue on blue and white on white, offset by a plain weave to simplify her surfaces; plain weave is the most basic of weave structures, and therefore the most deducible pattern to the lay "reader." The would-be reader is therefore guided in his or her ability to read the piece by sight alone; both works exaggerate the weft structure through their use of hand-spun wool, which is both the same color and material as the underlying warp. Hand-spun wool is irregular in texture, creating spontaneous peaks and valleys in the finished piece, resulting in a raised, boxy surface texture akin to Braille, the language of the visually impaired that can be traced or read by touch. In this way, the surface of each weaving becomes the text of an illegible letter, referencing a children's primer or a sampler. By assigning the art object its own subjectivity, Hicks offers her weavings the possibility of autonomous movement, the ability to occupy a previous historical situation or culture without the specificity of its tradition.

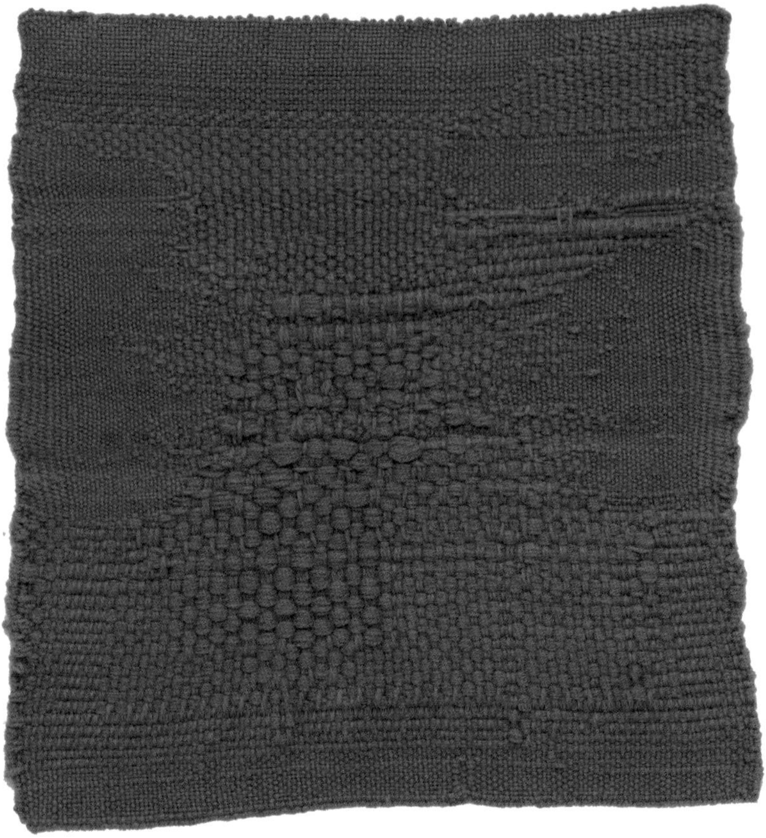

FIGURE 10.2. Sheila Hicks, *Blue Letter*, 1959. Hand-spun wool, 45.1 × 43.2 cm. Collection: Museum of Modern Art, New York. © Sheila Hicks, courtesy Sikkema Jenkins and Co., New York.

Willfully disassociated from the dominant trends of American artistic practice, Hicks continued to live abroad in Mexico and elsewhere throughout the 1960s.[42] She became one of the quintessential artists associated with the emergence of a disparate international endeavor known as the studio fiber movement. The 1960s saw an explosion in experimental textile practice throughout Western and Eastern Europe, the United States, and Canada. The break with the rigors of formal weaving, and its virtues of regularity and flatness is characteristic of what Hicks and peers such as Magdalena Abakanowicz sought to move beyond in their large-scale, expressionistic works. Other artists rejected weaving altogether, turning to alternative techniques to create substantial cloth

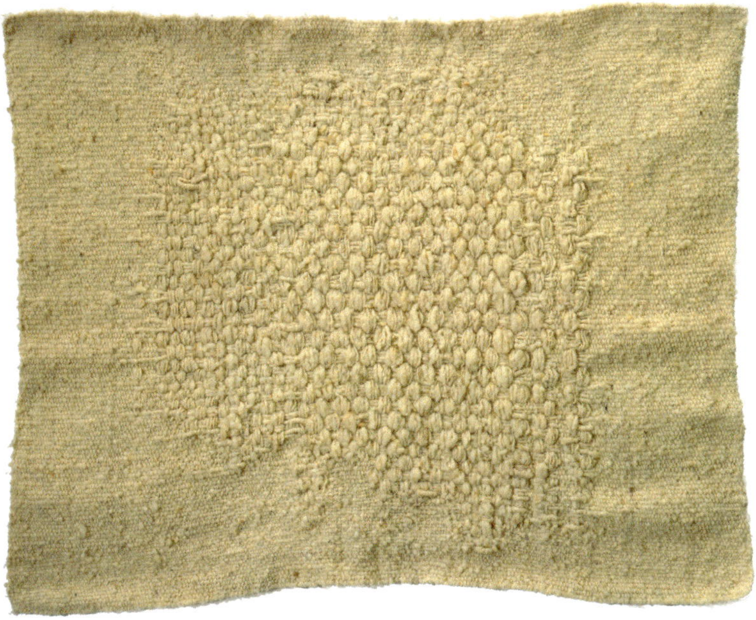

FIGURE 10.3. Sheila Hicks, *White Letter*, 1962. Hand-spun wool, 96.5 × 118.1 cm. Collection: Museum of Modern Art, New York. © Sheila Hicks, courtesy Sikkema Jenkins and Co., New York.

yardage, such as felting, knotting, looping, twisting, and wrapping through knitting, crochet, and even occasionally macrame. Because such techniques often conferred an amateur status, or an association with the ornamental and the decorative, curators and critics of the era turned to the primitive to substantiate the new off-loom production as worthy of the classification of "sculpture."

Through their materials, studio fiber artists during the 1960s made an assumption of translation, rendering their creation as culturally transcendent, or a nomadic extension of Deleuze and Guattari's "smooth space," a constant and ongoing displacement of fixed notions of spatialization through continuous fluidity, arrangement, and reconfiguration.[43] By appropriating ancient traditions and customs, as well as found natural materials such as shells, seed pods, bones, feathers, and porcupine quills into their warps, American artists tried to approximate the hunter-gatherer qualities found in ancient textiles.

It was against the backdrop of this cultural climate that Kubler's most famous book, *The Shape of Time*, was published. Written while Kubler convalesced at Gaylord Farm, a sanatorium for tuberculosis in Wallingford, Connecticut, the book was meant as a deathbed treatise, a potent, poetic, and altogether luminescent work that has become a theoretical staple in American art history departments. Much like Bird's *Paracas Fabrics*, the book had special resonance with contemporary artists for its transhistoricism, or what Pamela Lee describes as Kubler's "thinking about futurity," and its rejection of teleological notions of time. This was particularly the case for the sculptor Robert Smithson, who referred to Kubler in his own writings.[44]

Written in 1963, one of Bird's most important essays, "Technology and Art in Peruvian Textiles," made a tremendous impact on Hicks, and she chose to have it excerpted in the catalog for a 1964 group exhibition held at the Kunstgewerbemuseum in Zurich. Published in a volume alongside texts by noted anthropologists and colleagues Margaret Mead and Hans Himmelheber in 1963, Bird's essay seems intent on responding to *The Shape of Time*.[45] Using linguistic terminologies to classify textile techniques into categories of structure and superstructure, Bird puts forth the compelling argument that technical limits in weaving do not necessarily lead to the direct copy or "plagiarism" of patterns or motifs throughout time. This is in direct opposition to Kubler's notions of repetition and copying, which he sees as inferior, Indigenous, and prevalent in colonial architecture throughout Latin America as a symptom of misappropriation, rather than as a consequence of forced cultural exchange and the creative renegotiation by Indigenous craftsmen.

While neither Bird nor Kubler ever wrote directly on Hicks's work, it is clear from their personal papers that both continued to follow her career, carefully labeling and saving everything she sent. Hicks's catalogs and clippings are neatly labeled and filed away, as if for posterity. Now, in the twenty-first century, so many years later, the girl student Hicks has outlived all her mentors. She is the product of so many combined legacies, molded by archeology, art history, and Bauhaus-inflected art instruction, an artist who has continued to work with little regard for temporality. Yet the meteoric rise of her artistic profile is still wholly indicative of her gender, underscored by the ironic Guerilla Girls adage from their 1988 poster *The Advantages of Being a Woman Artist*: "Knowing your career might pick up after you're eighty."[46]

NOTES

1. Sheila Hicks, interview by Eleanor Munro, in Munro, *Originals*, 367.

2. For a close reading of Kubler's influence on Robert Smithson, see P. Lee, "'Ultramoderne.'"

3. Kubler, "Renascence and Disjunction in the Art of Mesoamerican Antiquity," 353.

4. Kubler, *Shape of Time*, 122.

5. This bias can be gleaned from a close reading of Kubler, "South Coast Valleys," in which he discusses taste rather than innovation.

6. Cleanth Brooks, letter to Randall and Mary Jarrell, January 19, 1963, box 5, folder 138, Cleanth Brooks Papers, Beinecke Collection of American Literature, Beinecke Rare Book and Manuscripts Library, Yale University.

7. For an excellent historiography, see Troy, *Anni Albers and Ancient American Textiles*. See also Albers, *Pre-Columbian Miniatures.*

8. Albers, *On Designing*, 73.

9. Albers, *On Designing*, 76.

10. George Kubler, letter to Anni Albers, March 6, 1952, box 12, folder 4, Anni Albers Correspondence, Josef and Anni Albers Foundation, Bethany, CT.

11. Kubler to Albers, March 6, 1952.

12. Anni Albers, letter to Junius B. Bird, April 21, 1952, Junius B. Bird Papers, Division of Anthropology Archives, Departmental Correspondence Files, box 141, folder 5, American Museum of Natural History, New York.

13. Wagner, *Three Artists (Three Women)*, 188.

14. Barber, *Women's Work.*

15. Sheila Hicks, interview by Monique Lévi-Strauss, February 3, 2004, 19, transcript, Archives of American Art, Smithsonian Institution, Washington, DC.

16. Hicks, interview by Lévi-Strauss, 19.

17. Pye, *Nature and Art of Workmanship*, 17; Bird and Bellinger, *Paracas Fabrics and Nazca Needlework*, 1.

18. Deleuze and Guattari, *Thousand Plateaus*, 477.

19. Bird and Bellinger, *Paracas Fabrics and Nazca Needlework*, 1.

20. Bird and Bellinger, *Paracas Fabrics and Nazca Needlework*, 1.

21. Kubler, *Shape of Time*, 60.

22. Kubler, *Art and Architecture of the Ancient Americas*, 287.

23. In *The Ticket That Exploded* (1962), William Burroughs made the fascinating assertion that language was a virus and would proliferate infinitely, an organic implosion that would continue outward, expanding beyond the confines of the human body to infect the written word. In his lexicon, the excretions of the mind were responsible for holding the body captive, a fashioning of human life through the dominion and, indeed, the domination of language. For Burroughs, this was the power of the word-virus, the shattering effect of writing, and the permanent restructuring of the text, a project that proved to be a lifelong engagement. See Burroughs, *Ticket That Exploded.*

24. M. Skinner, "Three Textiles from Huaca Prieta, Chicama Valley, Peru," 12.

25. Parker, *Saybrook Arras*, 36–37.

26. Junius B. Bird, letter to George Kubler, April 23, 1954, Junius B. Bird Papers, American Museum of Natural History, New York, Division of Anthropology Archives, Department of Anthropology Correspondence, box 166, folder 6.

27. Hicks, interview by Munro, 367.

28. Junius B. Bird, letter to Yale University, October 29, 1958, Junius B. Bird Papers, American Museum of Natural History, Division of Anthropology Archives, Department of Anthropology Correspondence, box 166, folder 8.

29. Lévi-Strauss, *Sheila Hicks*, 22.

30. Hicks, interview by Lévi-Strauss, 25.

31. Sheila Hicks, letter to Junius B. Bird, July 1957, Junius B. Bird Papers, American Museum of Natural History, New York, Division of Anthropology, Junius Bird laboratory. Hicks attached a sample of cochineal, used in making red dye, labeled and sealed behind cellophane tape.

32. Accession record, accession no. 1959–39, Department of Anthropology, catalog number 40.1/3707, American Museum of Natural History, New York.

33. Sheila Hicks, letter to Junius B. Bird, October 1, 1958, New Haven, CT, Junius B. Bird Papers, American Museum of Natural History, New York, Division of Anthropology, Junius Bird laboratory.

34. Constantine and Larsen, "Sheila Hicks."

35. Lévi-Strauss, *Sheila Hicks*, 22.

36. Bird, Hyslop, and M. Skinner, *Preceramic Excavations at the Huaca Prieta, Chicama Valley, Peru*, 207 (hereafter *Preceramic Excavations*).

37. Bird, Hyslop, and M. Skinner, *Preceramic Excavations*, 207.

38. Bushnell, review of *Paracas Fabrics and Naszca Needlework, Third Century BC–Third Century AD*, 175.

39. Bird, Hyslop, and M. Skinner, *Preceramic Excavations*, 198–99.

40. Bird, Hyslop, and M. Skinner, *Preceramic Excavations*, 198–99.

41. Sheila Hicks, letter to Anni Albers, May 9, 1969, box 3, folder 28, Anni Albers Correspondence, Josef and Anni Albers Foundation, Bethany, CT.

42. For a discussion of Hicks's use of workshops and commissions abroad in Mexico, Morocco, and India, see Parrish, "From Collectives to Corporations."

43. Deleuze and Guattari, *Thousand Plateaus*, 476.

44. P. Lee, "'Ultramoderne,'" 55.

45. Bird, "Technology and Art in Peruvian Textiles," 45–78.

46. Guerilla Girls, *The Advantages of Being a Woman Artist*, 1988, screenprint on paper, 43 × 56 cm, Tate, London.

Part IV

DECOLONIZING CONSTELLATIONS

11

Postwar Abstraction

Similarities, Differences, and Other Ophthalmologic Conundrums

ATREYEE GUPTA

Along with Frank Lloyd Wright, Ludwig Mies van der Rohe, Eero Saarinen, and Louis Kahn, Le Corbusier is now recognized as one of the canonical architects of the postwar decades.[1] But even more than others, it is Le Corbusier who exemplifies the utopian figure of the heroic architect, relentlessly resurrecting a whole new world after the ravages of the Second World War. Le Corbusier's largest built project, Chandigarh, a new capital city for the divided state of Punjab in newly independent India, has played a central role not just in Le Corbusier's oeuvre but also in the construction of the modernist architect's image as a visionary iconoclast. Having lost faith in the machine age, Le Corbusier had become increasingly engrossed in reconciling the aesthetic of industrial modernization with vernacular building practices, especially in the non-Western worlds. The Indian government's invitation in 1950 to build a new city provided the architect with an ideal opportunity to actualize what had until that point remained a visionary ideal.

The resultant architectural vocabulary as it was actualized in Chandigarh has been described by William Curtis as a "prodigious feat of abstraction in which devices from the classical tradition—the grand order, the portico—were fused with his own system of forms in concrete and in turn cross-bred with Indian devices like the 'chattri' (a dome on slender supports), the trabeated terraces, balconies and loggias of Fatehpur Sikri."[2] While Curtis finds Chandigarh's architecture exemplary in its synthesis of "the East and the West, ancient and the modern," not all critical assessments of Le Corbusier's work in Chandigarh have been equally affirmative.[3] Norma Evenson, for instance, critiques Le Corbusier for what she sees as a callous importation of Western forms to a non-Western context with complete irreverence toward the semi-industrialized and still largely agrarian local.[4] In both accounts, the modernizing aspiration of newly independent India plays a limited role. Instead, India becomes legible through its premodern, preindustrial form: the balconies and loggias of sixteenth-century Mughal architecture in Curtis's account and the still largely agrarian landscapes in Evenson's description. Postwar modernism and modernization then remain a Western imperative and the non-West merely its receptacle. Only very recently have scholars attempted to rework this binary. Recentralizing Chandigarh within the cultural fabric of modern India, Vikramaditya Prakash, for instance, has narrated a history of Chandigarh that not only closely attends to the aspirations of post-independence India but also foregrounds contending desires of modernism and modernization that shaped the city.[5]

The story of postwar modernism that I seek to recount bears more homogeny with Prakash's account of Chandigarh than it does with either Evenson's or Curtis's accounts. But unlike Prakash's, my interest is not centered on architectural modernisms. Le Corbusier plays only an ancillary role in this chapter. Instead of focusing on the materiality of Le Corbusier's architecture, I use Chandigarh like a mirage, an optical phenomenon, to make visible a peculiar dialectic between postwar abstraction and large-scale industrial modernization in 1950s and 1960s India. The dialectic between postwar modernism and the crisis of nuclearization has thus far functioned as a traction around which our present understanding of 1950s modernism remains organized. In inserting into this picture the recalcitrant trajectories of modernism and industrial modernization in the postcolony, my intention is not to dislodge this narrative but to open up the dialectic to heterogeneous global arrangements. I therefore propose to read the postwar archive against its grain, not only to open it up to plural desires but also to confront the art historical epistemic ruptures that such a reading necessarily engenders.

I.

Le Corbusier arrived in India in the pivotal moment of the former colony's transformation into a modern nation-state, when, guided by its first prime minister, Jawaharlal Nehru, the new country had just set forth on a course of accelerated industrial modernization shortly after its independence. Like many intellectuals in 1940s India, Nehru believed that only modernization could restore the erstwhile colony's place in the world by elevating its people out of poverty. This, then, was the promise of progress, plentitude, and equality, the promise of a postcolonial modernity. Over the subsequent decades, Le Corbusier was concerned with completing the administrative structures in Chandigarh's capital complex. Although the reinforced concrete buildings in the capital would become central in clinching Chandigarh's international stature as "a Mecca of contemporary architecture and urbanism," it was the city's housing complexes that first gave Chandigarh a prominent place in the Indian visualscape of the early 1950s.[6]

Repeatedly captured in photography, the cognitive affect of these structures far exceeded their architectural potential. When, for instance, *Marg*, an art journal central to debates on Indian modernism, first published photographs of these structures in 1953, their very materiality began to take on an abstract aesthetic dimension. Floating on a white background, the photograph adopted a slightly oblique angle. Collectively, the photographic angle and the strategic layout of the journal's page allowed for a focus on the geometricity of the structure's facade, highlighting the angular play of light and shadow on the built surface and magnifying the texture of brick and concrete. Thus, in 1953, sharply departing from the frontal perspective that was usually adopted for architectural photography in India, itself a legacy of colonial photographic practices, *Marg*, a journal whose early history was fundamentally conjoined with India's postwar modernist art, architecture, and design, introduced a distinctive visual vocabulary by opening up photography to the possibility of abstraction. I will revisit the intersections among photography, abstraction, and concrete later in the chapter. But first I want to foreground the immediate impact of abstraction in architecture photography on sculpture—a medium that encloses itself around space in a mode that is not dissimilar to that of architecture.

Dhanraj Bhagat, an artist whose work *Marg* had also prominently featured and who would eventually introduce an abstract turn in sculptural practices in India, produced his first reinforced concrete sculpture shortly after the publication of the 1953 *Marg* issue. While the architectonic quality of Bhagat's later works in concrete resonates with the sculpturesque forms of Chandigarh's architecture—a point I will also return to—his first reinforced concrete sculpture, *Burden*, took as its theme the laboring human body (fig. 11.1). The image of the laboring body had by this time accrued potency as a locus around which discourses of postindependence nationalism were aligned. If the vocabulary of nation-building dominated political discourse, labor undertaken by citizens emerged as the primary site through which both patriotism and the idea of the new nation was articulated in 1950s India. As Satish Deshpande writes, "The nation is not only the locus of all this work, but it is also the end towards which this work is moving: patriotism is quite literally the act of building a nation."[7]

Bhagat's decision to experiment with reinforced concrete at this specific historic juncture could hardly be a coincidence. Concrete—the material that made industrial modernization possible—was ubiquitously present in the visual and textual worlds of 1950s India. Given the monumentality of the state's building programs, India required enormous amounts of concrete. Concrete, a composite construction material made of cement, aggregate, and chemical compounds, was imperative for building gigantic hydroelectric projects and new planned cities—so much so that the very project of modernization was dependent on the availability of cement. But with partition, the country had lost five of its twenty-four cement-producing factories. The factories that remained in India met only a fraction of the country's requirements, forcing the government to begin a cement expansion scheme in 1948. By 1951, six new cement factories were established, increasing total production by one million tons.[8]

If in the 1950s one read detailed discussions on India's concrete-producing capacities in newspaper reports, one simultaneously encountered images of construction in progressive journals such as *Marg* and in the Bombay-based *Design Magazine of the Arts*, a monthly journal with an international editorial team of theorists, architects, and designers including Marcel Breuer, Walter Gropius, Isamu Noguchi, Eero Saarinen, and Sigfried Giedion. It is precisely at this juncture that Bhagat began to experiment with a material that was intrinsically related to the work of construction, of building, and charted an entirely new direction in abstract sculpture. Crucially, developments in architecture and photography had an important role to play in the sculptor's articulation of abstraction, as we will see.

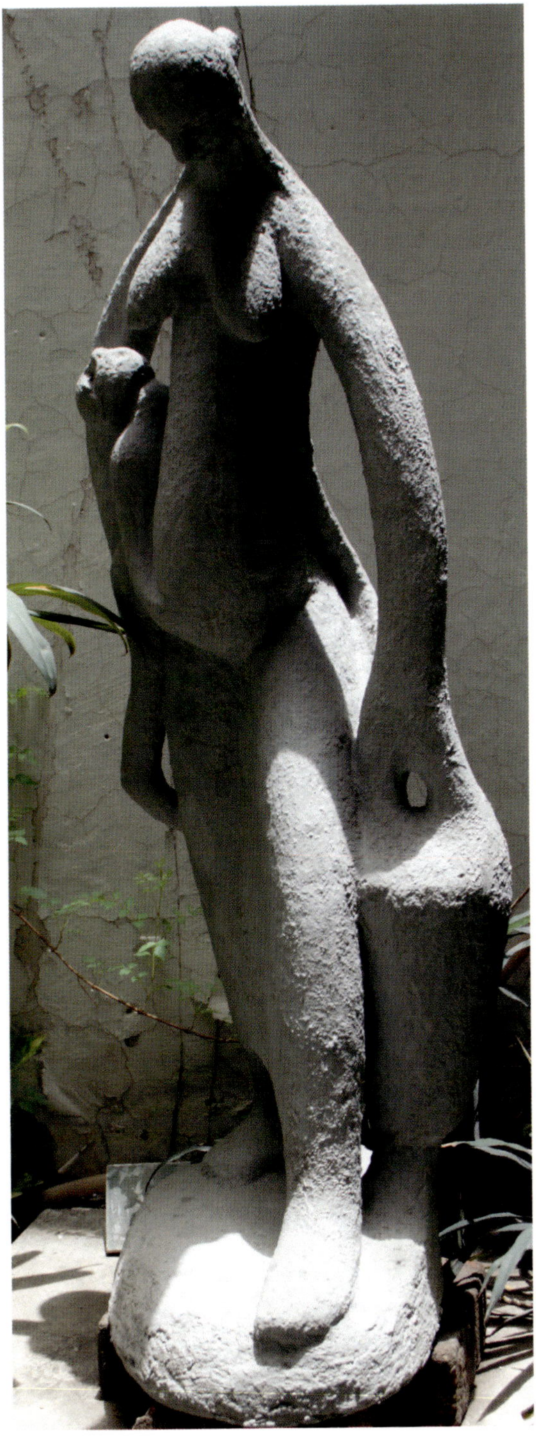

FIGURE 11.1. Dhanraj Bhagat, *Burden*, 1953. Reinforced concrete, h. 115 cm. Photograph courtesy Estate of Dhanraj Bhagat.

II.

In retrospect, 1955 emerges as a key year in the postwar trajectory that this chapter seeks to chart. This was the year that Le Corbusier's High Court was completed (fig. 11.2). The Hungarian-born, French-domiciled photojournalist Lucien Hervé accompanied Le Corbusier to Chandigarh to document the inauguration of this structure. The very next year, both India and Chandigarh entered the international media in a major way with journals such as *L'Architecture d'Aujourd'hui* prominently featuring Hervé's photographs of Chandigarh.[9] There was something distinctive about Hervé's photographs, which set them apart from earlier representations of India in the Western media, such as Margaret Bourke-White's and Henri Cartier-Bresson's now famous photographs of the partition or Werner Bischof's haunting photographs of the 1951 food grain crisis. Although deeply sympathetic to the momentous transformation taking place in India, Bourke-White, Cartier-Bresson, and Bischof almost inevitably foregrounded India's poverty and the plight of its teeming millions, reiterating not-yet-developed India's difference from the already industrialized West. In this sense, Bourke-White's, Cartier-Bresson's, and Bischof's photographs were somewhat out of step with the modernizing aspirations of the new nation. Their photographs found limited circulation in India, perhaps for this very reason. In contrast, Hervé presented the monumental mass of Chandigarh's buildings through an abstracted experience of fragmentary space, sharply delineated by the play of light and shadow, volume, and void.

Hervé's photographs of Chandigarh are almost inevitably devoid of human life. Within his oeuvre, portraits are also almost entirely absent—except, of course, for the figure of Le Corbusier, who appears often. But in all other instances, the heightened juxtaposition of light and shadow, that is, contrasting tones of blackness and iridescent illumination, achieves a complete eradication of sentimentality. The resultant is a close focus on the tactile surfaces of Le Corbusier's *béton brut de décoffrage*, stunning in the immediacy of concrete's materiality but alienating in the abstractness of the photograph's framing. Indeed, the images demand an exacting disciplining of vision, on the part of both the viewer and the photographer. "The architecture photographer's issues are as much mental as they are visual. His vision must be disciplined," Hervé reportedly stated.[10] This, in the South Asian context, would have been startlingly new. Never before had architecture been photographed in this manner in the subcontinent. Despite this, Hervé was a familiar name in 1950s India.

Essays published on Le Corbusier in journals such as *L'Architecture d'Aujourd'hui*, *Domus*, and *Jardin des Arts* almost exclusively used Hervé's photographs

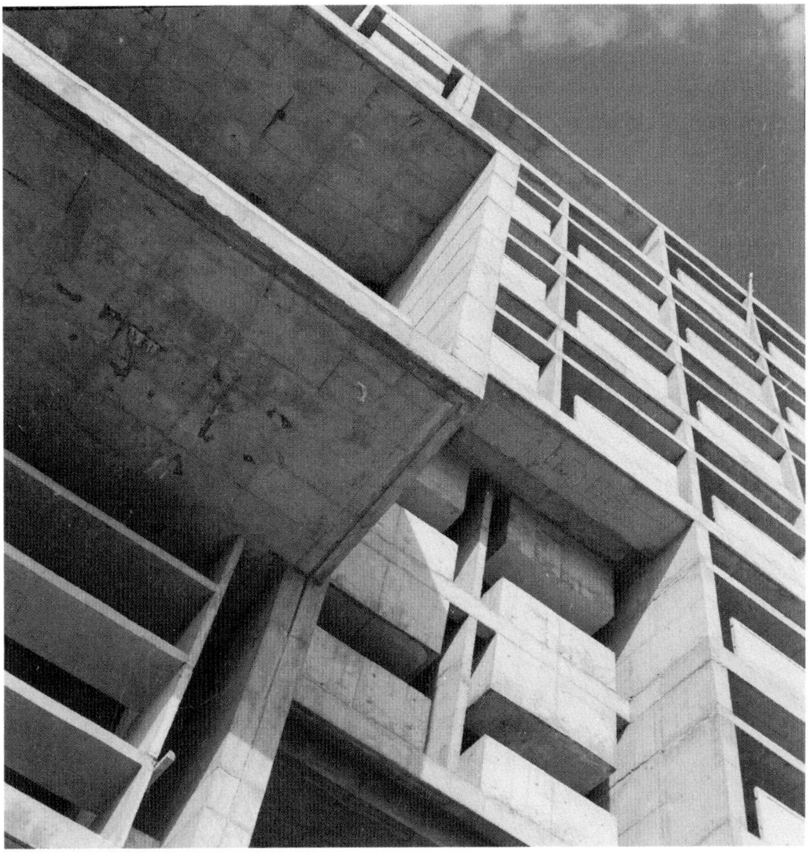

FIGURE 11.2. Lucien Hervé, *High Court, Chandigarh,* 1955. Black-and-white photograph. Collection: Getty Research Institute Archives, Los Angeles.

as illustrations of the architect's oeuvre. These essays, along with Hervé's photographs, were often reprinted in Indian journals such as *Marg*, *Design*, *Art in Industry*, and *Architect's Yearbook*. Yet unlike earlier frontal photographs of monuments that also circulated in the Indian media, Hervé's lens offered no knowledge, no comprehensive view of Chandigarh, so to speak. Still, Hervé's work was repeatedly circulated through art journals and government publications, thus becoming synonymous with Chandigarh, the city unlike any other in India, the city for which there existed no point of comparison. The monumental architecture of Chandigarh—residential blocks that filled up entire segments of the city, or the bold structures in the capital complex framed by acres of empty space—formed a corpus so vast, so new, and so alien, that it could perhaps only be assimilated through such fragmentation. Perhaps the modernizing aspirations of the new nation-state could not find adequate visual expression in photographic realism. Or perhaps the aesthetics of modernization required a new visual vocabulary. As the symbol of new India, Chandigarh may have readily lent itself to the working out of this new vocabulary. For embedded within this vocabulary was a new optics of disaggregation, which in turn precipitated a new vocabulary of abstraction, as we will see.

As far as Hervé's photographs of Chandigarh are concerned, it is difficult to surmise the extent to which they were governed by the strictures Le Corbusier placed on the photographer. Le Corbusier, we know, understood all too well the work that photography performed for architecture.[11] This was so much the case that his definition of architecture as "the masterly, correct and magnificent play of masses brought together in light" closely approximated the definition for the technology of photography.[12] The scribbled notes that accompanied the architect's sketchbooks reveal an astute awareness of landscape as a frame for architecture, which he distilled in his sketches into an amalgam of sharp geometrical outlines and blank surfaces. Then, he asked for certain buildings to be photographed from particular angles, against specified backdrops, at stipulated hours of the day.

Hervé, however, spent a limited number of days in India. In his absence, Jeet Malhotra, then a junior architect on Le Corbusier's team, served as the architect's designated photographer. Le Corbusier's instructions for Malhotra were exact. The framing, too, was delineated precisely: "One or two photographs story above the [G] the afternoon . . . +from the mezzanine of the [G], with the High Court in the background//Gr/from the mezzanine."[13] Always, the emphasis is on framing: "Malhotra Secretariat 12:30 PM// magnificent photographs to be taken perfect lighting//always facing the Himalayas//for Boesiger."[14] Seldom did Le Corbusier request the inclusion of figures. This is hardly surprising. The photographs that Hervé had taken for Le Corbusier do not include figures except as disembodied fragments that merge with the surface of architecture. The human figure is perhaps not of optimum essence here, but architecture is.

Certainly, Malhotra's photographs demonstrated an acute awareness of materiality. The architect-photographer adopted several strategies that Hervé had used. These included angular compositions, heightened juxtapositions of light and shade, and a close focus on the geometricity of architectural forms (fig. 11.3). But there was a crucial difference. If the Hungarian-born French photographer's depopulated images seemed to present Chandigarh's architecture in a way that was devoid of social comment, Malhotra adopted the essential formalist premises of Hervé's architectonics of abstraction but obdurately

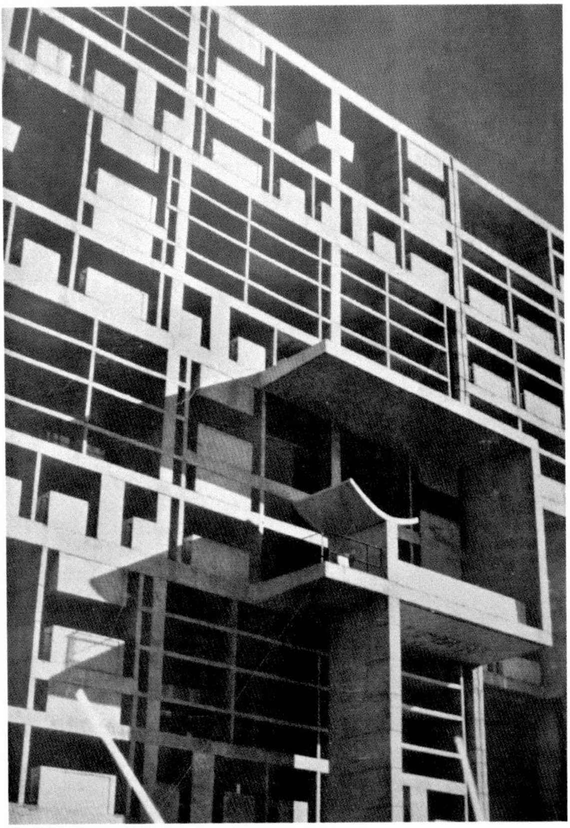

FIGURE 11.3. Jeet Malhotra, *High Court, Chandigarh*, 1956. Black-and-white photograph. Photograph courtesy Estate of Jeet Malhotra.

repopulated the photographs with human figures. If depopulation allowed Hervé to create images of global architectural modernism extracted from any historical and regional referent, Malhotra repopulated the images with social referents and laboring bodies. Thus, in the rare instance when Le Corbusier specifically demanded the inclusion of figures to accentuate the materiality of concrete—"Take photographs of the workers carrying sheet metal or piles onto the roof in the midst of concrete elements"—Malhotra took the opportunity to place the figure at the extreme foreground, making labor the subject of the photograph (fig. 11.4).[15]

Elsewhere, Malhotra managed to catapult the human body into photographic abstraction by using circular passages in architecture like viewing apertures, as if the viewer had in fact placed an eye at the circular viewing aperture in the building (fig. 11.5). The effect bordered on the voyeuristic, except here what is rendered to the voyeuristic eye is disembodied fragments of architecture. Such

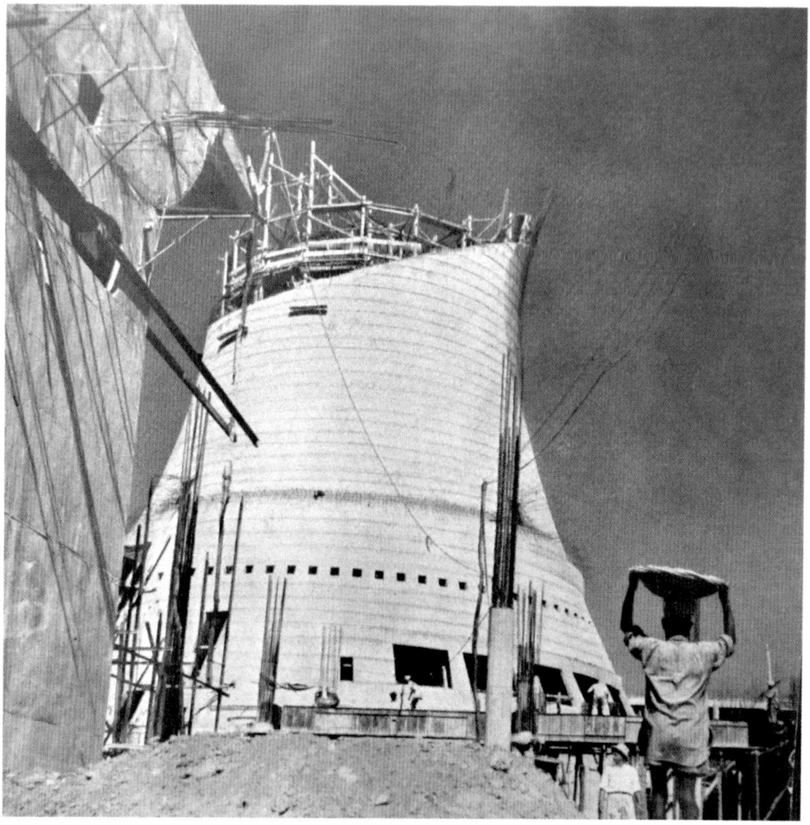

FIGURE 11.4. Jeet Malhotra, *Workers in Chandigarh*, 1955. Black-and-white photograph. Photograph courtesy Estate of Jeet Malhotra.

a framing strategy allowed Malhotra to produce a view that was intimate, even embodied, and grounded in the everyday spaces of the new city. Almost always, figures dotted Malhotra's frames, even if in the form of minuscule specks in the distance. In this sense, his photographs then were not timeless and placeless in quite the same way as Hervé's could claim to be. Malhotra's photographs of Chandigarh, in other words, could not function as a supplement for Le Corbusier's buildings in any other part of the world. Perhaps because of their precision, their placedness, their grounding in postcolonial India, as it were, Malhotra's work initiated a new turn in photographic practices, one that was further developed in the hands of a younger generation of architecture photographers such as Madan Mahatta.

By the end of the 1950s, modernist photography would be free from pictorialism, and in this process, modernist architecture had certainly been of service.

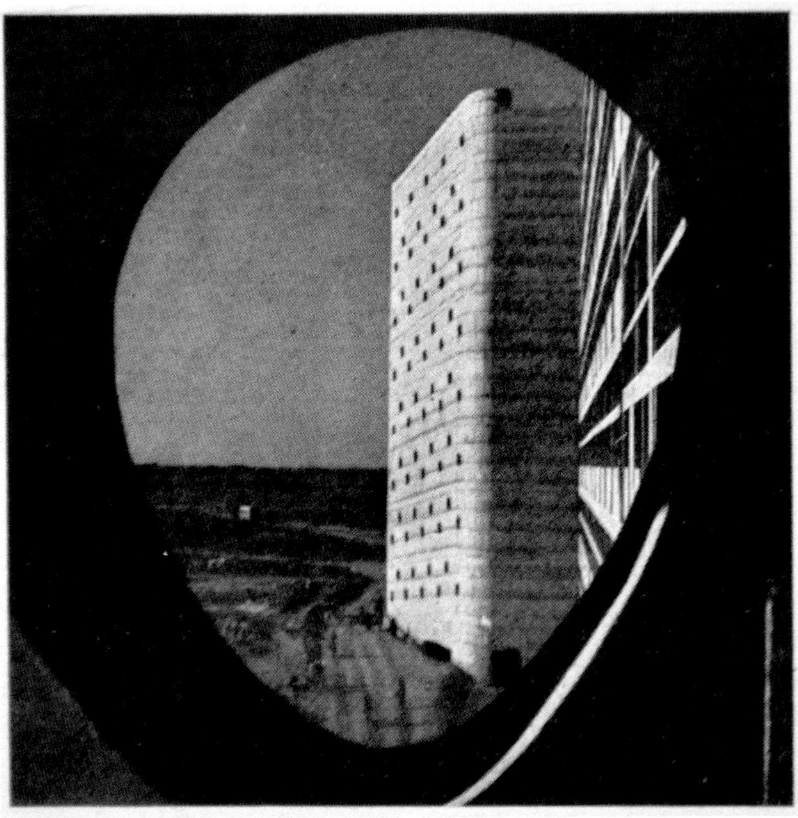

FIGURE 11.5. Jeet Malhotra, *Central Secretariat, Chandigarh*, 1961. Black-and-white photograph. Photograph courtesy Estate of Jeet Malhotra.

In this sense, postwar architecture and photography shared a close affinity, as Adrian Forty, too, has observed in the European context.[16] Perhaps this relationship was a fundamentally global one. But in the postcolony, this new strand within photography would remain restricted to images of modernist architecture and the industrial landscape, further underscoring the fundamental link between new abstractionist tendencies and the new topographies of development that served as its cultural premise and historical ground.

III.

From this cauldron of modernization emerged an architectonic optics of abstraction in the visual arts. Prior to its manifestation in painterly practices, a new aesthetic of abstraction found recognition in midcentury India in a new kind of sculpture, one that eschewed monumentality and volume to highlight sculpture's optical effect. Only a few years earlier, Clement Greenberg, the doyen of modernism in America, had heralded new sculpture as "the representative visual art of modernism."[17] In 1958, elucidating sculpture's effect, Greenberg had asserted: "A building and a picture, too, coinciding with its support, each require a greater amount of palpable stuff than does a piece of sculpture to convey a qualitatively equivalent spatial effect. Feats of 'engineering' that aim to provide the greatest possible amount of visibility with the least possible expenditure of tactile surface belong categorically to the free and *total* medium of sculpture."[18] Contra the tactility of solidity and mass, it was the optical qualities of sculpture that interested Greenberg the most. In the 1949 essay "New Sculpture," he had already elaborated on the intersections between sculpture and engineering.[19] Now, Greenberg's discursive delineation of "*total* sculpture" rested squarely on the medium's graphic, anti-illusionistic, and ocular potentialities. "Now it is eyesight alone," the critic declared.[20]

It is likely that Greenberg's point of reference was the American sculptor David Smith, whose work he had been writing about since the 1940s and around whose work he had constructed an entire discourse about New Sculpture.[21] But Greenberg might just as well have been speaking about Dhanraj Bhagat, whose work was emblematic of a new form of sculpture that emerged in midcentury India. Bhagat himself was conversant with Smith's repertoire, having spent time in New York on a Rockefeller scholarship in 1952, the year that also saw the organization of the Museum of Modern Art (MoMA) symposium on New Sculpture.[22] He was acquainted with Greenberg's discursive formulation of New Sculpture as well. Yet he did not embrace the anti-illusionist, ocular-centralism of sculptural abstraction in the same way that Smith did or Greenberg demanded.

From the mid-1950s onward, architectonic forms began to creep into Bhagat's oeuvre. Increasingly, the sculptor turned to industrial materials such as steel, aluminum, reinforced concrete, and iron. Combining concrete with wood and terra-cotta, materials used in vernacular building practices, Bhagat began constructing linear totemic forms and assemblages of boxlike shapes (fig. 11.6). "The elements of construction grew more obsessive with him," the art critic Richard Bartholomew noted.[23] So did his engagement with the optical experience of positive and negative space. Here, then, was an entirely new departure, one that occasioned a conceptual rupture from the predominantly realistic figuration that had marked contemporaneous Indian sculpture until this time.

Bhagat began working out the relationship between positive and negative space in his sketchbooks (fig. 11.7). With outlines, he delineated the space that sculpture's volume perceptibly occupied. He demarcated the internal spaces of

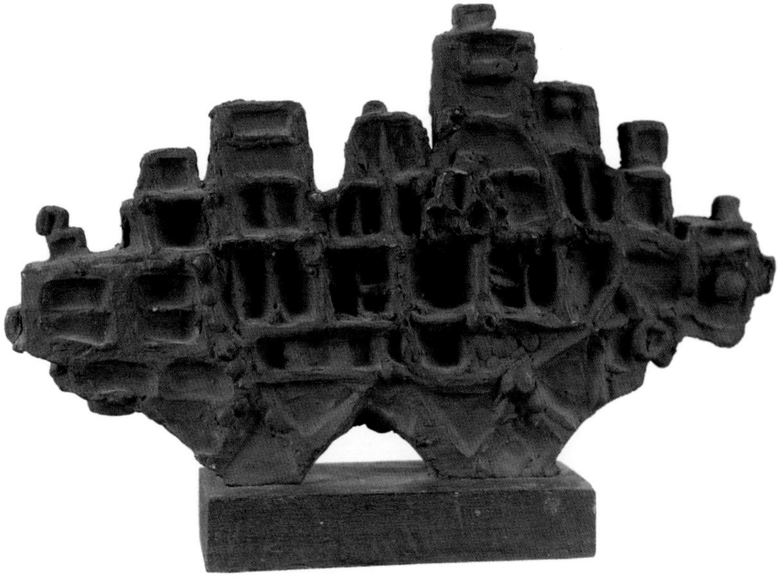

FIGURE 11.6. Dhanraj Bhagat, *Untitled*, ca. 1955. Terra-cotta, 17.3 × 29.2 × 4.3 cm. Collection: Delhi Art Gallery.

sculpture with black highlights, which he then translated into accentuations and recessions in his abstract three-dimensional boxlike forms. These clustered around windowlike passages that framed the empty space. We could call this emptiness sculpture's negative space, which was, in turn, appropriated and made visible as sculpture by Bhagat. The resultant effect was optical rather than tactile—a characteristic that his contemporary critics repeatedly underscored. "These sculptures are naked and we see them vividly with the exploring eye," Bartholomew put it in 1968.[24] Bhagat's work thus inaugurated a new phase in Indian sculpture, a phase that was, in some senses, an Indian counterpart to Greenberg's New Sculpture. But unlike Greenberg's conceptualization of New Sculpture, which privileged the extension into sculpture of the optics of painterly abstraction, this new abstract sculpture's realization lay imbricated in the concreteness of construction. Industrialization and modernization, then, served as this abstraction's condition of possibility.

Abstraction, however, did not amount to an erasure of the figure. The abstract sculptures, which dominated Bhagat's repertoire in the late 1950s and the early 1960s, appear to stand on architectonic tubular leglike shapes that allude to the human body. It is as if the human body is transformed into architecture,

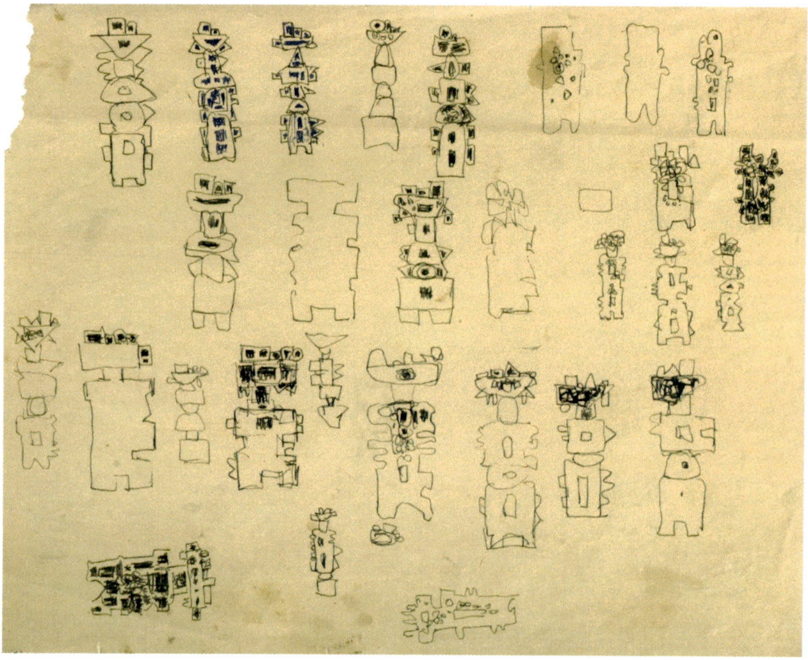

FIGURE 11.7. Dhanraj Bhagat, pages from sketchbook, 1963. Pen and ink on paper, 25.8 × 32.2 cm. Collection: The Osian's Collection.

and architecture, in turn, is humanized. Consistently, Bhagat returns to the figure. But now, the figure functions much like a simile for architecture, as the art critic Charles Fabri observed in 1964: "Eyes are like windows, mouths like doors, heads are like columns or pillars."[25] In context of the broader history of abstraction, formal considerations, it then follows, were not governed by the demands of a particular medium. Neither did Indian modernism produce a critical discourse that privileged form, purity of medium, or medium specificity. Nor was abstraction as epistemologically opposed to figuration as the Euro-American tradition would presuppose. Thus, although conceived in the shadow of postwar abstraction in the West, when annunciated in a postcolonial diction, abstraction, too, was revealed as constitutively *different*.

IV.

Constitutive differences resisted an easy equivalence; even as Indian artists such as Bhagat saw themselves as participating in the international field of postwar abstraction, they systematically challenged its discursive structures. This challenge was perhaps most perceptible in 1967, when Clement Greenberg arrived in New Delhi, chaperoning *Two Decades of American Painting*, a traveling exhibition of American art organized by New York's MoMA as a form of Cold War cultural diplomacy.[26] Consisting of ninety-eight paintings selected by Waldo Rasmussen, the exhibition's curator and MoMA's executive director of circulating exhibitions, *Two Decades* was the largest and purportedly the most comprehensive exhibition of postwar American art to be shown outside the United States until that time. The exhibition featured abstract expressionist works, color-field paintings, and examples of pop art. By this time, abstract expressionism, and by extension artists such as Jackson Pollock, Mark Rothko, and Barnett Newman, had become synonymous with America's Cold War political ideology and its attendant rhetoric of democracy and cultural freedom. At face value, then, the inclusion of a younger generation of artists such as Frank Stella, Ellsworth Kelly, and Roy Lichtenstein could be read as exemplary of Rasmussen's attempt to disengage the aesthetic and the political at the level of institutional patronage. Contra the curator's attempt to reorganize the politics of postwar American art, the exhibition's official catalog nevertheless stated that the primary aim of *Two Decades* was to foreground the spirit of freedom that purportedly made America distinct from the communist world by making space for avant-garde dissent as an essential practice of democracy.[27]

The exhibition arrived in India only six years after the Non-Aligned Movement, a network of thirty colonized and formerly colonized countries, had been formalized in Belgrade under the leadership of Nehru of India, Kwame Nkrumah of Ghana, Gamal Abdel Nasser of Egypt, Sukarno of Indonesia, and Josip Broz Tito of Yugoslavia. Together, the nonaligned nations, which represented more than half of the world's population in the 1960s, had declared their neutrality to the Cold War's seemingly hegemonic capitalist/socialist binary.[28] The Cold War powers, however, perceived nonalignment as a deliberate provocation to the Cold War axis. The *Two Decades* exhibition thus revealed America's fears about India's alliances in the Cold War struggle, as did the increase in the circulation in India of exhibitions organized by MoMA.[29] The United States' efforts to secure India's cooperation through cultural diplomacy, however, paralleled the emergence of a different kind of cultural solidarity. Through the nonaligned political networks, the term *Third World* was gradually accruing currency as an alternative intellectual and ideological position in both modernity and cultural modernism.[30]

That Greenberg's visit was orchestrated and funded by the US Bureau of Educational and Cultural Affairs, an organization that played an important role in postwar cultural diplomacy, certainly serves to situate *Two Decades* well within the Cold War frame.[31] Far from the terse terrains of Central Europe and North America, Greenberg's reception in India also projects onto the postwar art historical matrix a series of global entanglements that stood outside Cold War's East–West divide yet exerted a contrapuntal pressure on its aesthetic and ideological arrangements.

By way of addressing the emergent modernist discourse in India and across the nonaligned worlds, the American art critic delivered a lecture titled "Painting in the United States Today" for the All India Radio. The lecture succinctly summarized for his Indian audiences the key tenets of Greenbergian modernism: the absolute primacy of pure form, the unconditional superiority of medium over subject matter, the idea that flatness was an inviolable component of modernist aesthetics, and perhaps most important, opticality, or the universality of the disembodied gaze, as the only criterion for appreciation and evaluation of postwar abstraction. Categorically situating modernism within an optical regime, the American art critic thus presented abstraction as both universal and hermeneutically resistant to ideological and political manipulation—an assertion that was strangely out of step with the immediate political context that had made Greenberg's visit to India possible in the first place. But as such, the content of Greenberg's talk derived from a lecture that he had already presented for the Voice of America's Forum Lectures in 1961 and had subsequently published as an essay in the same year.[32] In addition, as if to prepare Indian audiences for a proper appreciation of postwar abstraction, Greenberg traced a genealogy of midcentury abstraction as a fundamental break with perspectivalism, mapped through the critique of single-point perspective as defined by late nineteenth-century impressionism, the radical fracturing of space as symptomized by early twentieth-century cubism, and the realignment of figure and ground in mid-twentieth-century abstraction. But such a particularized characterization of twentieth-century modernism may have seemed trivial to his Indian audiences, for neither had perspectivalism presented itself as an aesthetic priority in the colonies nor was realism produced as a privileged syntax at any specific historical juncture. Instead, an advanced vocabulary of abstraction had emerged precipitously in twentieth-century India.

Consequently, both the art critic and the exhibition received responses ranging from utter incomprehension and ambivalence to outright rejection.[33] The paintings in the exhibition were described by Indian audiences as "decadent," "boring," "inexplicable," even "tragic."[34] If Greenberg presented the American paintings on display as symptomatic of a positive alignment between art and its self-referentiality in the face of tumultuous postwar social transformations, Indian artists and critics described the exhibition as merely conveying the "exasperation, depression and impotent anger of a generation of Americans."[35] Greenberg's appeal that content be "dissolved so completely into form that the works of art or literature cannot be reduced in whole or in part to anything but itself" found little resonance in India, where building, that is, construction, rather than dissolution was still the predominant intellectual and political concern.[36] Summarizing the responses to Greenberg's 1967 lecture in New Delhi, the artist Gieve Patel noted that however important the contribution of American abstraction may be for postwar modernism, "the American statement seemed too complete in its own context, and offered an impassive façade" to its Indian viewers.[37] Thus, even as Indian artists perceived themselves as equal participants in international aesthetic discourses, Greenberg's ocular-centrism presented an impassive facade.

Greenberg, for his part, found postwar Indian abstraction to be lacking an essence of Indianness. Paradoxically, to him, postwar Indian abstraction looked remarkably *similar* to art produced in America, the proverbial center of postwar abstraction. In contrast, Greenberg was drawn to premodern Indian art and architecture, especially the Taj Mahal, where he may have discerned a distinctive Indianness that he also sought in postwar Indian art (fig. 11.8). Explicitly, he drew attention to the question of the exportability of art. By this, he meant a perceptible quality that purportedly marks art produced in specific national contexts and sets it apart from art produced elsewhere when presented internationally. And when he encountered the work of Bhagat during his visit to the National Gallery of Modern Art in New Delhi, the sculptor's abstract forms reminded him all too vividly of David Smith.

The ophthalmologic conundrum that was revealed as Greenberg and his Indian interlocutors stood facing each other in New Delhi offers a felicitous passage that allows me to conclude by recentralizing the argument that I make here. Although Indian artists and critics recognized the formal exegeses of abstraction in their own practice, they read Greenberg's championing of postwar abstraction's optical imperatives as an unyielding, impassive facade that defied comprehension. In turn, having already situated an essence of Indianness in the Taj Mahal, the American art critic could only comprehend in postwar Indian abstraction ostensibly derivative echoes of Western modernism. At the core, then, was a peculiar ocular problem that played out through seemingly counterintuitive negotiations between similarity and difference.

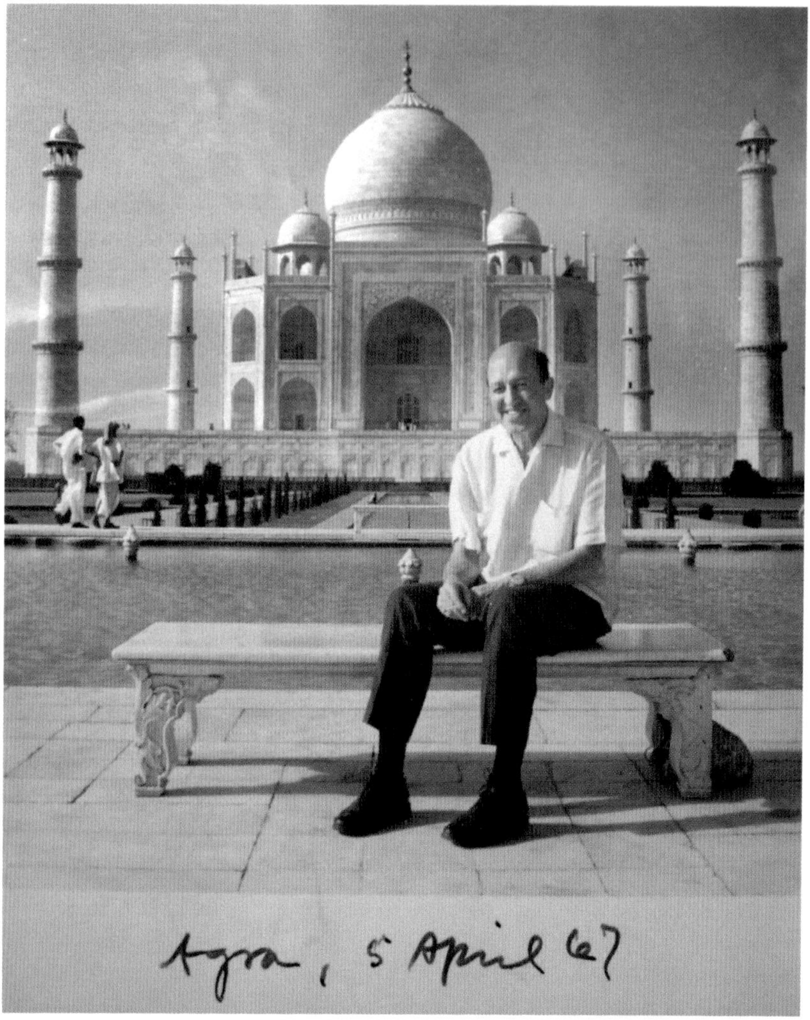

FIGURE 11.8. Unknown photographer, Clement Greenberg at the Taj Mahal, Agra, 1967. Black-and-white photograph. Collection: Getty Research Institute Archives, Los Angeles.

Certainly, postwar abstraction in India remained embroiled with the haphazardness with which modernism as an aesthetic discourse worked itself out in the colony and the postcolony. The crises of representation at the core of European modernism had taken on different shadings in the former peripheries, where modernist genealogies and impulses were both distinct and dissonant. The resultant effect was an array of artistic practices that looked like they fit well within the formal exegeses of European and American modernisms but ultimately did not concede to Western modernism's visual codes. That it is impossible to chart a mediatic unfolding of sculptural abstraction or even painterly or photographic abstraction in India only reiterates the deep-rooted heterogeneities that structured the global field of postwar modernism. Indeed, no systematic formal groundwork in India led from realism to cubism and ultimately to painterly abstraction, New Sculpture, minimalism, earthworks, and onward. Neither did Indian modernism produce a critical discourse that privileged form, purity of medium, or medium specificity. An engagement with this difference then requires new methodological approaches that can account for the creative adaptations that were undertaken to reconfigure form to address the exigencies of a postcolonial context.

Then, if we are to redraw the cartographies of postwar modernism—in other words, if we are to think in terms of postwar modernism's global frame—it may not be sufficient to stop alluding to a similarity in form and difference in context. In order to think more productively about postwar modernism's global frame, it is necessary to further probe the similarity/difference dialectic by taking seriously Dilip Gaonkar's suggestion that we recognize and problematize both similarity and difference. "It is customary," Gaonkar writes, "to think about convergence in terms of institutional arrangements, such as a market economy, a bureaucratic state, modes of popular rule, and so on. Similarly, one thinks of divergence primarily in terms of lived experience and cultural expressions of modernity. . . . An alternative modernities perspective complicates this neat dichotomy by foregrounding that narrow but critical band of variations consisting of site-specific 'creative adaptations' on the axis of convergence (or societal modernization)."[38] In such an approach, what appears to be dissimilar could perhaps be made intimately proximate and what appears to be similar productively rendered strange.

NOTES

1. An early version of this chapter was published as Gupta, "Dwelling in Abstraction."
2. Curtis, *Modern Architecture since 1900*, 428.
3. Curtis, *Modern Architecture since 1900*, 428.
4. Evenson, *Chandigarh*.
5. Prakash, *Chandigarh's Le Corbusier*.
6. Quote from von Moos, introduction to *Chandigarh 1956*, 17; Evenson, *Chandigarh*, 49.
7. Deshpande, "Imagined Economies," 24.
8. Das, *Cement Industry of India*.
9. See the double issue of *L'Architecture d'Aujourd'hui* on tropical modernist architecture (no. 67–68 [October 1956]), which features Lucien Hervé's photographs of Chandigarh

and includes an essay by Pierre Jeanneret. Jeanneret, "Incidences des techniques locales et du climat sur la construction à Chandigarh."

10. Hervé quoted in Beer, *Lucien Hervé*, 24.

11. For a discussion, see Colomina, "Le Corbusier and Photography"; Piotrowski, "Le Corbusier."

12. Le Corbusier, *Towards a New Architecture*, 31.

13. Franclieu and Architectural History Foundation, *Le Corbusier Sketchbooks*, 776–78. Notations in original.

14. Franclieu and Architectural History Foundation, *Le Corbusier Sketchbooks*, 741. Notations in original.

15. Franclieu and Architectural History Foundation, *Le Corbusier Sketchbooks*, 776–78.

16. Forty, *Concrete and Culture*.

17. Greenberg, "Sculpture in Our Time," 61.

18. Greenberg, "Sculpture in Our Time," 61.

19. Greenberg, "New Sculpture," 319.

20. Greenberg, "Sculpture in Our Time," 59.

21. For Greenberg, Smith had begun to assume an importance like that of Jackson Pollock, as David J. Getsy has noted. See Getsy, "Tactility or Opticality," 105–21.

22. For the transcript of the symposium, see "New Sculpture, a Symposium."

23. Bartholomew, "Contemporary Indian Artists," 329.

24. Bartholomew, "Vivid Metal and Wood Sculptures," 434.

25. Fabri, *Bhagat*, n.p.

26. Prior to its arrival in New Delhi, the exhibition had been sent to Japan, where it had opened in Kyoto in October 1966 to an ambivalent public reception. Although not part of its original itinerary, the exhibition's international sojourn concluded in Australia, where the paintings traveled by sea from Mumbai, in part due to the persistence of its curator, before finally returning to New York on a fleet of Qantas aircraft. Greenberg's offer to accompany the exhibition to Australia, however, was declined, perhaps because Australia's alignment with the United States in the Cold War was hardly a matter of dispute. Unlike in Kyoto and New Delhi, in Australia, *Two Decades* was heralded as "the most important exhibition ever seen," commended "enthusiasm and awe," and caused "fantastic traffic jams" of eager viewers who reportedly flocked to see the show in Melbourne. See Thomas, "Australia's Most Important Exhibition."

27. Rasmussen, *Two Decades of American Painting*.

28. For a political history of the Non-Aligned Movement, see Prashad, *Darker Nations*.

29. See Department of Circulating Exhibitions Records, series II.1, II.2, Museum of Modern Art Archives, New York.

30. For an intellectual history of the Third World, see Young, *White Mythologies*.

31. This aspect becomes clear in several letters and notes in the Clement Greenberg Papers, 1928–95, accession no. 950085, Getty Research Institute, Los Angeles.

32. Greenberg, "Modernist Painting."

33. The intention of the show was to foreground the ideologies of freedom that distinguished America from the communist world. Governed by a code of artistic autonomy and individualism, contemporaneous American art lent itself to the United States' Cold

War rhetoric of democracy and freedom, as Serge Guilbaut has suggested. Guilbaut, *How New York Stole the Idea of Modern Art*.

34. Quotes from Lelyveld, "Modern U.S. Art Stirs New Delhi."

35. *Patriot*, "Two Decades of American Paintings."

36. Greenberg, "Avant-Garde and Kitsch," 6.

37. Gieve Patel, "Decades and the Seminar," 6.

38. Gaonkar, "On Alternative Modernities," 16.

12

Enemy of the People

Jewad Selim and the Baghdad Group for Modern Art

NADA SHABOUT

Modern art truly is the art of the age, and its complexity is a result of the complexity of this era. It expresses many things: anxiety, fear, great disparities in most things, human massacres, man's distancing himself from God, and then the new perspectives on everything, generated by modern theories in psychology and other disciplines.—JEWAD SELIM, 1951

In his 1991 book *Jewad Selim, al fanan wa al-akharun* (Jewad Selim, the artist and the others), Shakir Hassan Al Said (1925–2004) posed a question that effectively sums up the Iraqi artist Jewad Selim's short but poignant career. He asked, "How could [Selim] at once be concerned with local and global humanity in his art and draw from various roots his relationship with his environment, that vast ocean, an objective relationship that does not denigrate the value of his local or global environment?"[1] Arguably Iraq's best-known artist, Jewad Selim (1919–61) is credited with constructing Iraq's modern visual and intellectual iconography. More important, through the Baghdad Group for Modern Art, Selim instigated a process of negotiation that became the mark of Iraqi modernism. This chapter contextualizes specific works and analyzes his contribution in shaping a postwar modernism that joins the national with the international in Iraq.

JEWAD SELIM PERCEIVED the years of the Second World War and its immediate aftermath as the beginning of a critical shift that marked a unique Iraqi engagement with modernism. The political tension and local unrest between the pro-Allies (as per the 1930 British-Iraqi treaty) and pan-Arabs (pro-Axis) brought about a rude awakening for artists. Newly formed art groups played a pivotal role during the 1940s and the 1950s in Iraq in promoting new methods of expression and modern art.[2] Collectively they exemplified the artists' struggles to carve a socially accepted space for their local and world vision.

Selim, who was a member of al-Ruwwad (initially Société Primitive) after his return from Europe, went on to co-establish the second group with Shakir Hassan Al Said in 1951, the Jamaat Baghdad Lil Fan al-Hadith (Baghdad Group for Modern Art).[3] This became arguably Iraq's most significant art group, and Selim perceived it as a necessary step beyond al-Ruwwad to introduce a new way of thinking about making art and to fulfill the notion of negotiating both the past and the present. It was the first group that not only gathered around specific goals but also constituted a movement or a school of thought and style instead of a congregation of artists who shared a philosophy or were united through a shared context but not style.[4]

The Baghdad Group for Modern Art was formed to begin a necessary negotiation between a new postcolonial national consciousness and European (albeit perceived as international and transnational) modernism. In statements written by Iraqi artists from the 1940s to the 1960s and in their memoirs, one is immediately struck by the distinct ease they felt in moving across and within various borders. They simply operated within global parameters.[5] Baghdad was a cultural hub, in which one could find references to George Wilhelm Friedrich Hegel, Giacomo Puccini, Iraqi *maqam*, Umm Kulthum, and Taha Hussein. Nevertheless, works created before the 1950s had directly appealed to Iraqis for their subjects' simplicity and familiarity: images of the desert by Faiq Hassan, working people and peasants by Jewad Selim, and nature in Atta

Sabri's work. At a time when Iraqis became accustomed to seeing aspects of their lives on canvas, Iraqi artists realized that it was time to move away from the naturalism of nineteenth-century European styles. This realization, some artists tell us, was arguably aided by Poles, as referred to in the writing of the period.[6] On September 9, 1943, Selim noted in his journal:

> Then there was the war, few of them [i.e., Polish artists, such as Józef Jarema, Edward Matuszczak, and Józef Czapski] were transferred to Baghdad, they attended our annual exhibition and met me and Faiq [Hassan] in 1941. It was a very passionate meeting when they learned that we were part of the School of Paris as well. [The Polish artists had studied with Pierre Bonnard twenty years earlier.] ... I learned about the Impressionists and post-impressionists from them.... I learned the value of time and color.[7]

The importance of these Polish artists is in the fact that they gave Selim and other Iraqi artists the opportunity to discuss ideas and new experiments beyond academic styles. Artist Ismail al-Shaikhly, who was a third-year student at the Institute of Fine Arts in Baghdad at the time, recalls that after several meetings with Polish artists, his teacher Faiq Hassan asked the class to tear apart all that they had painted thus far, calling it shallow, and changed his teaching methods to include discussing new ideas.[8] Perceivably, the Polish artists provided the students with a Western art historical education that was missing from their curriculum, particularly as this preceded the major scholarships to Europe. Consequently, the rebellious nature of modern art motivated Iraqi artists to rebel against their academic style.

Selim's first scholarship to study art in 1938 in Paris was abruptly terminated in less than a year with the beginning of the Second World War. He was sent to Rome (1939–40) instead, but the war soon followed, so he had to return to Baghdad and was appointed as an instructor at the Institute of Fine Arts. His period abroad was short but served as an introduction to various concepts, particularly to the notion of experimentation. Novelist and thinker Abd al-Rahman Munif considers it a decisive one, during which Selim's priorities were formed in terms of stimuli and styles.[9] He argues that given the short duration of his time abroad, Selim's return to Baghdad and his stint teaching at the institute before embarking on further travel made him more mature and exposed him to multiple styles without one school or approach becoming dominant, particularly as Baghdad at that time reflected the political, social, and intellectual turmoil of the period. It was a time of challenging the status quo at every level. Thus artists and critics, Polish and British, passing by or stationed in

Baghdad during the war years were a supplement to his education and provided him with the tools to rebel.

After the end of the war, Selim was sent on a scholarship to England (1946–48), to study at the Slade School, where he met his future wife, Lorna. Selim returned to Iraq in 1949 and became the head of the sculpture department at the Institute of Fine Arts. Lorna joined him in 1950 and they were married. In Baghdad, Selim was part of a wider conversation that included challenges to poetry, architecture, and theater. The first meeting of the Baghdad Group for Modern Art took place in April 1951 in Jewad Selim's house and was attended by Naziha Selim, Lorna Selim, Nizar Selim, Shakir Hassan Al Said, Mohammed Ghani Hikmat (a sculptor), Jabra Ibrahim Jabra, and four other members, including an architect who later left the group.[10] Two years later other important artists, including Ismail Fatah al-Turk, also a sculptor, and the ceramicist Saleh al-Ameri joined. They later specified in their manifesto that the group consisted of painters and sculptors, which was their way of asserting the importance of sculpture, for which there was no recent history in Iraq. They further affirmed that each member was to retain a unique style but all aimed to navigate the history of Iraqi culture to further develop that individual style and be able to visualize the country, the land, and its cultures in a modern manner.

As the charismatic leader of the group, Selim emphasized and promoted the notion of *istilham al-turath*, a term that encompasses finding ways to be informed by heritage through innovative engagements, to initiate a new way of thinking about making art, and to develop an artistic vision that would be equally historio-cultural and modern.[11] *Istilham* is a concept that supports mediation between the past and the present, as a form of negotiation of heritage and tradition, to project forward and realize a new contemporary aesthetics. *Istilham* perceives a spiritual relationship between the two periods regardless of temporal distance and "establishes a new spatial and temporal relationship with our surroundings," Al Said argued.[12] For Selim, however, it had its basis in the humanistic tradition. His understanding of modern art in Iraq expressed the problematic of the new art they had learned—oil painting on canvas engaging modern styles—and the past that Selim had perceived in the medieval work of Yahya al-Wasiti. Thus, he affirmed the group's *istilham* as a renewal of painting in Iraq.

These ideas found concrete shape in the image on the cover of the fourth issue of *Al-fikr al-hadith: Majalla shahriya lil fan wa al-thaqafah al-hura* (Modern thought: Monthly journal for the free arts and culture), a journal of international contemporary arts, both visual and literary, launched and edited by the

Iraqi artist Jamil Hamoudi in 1949 (fig. 12.1). The image is a sketch of a statue, commissioned by the Baghdad Municipality, that Selim designed and built for the Directorate of Public Transportations. Selim's intention, as argued by Hamoudi, was to "convey the concept of transportation through his design, which clearly exhibits elements of the Assyrian tradition."[13] Hamoudi further explained that the masculine human form signifies strength and balance. The wing signifies speed, while the Assyrian-looking wheel suggests its origin in Mesopotamia. This statue, which combines speed, power, forward motion, and the history of transportation, embodies Selim's life "efforts to construct a modern spirit in the renewal of the Iraqi taste."[14]

A few years later, in the inaugural speech delivered at their first collective exhibition in 1951, Selim, speaking for the Baghdad Group for Modern Art, declared, "We dream that there is a dream that connects us with all the beings that simply dream. A dream we call Baghdad."[15] Selim focused on explaining the evolution of art and its role, and that of the artist in maintaining culture and serving humanity in a global context. He specifically questioned the status of Iraqi artists in Baghdad and located modern art in the margins. His speech problematized the development of a market driven by bourgeois taste that adapted to the latest international trends in music, furniture, and film but had remained distant from modern visual art. He essentially disapproved of the dominant mainstream preference for academic style.[16] The artists' revolutionary and ambitious thought, however, embraced the spirit of *turath* (tradition). Their understanding of "international" art was thus rooted in their notion of "identity," which they believed was their only claim for distinctive creativity. This notion in particular is what connected them directly to the Iraqi society then and keeps their experiments relevant today.

Selim, the man and the artist, has been almost an obsession for anyone who writes about Iraqi art, to the point of finding it impossible to move beyond him. Selim was born in Ankara in 1919 to Iraqi parents in a family of artists.[17] A charming person and somewhat of a dandy who became a myth after his untimely demise in 1961, Selim was a passionate man but an intellectual artist. He loved music and played the guitar; he loved poetry, theater, and all other cultural productions and presented as a model citizen for the newly formed middle-class society of the period. Moreover, Selim was as pragmatic as he was romantic. He was an activist, a cultural agent who professed it to be his duty to exact change. Selim's wife, Lorna, writes that he "tried to define in artistic terms the emerging national aspirations of his country and in that his work undoubtedly reflects the feelings of the time. . . . He set out to prove that they

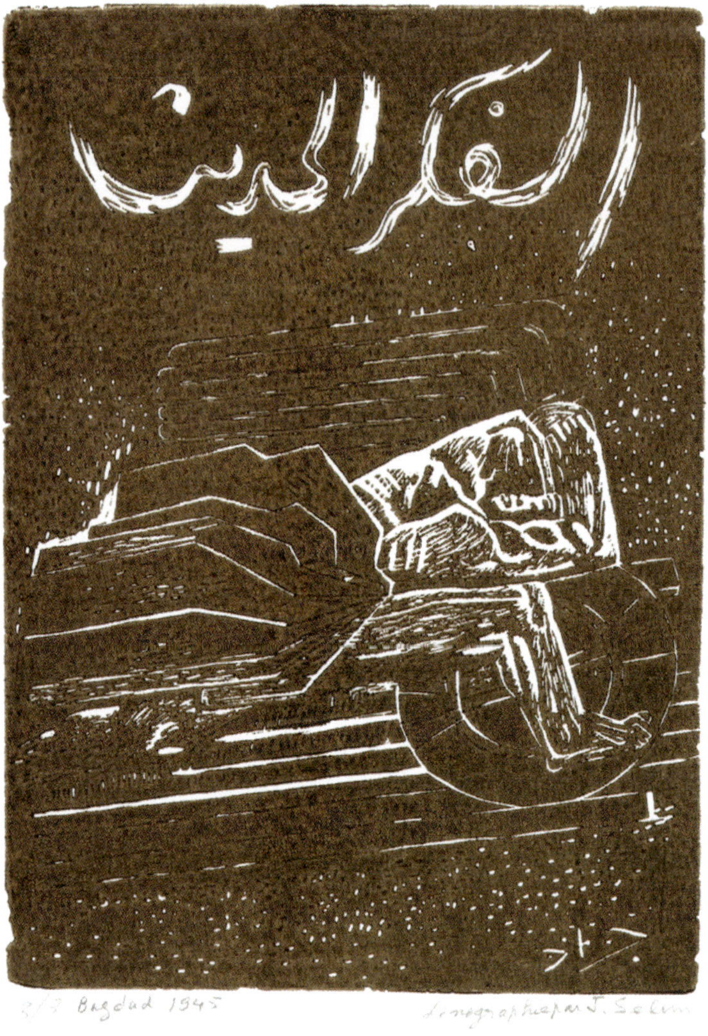

FIGURE 12.1. Jewad Selim, *Al-fikr al-hadith* (Modern thought), 1945. Linocut on paper, 28.8 × 20.3 cm. Collection: Mathaf: Arab Museum of Modern Art, Doha.

could be proud of their ancient heritage and did not need to feel inferior to anyone."[18] More than that, he wanted to visualize the national revolutionary discourse.

Constructing Iraqi Iconography

Selim's experimentation with form and content did not end until he died. He was continuously in search of possibilities, not answers or solutions. Among his key goals was creating a culture that understood art as well as appreciated it—an audience that would parallel and reflect the social and artistic progress of the period. Having spent time in three major European cities before the Second World War (which was also the post–First World War period) and after, he was exposed to the instability and anxiety felt in Europe. The Iraqi art historian Adel Kamel sees in this particular narrative Selim's return to his heritage in which he located his value in humanity.[19] Nonetheless, Selim's work fluctuated between the local—such as in his *Baghdadiat* series that articulated modern life in Baghdad by depicting scenes of street life and domestic intimacy (fig. 12.2)—and the global, with transnational themes like the political prisoner.[20] Essential in Selim's iconography is the visual rhythm created by the duality of the two basic shapes of circle and square or their components. Duality, a concept present in all of his work, conveys the global and eternal totality of the human experience, both as a method of compositional organization and as a psychological value. It also creates visual dynamism through contrast, be it in parities of the primordial elements of male and female, consciousness and unconsciousness, straight lines and curvilinear lines, or decorative and representational elements.

In naming his 1950s series *Baghdadiat*, Selim referenced both the Abbasid Baghdad School of painting and the contemporary city of Baghdad. *Baghdadiat* thus at once forges a historical continuity and expresses the contemporaneity of his manifestation. The series consisted of three groups of paintings: one having its source in folk life and tradition, the second in vernacular artifacts, and the third in children's innocence and joy.[21] *Baghdadiat*, however, presented a very provocative discourse in the context of the historical and political realities of the city ruled under emergency law by Nuri al-Said, and its people facing corruption, a shortage of food, and political oppression. Thus by negating reality, the *Baghdadiat* images ideologically resisted the status quo and projected a better, yet imagined, future that nevertheless seemingly romanticized an imaginary. Selim systematically intellectualized folk themes into high art, which sought to methodically de-exoticize and deorientalize representation.

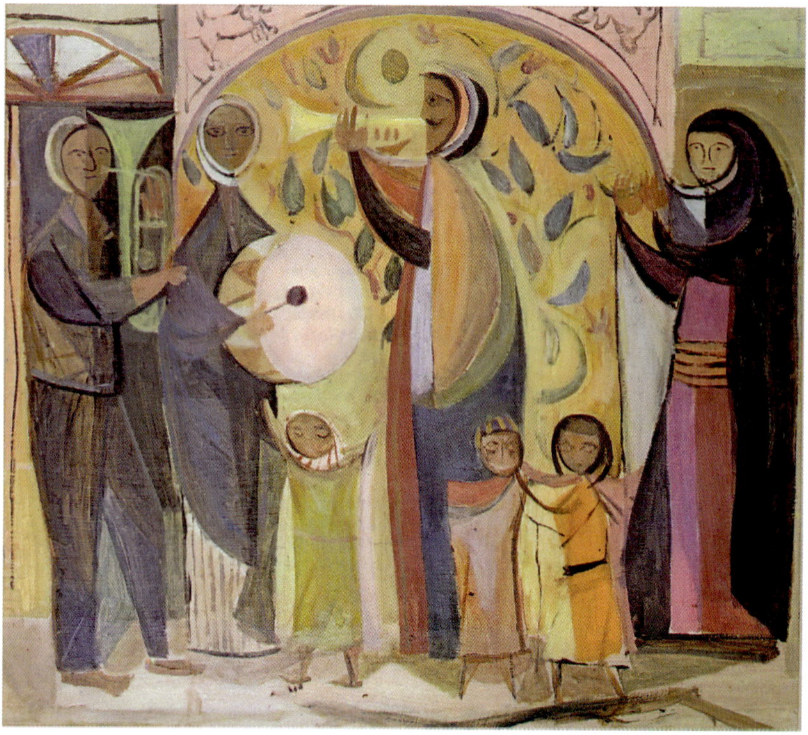

FIGURE 12.2. Jewad Selim, *Street Musicians*, 1956. Oil on canvas, dimensions unknown. Looted from the National Museum of Modern Art, Baghdad, in 2003.

Selim's paintings from the 1950s are also dubbed *hilaliat* (crescent-like). In these works, Selim abstracts both ideas and forms into gestural, stylized articulations in crescent shapes that further exemplify the tension of the concept of duality. The frontality of the faces of his figures and their big almond-shaped eyes, formed by two horizontally joined crescents, negotiate Sumerian traditions. The repetition of shapes, curvilinear and angular, creates a rhythm akin to that of Islamic arabesques. One can argue that his nonlinear approach to repetition implements an important aspect of Islamic aesthetics based on interaction and juxtaposition of diverse units. The duality of past and present is further presented at times by the tension between the two-dimensionality of the figures and the three-dimensionality of some of the objects in the scene. Moreover, while figures generally dominate Selim's compositions, emphasizing the centrality of humanity in his work, they are equally transformed into objects of aesthetics. For example, the figures in *Children Playing* are abstracted and ornamented into linear patterns.

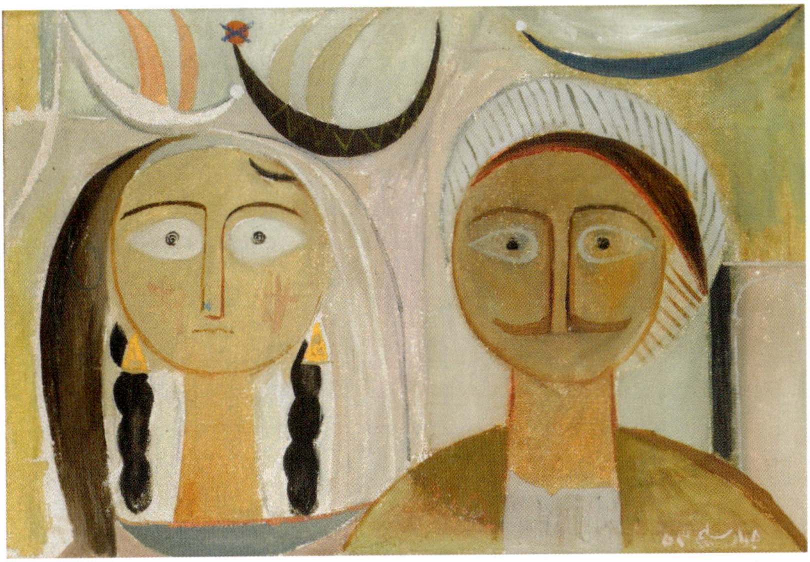

FIGURE 12.3. Jewad Selim, *Young Man and Wife*, 1953. Oil on canvas, 51 × 76 cm. Private collection.

The 1953 painting *Young Man and Wife* (also known as *A Farmer and His Wife* and *A Groom and His Bride*), considered by Al Said to be one of Selim's most important works, exemplifies Selim's growing interest in ancient Iraqi heritage reinterpreted in contemporary settings (fig. 12.3).[22] The painting is a closeup portrait of a man and a woman, who, it has been argued, recall the subjects of Sumerian sculptures like *Abu and His Wife*. Most notable are the couple's Sumerian-like eyes and attires referencing traditional Baghdadi dress of the 1950s. Moving away from earlier representations of marginalized and working classes, Selim stylistically references the Baghdad School of painting, drawing on the work of Yahya al-Wasiti's thirteenth-century illustrations for the *Maqamat al-Hariri*.[23]

A recurrent concept in Selim's work, also seen in the work of other artists of the time, is motherhood. The symbolism embodied by motherhood creates a link between the past, present, and future. It is a direct reference to the ancient concept of fertility as embodied by various visual manifestations of goddesses and the relationship with the land, on one hand, and by modern ideas of nationalism and motherland, on the other. It signifies homeland and cultural roots. In his 1954 sculpture *Mother and Child*, Selim furthers his negotiation of *hilaliat* within the theme of motherhood (fig. 12.4). Al Said argues that the expression of the concept of motherhood in Selim's work transcends the subject matter to the being of the work itself. This is expressed in the images of the crescent and circle, in reference to ancient symbolism: the circle (feminine), such as the sun, the moon, or a womb, as a symbol of the universe and the square (masculine) as a symbol of a house.[24] In Selim's work, thus, motherhood takes the form of a circle or crescent.

As an artist, Selim lived the tension between being a painter and a sculptor. He eventually relinquished painting in favor of sculpture. Selim's ideas, exploration, and experience culminated in his last masterpiece, which became a landmark of and for Baghdad, the Nasb al-Hurriyah (Monument of Freedom) in al-Tahrir (Liberation) Square, commissioned by the new Iraqi military regime in 1959 to celebrate the revolution of 1958 (fig. 12.5).[25] The largest monument to be built in Iraq in 2,500 years, it was the first modern outdoor sculpture to be designed and constructed by an Iraqi artist. The bas-relief mural in bronze (50 × 8 m) was a collaboration between Selim and the Iraqi architect Rifat Chadirji, who was appointed by the new government to design and execute the project. Its twenty-five connected figures, divided among fourteen bronze units, visually narrate the revolution and the events that surrounded it from the perspective of the people and without any direct references to the politics of its commission. Equally the units resemble the letters of an Arabic verse in their movement and flow. Here Selim succeeded in combining the linear quality of Arabic characters and the stylized forms of the Sumerians and Babylonians with modern styles. The narrative was organized into several interconnected groups, expressing injustice, resistance, solidarity, hope, and ambition, and portrayed in a style of symbolic realism. As a humanistic composition, it juxtaposed several familiar concepts in Selim's oeuvre: eternal calamity, motherhood, and fertility. The project caused him tremendous stress, and Selim died before it was completed.[26]

In his work Selim did not simply adapt modern abstraction to Islamic or ancient representations. Rather, he succeeded in negotiating innovative visual iconography that addressed and theorized the principles of abstraction, ornamentation, mythology, and symbolism throughout the history of art but was also capable of expressing his contemporary self and realities. His discourse was confrontational, both national and modern, forcing his public to engage with the new traditions he and other contemporary artists were creating. His work forced his contemporaries to find renewal within historical roots. This was specifically why the legacy of Jewad Selim became much larger than his short life and career. Other artists contributed to the search and change in direction along similar principles. Madiha Umar's experimentation with Arabic letters became the basis for a theory of Arab identity art throughout the Arab world. She introduced examples of the contextualization of the Arabic letter in Iraqi

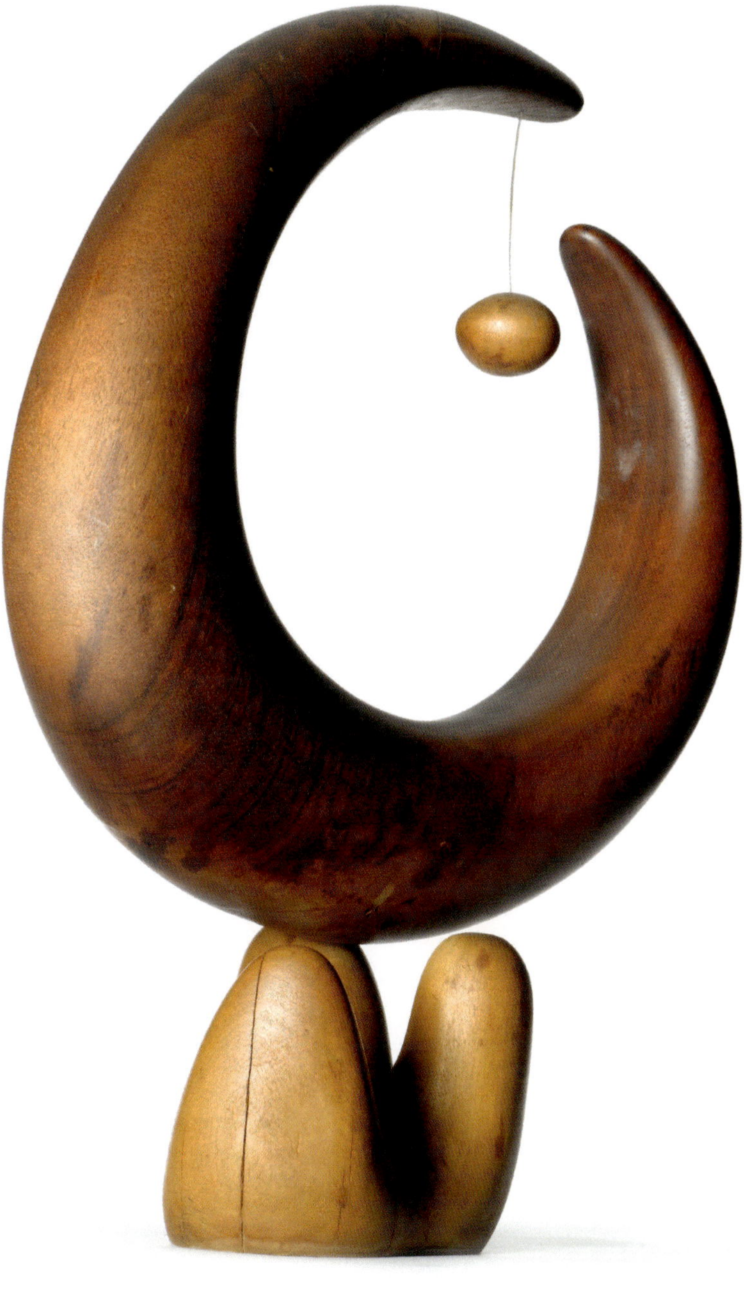

FIGURE 12.4. Jewad Selim, *Mother and Child*, 1954. Fruitwood and mixed media, 43 × 30 × 14 cm. Private collection.

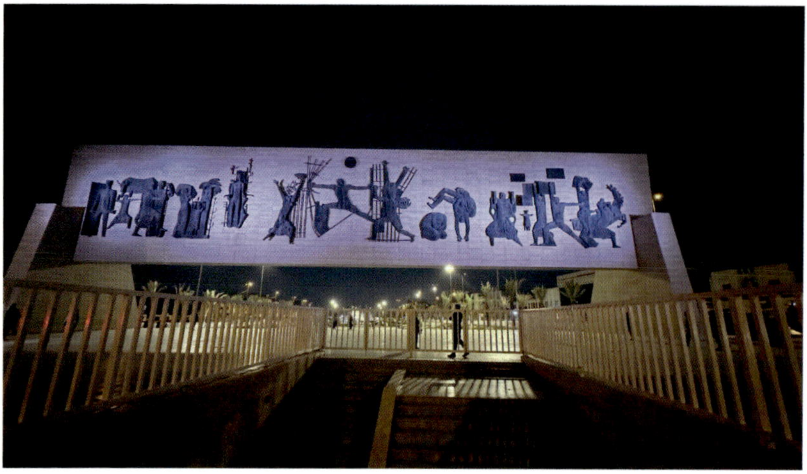

FIGURE 12.5. Jewad Selim, Nasb al-Hurriyah (Monument of Freedom), al-Tahrir Square, Baghdad, 1959–62. Concrete, marble, and bronze, 50 × 10 m. Photograph by the author.

modern art. Umar has been credited with the initiation of the use of the Arabic letter in art through a number of works she started in 1944 and is thus considered a precursor to *horofiyah*, the style of visual manipulations of Arabic letters in visual art that was widely employed in the second half of the twentieth century and became a long-lasting trend. Another example is Ismail Al-Shaikely. One of the founders of the al-Ruwwad group, upon his return from France in 1952 he faced the same dilemma of attaining a balance between an individualism that incorporated an understanding of European styles and a nationalism that shared Arab intellectual, social, and political concerns.

Legacy and Projection

Ismail Al-Shaikely cites two specific exhibitions he considered important during that period, one of Indian art, in 1948, and the other of Mexican art, in 1950.[27] He argued that their emphasis on national being had a direct impact on Iraqi artists. Moreover, these exhibitions seem to have offered an alternative to the styles and subjects that the Iraqi artists studied in Europe. The exhibitions inspired them to reevaluate the perceived universality of European modern art. They saw European art as the product of change in European societies, based on events directly related to specific developments—industrial, intellectual, and political—that in turn facilitated Europe's hegemony over Third World countries. This reevaluation and thus contextualization of modernism within local histories was the motivation for Iraqi artists to create a national art that was predicated on visual correspondence to Iraq's geography, environment, and intellectual history.

The legacy of the Baghdad Group for Modern Art is specifically in negotiating Iraq's visual heritage in a new national iconography grounded in the rhetoric of national history. The group reached a broad audience, which they saw as a means of democratizing visual production and of ensuring the dissemination of a visual character that was identifiably Iraqi by reconnecting with the daily life of citizens and urban life rather than focusing only on peasants. The Ministry of Culture and Communications, formed after the 1958 revolution, through its patronage and support, also played a role in bridging the gap between artists and the people. In Selim's speech at the opening of the Baghdad Group for Modern Art's first exhibition, in 1951, he stated that a journalist of his acquaintance had called him and his colleagues "enemies of the people." Selim said that while he forgave him, he knew that at least 97 percent of people would no doubt oppose what members of the group were trying to express and the modern styles in which they did it. The 1951 exhibition in effect launched a series of debates among the artists themselves that, through successive exhibitions, centered on their objectives. The discussions were taken up by students as well, and related articles frequently appeared in Iraqi newspapers.

Jabra Ibrahim Jabra (1919–94), Iraq's preeminent art critic (and poet, novelist, and artist), wrote that "from the beginnings of the 1950s, Iraqi art achieved a unique status in a very challenging field."[28] While acknowledging the numerous creative directions in which European art was continuously heading and the strong relationship between its formal and technological developments, Jabra placed Iraqi art on the same level as that of any developed country on the basis of the essential relations between an individual and their creativity and the materiality of the artwork. Jabra also noted that, aside from providing young artists with art scholarships to study abroad, Iraq as a state officially began to acknowledge and value its artists during the 1950s. The state organized the first comprehensive exhibition of Iraqi art at al-Mansur Club in February 1956. Jabra argued that the sweeping success of the exhibition, during which the government gave artists awards for excellence, motivated the establishment of the Association of Iraqi Artists. One could clearly see the connection between the activities of the first two groups of artists that led to this recognition, but more specifically that of the Baghdad Group for Modern Art.

Members of the Baghdad Group for Modern Art understood that art is capable of facilitating and shaping new spaces within which new identities could be negotiated and contested and new and renewed visual cultural icons formed. The 1958 revolution that overthrew the monarchy and formed the Republic of Iraq instigated a pronounced turn in the city's energy. Selim interpreted this new vigor as an "explosive continuation" of the past insofar as it represented an art historical persistence charged with creative experiments. And this is something he tried to visualize in his best-known work and finale, the Monument of Freedom. Ultimately, the experiments by these early twentieth-century Iraqi artists resulted in a visualization of a modern national culture that even today remains the basis of all new visualizations of Iraq. Perhaps more significant, their work aimed at a true globalization that would encompass self and other, thus shattering the binary observed in the West without losing local and national distinctions.

NOTES

Epigraph: Selim, "Renewal of Art (1951)," 154. This text is a translation of Jewad Selim's inauguration speech for the Baghdad Group for Modern Art, delivered at its first exhibition, in 1951, and subsequently published in the newspaper *Sada Al-Ahali*. See Jewad Salīm, "Tajdīd al-Fann," in Jabra, *Jawad Salim wa-nusb al-hurriyyah*, 189–94.

1. Al Said, *Jewad Selim*, 9. Unless otherwise noted, all translations are by the author.

2. Three focal and extremely active groups, each centered around a noted artist, dominated the scene. Prior to these groups, the Friends of Art Society was established in 1941, with a membership that included many of Iraq's leading artists. They organized three exhibitions, in 1941, 1943, and 1946. Noted artist Abdul Qadir al-Rassam, who was one of Iraq's first art teachers, was an honorary member of the group. They also organized a number of cultural lectures.

3. On December 22, 1950, the Société Primitive organized its first annual exhibition in Khalid al-Qassab's family house and adopted a new name in Arabic, al-Ruwwad, "Researchers on the Move" (widely translated as "The Pioneers"). Their second exhibition took place in the Costumes Museum in 1952 and included sculptural works as well. In response to the exhibition, the United Nations Educational, Scientific, and Cultural Organization (UNESCO) wrote the group a letter describing them as the most influential art group in Iraq and invited them to participate in the Venice Biennale. Arguably, the success of the exhibition helped the formation of other art groups.

4. The third influential group of the period was the Impressionists group (most of whom actually experimented with postimpressionist and cubist styles), formed in 1954 by Hafidh al-Droubi. The three groups together comprised about fifty painters and sculptors who, while sometimes acting collectively, remained very active individually. Art groups multiplied during the 1960s.

5. To Al Said, what distinguished Arab and Iraqi artists was their persistence in the face of what he perceived as the abyss of international/global art through mastering their work as global artists and being in control of all of their personal and global histories. See "Interview with Shakir Hassan Al Said."

6. The role of Polish artists in the progress of Iraqi modern art may have been exaggerated in various recollections and with time simplified into a direct influence. This is partly caused by the repetition of the story and partly relies on parts of Selim's diary, selectively published by Jabra Ibrahim Jabra. New research and archival material tell a different story, in which Polish artists are not as prominent.

7. Jewad Selim, diary entry, July 23, 1943, in Jabra, *Al-rihla al-thaminah*, 159–60.

8. Al-Roabie, "Interview with Ismail Al-Shaikhly," 175. Al-Shaikhly explained, "During Matuchak's visit to Faiq Hassan's class, he sketched the next door café for 4 hours during which the students watched in amazement."

9. Munif, "In His Own Words."

10. Al-Roabie, "Jewad Selim and the Founding of the Baghdad Group." The four other members were Ali al-Shaalan, Khalil al-Ward, Qahtan Awni, and Tareq Madhloom. Later Faraj Abo and Mohammed al-Husaini joined the group, followed soon after by other key artists in the development of modern art in Iraq, including Miran al-Saadi, Ghalib Nahi, and Bougous Bablanian, who left the group in 1965.

11. The verb *istilham* is derived from *ilham*, or inspiration; *ilham* is derived from the root *lahm*: to inspire, to pray.

12. Al Said, *Hiwar al-fan al-tashkili*, 49–50.

13. Hamoudi, *Al-fikr al-hadith*, 4 .

14. Hamoudi, *Al-fikr al-hadith*, 4.

15. Jewad Salīm, "Tajdīd al-Fann," in Jabra, *Jawad Salim wa-nusb al-hurriyyah*, n.p. Nine artists participated in the first exhibition of the Baghdad Group for Modern Art: Jewad Selim with eight paintings, Shakir Hassan Al Said with twenty-four paintings, Lorna Selim with seven paintings, Mohammed Housni with fourteen paintings, Qahtan Awni with three paintings, Nazar Ali Jawdat with two drawings, Richard Ghanada with four paintings, Mahmoud Sabri with eleven paintings, and Jabra Ibrahim Jabra with six paintings.

16. For English translations of Selim's inaugural speech and the manifesto of the Baghdad Group for Modern Art, see Selim, "The Renewal of Art (1951)," and Baghdad Group for Modern Art, "Manifesto (1951), both in Lenssen, Rogers, and Shabout, *Modern Art in the Arab World.*

17. His father was one of the first teachers of art in Iraq. His brother Suad, brother Nizar, and sister Neziha were artists.

18. Al-Khamis, "Lorna Selim Remembers," 43.

19. Kamel, *Al-harakah al-tashkiliyah fi al-Iraq*, 27.

20. Selim's *Political Prisoner* sculpture was one of the eighty-six works awarded prizes in the worldwide sculpture competition called the Unknown Political Prisoner, organized by the Institute of Contemporary Arts in London in 1952. There were 3,500 entries from fifty-seven countries. Reg Butler won first prize; second was shared by four artists, including Barbara Hepworth, Antoine Pevsner, and Naum Gabo. One hundred and fifty works were exhibited.

21. Bahnassi, *Ruwwad al-fan*, 126.

22. Al Said, *Jewad Selim*, 123.

23. The Abbasid painter Yahya al-Wasiti lived in Baghdad around the twelfth to thirteenth century. The most famous of his works are his celebrated illustrations for the

1237 book *Maqamat al-Hariri* (al-Hariri's Assemblies), a series of anecdotes of social satire written by al-Hariri, the head of the police department in the city of Basra, Iraq.

24. Sumerian fertility symbolism was connected to the agricultural cycle's dependency on the lunar calendar. See Al Said, *Fusul min tarikh*, 211.

25. The monument is one of the very few that survived the destruction following the 2003 invasion. On January 23, 2004, the interim minister of culture, Mufid al-Jazairi, initiated a renovation-and-restoration operation.

26. The monument was analyzed by many Iraqi critics at the time, most notably by Jabra and Al Said. For a detailed reading of the iconography, see Bahrani, "Revolutionary Monument."

27. There are references to these exhibitions in the writings of Iraqi artists of the period but unfortunately no specific information. The interest in Indian art, however, is mentioned on several occasions. Khalid al-Qassab writes about a specific engagement following one of al-Ruwwad's exhibitions, which coincided with the opening of the All India Art Exhibition (I assume the one in London in 1948 at the Royal Academy), when the group was invited to the Indian Embassy in Baghdad and shown a film about the Indian artist Jamini Roy (1887–1972). Al-Qassab remarked that it was the first time they had learned about India directly, without European mediation. Muzaffar, *Al-Qassab*, 79.

28. Jabra, quoted in Al Said, *Fusul min tarikh*, 100. A poet, novelist, translator, and literary critic, Jabra was of Palestinian origin and settled in Iraq after 1948.

13

Decolonization and Calligraphic Abstraction

IFTIKHAR DADI

Postwar decolonization engendered the rise of modernist calligraphic abstraction in the Middle East, North Africa, and South Asia (the MENASA region). The challenges that decolonization posed for culture in Asian and African nations formerly under direct or indirect British rule were especially acute in the decades since the mid-1950s.[1] A profound and intensive search for new artistic languages began at that time, which would seek to recover expressivity that had been repressed under colonialism but that would also actively produce a new modern culture. The demands placed on cultural production were highly overdetermined: the new culture was to be individuated, yet collective; it was to be completely modern in the sense of being in dialogue with artistic production in the industrialized world, yet it was also mandated to represent local histories and lived practices that were hitherto suppressed.

From the mid-1950s, artists from North Africa, the Middle East, and South Asia contributed to a movement that transformed aspects of Arabic calligraphy into modern art—mostly without direct knowledge of one another's work.[2] Not only were earlier attitudes about classical Arabic calligraphy decisively modified, but modern Western genres such as academic realism in portraiture, landscape, and still life were also reshaped by a renewed concern with the abstract and expressive possibilities of the Arabic script, which was now imbued with figuration and abstraction to a degree that resisted a straightforward literal or narrative meaning.[3] Their groundbreaking artistic projects can be understood in a variety of ways: as individual and subjective expressions, as enacting a dialogue with nationalism, and as a critical engagement with metropolitan modernism and cosmopolitanism. Artists whose work can be understood with reference to "calligraphic abstraction" include the Iranians Charles Hossein Zenderoudi (b. 1937) and Parviz Tanavoli (b. 1937); the Iraqi artist Shakir Hassan Al Said (1925–2004); the Pakistani artists Hanif Ramay (1930–2006), Sadequain (1930–87), and Anwar Jalal Shemza (1928–85); and the Sudanese artist Ibrahim El-Salahi (b. 1930).[4]

Zenderoudi worked out these possibilities in his paintings of the late 1950s, inspired by Shi'ite talismanic designs and popular posters and shrines. He was one of the founders of an Iranian artistic approach to calligraphy that was named Saqqa Khaneh in 1962. The term refers to public places for drinking water and has populist associations with the martyrdom of Shi'ites at the battle of Karbala in 680, in which they were deliberately deprived of water.[5] For modernist Arab artists, the word *hurufiyyah* (from the Arabic *harf*, meaning "letter"), which already carried an intellectual, esoteric, and Sufi charge, was now invested with a new connotation of formal abstraction—in distinction to the word *khattat*, which denoted the traditional calligrapher.[6] The Iraqi theorist and artist Al Said was part of a group that discarded mimetic representation in favor of a "purer" calligraphic form. Al Said was a key participant and theorist in the movement that mounted the One Dimension Group exhibition, held in Baghdad in 1971.[7] This important exhibition also included the US-based Syro-Iraqi artist Madiha Umar, who was a pioneer in developing abstract calligraphic paintings from as early as 1945 and held one of the first exhibitions of modern Arabic calligraphic works at the Georgetown Public Library in the United States in 1949.[8] Working in Pakistan, Hanif Ramay and Sadequain explored calligraphy in relation to modernist abstraction. Sadequain transformed calligraphy into figuration in a painterly manner in the late 1950s,

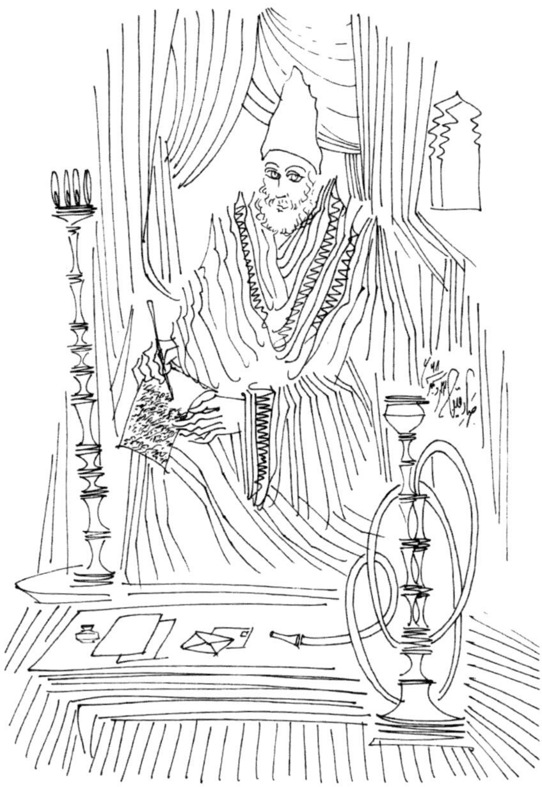

FIGURE 13.1. Sadequain, portrait of the Persian and Urdu poet Ghalib, from Sadequain, *Ghalib* (Karachi: Elite Publishers Limited, 1969), n.p.

but his work became more linear and graphic by the mid-1960s, leading him to visually explore the poetic subjectivity of the Indo-Persian cultural milieu that characterizes South Asian Muslim culture (fig. 13.1).[9] And during the late 1950s and early 1960s in Sudan, El-Salahi created a dialogue between calligraphy and figuration that introduced West African motifs to his multifaceted response to the heterogeneity of the linguistic, religious, and cultural landscape of the region; his paintings also acknowledged the persistent Islamic influences in Africa.[10]

Artists from these regions traveled to Europe to study there or were exposed by print to modernism associated with the School of Paris. For mid-twentieth-century non-Western artists, the aftermath of Pablo Picasso's cubism, Wilfredo Lam's surrealist synthesis of cubism with Africana religions in Cuba during the 1940s, and such mid-twentieth-century movements as lettrism, art brut, and art informel were far more compelling modalities than older perspectival and realist European academic styles.[11] A genealogy of European-inflected training was a common factor for many artists. For example, Zenderoudi studied in Tehran in the late 1950s with teachers who had trained in Paris and Italy, and he has resided primarily in France since 1961.[12] Al Said, who visited Paris on a scholarship in 1956, was a member of a group of Iraqi impressionist painters who maintained extensive contact with Western Europe during the 1950s.[13] Sadequain was self-taught, but after he won a prize at the Biennale de Paris in 1961, he spent the next seven years working mostly in Paris.[14] El-Salahi trained in London from 1954 to 1957 and then traveled extensively during the 1960s in West Africa, Europe, and Mexico and held extended fellowships in the United States. The significance of the work of these artists, however, is by no means reducible to European and American prototypes.

This growing awareness of national independence and sovereignty created a demand for a new aesthetic of decolonization, one that would remain in dialogue with metropolitan developments but would also account for regional and nationalist specificities. Artists attempted to find visual languages adequate to the aspirations of decolonization by creating work that appeared to fulfill the expectations of a "national art"; hence, it is no surprise that this intensive and fertile period of artistic creativity has been primarily understood as a nationalist undertaking. Indeed, one can find numerous studies in which the artistic and aesthetic developments during this period are understood as "national" ventures. Clearly the stakes were very high, as artists were expected to do nothing less than to develop a new cultural language that would exploit the opening provided by decolonization—understood at the time as an opportunity to enact a truly world-historical shift in politics and culture—but these demands could not be reconciled easily.

The artists who grappled with these challenges in their sweeping, highly charged careers have become national legends. The importance of the national framework remains highly significant in the specific context of calligraphic abstraction. Indeed, since the beginning of his career in 1955 and certainly after his return from Paris in 1968, Sadequain enacted the persona of the supreme Pakistani national artist.[15] In Sudan, El-Salahi is regarded as one of the founders of the Khartoum School of Art and through his teaching and artwork became a highly influential and dynamic exemplar for successive generations of Sudanese and African artists. In Iran, Zenderoudi's paintings were highlighted in a number of state-sponsored exhibitions, including numerous Tehran Biennials during the 1960s, and in a 2001 retrospective at the Tehran Museum of Contemporary Art.[16] Since 1958, the Iraqi government has been a major patron of the arts, sponsoring numerous public works, planning exhibitions of modern art within Iraq and in international venues, and encouraging scholarship and publications on ancient, classical Arab, and modern Iraqi art and culture.[17]

The national framework is thus fundamental in situating these artists as eminent cultural personae who each developed schools of national artistic practice. However, the link between national art and the diaspora also needs to be considered. It is in the diaspora that many such artists encountered the range and strength of Western artistic practices firsthand. They were able to visit the great Western museums, filled with canonical works, which many had previously seen only in magazine reproductions. It is in the diaspora that many of these artists met with other Western and non-Western artists, learning about one another's methods and concerns. Moreover, artists frequently sought institutional support to develop their careers in the diaspora, as such support was not as well established in their own countries. Comparatively speaking, the governments of Iran and Iraq were able to provide better opportunities for artists during the period from the late 1950s to the late 1970s. Mostly, national support meant showing in a limited number of galleries and in private collections, participating in a few official exhibitions and public art projects, and on occasion traveling for the purpose of providing national representation in international fairs.

I will now focus more closely on two artists: Ibrahim El-Salahi (b. 1930) and Anwar Jalal Shemza (1928–85). Coming from widely separated geographic regions that bookend the Middle East (Sudan and Pakistan), their common training and their subsequent aesthetic developments are insightful in understanding the scope of calligraphic abstraction across the MENASA region. Both artists also spent an important part of their career in diaspora, which is instructive in understanding the transnational implications of calligraphic abstraction. Both artists studied in London at the Slade School of Fine Art during the 1950s, and both had become painfully aware of the marginal status accorded to Islamic art in the public lectures delivered by the celebrated art historian Ernst Gombrich.[18]

Ibrahim El-Salahi

El-Salahi's painting *The Last Sound* (1964), executed on a square canvas with a carefully limited palette of grays and earth tones, is organized around a central circular dynamic core (fig. 13.2). Radiant lines thrust outward from a barely perceptible African mask–like form. Celestial bodies, elements of calligraphic geometric and animate shapes, and actual palimpsest-like Arabic calligraphic prayers surround the central form, creating a metaphoric universe in which the last sound is echoed. The title of the work refers to the Islamic practice of reciting

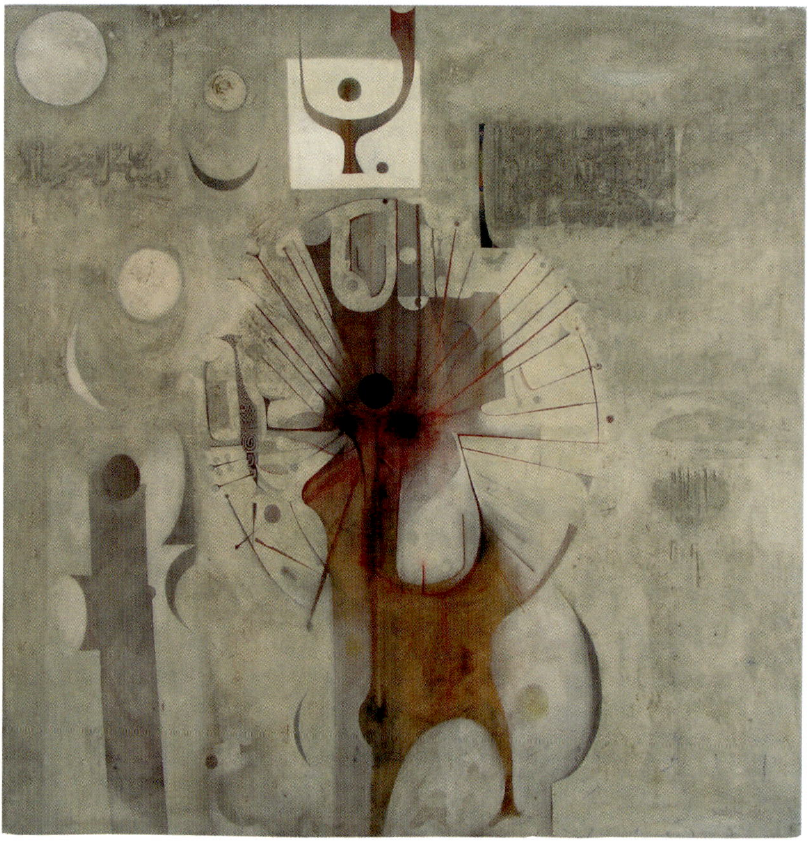

FIGURE 13.2. Ibrahim El-Salahi, *The Last Sound*, 1964. Oil on canvas, 121.6 × 121.6 cm. Collection: Barjeel Art Foundation, Sharjah.

prayers for the dead and dying. In the work, El-Salahi renders the soul's passage from the corporeal to the celestial as it travels toward heavenly forms inhabiting the universe and beyond. *The Last Sound* is, however, not a narrative or realist work but a manifestly modernist one, in which the terrifying event is metaphorized in a dynamic formal composition. Here, the abstraction of African sculptural forms and calligraphy serves to universalize the event—no realist or academic visual language could obviously be adequate to the scope of the subject. The relation El-Salahi creates between African abstract forms and Arabic calligraphy that itself refers to Islamic discursive textuality invokes the gravitas of its theme.

The assured handling of the visual language with which *The Last Sound* is painted might lead one to imagine that El-Salahi is working from an aesthetic grammar already in place, perhaps developed much earlier. But it was only very recently that El-Salahi himself had articulated the linkage between Arabic calligraphic and African sculptural forms. *The Last Sound* was painted during the middle of an intense period of modernist experimental effort carried out by the artist between 1958 and the late 1960s. Born in Sudan, El-Salahi was formally trained as an artist in Khartoum, then studied at the Slade from 1954 to 1957, and subsequently returned to Khartoum. It is the working out of his concerns by praxis and the overthrowing of his academic training at the Slade that mark El-Salahi's intellectual concerns during that era. El-Salahi's rejection of the academic training he had received in England was prompted by his awareness, when he returned to Sudan, of his training's inadequacy and irrelevance to the role that art ought to play in postcolonial Sudan. Reflecting on the lack of interest among the Sudanese for an exhibition of his work in Khartoum during the late 1950s, El-Salahi states:

> I understand that every artist has a message to deliver in his or her society. . . . By nature, to start with, one has to address one's *Self*, the satisfaction of which is initial and crucial in the creative process. Secondly, one addresses *Others* in one's own society and culture from which one has borrowed and absorbed a great deal that is to be repaid in kind. And thirdly, last but not least, one ultimately does address All, meaning humanity and human society at large.[19]

By the late 1950s and the early 1960s, academic painting's failure to break out of the narrow elite salon and gallery exhibition circuit of Khartoum and engage with a more democratic and vernacular visual culture impelled El-Salahi toward a radical aesthetic shift. As he describes it, this transformation demanded breaking open the Arabic letter and exploring the new aesthetic universe that emerged from the fragments and the interstices. Fracturing the Arabic letter also broke the classical calligraphic text as a repository of received meaning. This is evident in a series of paintings whose very title, *They Always Appear* (1964–65), signifies the emergence of figural forms among the spaces defined by the figure-ground relationship of abstracted calligraphic shapes (figs. 13.3 and 13.4). The artist recalls:

> I limited my color scheme to somber tones. . . . In the next step I wrote letters and words that did not mean a thing. Then came a time when I felt I had to break down the bone of the letter, observing the space within a letter and the space between a letter and the other on the line. I wanted to see what was there and find out their basic components and origins.

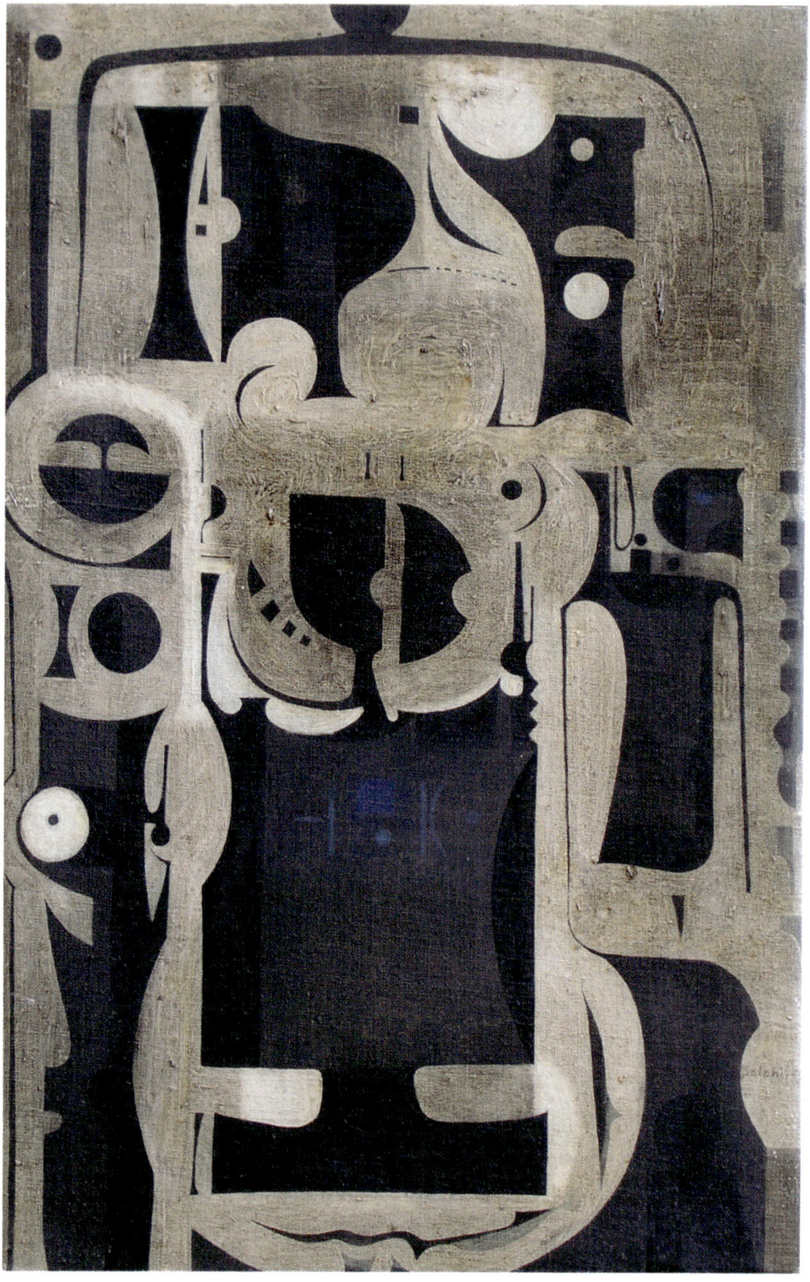

FIGURE 13.3. Ibrahim El-Salahi, from the series *They Always Appear*, 1964–65. Oil on canvas, 45.8 × 30.5 cm.

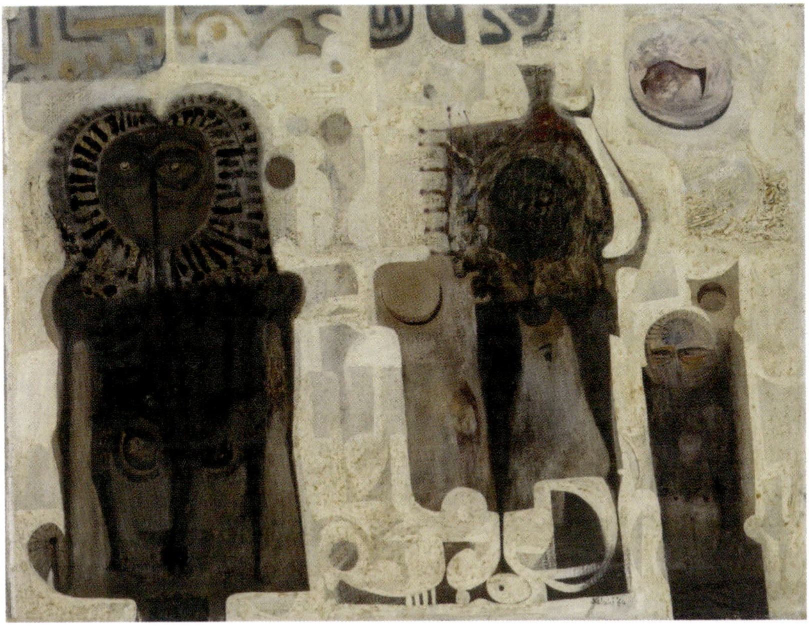

FIGURE 13.4. Ibrahim El-Salahi, from the series *They Always Appear*, 1964–65. Oil on canvas, 46 × 61 cm.

> There the Pandora's box opened up wide before my eyes. . . . In place of those broken-up letters I discovered animal and plant forms, sounds, human images, and what looked like skeletons with masked faces.[20]

El-Salahi's intellectual formation further broadened during his travels in the United States in the early and mid-1960s, when he had a chance to meet with artists, jazz musicians, political activists, and Black intellectuals. He also traveled to Mexico to meet with artists there and to China to study its artistic pedagogy. As the example of Négritude, the francophone Black cultural movement that emerged in the 1930s, shows, in an important sense, the experience of diaspora engendered transnational aesthetic movements as well as new affiliations of identity and community.[21] El-Salahi also facilitated the imagining of a broader Africanist aesthetic, not least by participating in exhibitions in Nigeria in 1961 and in Senegal in 1966.[22] El-Salahi's experiments thus resulted in an abstraction that was regional, yet modernist, and that referred to a vast ensemble of iconic and textual material, traversing the Arabic-Islamic discursive tradition and West African iconography. While his contribution is distinctive in developing an aesthetic of decolonization for Sudan and much of Africa—situated among Islamic textuality, African plastic forms, and transnational modernism—it can be usefully compared to other modernist artists from the Islamic world who were engaged with similar cultural problems in the wake of decolonization from the mid-twentieth century onward.

Anwar Jalal Shemza

An important modernist in his own right, Shemza is representative of a generation of artists who emerged in the wake of the decolonization of Asia and Africa. The partition of South Asia marked Shemza's formation in 1947, and his work grapples also with issues of belonging in the diaspora, as he lived in the UK from the mid-1950s till his death in 1985. Based on a study of Shemza's writings and a significant part of his artistic oeuvre, this chapter traces the development of the artist's career with reference to calligraphic abstraction. Born in Simla in 1928 to a Kashmiri and Punjabi family who, at the time, owned a carpet and military embroidery business in Ludhiana, Punjab, Shemza attended high school in Lahore. After a year in university studying philosophy, Persian, and Arabic, he convinced his father of the seriousness of his artistic vocation and joined the Mayo School of Art in 1944, where the Bengal School aesthetic still reigned.[23] Upon graduating in 1947, he set up a commercial design studio in Simla. The beginning of his career coincided with the bloody trauma of the partition in the same year, dividing colonial India into the postcolonial states of India and Pakistan. Many of Shemza's family members in Ludhiana were killed during the partition, a memory that continued to haunt him throughout his life. Shemza taught at various schools and colleges in Lahore until 1956, when he left to study at the Slade School of Fine Art in London.[24] His interest in art education remained of abiding concern throughout his life.

From the late 1940s through the mid-1950s, Shemza was associated with the Urdu literary intelligentsia and contributed to this sphere through his writings and organizational work. The writer Zulfiqar Tabish has noted that during this period, literature, poetry, and especially fictional writing dominated Lahore's intellectual atmosphere.[25] Even while working on his paintings Shemza actively participated in this literary sphere; he published several novels in Urdu, edited the journal *Ehsas* for three years, wrote and performed a number of radio plays, and contributed poetry to various publications under pseudonyms. At that time, competing stylistic and ideological groups—including the secularist and non-nationalist Progressive Writers, those associated with the Halqa-i Arbab-i Zauq (Circle of Aesthetes), and others who were promulgating a right-wing Pakistani ideology—were engaged in lively and fractious

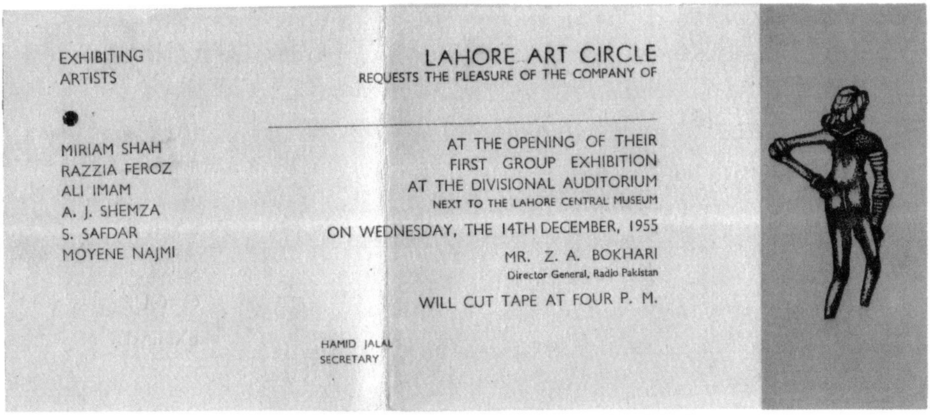

EXHIBITING
ARTISTS

MIRIAM SHAH
RAZZIA FEROZ
ALI IMAM
A. J. SHEMZA
S. SAFDAR
MOYENE NAJMI

LAHORE ART CIRCLE
REQUESTS THE PLEASURE OF THE COMPANY OF

AT THE OPENING OF THEIR
FIRST GROUP EXHIBITION
AT THE DIVISIONAL AUDITORIUM
NEXT TO THE LAHORE CENTRAL MUSEUM
ON WEDNESDAY, THE 14TH DECEMBER, 1955
MR. Z. A. BOKHARI
Director General, Radio Pakistan
WILL CUT TAPE AT FOUR P. M.

HAMID JALAL
SECRETARY

FIGURE 13.5. Invitation card for the Lahore Art Circle's first group exhibition, Divisional Auditorium, Lahore, 1955.

debates in meetings and journals.[26] Much of this debate continued shifting the contours of the ongoing battle between progressivism (*taraqqi pasand*), equated with "art for life's sake," and literary modernism (*jadidiyat*), termed "art for art's sake."[27] The move toward painterly modernism (*tajridi*) needs to be situated accordingly as an affirmation of its metaphoric and allegorical potentialities in offering deeper insights into the self and society than the kind of reductive realism the progressives had increasingly embraced from the late 1930s.

Shemza was a founder of the Lahore Art Circle, a group of young artists who aspired toward modernism and abstraction during the early and mid-1950s (fig. 13.5). Artist Shakir Ali's (1914–75) return to the Lahore art scene in 1952 from Europe also decisively contributed to the gathering movement toward modernism. And in 1953, a group of young writers and modern artists began issuing a short-lived journal, *Khayal*, which was intended to address issues faced by modernist thinkers. Their discussions included the relevance for contemporary culture of the modernism of writers such as T. S. Eliot, Ezra Pound, and Charles Baudelaire; the painterly modernism of Paul Cézanne, Henri Matisse, Paul Klee, and Wassily Kandinsky; and the significance of Kabir, Mirabai, and numerous historical Muslim thinkers.[28] Shemza's exposure to these debates in his later career may be seen in his response to the writings of Rainer Maria Rilke and the art of Klee, in his embrace of modernism as praxis in a highly disciplined and rigorous fashion, and most significant, in the role that textuality and lettrism plays in the construction of history and memory in his works.

Part of a generation of artists and intellectuals from nations that had recently attained independence from the British Empire, Shemza moved to the UK to study at the Slade from 1956 until 1960. Stuart Hall has identified postwar British diaspora artists as arriving in "three distinct 'waves.'" The first wave consisted of artists such as Frank Bowling, Avinash Chandra, Li Yuan-Chia, Uzo Egonu, Donald Locke, David Medalla, Ahmed Parvez, Francis Newton Souza, Aubrey Williams, and Shemza. Hall remarks: "The first generation was born in the 1920s and 1930s in the far-flung corners of the British Empire. They came to Britain, as the last 'colonials,' in the 1950s and 1960s . . . to fulfil their ambitions to become practicing artists."[29] Noting that the concerns of the second wave differ from the first (in moving beyond modernism and confronting the question of race in the UK), Hall characterizes the first-wave artists as seeing themselves as practitioners in an egalitarian ethos of transnational modernism:

> One immediate contrast between these two "waves" lies in their attitude to Modernism. Broadly speaking, the artists of the first wave came to London in a spirit not altogether different from that in which Picasso and others went to Paris: to fulfil their artistic ambitions and to participate in the heady atmosphere of the most advanced centres of artistic innovation at that time. As colonials, they had been—and are still thought of as—marginalized from such developments. In fact, they came to Britain feeling that they naturally belonged to the modern movement and, in a way, it belonged to them. The promise of decolonization fired their ambition, their sense of themselves as already "modern persons." It liberated them from any lingering sense of inferiority.[30]

However, far from being accepted as an equal as a modern artist, Shemza experienced an existential crisis during his Slade years, which he lucidly summarized in a statement written in 1963. This perceptive reflection is reproduced at length here because of its importance not just for understanding the artist's subsequent career but also for its prescience in clearly articulating the exilic dilemmas of many other artists since:

> Before I came to England I was a very happy man, a celebrated artist, who had had several one-man exhibitions, who had his work in the national collections of his country and among very many private collections. I was, indeed, represented in dozens of countries.
>
> The dream of this already happy man came true in 1956, when I arrived in London. . . . Next month, I joined the Slade, and met young and

> very English students trying Englishly not to be English. But within a few months' time, I had failed my drawing test, and all the paintings I'd submitted for the annual Young Contemporaries Exhibition were rejected. These two shocks were too much for me. I could not forget that at home I was an "established" painter.
>
> But one day I locked myself in my room, stood in front of a mirror, and had a heart to heart talk. It was a bitter experience. The result was a decision to start again from the beginning. And to hide the face of that "celebrated artist," I grew a beard. This worked rather well.
>
> It was a wonderful, depressing time. I read a lot, including [Rilke's] "Letters to a Young Poet." It sounded fascinating in the books, that if you go wrong, just start again—but in real life, it was a painful process, especially when you didn't know from where to start.[31]

Especially devastating was how the celebrated art historian Ernst Gombrich regarded the art of the non-West.[32]

> One evening, when I was attending a Slade weekly lecture on the history of art, Prof. Gombrich came to the chapter on Islamic Art—an art which was "functional"—from his book, "The Story of Art." I remember leaving the room a few minutes before the lecture finished, and sitting on a bench outside. As the students came out, I looked at all their faces; they seemed so contented and self-satisfied. I went home and looked again in the mirror. This time I couldn't find any familiar face at all, neither the beginner at the Slade, nor the "celebrated artist." I couldn't talk; I just stared. After all, it wasn't a very pleasant sight.
>
> All evening I destroyed paintings, drawings, everything that could be called "art." All night I argued with somebody—as I was told next morning by my hostel neighbor. All day restlessness sent me from place to place, until I found myself in the Egyptian Section at the British Museum. For the first time in England, I felt really at home.
>
> No longer was the answer simply to begin again; the search was for my own identity. Who was I? The simple answer was: A Pakistani. But this wasn't enough. I could see Pakistan in my mind's eye: Lahore, where I came from, my friends, painters, their work—all little Picasso's, Cezanne's, Braque's, Van Gogh's [*sic*]. I could see a third-rate "Paris." The "celebrated artist" was lost at last, as was also the beginner at the Slade. What's more, I had lost my home. I was an exile, homeless, without a name.
>
> Although I was a regular student at the Slade, I hated much of my time there, that was the only place that gave me unhappiness, a source to find

happiness. Happiness was in the British Museum, and at the Victoria and Albert. I started painting again, strange paintings. And at the Slade, Andrew Forge was "father and confessor." His encouragement meant more to me than anything else that had happened to me in England. I worked between fourteen and eighteen hours a day. Further encouragement from George Butcher and W. G. Archer confirmed only one thing, that my search for myself was leading in the right direction.

Such searching has its own fascination. One "enjoys" it even when tired, depressed, annoyed. But that is the nature of the creative process, perhaps even of life itself. Thus far have I come. It is for others to look for themselves in what I have done. Either way, we have all only just begun.[33]

Shemza's existential crisis was artistic as well as personal. As exhilarating a city as London was, it was also a profoundly alienating place. In a letter postmarked August 7, 1957, the artist notes, "London—the world's biggest city, but if one is alone, it instantly becomes a forlorn and frightening jungle."[34] Precisely due to this sense of dislocation, and because even his previous artistic achievements offered no solace, the Slade years were highly productive for him. Not only did he work intensively on his own paintings, but he was also exposed to the range of global art housed in British museum collections and engaged in a sustained study of Islamic art from various regions and periods—an opportunity that was simply unavailable in Pakistan, where even Mughal paintings produced in Lahore are not well-represented in the city's museum.

During these years, the example of Klee's work also proved decisive for Shemza's subsequent formation, which Shemza fully acknowledged. In a letter to his friend Karam Nawaz, a Lahore-based author, dated April 23, 1957, Shemza expresses his desire to travel to continental Europe in order to study Klee's paintings firsthand.[35] Shemza had planned to write a book on Klee and even traveled to Bern in 1957 to meet Klee's son. Nevertheless, Shemza also realized the need to *creatively* appropriate formalist and thematic modalities from Klee, as evident in a letter dated July 20, 1957, to Karam Nawaz, in which the artist notes, "I have been deeply struck by Paul Klee. He is a Swiss painter and I am planning to travel to Switzerland for this purpose. I realize that being afflicted by Paul Klee may have a positive outcome or a negative one."[36] Although Shemza never completed his book project, among the lessons he learned from Klee was the importance of *surface* as the plane of modernist experimentation, rather than a stress on modeling, and the freedom and ability to deploy abstraction, geometry, and pattern—much of it derived from Islamic art—in modernist exploration.[37] As Andrew Forge, Shemza's tutor and supporter at the Slade, judiciously put it, "Shemza has been intelligent enough to grasp European art at the point at which it was stretched nearest to the East: in the work of Paul Klee. He has made a special study of Klee and has been able to use his influence positively, applying his principles of growth and development to the sort of forms which he knows intimately himself."[38] Shemza now began to develop work based on his own lived and studied knowledge and experience: of carpet patterns, Mughal architecture from Lahore, and calligraphic forms. For this purpose, he continued to collect motifs and materials; for example, in a letter dated March 23, 1958, presently housed in the artist's estate, he requested that Karam Nawaz send him popular cards with calligraphy bearing *Ya Allah*, *Ya Muhammad*, *Ya Ali*, and similar Arabic phrases "preferably written in older styles."

It was during his Slade period that Shemza abandoned his earlier illustrative approach to modern art and began his search for a deeper compositional schema for a calligraphic modernism; this quest occupied him intensively for the remainder of his career. The artist considered *Still Life* (1957) to be a breakthrough into his mature phase (fig. 13.6). It dramatically moves from a volumetric depiction of space and objects in the lower part of the painting to an abstract flattened and calligraphic rendering at the upper middle of the canvas, prefiguring his later work.

Shemza met Mary Taylor in 1957 and they were married soon after. Their eldest daughter, Tasveer, was still a baby when the artist decided to move with his family permanently to Pakistan in 1960. Deeply interested in art education, Shemza wished to join the National College of Art (previously the Mayo School of Art) in a senior capacity. The artist was well aware of his responsibility to his "home" as a postcolonial intellectual and artist.[39] He was, however, not able to obtain a suitable position in Lahore and was forced for a while to work for an advertising firm in Karachi. Deeply unhappy with the poor career choices available to him in Pakistan, he decided to move permanently to England in 1961, choosing to live in the Midlands, where the family would be close to Mary's parents. Thereafter, Shemza taught art education in schools, and the relative isolation of the Midlands meant that he could devote himself to an intense exploration of his mature artistic project. Nevertheless, the artist showed work extensively in the UK, in Pakistan, and internationally in solo and group exhibitions, but diasporic existence was now to be lived as an immanent, indefinite, and unending condition.

London, from the mid-1950s till the mid-1960s, was an important center for artists of diverse backgrounds making and exhibiting innovative work. Significant modernist artists from South Asia who resided there included

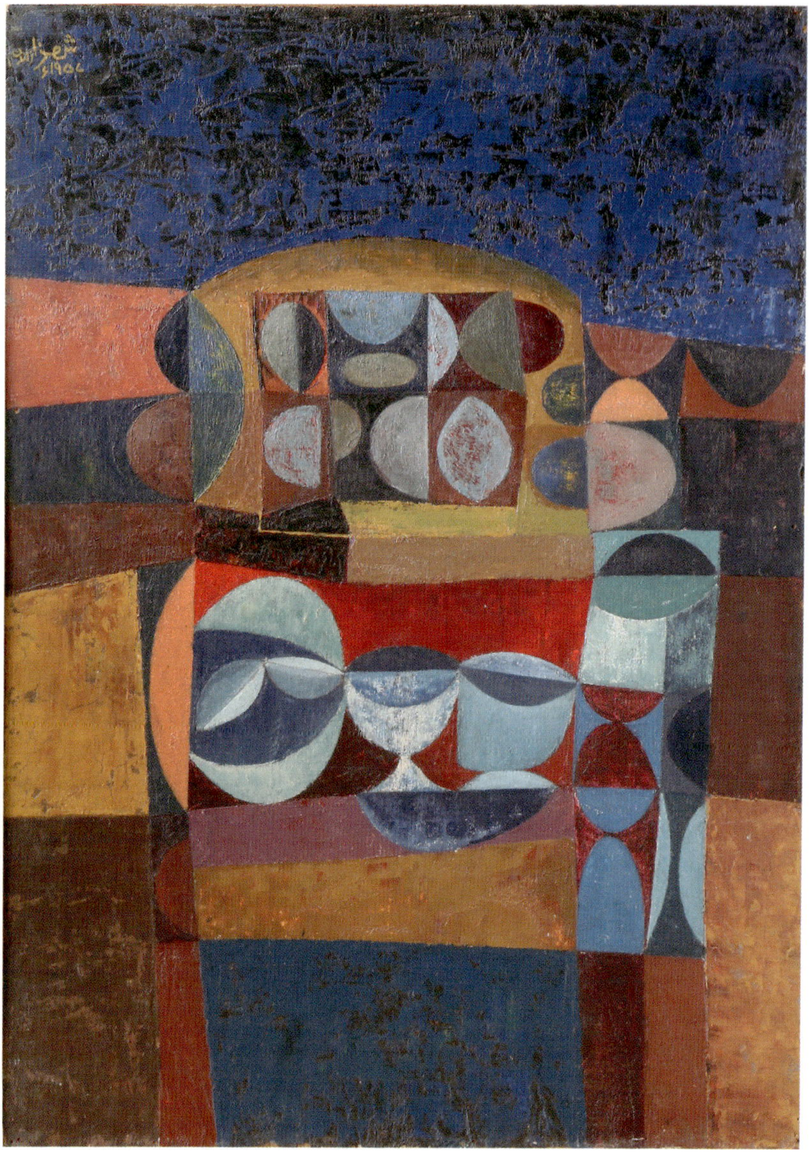

FIGURE 13.6. Anwar Jalal Shemza, *Still Life*, 1957. Oil on fiberboard, 64 × 46.4 cm. Collection: Estate of Anwar Jalal Shemza.

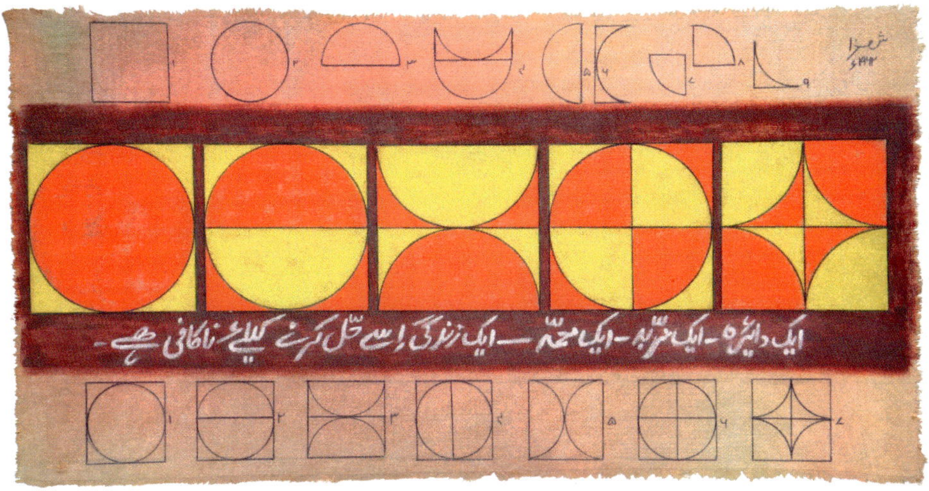

FIGURE 13.7. Anwar Jalal Shemza, *One to Nine and One to Seven*, 1962. Oil on hand-dyed cloth, mounted on board and hardboard, 30.2 × 55.5 cm. Collection: Estate of Anwar Jalal Shemza.

Avinash Chandra, Iqbal Geoffrey, Ahmed Parvez, and Francis Newton Souza. While the work of many modern artists from formally colonized regions was being subsumed and even contained under the "Commonwealth" rubric, this term also provided for exhibition opportunities. Shemza had solo shows at the influential New Vision Centre (1958) and at Victor Musgrave's Gallery One (1960), where he also showed work alongside Chandra and Souza.

Shemza continued to investigate the relation between visual and textual practice in his modernist compositions, referencing especially "Islamic" visual motifs and calligraphic forms. He investigated a small number of themes: city walls and architecture, electronic circuit boards, chessmen, the letter *meem* (the first letter of the name of the Prophet Muhammad), and a few others. He experimented with innovative technical procedures, and worked to introduce references to fabrics, textiles, and textures in numerous works. The artist's sketchbooks form the basis for his experimentation, and the numerous compositions he developed there are peppered with marks and notations in English and Urdu; the sketchbooks consequently merit detailed study with reference to his evolving praxis and how he realized his ideas in finished works such as prints and paintings.

Shemza distilled his experiences into a disciplined formalist practice, much of it based on geometry. For example, in the work *One to Nine and One to Seven* (1962), he notes in Urdu: "A circle—a square—a puzzle—for which a lifetime is not enough" (translation mine) (fig. 13.7). These geometric forms would provide him with a set of finite, yet flexible, building blocks. Much of his work contains references to the shapes of the letters *B* and *D*. However, the calligraphic dimensions in many of his works, especially the *Roots* series, draw from the sinuous lines of the Arabic alphabet as well and thus venture far beyond rigid geometric abstraction. Many of Shemza's works draw on a creative tension between geometric abstraction derived from the Roman alphabet and the sinuous character of many Arabic scripts. For example, in works such as the 1969 *Love Letter One*, one sees the composition bound by geometric reticulation in passages of varying modulation and frequency, yet here, using the Roman alphabet, the work strains against its strict geometric form (fig. 13.8). On the other hand, in the 1967 *Meem One*, the Arabic letter *meem*, often written in a sinuous manner, is now interpreted in the opposite direction, as a strict optical geometry of circles and lines (fig. 13.9).

Shemza's career culminated in the *Roots* series, created from 1977 until his death in 1985. Structurally, these works often delineate an imagined plant form on the upper half of the picture, while the lower half depicts root forms. In the works developed in 1977, both upper and lower forms are rendered in flat, optical shapes on a richly textured hand-dyed cloth, while works developed from 1983 on, such as *Roots Three* (1984), are more frequently based on abstracted Arabic cursive scripts that are, however, not legible (fig. 13.10). Shemza's sketchbooks and prior works suggest that the series involved extensive preparation and much forethought. These works relay the anguish of diaspora in a formally restrained language based on calligraphy and ornamental designs inspired by oriental carpets and textiles, perhaps a reminiscence of his family's carpet business in pre-partition South Asia. Made in a small format, their moveable character recalls works by other artists who have grappled with issues of the portability of artistic form with reference to exile and diaspora.[40] Moreover, *Roots*, while retaining a strong sense of formal discipline in its serial execution, is unabashedly more decorative than much of Shemza's earlier work.

Adolf Loos has famously declared that modern man's love of ornament is a sign of his criminality and degeneracy.[41] There are any number of thematic and formal ways by which modernism strove very hard to distinguish itself from simply being equated with decoration and ornament.[42] It may be noted that Islamic art has been characterized in art historical scholarship precisely as ornamental, decorative, and applied—or "functional," in the way Gombrich described it in the lecture that proved to be so shattering to Shemza earlier. For modern artists drawing inspiration from "Islamic art," however, the relationship between modernism and decoration cannot be so easily disavowed. In one

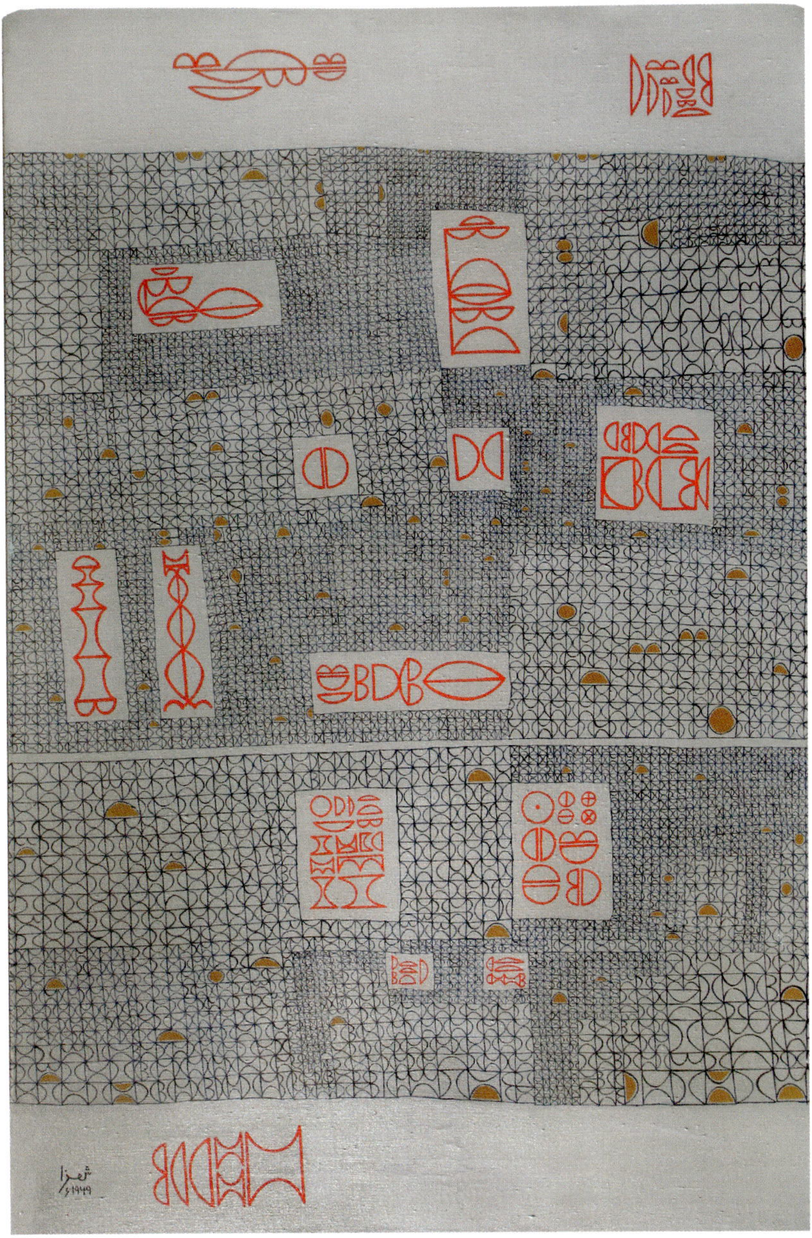

FIGURE 13.8. Anwar Jalal Shemza, *Love Letter One*, 1969. Oil on canvas, 91.5 × 61 cm. Collection: Metropolitan Museum of Art, New York, purchase, The George Economou Collection Gift, 2013.

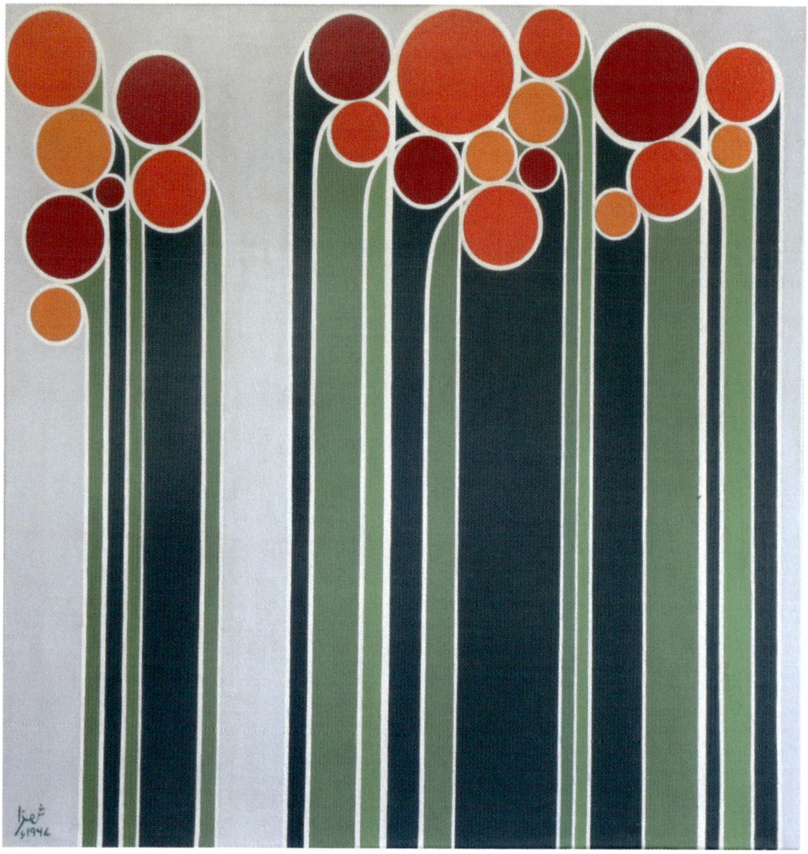

FIGURE 13.9. Anwar Jalal Shemza, *Meem One*, 1967. Oil on canvas, 91.5 × 91.5 cm. Collection: Estate of Anwar Jalal Shemza.

sense, Shemza's *Roots* series brings the dangerous question of ornament and its relation to modernism to a point of crisis, especially with reference to modernism's intimate yet unacknowledged relation to the "decorative arts" of the non-Western world. Moreover, the "roots" of the plant forms in the later works are textual and lettrist, suggesting that a return to one's roots can no longer be based on a blood-and-soil or "national" affiliation, but the roots themselves become transnational in their historic and contemporary valences.[43]

THE MODERNIST EXPERIMENTS in calligraphic abstraction of artists such as El-Salahi, Shemza, and others of the era of decolonization from South Asia, the Middle East, and North Africa emphasize form over content, quite

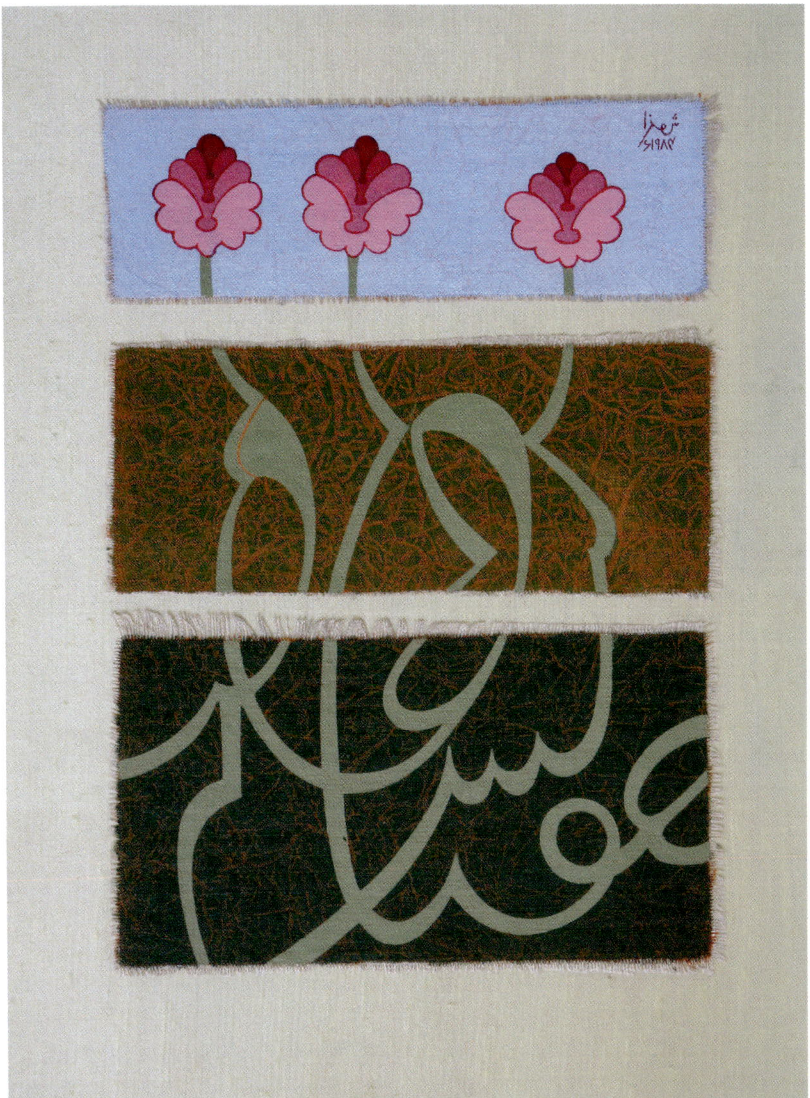

FIGURE 13.10. Anwar Jalal Shemza, *Roots Three,* 1984. Oil on canvas, mounted on silk and hardboard, 40 × 30 cm. Collection: Estate of Anwar Jalal Shemza.

unlike the premodern convention of rendering sacred or wise quotations in ornamental form. These artists have foregrounded textual, abstract, and calligraphic modes and evacuated iconic signifiers from their works. The illegibility of calligraphy—in its dialogue with postcubist figuration and in its nonornamental renderings—reterritorializes the Arabic script, foregrounding its discursivity while also making its aesthetic permeable to the outside, thus problematizing a simple binary homology between art and national identity. By their sustained practice, these artists relayed aesthetic and affective potentialities across the heroic age of decolonization into the present. Their endeavors have retained critical affiliations and differences from metropolitan modernisms that were not merely local or national but gestured toward imagining broader regional concerns that were aesthetic as well as social and political.[44]

NOTES

1. While Iran was never formally colonized, its intellectuals remained caught in many of the same perceptions as those from formally colonized areas, namely of seeing the country as economically, socially, and culturally backward. In this sense, decolonization as an intellectual and cultural idea is applicable to Iran. Also see Prashad, *Darker Nations*, 75–94.

2. For a fuller account of Ibrahim El-Salahi's contributions, see S. Hassan, *Ibrahim El-Salahi*. By *Arabic calligraphy*, I also refer to Persian and Urdu, which share the Arabic alphabet.

3. On the traditional role of the calligrapher in the Islamic world, including examples from South Asia, see Schimmel, *Calligraphy and Islamic Culture*.

4. For an attempt at a taxonomy of modern calligraphic paintings, see Ali, *Modern Islamic Art*, 137–60. On the lettrists in the Arab world, see Daghir, *Al-hurufiyah al-'arabiyah*. On the modern art of Iraq, see Faraj, *Strokes of Genius*; Jabra, *Iraqi Art Today*; Jabra, *Grass Roots of Iraqi Art*; Muzaffar, "Iraqi Contemporary Art," 63–89; and Naef, *À la recherche d'une modernité Arabe*. The art history of modern Iran is outlined in Balaghi and Gumpert, *Picturing Iran*; and Issa, Pakbaz, and Shayegan, *Iranian Contemporary Art* . On developments in Pakistan, see Dadi, *Modernism and the Art of Muslim South Asia*.

5. Emami and Wilson, *Saqqakhaneh*; Keshmirshekan, "Saqqa-Kana School of Art"; Daneshvari, "Seismic Shifts across Political Zones in Contemporary Iranian Art."

6. Naef, "Reexploring Islamic Art."

7. Muzaffar, "Iraq," 166; Al-Khamis, "Historical Overview 1900s–1990s," 29; Selim, "Diaspora, Departure, and Remains," 52.

8. Nashashibi, Nader, and Adnan, "Arab Women Artists," 33.

9. Dadi, *Modernism and the Art of Muslim South Asia*, 135–76; Akhund, Said, and Yusuf, *Sadequain*; Araeen, "Modernism, Postcolonial Nation States Art Criticism."

10. Beier, "Right to Claim the World"; Beier, *Drawings: Ibrahim El Salahi*; S. Hassan, "Khartoum and Addis Connections."

11. For an anecdotal account of the life of diaspora intellectuals in Paris, see Mphahlele, "Paris in the 1960s." On the postwar status of the School of Paris, see Adamson, *Painting, Politics and the Struggle for the École de Paris, 1944–1964*.

12. Daftari, "Another Modernism," 67–78.

13. Naef, *À la recherche d'une modernité Arabe*, esp. 250–53; Al-Khamis, "Historical Overview 1900s–1990s," 29; Muzaffar, "Iraq," 162.

14. For a description of his experience in Paris, see his letters reproduced in Naqqash, *Ruq'at-i Sadiqaini*.

15. See esp. the critical essay by Vazira Fazila-Yacoobali, "The Making and Unmaking of a National Artist."

16. *Two Modernist Iranian Pioneers—Hossein Zandehroudi, Massoud Arabshahi*, Tehran Museum of Contemporary Art, December 25, 2001–March 31, 2002. See the relevant web page at Artfacts, accessed August 6, 2024, https://artfacts.net/exhibition/two-modernistiranian-pioneers-hossein-zandehroudi-massoud-arabshahi/19084.

17. Among the public works is Jewad Selim's 1961 Nasb al-Hurriyah (Monument of Freedom) in Baghdad. See the chapter by Nada Shabout in this volume; Al-Khamis, "Lorna Selim Remembers"; Jabra, *Jawad Salim*. As an example of modern art exhibitions, the Iraqi Cultural Center, London, held exhibitions during the 1970s and 1980s, including one of works by a traditional twentieth-century calligrapher. See Hashim, *Hashem al-khattat*. And on scholarship, see E. Davis, *Memories of State*, 109–75.

18. This created a profound crisis in Shemza, leading him toward his mature work. See J. Holt, "Anwar Jalal Shemza," 105.

19. El-Salahi, "Chronologue," 34.

20. El-Salahi quoted in Beier, "Right to Claim the World," 29.

21. Lambert, "From Citizenship to Négritude."

22. El-Salahi, "Chronologue," 96.

23. On the Bengal School, see Mitter, *Art and Nationalism in Colonial India, 1850–1922*; and Guha-Thakurta, *Making of a New "Indian" Art*.

24. For biographical accounts of Shemza's years in Lahore, see I. Hassan, "Way It Was"; and Siddiqui, "Shemza." An insightful personal recollection in Urdu is in Aqeel, *Char jadid musavvir*.

25. Tabish, "Anwar Jalal Shemza." Khursheed Kamal Aziz describes Shemza in Aziz, *Coffee House of Lahore*, 136–40.

26. Toor, "Culture/Nation/State"; Husain, *Chiraghon ka dhuan*, 28–79. On the latter group, see Javed, *Halqa-e-Arbab-e-Zauq*.

27. Discussions in English include Pue, *I Too Have Some Dreams*; and Geeta Patel, *Lyrical Movements, Historical Hauntings*.

28. Husain, *Chiraghon ka dhuan*, 112–26. For a detailed discussion of Lahore's artistic milieu at midcentury, see Dadi, *Modernism and the Art of Muslim South Asia*, 93–133.

29. Hall, "Black Diaspora Artists in Britain," 4–5.

30. "Whereas the leading early figures of the second 'wave'—people like Eddie Chambers, Keith Piper, Donald Rodney, Sonia Boyce, Lubaina Himid, Claudette Johnson, Mona

Hatoum, Maud Sulter, Gavin Jantjes and others—were not born until the 1950s or 1960s and did not exhibit work until two decades later." Hall, "Black Diaspora Artists in Britain," 4–5.

31. Shemza, "Artist's Statement, July 1963," 2–4.

32. The Sudanese artist Ibrahim El-Salahi was a fellow student at the Slade at that time, and his career was also decisively shaped in response to the marginal status accorded to Islamic art in the same public lectures delivered by Gombrich.

33. Shemza, "Artist's Statement, July 1963," 4.

34. Anwar Jalal Shemza, letter to Karam Nawaz, August 7, 1957, estate of Anwar Jalal Shemza, UK.

35. Anwar Jalal Shemza, letter to Karam Nawaz, April 23, 1957, estate of Anwar Jalal Shemza, UK.

36. "Ab Paul Klee ka ho jana achcha bhi ho sakta hai aur bura bhi." Anwar Jalal Shemza, letter to Karam Nawaz, July 20, 1957, estate of Anwar Jalal Shemza, UK.

37. In the same letter dated July 20, 1957, he claims that he has already started work on the book.

38. Forge quoted in Butcher, "Shemza," 10.

39. In a moving letter to Karam Nawaz dated September 15, 1960, before he embarked on his journey, Shemza describes the sacrifices Mary and Tasveer would make in sundering their links to Mary's family in England and writes: "Whatever I have obtained in this country (England), it was solely for the sake of students in my country. I have tirelessly struggled to master the intricacies of artistic technique—this research was for the people of my nation who are anxious to benefit from Western experiments. But will I be able to convey this trust to them, I wonder? This is an aching question for which I see no clear answer." Anwar Jalal Shemza, letter to Karam Nawaz, September 15, 1960, estate of Anwar Jalal Shemza, UK.

40. See Lyford, "Noguchi, Sculptural Abstraction, and the Politics of Japanese American Internment"; Demos, *Exiles of Marcel Duchamp*.

41. Cernuschi, "Adolf Loos, Alois Riegl, and the Debate on Ornament," 45–56.

42. Trilling, *Ornament*.

43. This interpretation contrasts with explanations about the *Roots* series that focus solely on Shemza's attachment to the soil, architecture, and flora of Lahore. See, e.g., Tabish, "Anwar Jalal Shemza."

44. Examples include the Dhaka-based artist Zainul Abedin (1914–76), who, upon invitation by the Arab League, met with and created a series of sketches of Palestinian guerrillas and refugees in 1970; see Dadi, *Modernism and the Art of Muslim South Asia*, 101. Concern with Palestine also found expression in literature; see Ahmad, "Poetics of Solidarity."

14

Postwar Imaginings

Négritude Legacies and Thwarted Universalisms in Dakar and Paris

ELIZABETH HARNEY

In Paris in September 1956, two visual artists, one from South Africa, the other from Nigeria, took their turn at the podium to address the delegates of the First International Congress of Black Writers and Artists. As their voices filled the lofty halls of the Sorbonne, Gerard Sekoto and Ben Enwonwu chronicled the predicaments they faced in the postwar moment. While detailing the colonial mechanisms that had long hindered their creative expressions, they pondered the weighty task of articulating the aspirations of an emancipatory age.

Enwonwu, working in the last days of colonial rule in Nigeria, noted, "Every true artist is bound by the traditional artistic nature of his country, to express, even unconsciously, the political aspirations of his time." But, he continued, "it would not have been necessary for the African artist of today to prove to the world that he can create objects, had the political problems that he had to face not affected him so deeply."[1] He spoke of the disbelief and humiliation he felt each time he was "schooled" by a European ethnographer on examples of his own heritage, through artworks held within the wealth of colonial collections. When it was his turn to speak, Sekoto, having fled the restrictions of South Africa's apartheid state for a life of prolonged exile in Paris, noted with remarkable understatement, "The Negro artist feels often deprived of his rights as a full citizen to contribute an art towards the pride and dignity of his country in which he is made an outcast."[2] He recalled repeated expulsions from whites-only gallery spaces and harassment at the hands of police as he traversed the very city streets he hoped to draw and paint. In their devotion to the stylized, modernist figure, whether in painted, sketched, or sculpted form, Sekoto and Enwonwu married pan-African visual sources with strategically mediated modernist forms. They, like others of their generation, were cosmopolitans, meeting within the networks of the postwar era. Each had known and digested numerous artistic approaches from their British or French training in the metropole and often reimagined or rehabilitated denigrated artistic traditions from home. With this mixing of African vernacular and European approaches, the works of these and other artists of the era sought to synthesize the complexities inherent to the colonial modernist experience—a process which the Malagasy writer Jacques Rabemananjara would later describe as "the double chewing over" of different parts of themselves.[3]

The cultural exchanges at the 1956 conference between Black intellectuals from Africa and its diasporas focused on the key role that art and culture would play in challenging European self-evidentiary claims to universalism. Many of the same thinkers and activists at the 1956 congress would gather once again in 1959, in Rome, and in 1966, in Dakar (fig. 14.1). Indeed, both Enwonwu and Sekoto would participate, a decade later, in the 1966 First World Festival of Negro Arts in Dakar (fig. 14.2). Enwonwu also took part in an accompanying colloquium on the role and function of African art in society.[4] Sekoto showed his work not only in the contemporary art exhibition of the festival, *Tendances et Confrontations*, but again the following year, at the behest of Senegal's president Léopold Senghor, at the newly built national theater space.

Both artists were part of a generation of pioneering modernists that rode the wave of decolonization from communities of affiliation in Paris and London to national filiation in arenas a decade later.[5] It is this pattern of exchanges, around the character of Black modernity and liberation, occurring across differing political spaces and circumstances from 1945 to 1965, to which I want to

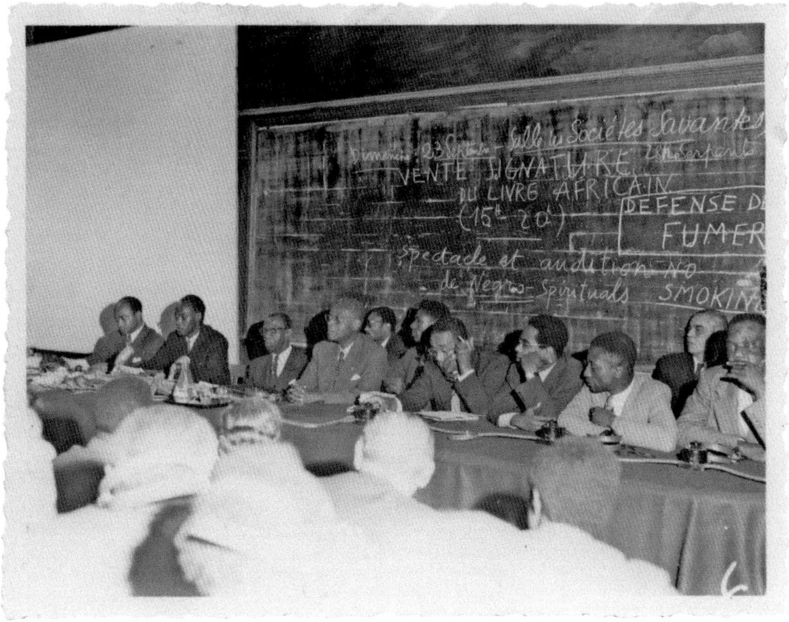

FIGURE 14.1. First International Congress of Black Writers and Artists, Sorbonne, Paris, September 1956. Photograph courtesy Horace Mann Bond Papers (MS 411), Special Collections and University Archives, University of Massachusetts Amherst Libraries.

draw further attention. Histories of modernism in Africa have often focused on postindependence, nation-state models.[6] Furthermore, scholars such as Chika Okeke-Agulu and Okwui Enwezor have insisted that political liberation must precede any set of practices we might call modernism.[7] However, while the container of the nation-state no doubt held great sway, its rhetoric has tended to obscure the longer-functioning networks between intellectuals operating in the last stages of empire, in Europe and in Africa.[8]

This chapter recalls the numerous efforts by Black intellectuals in France and its colonies to invest heavily in cultural expressions (literary, visual, theatrical, exhibitionary) as essential tools to imagine liberated futures and new forms of postwar humanism. It builds on my work on the development of the Négritude philosophy and the ways in which its principles informed the dynamics and parameters of a Senegalese art world after independence. While many of these efforts would eventually manifest as public events in new nations, they were formed in a discursive arena that was not, in the first place, geared solely toward this eventuality. In particular, I want to ask how art historians might productively revisit the crucial two decades between the end of the Second

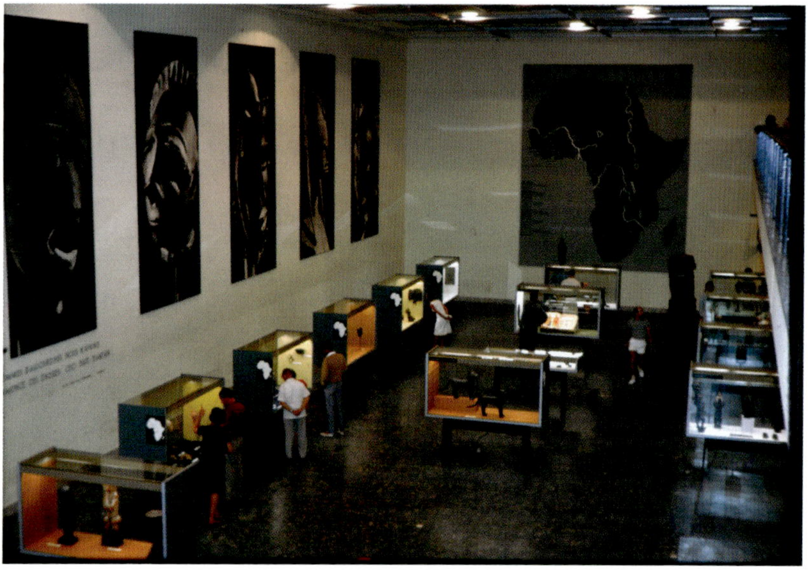

FIGURE 14.2. Installation view, *L'art négre: Sources, evolution, expansion*, exhibition at the Musée Dynamique, Dakar, 1966, during the First World Festival of Negro Arts. Photograph courtesy Roland Kaehr, Fonds PANAFEST Archives–Musée du Quai Branly 35AP/22, courtesy Cédric Vincent.

World War and the rise of postcolonial nation-states in Africa to better shape our understanding of the fluidity and rapidity with which ideas of cultural particularism and universalism reshaped the narratives of modernism.

The central role that the arts should play in anticolonialist politics was already well established by the early 1950s, thanks in part to the prolific output of poets from French colonies in the Caribbean and Africa. Young intellectuals like Léon Damas, Etienne Léro, Léopold Senghor, Aimé and Suzanne Césaire, and Jacques Rabemananjara met in Paris as students in the interwar years and created short-lived student publications like *La Dépêche Africaine*, *La Revue du Monde Noir*, *Légitime Défense*, and *L'Étudiant Noir* that strategically harnessed Marxist and surrealist ideas to advance anticolonial thought.

Their efforts found a lasting platform in the pages of *Présence Africaine*, the journal of the Society for African Culture, an organization established in 1947 by Senegalese author and activist Alioune Diop.[9] This journal had grand ambitions to reinvigorate African cultures, fostering the knowledge networks necessary to support the next generation of artists. Its aim was "to define African originality and hasten its entrance into the modern world."[10] Starting with the premise that humanism was both defective and defunct without the participation of the colonized, Diop wrote of "the responsibility to think and improve the fate of the human race."[11] In this way, anticolonialism and new models for humanism were framed through the ascendance of cultural particularism and postcolonial consciousness.

The process of reclaiming lost, disfigured, or forgotten cultural histories was critical to the Society for African Culture's broader agenda. Speaking in the late 1940s, Diop insisted that "among the most severe crimes of the colonial project, one of the most extreme, which has for such a long time gone unadmitted in the West, was the notion of a people without culture."[12] At the 1956 meeting, Martinican poet, philosopher, and politician Aimé Césaire echoed these sentiments in a now famous address entitled "Culture and Colonialism." Frankly outlining the condition of colonized peoples and their shared call to action he stated: "We find ourselves today in a cultural chaos. And this is our role: To liberate the forces, which alone, can organize from this chaos a new synthesis; a synthesis which will deserve the name culture, a culture which will be the reconciliation—*et dépassement*—of the old and new. We are here to proclaim the right of our people to speak, to let our people, black people, make their entrance on the great stage of History."[13] The inhumanity of the colonial project was decidedly and openly exposed on Europe's savage battlefields. And the hypocrisy of claims to civilization were laid bare for all to see, particularly for large numbers of colonial soldiers who fought and died in the name of empire. By the end of the 1950s, the world had "reached a solemn hour, an hour when colonialism [was], not, alas! dead, but when at least it recognize[d] itself to be mortal."[14] And while the Artists and Writers Congress took place a full decade after the official end of the war, it operated in what was still an extremely fluid, volatile cultural arena, marked by the horrifying revelations and deprivations of conflict. Though ostensibly its discussions addressed the work of Black artists and writers in Africa and its diasporas, its exchanges rested upon a broader belief that participants would reckon with Césaire's call or, indeed, build upon it to imagine the contours of a world after empire.

The 1956 meetings formed part of an important lineage of cross-cultural and transatlantic exchanges. Undoubtedly, they harnessed the political momentum of the 1945 Pan-African Congress in Manchester, a gathering that itself had an illustrious international history stretching back into the nineteenth century. In its postwar guise, the gathering featured a number of charismatic student leaders from the continent—Jomo Kenyatta of Kenya, Kwame Nkrumah of Ghana, and Julius Nyerere from Tanzania, among others—who drew strength and certainty from newly forged alliances between labor unions and liberation struggles.

But the Bandung (Asian-African) conference, held just a year earlier in Indonesia, was an equal, if not greater, spiritual lodestar for the 1956 meetings (in fact, as convener of the Paris meetings, Diop referred to his gathering as the cultural Bandung). At this unprecedented 1955 gathering of twenty-nine newly independent, unaligned nations, designates committed to "political self-determination, mutual respect for sovereignty, non-aggression, non-interference in internal affairs, and equality."[15] Because it was held while decolonization was still unfolding, particularly in many parts of the African continent (the atrocities in Algeria were mounting), the designates took it upon themselves to speak on behalf of their brethren and to advance possibilities of utopian community beyond either colonial or Cold War paradigms.[16]

Navigating the "Global Turn"

Over the last two decades, art historians have increasingly focused on the histories of art schools that arose in conjunction with the aspirational African nation-state—in Senegal, Tunisia, Sudan, Ethiopia, and Morocco.[17] These studies aimed, in the first instance, to challenge the putative canon of modernism, which in the late 1990s remained overwhelmingly Eurocentric and parochial. Many artworks associated with anticolonial struggles and emergent nationalisms were dismissed in the broader Western art world as blind, ineffectual mimicries of earlier European forms. Deeper archival studies into specific local histories have elicited complex, sometimes contradictory stories of modernism, where artists sought to define their present condition through concerted efforts to reach backward to lost or silenced traditions.[18]

For example, in Senegal, artists working under the patronage of Léopold Senghor envisioned Négritude not only as a theory of racial belonging for Black people worldwide but also as a cultural rallying point with which to begin the crucial postcolonial process of nationalist affirmation. Within the Négritude philosophy, Senghor also established a concept of the "civilization of the universal," which posited that by incorporating unique elements from each culture, a great and more equitable world civilization could be formed. He believed that Africa's approach to and participation in this community would be most clearly expressed through the imagery and symbolism of artistic form. With this goal in mind, he identified "rhythm" as Africa's unique characteristic of artistic expression. Senghor's promotion of the École de Dakar, with its synthesis of pan-African iconographies and European modernist painting, was aimed at defining cultural particulars suited to contributing to a global humanism he had envisioned in his interwar days in Paris. The means through which he came to this argument have preoccupied and disturbed a generation of scholars and critics, laboring with the knowledge that this prolific writer and thinker would turn to European philosophical and ethnographic literature to sketch the parameters of a postwar vision of pan-African modernism.[19]

Early studies of modernism in Africa were also designed to disrupt the conservative field of African art scholarship, which had either stubbornly ignored or intentionally dismissed the modernity of African societies. Many Western art historians of the generation writing after the Second World War held on to anachronistic ethnographic tropes about the continent, avoiding its cities to conduct "fieldwork" in what they hoped were authentic small-scale sites.[20] They thus bemoaned what they saw as the contamination or destruction of "authentic" cultures by colonial modernist forces. Therefore, they were also remarkably blind to the aspirations of African intellectuals eager to make their words and images visible in the postwar era.[21] The evident hybridity of many modernist forms particularly disturbed long-established canonical measures of value.

With the critical amassing of further in-depth and considered histories of modern art practices from former colonial regions and, indeed, with the passing of time, we are now able to further complicate some of these earlier studies. Okwui Enwezor's significant efforts to resituate "decolonization, and its attendant ideological and philosophical contestation of Western imperialism," as "one of the most significant events of the twentieth century," most evident in his *Short Century: Independence and Liberation Movements in Africa, 1945–1994* (2001), were instrumental in finally forcing the art world to revisit unfinished conversations about modernity and its global networks.[22]

"Unfinished Conversations" of the Postwar and the Postcolonial

Three strands of revisionist scholarship have coalesced over the last several years to enable a more nuanced reading of the political and cultural machinations at work in the critical postwar years and to highlight the prescience of the anticolonial aesthetic archive: first, challenges to the very category of *postwar* and consequent debates around the cultural politics of temporality have encouraged new modes of "decolonial looking," enabling us to recognize how the art historical canon has continuously obscured anticolonial struggles and naturalized their absence from the canon; second, nostalgic retrospectives surrounding the fiftieth anniversary of independence in many African sites; and third, reconsiderations of the overlaps between the erection of a postcolonial consciousness and new forms of humanism.[23]

These discussions revisit archival sources and bring attention to the intricacies of earlier scholarship, much of which has been passed over too hastily, to allow us to give further context to the poignancy of the artists' testimonials in 1956 and to broaden our narrow readings of cultural nationalism and the structures that supported many modernist practices in the era.[24] A plethora of writings, art projects, and exhibitions have turned a retrospective (often nostalgic) lens on the promises of Third Worldism, nonalignment, and postcolonial consciousness, inspired by the fiftieth anniversary of the Bandung conference in 2005 and, five years later, by the widespread commemorations of fifty years of political independence in many African nations.[25] For instance, productive close readings of the content and impact of vanguard journals—such as *Souffles*, *Lotus*, or *Black Orpheus*—reveal the extent to which writers, poets, and visual artists experimented with diverse strategies to produce artistic expressions suitable for revolutionary times. The featured aesthetics did not always lead to the desired results, but revisiting them now does require us to recognize the specific contours of the cultural and political spaces in which they operated and the real limits of both their tools and their dreams.[26]

A project like PANAFEST, for example, aimed at revisiting the impact and import of four Pan-African festivals of arts and culture that took place in the 1960s and 1970s—the First World Festival of Negro Arts, Dakar, 1966; the First Pan-African Cultural Festival, Algiers, 1969; the Second World Festival of Black Art and Culture, Lagos, 1977; and Zaire 74, Kinshasa, 1974—is a case in point. While these gatherings fall outside the time frame of this volume, there is little doubt that their organization and conceptualization drew significantly on and extended the debates of the postwar era.[27] With the archival work on Dakar, we now have a better idea of the extent to which Senghor's government constructed art-world institutions to produce local artworks that could travel through national, international, and intercontinental networks (the large tapestries created at the Manufactures Sénégalaises des Arts Décoratifs, a government-sponsored workshop, most notably, were commissioned to use as diplomatic gifts).

A number of artistic projects over the last decade have also moved us away from an "ambivalent fascination" with past (postwar) visions for the future and toward those that seek not "the reiteration of the actual past, but the persistence of what never actually happened, but might have."[28] *Postwar: Art between the Pacific and the Atlantic, 1945–1965* at the Haus der Kunst in Munich (launched in 2014; exhibition in 2016–17) was able to build upon other exhibitions from the mid-2000s that operated as places "for enacted research," such as Simon Njami's poignant show *A Useful Dream: African Photography, 1960–2010* (2010), in which the curator addressed the desperate utopianism of decolonization.[29] Similarly, in 2013 the Haus der Kulturen der Welt in Berlin mounted *After Year Zero: Geographies of Collaboration since 1945*, fundamentally challenging standard narratives of midcentury to foreground decolonization networks and collaborative thinking aimed at creating anticolonial modernity.[30] While this widespread retrospective work has often highlighted the failures of and profound disappointment in modernization—where anticipated benefits never materialized and thwarted promises made at independence cast shadows on contemporary life, it also has a speculative, promissory note to it, where collecting and filling out the archive can be viewed as "a celebration of the Africa yet to come."[31]

Fluid Spaces and Horizons of the Possible: Between Metropole and Colony

The further opening of archives to researchers in the last decade has complicated pat stories of nationalism by reactivating the details of "futures past."[32] In particular, historians have begun to pay greater attention to the convoluted micropolitics at work, as budding politicians and intellectuals from the colonial sphere mounted repeated attempts to craft and refine postwar models of engagement that could establish equitable cultural networks of exchange between the metropole and former colonies.

As Frederick Cooper explained, "Perhaps the most important lesson we might learn from returning to this moment is not that any one of the political aspirations articulated at the time should be resurrected, but that the very sense of alternatives can broaden our sense of possibilities for the future."[33] These attempts often emphasized cosmopolitanism and shared responsibilities, rather than nationalism and independence. But scholars have read these attempts as reflections of misplaced, colonialist thinking. Most frequently, Léopold Senghor's stance on relations with France, which focused on obtaining greater educational and political freedoms while keeping ties close economically and culturally, branded him an accommodationist. Reflecting back on his writings in 2010, Nancy Jachec noted that in the late 1950s, at the moment of anticolonial determinations, Senghor described himself as "a Eurafrican cultural hybrid," and while he insisted repeatedly that Africans should not *be* assimilated, but rather assimilate, his attempts to articulate the unique contributions that Africans could make to a broader world often rang out in self-primitivizing tones.[34]

Surely the scholarly work of decolonization can only continue to flourish if we are better able to unfix the image of postwar liberation and place it into the fluid circumstances of the era. For example, against the backdrop of the famous "*oui* or *non*" vote, called by French president Charles de Gaulle in 1958, a number of colonial deputies in the French assembly envisioned some form of French-African federation—what was known as "layered sovereignty."[35] Theirs was an anticipatory self-determination focused on crafting a power-sharing relationship that may or may not have involved state sovereignty. Gary Wilder's writings have refocused attention on the fathers of Négritude (Senghor and Césaire), rescuing them, to some degree, from expedient critiques that bound their writings too tightly to narratives of blind nationalism, nativism, or accommodationism. Wilder and others suggest that it is perhaps time to situate these thinkers in a more radical politics of humanism and transnational solidarity.[36] Wilder writes, "Senghor challenged the reification of Africa and France as entities supposedly standing in an external relation to one another. His task was to fashion a political form that could build upon this history of imperial interdependence and end colonialism, without retreating into what he regarded as the territorialist trap of 'national autarchy,' which he argued was an outmoded and inadequate framework for postcolonial democracy and development."[37] Elsewhere Wilder argues, "Scholarship long promoted one-sided understandings of Césaire and Senghor as either essentialist nativists or naïve humanists," and thus, "Negritude, whether embraced or criticized, was treated as an affirmative theory of Africanity rather than a critical theory of modernity."[38]

Senghor, the 1950s, and the Making of African Modernity

In the immediate years after the war, Léopold Senghor, successful poet, philosopher, and aspiring professor, was tapped by his senior Lamine Guèye, deputy to the French assembly, to join him as a junior representative in the Socialist Party. Senghor reluctantly agreed to a life in politics, and with his intelligence, rhetorical skills, and established connections to powerful French figures (such as Georges Pompidou and Charles de Gaulle), he became a central figure in the repeated, unfolding efforts to navigate the chaos of postwar Europe while bettering the conditions in the colonies.[39]

It is worth noting that before he assumed power in his new nation and established one of the most extensive arts patronage systems in the postcolonial era, Senghor spent more than a decade in the French National Assembly, from 1945 to 1958.[40] Soon after his appointment, Senghor returned home for what his engaging biographer, Janet Vaillant, called his "listening tour"—during this period he traveled around the hinterland, meeting with local leaders (particularly

Mamadou Dia, with whom he would later govern) and reconnecting to traditions that he had left (as a Serer boy, he had lived outside the Four Communes, areas that granted inhabitants status as French citizens, but had soon been swept up into the French educational system). In the midst of this homecoming, he witnessed the rapidly changing demands of a new generation, aware of the hypocrisy of French claims to a *mission civilisatrice* (or a policy of assimilation) and ready for greater rights. Fresh from the horrors of wartime imprisonment himself, Senghor delivered a militant speech in the National Assembly chambers (1946), saying: "I would like to assure the whites of our unshakeable will to win our independence and that it would be stupid as well as dangerous for them to wish to make the clock march backwards. We are ready, if necessary, as a last resort, to conquer liberty by any means, even violent ones."[41]

The following year, Senegal endured a major railway strike, lasting over five months and paralyzing transport systems across large swathes of French West Africa. This labor dispute was essentially a social movement to fight French attempts to redefine status in a postwar colonial sphere, perhaps best remembered and mythologized by Ousmane Sembène's popular 1960 novel *Les bouts de bois de Dieu* (*God's Bits of Wood*). Vaillant reminds us that the intellectual residue of years of negotiating within the French imperial machine had left their mark on the young deputy. His attempts to craft a federation with Mali were evidence of these years, as too were the very real improved educational improvements he achieved for those living both within and beyond the Four Communes.[42] But perhaps most important for a deeper understanding of his journey through the era of decolonization toward the presidency is that, beginning in the 1950s, Senghor began to share his ideas about Négritude, his pride in Africa, his rediscovery of its histories, and his plans for a universal civilization in a locally produced newspaper, *La Condition Humaine*. In these pages, Senghor tested many of his philosophical ideas locally before they would take political form, encouraging dialogue in a shifting public sphere and cultivating new (not necessarily nationalist) models of citizenship. Vaillant provides us with a telling passage from one of Senghor's pieces in the newspaper: "And we say that assimilation is an illusion in a world where people have become conscious of their personality and we also affirm that independence is a dream in a world where the interdependence of peoples affirms itself so clearly."[43]

These political ideas were punctuated by poems and prose by Senghor's friends from Paris, Étienne Léro, Aimé Césaire, and Birago Diop, who were presented for the first time to an African audience. Senghor encouraged his fellow colonial subjects to seek out "self-awareness through poetry and literature" as "a critical part of the education that would lead to an improvement in the position of Africans, and that West Indian and black American writers could contribute to the African cause."[44] Knowing this broader historical account counters the oft-repeated criticism that the Négritude philosophy was purely an elitist, Parisian phenomenon unavailable to a larger Senegalese public (though it still reached only a literate one there).

These writings also point us to the dynamics of evolving notions of citizenship and the varied ways in which colonial deputies dared to imagine political rights against an active scene of union strikes and student organizing. While one might argue that the strategic decisions these African deputies made would affect and eventually populate the theater of nationalism, Frederick Cooper argues that "whether the territorial nation state was what African activists wanted or not, that was what they could get."[45]

In 1959, two of the largest regions of French colonies, Senegal and the Sudanese Republic, formed the Mali Federation, but it lasted a mere two months and Senegal soon declared its independence in 1960.[46] Once the federation failed, Senghor got to work crafting a cultural framework for national citizenship.[47] In particular, he, along with his younger colleague Papa Ibra Tall, sought to develop art forms that would facilitate a wide, even grand, public address. In numerous interviews, Tall has recalled their early considerations of mosaic work and murals before eventually choosing large-scale tapestries, based on the long tradition of French Aubusson works, that had been used in the service of royal and state power.[48] These tapestries, woven after painted models, played the part of narrative history painting and proved to be ideal forms for retelling myths, articulating moral boundaries, and instilling overarching responsibilities of citizenship. But they also drew from extant traditions of oral history recitations in griot cultures that sang the praises of great leaders and kingdoms.[49]

For critics of both yesterday and today, however, Négritude has represented "a messy and untimely insurrection of particularism" at a time when formerly colonized peoples sought access to the wider platforms of world history.[50] But Denis Ekpo reminds us that "the anti-colonialistic, nationalist generation had ears only for the Senghor who spoke *Négritude*" but often failed to consider the flexibility of Senghor's thought and sustained engagement with questions of universalism: "Senghor spoke almost simultaneously out of both sides of his mouth: he spoke Négritude but also that which exceeds and annuls Négritude, namely, modernity, universality. He embodied both the politics of difference and the politics of integration into universal civilization."[51]

We began with the stories of Ben Enwonwu and Gerard Sekoto. Enwonwu, who had befriended Senghor in Paris and worked repeatedly with notions of

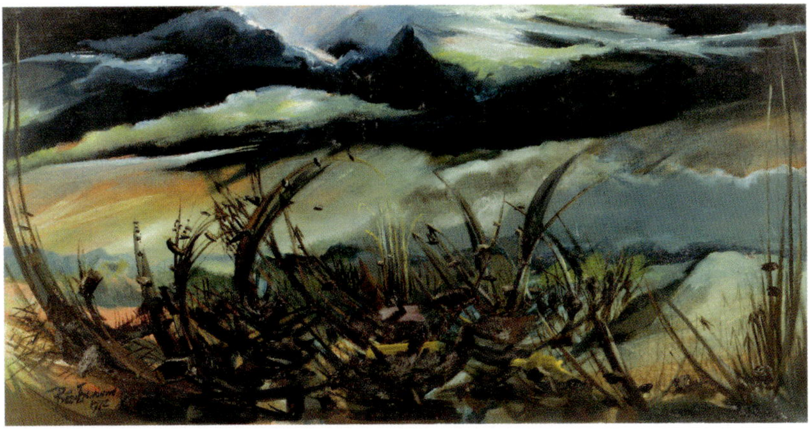

FIGURE 14.3. Ben Enwonwu, *Storm over Biafra,* 1972. Oil on canvas, 78.6 × 154.3 × 5.2 cm. Collection: National Museum of African Art, Smithsonian Institution, Washington, DC. Photograph courtesy Ben Enwonwu Foundation.

Négritude, was invited to lead the Nigerian delegation to the 1966 festival in Dakar (Nigeria had been given a special place in celebrations because Senghor was so enamored with its ancient histories, calling it the Greece of Africa). As far as we know, Enwonwu did not show any of his work but did deliver an important speech at the "Colloque sur l'art nègre."[52] In Dakar and elsewhere, Enwonwu continued to push against attempts by Western critics to limit his work and that of other African modernists. Ultimately, he sought to better control the manner in which he brought his cultural heritage to bear on his own modern art practice—a practice that he hoped would speak to his new nation of Nigeria and to these wider cosmopolitan networks to which he had always belonged. He would have great success in his career, as both a visual artist and an ambassador for pan-African cultural expressions (fig. 14.3).

After befriending a nephew of Senghor's in Paris, Sekoto returned to Africa for the first time since entering exile from South Africa, to exhibit at the First World Festival of Negro Arts. Eager to be back on the continent and overwhelmed to witness strong, liberated communities, Sekoto quickly decided to stay longer. He would have a revelatory time in Senegal's southern Casamance region, where he immersed himself in the local cultures and produced a series of whimsical sketches of local life, which have only recently been examined as an important part of his oeuvre (fig. 14.4).[53] In his return, Sekoto's desire to return home to a viable experience of Black modernity after apartheid takes aesthetic form in his Senegalese work.

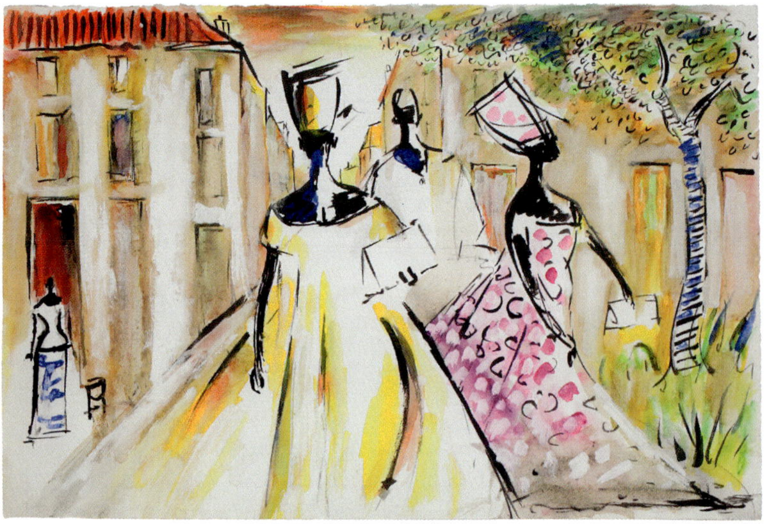

FIGURE 14.4. Gerard Sekoto, *Senegalese Women*, 1966. Gouache on paper, 35.5 × 55.8 cm. Collection: Iziko Museums, South Africa. © Gerard Sekoto Foundation/Darlo.

The two decades between the end of the Second World War and the rise of nation-states proved to be a fertile period not only for reckoning with the cultural loss and destruction wrought by the colonial project but also for imagining new solidarities, new modernist expressions, and new horizons for intercultural and international relations. While narratives addressing the development of Négritude and other forms of pan-African belonging are well known, the last several decades of scholarship (in academia, in the space of exhibition, and in the artist studio) have brought fresh interrogatories into these histories, enabling the anticolonial archive to speak to us in renewed, often surprising ways.

NOTES

1. Enwonwu, "Problems of the African Artist Today," 174.
2. Sekoto, "South African Artist," 281–82.
3. Rabemananjara, "Foundations of Our Unity Arising from the Colonial Epoch," 83. The artists' talks were rather innocuously titled: "A South African Artist" (Sekoto) and "Problems of the African Artist Today" (Enwonwu).
4. See World Festival of Negro Arts, *Colloque*.

5. Said, *World, the Text, and the Critic.*

6. My own early work represents one such project. However, in writing this early account of the ways in which the first president of Senegal, Léopold Senghor, parlayed his complex ruminations on Black modernity (in the form of Négritude philosophical tenets) into statecraft, I was careful to insist that these processes were much more complicated than met the eye and were geared as much toward supranational concerns in the era of decolonization as they were in announcing nationalist ones. See Harney, *In Senghor's Shadow.*

7. Okeke-Agulu, *Postcolonial Modernism*; Enwezor and Okeke-Agulu, *Contemporary African Art since 1980.*

8. Harney, "Constellations and Coordinates."

9. The Society for African Culture also organized the writers and artists congresses.

10. Diop, "Niam n'goura," 7.

11. "La responsabilité de penser et d'améliorer le sort du genre humain." Diop, "Niam n'goura," 7 (my translation).

12. "Parmi les péchés capitaux du colonialisme, l'un des plus nocifs, pour avoir été admis longtemps sans discussion par l'Occident, fut la notion de peoples sans culture." Diop, "Notre politique de la culture," 5.

13. Césaire, "Culture and Colonialism"; as quoted in Baldwin, "Princes and Powers," 53.

14. Irele, "1956 and After," 231.

15. "Bandung Conference (Asian-African Conference), 1955," Office of the Historian (website), US Department of State, accessed September 1, 2022, https://history.state.gov/milestones/1953-1960/bandung-conf.

16. Sherwood, "Pan-African Conferences 1900–1953." Although historical documents seem to indicate that none of the well-known names of anticolonialism operating within the French sphere (Léopold Senghor, Félix Houphouët-Boigny, Aimé Césaire, or Alioune Diop) attended the 1945 Manchester Pan-African Congress, students, and particularly trade unionists, may indeed have been in attendance, and archives do show that Kwame Nkrumah, then the head of the West African National Secretariat and the West African Students Union and one of the organizers of the congress, had sent representatives to Paris in 1946–47 to meet expressly with his counterparts there.

17. See Harney, *In Senghor's Shadow.*

18. See Okeke-Agulu, *Postcolonial Modernism*; Kwami, *Kumasi Realism*; Gerschultz, *Decorative Arts of the Tunisian École*; S. Hassan, *Ibrahim El-Salahi*; Sanyal, "'Being Modern.'"

19. Wilder, *Freedom Time*; Diagne, *African Art as Philosophy*; Irele, *Negritude Movement.* The literature on this topic is vast, so I have chosen here to cite just several of the most recent investigations of this history of thought.

20. But important studies done by Marshall Mount, Kojo Fosu, Ulli Beier, and Evelyn Brown between the 1960s and 1980s should not be dismissed. See Beier, *Contemporary Art in Africa*; Brown, *Africa's Contemporary Art and Artists*; Fosu, *20th Century Art of Africa*; Mount, *African Art.*

21. Harney, "Narratives of a Reluctant Modernist."

22. Enwezor, *Short Century*, 10.

23. On the first point, see Feldman, *From a Nation Torn*; and Lebovics, *Bringing the Empire*. On the third point, see Kamola, "Time for Anticolonial Theory."

24. Artist John Akomfrah titled his moving three-channel documentary film—a tribute to the Jamaican-born cultural theorist Stuart Hall—*The Unfinished Conversation* (2012). Discussions are taken up here in the same spirit.

25. C. Lee, *Making a World after Empire*.

26. Irele, "1956 and After," 230.

27. PANAFEST Archives, accessed August 2, 2019, http://webdocs-sciences-sociales .science/panafest/index.html.

28. Eshun, "Further Considerations of AfroFuturism"; Handberg, "World Goes Modern." On "ambivalent fascination," see Latham, "Our Jaded Tomorrows."

29. Sheikh, "Towards the Exhibition as Research," 40; Njami, *Useful Dream*, 9. Njami drew his title from the writings of Guinean novelist Thierno Monénembo.

30. "After Year Zero," Haus der Kulturen der Welt, accessed August 15, 2019, https:// archiv.hkw.de/en/programm/projekte/2013/after_year_zero/start_after_year_zero.php.

31. Lachenal and Mbodj-Pouye, "Politique de la nostalgie"; as quoted in Malaquais and Vincent, "Entangled Panafrica."

32. Koselleck, *Futures Past*.

33. Cooper, "Possibility and Constraint," 168.

34. Jachec, "Léopold Sédar Senghor," 195.

35. The slogan, however, in Guinea with Sekou Toure's party, which ultimately chose to vote for cutting ties with France, was "Better independence with poverty than servitude with plenty."

36. See Wilder, *Freedom Time*; Amselle, "Négritude, créolisation, créolité"; Kliger, "Humanism and the Ends of Empire."

37. Wilder, "Eurafrique as the Future Past of 'Black France,'" 75.

38. Wilder, *Freedom Time*, 8.

39. Senghor's successes were most evident in a series of educational projects and in his support for the dismissal of the dreaded corvée system (which his friend Félix Houphouët-Boigny, later president of Côte d'Ivoire, succeeded in forcing through the French National Assembly).

40. Senegal began sending deputies to the French National Assembly as early as 1872. The early cosmopolitan trading communities along the Atlantic coast known as the Four Communes (Saint-Louis, Dakar, Gorée, and Rufisque) developed long-standing, sophisticated understandings and expectations of their rights as citizens, both of France and of the world. The African inhabitants of the Four Communes, called the *originaires*, had the status of French citizens and thus were unlike other African inhabitants, who were subjects of the French Empire and controlled by the *code de l'indigénat*, or colonial penal code.

41. "The Story of Africa: Independence," BBC, accessed August 2, 2019, www.bbc.co.uk /worldservice/africa/features/storyofafrica/14chapter2.shtml. Senghor spent almost two years in a prisoner-of-war camp in Vichy France.

42. Vaillant, *Black, French and African*.

43. Senghor, quoted in Vaillant, *Black, French and African*, 225.

44. Vaillant, *Black, French and African*, 226.

45. Cooper, "Possibility and Constraint," 168.

46. *Africa Report*, "Collapse of the Mali Federation," 5.

47. It is worth noting that infrastructure-building for the ill-fated federation had already included an extensive Maison des Arts, which would have featured training in visual arts, music, theater, design, and film. See Cohen, "Locating Senghor's École de Dakar."

48. Cohen, "Locating Senghor's École de Dakar," 17–18.

49. Other well-known actor-statesmen in this era also made their way through the local circuitries of power and access in order to rise to power. Houphouët-Boigny spearheaded the overturning of the corvée system.

50. Diagne, *African Art as Philosophy*, 244.

51. Ekpo, "Slaying Négritude's Last Shadows."

52. Enwonwu, "The African View of Art and Some Problems Facing the African Artist."

53. Eyène, "Sekoto and Negritude."

Bibliography

Abinales, Patricio N., and Donna J. Amoroso. *State and Society in the Philippines*. Lanham, MD: Rowman and Littlefield, 2005.

Adamson, Natalie. *Painting, Politics and the Struggle for the École de Paris, 1944–1964*. Farnham: Ashgate, 2009.

Adorno, Theodor. "From 'Commitment: The Politics of Autonomous Art,' *New Left Review* (1962)." In *Debating the Canon: A Reader from Addison to Nafisi*, edited by Lee Morrissey, 71–72. New York: Palgrave Macmillan, 2005.

Adorno, Theodor. *Prisms*. Translated by Shiery Weber Nicholsen and Samuel Weber. Cambridge, MA: MIT Press, 1983.

Africa Report. "Collapse of the Mali Federation." Vol. 5, no. 12 (December 1960): 5–7.

Agamben, Giorgio. *Homo sacer: Sovereign Power and Bare Life*. Translated by Daniel Heller-Roazen. Stanford, CA: Stanford University Press, 1998.

Agamben, Giorgio. *The Open: Man and Animal*. Translated by Kevin Attell. Stanford, CA: Stanford University Press, 2004.

Ahmad, Shahab. "The Poetics of Solidarity: Palestine in Modern Urdu Poetry." *Alif: Journal of Comparative Poetics*, no. 18 (1998): 29–64.

Akhund, Abdul Hameed, Farida Munavarjahan Said, and Zohra Yusuf, eds. *Sadequain: The Holy Sinner*. Karachi: Mohatta Palace Museum, 2003.

Albers, Anni. *On Designing*. Middletown, CT: Wesleyan University Press, 1971.

Albers, Anni. *Pre-Columbian Miniatures: The Josef and Anni Albers Collection*. New York: Praeger, 1970.

Albert, Melissa, Satyavrat Nirala, and Surabhi Sinha. "Bandung Conference." In *Encyclopaedia Brittanica* online. Article published July 20, 1998. Last modified August 5, 2014. http://www.britannica.com/EBchecked/topic/51624/Bandung-Conference.

Ali, Wijdan. *Modern Islamic Art: Development and Continuity*. Gainesville: University Press of Florida, 1997.

Al-Khamis, Ulrike. "An Historical Overview 1900s–1990s." In *Strokes of Genius: Contemporary Iraqi Art*, edited by Maysaloun Faraj, 21–40. London: Saqi Books, 2001.

Al-Khamis, Ulrike. "Lorna Selim Remembers." In *Strokes of Genius: Contemporary Iraqi Art*, edited by Maysaloun Faraj, 41–46. London: Saqi Books, 2001.
Al-Roabie, Abd al-Rahman. "Interview with Ismail Al-Shaikhly." *Al-Muthaqaf al-Arabi*, no. 3 (1971): 171–77.
Al-Roabie, Abd al-Rahman. "Jewad Selim and the Founding of the Baghdad Group," *Al-Aqlam* 4, no. 10 (June 10, 1968):131–137.
Al Said, Shakir Hassan. *Fusul min tarikh al-haraka al-tashkiliah fi al-'Iraq, al-juz' al-thani*. Vol 1. Baghdad: Ministry of Culture and Information, 1983.
Al Said, Shakir Hassan, ed. *Hiwar al-fan al-tashkili*. Amman: Abd al-Hamid Shouman Foundation-Darat al-Funun, 1995.
Al Said, Shakir Hassan. *Jewad Selim, al fanan wa al-akharun*. Baghdad: Ministry of Culture and Information, 1991.
Amselle, Jean-Loup. "Négritude, créolisation, créolité: L'ethnicisation de la société française au prisme des auteurs martiniquais." *Les Temps modernes* 662-63, no. 1-2 (2011): 340–56.
"The And: An Expanded Questionnaire on the Contemporary." Special issue, *Field Notes*, no. 1 (2012). https://aaa.org.hk/archive/202583.
Anderson, Laurie. "Time and Beauty." In *Buddha Mind in Contemporary Art*, edited by Jacquelynn Baas and Mary Jane Jacob, 113–22. Berkeley: University of California Press, 2004.
Applebaum, Anne. "A Warning from Europe: The Worst Is Yet to Come." *Atlantic Monthly*, October 2018.
Aqeel, Shafi. *Char jadid musavvir: Ahmad Parvez, Sayyid Ali Imam, Anwar Jalal Shemza, Qutub Shaikh*. Karachi: Akadami Bazyafat, 2006.
Araeen, Rasheed. "Modernism, Postcolonial Nation States Art Criticism: A Reflection on the Work of Hanif Ramay and Sadequain." *Nukta: An Art Discourse*, no. 1 (2005): 22–29.
Araeen, Rasheed, ed. *The Other Story: Afro-Asian Artists in Post-war Britain*. Exhibition catalog. London: South Bank Centre, 1989.
Arendt, Hannah. *The Human Condition*. Chicago: University of Chicago Press, 1958.
Arendt, Hannah. Introduction to *Illuminations: Essays and Reflections*, by Walter Benjamin, 1–51. Edited by Hannah Arendt. Translated by Harry Zohn. New York: Schocken Books, 1968.
Arendt, Hannah. *The Origins of Totalitarianism*. San Diego, CA: Harcourt Brace, 1985.
Asad, Talal. "Religion, Nation-State, Secularism." In *Nation and Religion: Perspectives on Europe and Asia*, edited by Peter van der Veer and Hartmut Lehmann, 178–96. Princeton, NJ: Princeton University Press, 1999.
Atkins, Guy. *Jorn in Scandinavia, 1930–1953*. London: Lund, Humphries, 1968.
Auping, Michael. "An Interview with Jess." In *Jess: A Grand Collage, 1951–1993*, edited by Michael Auping, 19–30. Buffalo, NY: Albright-Knox Art Gallery, 1993.
Auping, Michael. *Jess: Paste-Ups (and Assemblies), 1951–1983*. Sarasota, FL: John and Mable Ringling Museum of Art, 1983.
Aziz, Khursheed Kamal. *The Coffee House of Lahore: A Memoir, 1942–57*. Lahore: Sang-e-Meel, 2008.

Baciu, Stefan. *Carlos Mérida, um maia na era atômica: Um diálogo*. Rio de Janeiro: Associação Brasileira do Congresso pela Liberdade da Cultura, 1961.
Baghdad Group for Modern Art. "Manifesto (1951)." Translated by Dinah El Husseiny. In *Modern Art in the Arab World: Primary Documents*, edited by Anneka Lenssen, Sarah Rogers, and Nada Shabout, 150–51. New York: MoMA Publications, 2018.
Bahnassi, Afif. *Ruwwad al-fan al-hadith fi al-bilad al-arabiyah*. Beirut: Dar Al-Raed Al-Arabi, 1985.
Bahrani, Zainab. "A Revolutionary Monument: Reclaiming the Naṣb al-Ḥurrīyya in Baghdad." *Journal of Contemporary Iraq and the Arab World* 15, no. 1–2 (March 2021): 27–40.
Balaghi, Shiva, and Lynn Gumpert, eds. *Picturing Iran: Art, Society, and Revolution*. London: I. B. Tauris, 2002.
Baldwin, James. "Princes and Powers." In *The Price of the Ticket: Collected Nonfiction, 1948–1985*, 41–63. Boston: Beacon, 2021.
Balzac, Honoré de. *The Unknown Masterpiece*. Translated by Richard Howard. New York: New York Review of Books, 2001.
Banaji, Jairus, ed. *Fascism: Essays on Europe and India*. Gurugram: Three Essays Collective, 2013.
Barber, Elizabeth Wayland. *Women's Work: The First 20,000 Years; Women, Cloth, and Society in Early Times*. New York: W. W. Norton, 1994.
Bardaouil, Sam. *Surrealism in Egypt: Modernism and the Art and Liberty Group*. London: I. B. Tauris, 2017.
Barthes, Roland. *Image-Music-Text*. Translated by Stephen Heath. New York: Hill and Wang, 1977.
Bartholomew, Richard. "Contemporary Indian Artists: Dhanraj Bhagat." In *Art Critic*, edited by Rati Bartholomew, Carmen Kagal, and Pablo Bartholomew, 329–32. Noida: BART, 2012.
Bartholomew, Richard. "Vivid Metal and Wood Sculptures by Dhanraj Bhagat." In *Art Critic*, edited by Rati Bartholomew, Carmen Kagal, and Pablo Bartholomew, 432. Noida: BART, 2012.
Bataille, Georges. *The Cradle of Humanity: Prehistoric Art and Culture*. Edited by Stuart Kendall. New York: Zone Books, 2005.
Bataille, Georges. *Prehistoric Painting: Lascaux or the Birth of Art*. Translated by Austryn Wainhouse. Lausanne: Skira, 1955.
Baumgartner, Michael, Jonathan Fineberg, and Rudi Fuchs, eds. *Klee and Cobra: A Child's Play*. Ostfildern: Hatje Cantz, 2011.
Beer, Olivier. *Lucien Hervé: Building Images*. Los Angeles: Getty Research Institute, 2004.
Beier, Ulli. *Contemporary Art in Africa*. London: Pall Mall Press, 1968.
Beier, Ulli. *Drawings: Ibrahim El Salahi*. Exhibition catalog. Ibadan, Nigeria: Mbari, 1962.
Beier, Ulli. "The Right to Claim the World: Conversation with Ibrahim El Salahi." *Third Text* 7, no. 23 (Summer 1993): 23–30.
Belting, Hans. *Art History after Modernism*. Chicago: University of Chicago Press, 2003.
Belting, Hans. "Contemporary Art as Global Art." In *The Global Art World: Audiences, Markets, and Museums*, edited by Hans Belting and Andrea Buddensieg, 39–40. Ostfildern: Hatje Cantz Verlag, 2009.

Benedict, Ruth. *The Chrysanthemum and the Sword: Patterns of Japanese Culture.* Boston: Houghton Mifflin, 1946.
Benhabib, Seyla. *The Reluctant Modernism of Hannah Arendt.* Lanham, MD: Rowman and Littlefield, 2003.
Benjamin, Walter. "Critique of Violence." In *1913–1926*, edited by Marcus Bullock and Michael W. Jennings, 236–54. Vol. 1 of *Selected Writings.* Cambridge, MA: Harvard University Press, 1996.
Benjamin, Walter. "Experience and Poverty." In *1927–1934*, edited by Michael W. Jennings, Howard Eiland, and Gary Smith, 731–36. Vol. 2, pt. 2, of *Selected Writings.* Cambridge, MA: Harvard University Press, 1999.
Berger, John. *Art and Revolution: Ernst Neizvestny and the Role of the Artist in the U.S.S.R.* London: Penguin Books, 1969.
Bethune, Ade. "Philippine Adventure." *Liturgical Arts* 19, no. 4 (August 1951): 110–13.
Biesenbach, Klaus Peter. *Mexico City: An Exhibition about the Exchange Rates of Bodies and Values; A Thematic Exhibition of International Artists Based in Mexico City.* Exhibition catalog. Long Island City, NY: PS1 Contemporary Art Center, 2002.
Billig, Michael S. *Barons, Brokers, and Buyers: The Institutions and Cultures of Philippine Sugar.* Quezon City: Ateneo de Manila University Press, 2003.
Bird, Junius B. "Technology and Art in Peruvian Textiles." In *Technique and Personality*, edited by Margaret Mead, Junius B. Bird, and Hans Himmelheber, 45–78. New York: Museum of Primitive Art, 1963.
Bird, Junius B., and Louisa Bellinger. *Paracas Fabrics and Nazca Needlework, 3rd Century BC–3rd Century AD.* Washington, DC: National Publishing, 1954.
Bird, Junius B., John Hyslop, and Milica Dimitrijevic Skinner. *The Preceramic Excavations at the Huaca Prieta, Chicama Valley, Peru.* Vol. 62, pt. 1. New York: Anthropological Papers of the American Museum of Natural History, 1985.
Birtwistle, Graham M. *Living Art: Asger Jorn's Comprehensive Theory of Art between Helhesten and Cobra, 1946–1949.* Utrecht: Reflex, 1986.
Bix, Herbert P. *Hirohito and the Making of Modern Japan.* New York: HarperCollins, 2000.
Blocker, Jane. *Becoming Past: History in Contemporary Art.* Minneapolis: University of Minnesota Press, 2015.
Breuil, Henri. *Four Hundred Centuries of Cave Art.* Translated by Mary E. Boyle. Montignac: Centre d'Etudes et de Documentation Préhistorique, 1952.
Breton, André. "On the Time When the Surrealists Were Right (1935)." In *Manifestoes of Surrealism*, translated by Richard Seaver and Helen R. Lane, 243–54. Ann Arbor: University of Michigan Press, 1969.
Brown, Deidre. "Mana Modernism." *Off the Wall*, no. 4 (January 2014): 1–6.
Brown, Evelyn S. *Africa's Contemporary Art and Artists.* New York: Harmon Foundation, 1966.
Brown, Gordon H. *Towards a Promised Land: On the Life and Art of Colin McCahon.* Auckland: Auckland University Press, 2010.
Brown, Jeremy. *City versus Countryside in Mao's China: Negotiating the Divide.* New York: Cambridge University Press, 2012.
Browning, Christopher R. "The Suffocation of Democracy." *New York Review of Books*, October 25, 2018.

Bruchet, Liz, and Ming Tiampo. "Slade, London, Asia: Contrapuntal Histories between Imperialism and Decolonization 1945–1989 (Part 1)." *British Art Studies*, no. 20 (July 2021). https://doi.org/10.17658/issn.2058-5462/issue-20/tiampobruchet.

Bryan-Wilson, Julia. *Art Workers: Radical Practice in the Vietnam War Era*. Berkeley: University of California Press, 2009.

Buchenau, Jürgen. "Ambivalent Neighbor: Mexico and Guatemala's 'Ten Years of Spring,' 1944–1954." *Latin Americanist* 61, no. 4 (December 2017): 458–73.

Buchloh, Benjamin H. D. "Beuys: The Twilight of the Idol, Preliminary Notes for a Critique." In *Neo-Avantgarde and Culture Industry: Essays on European and American Art from 1955 to 1975*, 41–64. Cambridge, MA: MIT Press, 2000.

Buchloh, Benjamin H. D. "Theorizing the Avant-Garde." *Art in America*, November 1984.

Burger, Peter. *Theory of the Avant-Garde*. Translated by Michael Shaw. Minneapolis: University of Minnesota Press, 1984.

Burroughs, William S. *The Ticket That Exploded*. Paris: Olympia, 1962.

Bushnell, G. H. S. Review of *Paracas Fabrics and Naszca Needlework, Third Century BC–Third Century AD*, by Junius B. Bird and Louisa Bellinger. *Man*, no. 55 (November 1955): 175.

Butcher, G. M. "Shemza: Years in London." *Contemporary Arts in Pakistan* 2, no. 2 (Summer 1961): 8–13.

Butler, Rex, and A. D. S. Donaldson. "Against Provincialism: Australian-American Connections 1900–2000." *Journal of Australian Studies* 36, no. 3 (2012): 291–307.

Büttner, Christof. "The Transformations of a Work of Art: 'Rent Collection Courtyard,' 1965–2009." In *Art for the Millions: 100 Sculptures from the Mao Era*, edited by Esther Schlicht and Max Hollein, 20–48. Munich: Hirmer Verlag, 2010.

Čapková, Helena. "Influence of Spirit and Not of Form: Antonín Raymond, Le Corbusier, and Architectural Piracy in the Transwar Era." In *A Pirate's View of World History: A Reversed Perception of the Order of Things from a Global Perspective*, edited by Shigemi Inaga, 85–93. Kyoto: International Research Center for Japanese Studies, 2017.

Carroll, Noël. "Art and Globalization: Then and Now." *Journal of Aesthetics and Art Criticism* 65, no. 1 (2007): 131–43.

Cernuschi, Claude. "Adolf Loos, Alois Riegl, and the Debate on Ornament in Fin-de-Siècle Vienna." In *Cosmophilia: Islamic Art from the David Collection, Copenhagen*, edited by Sheila S. Blair and Jonathan M. Bloom, 45–56. Chestnut Hill, MA: McMullen Museum of Art, 2006.

Césaire, Aimé. "Culture and Colonialism." *Présence Africaine*, no. 8/10 (June–November 1956): 190–205.

Césaire, Aimé. *Discourse on Colonialism*. Translated by Joan Pinkham. New York: Monthly Review Press, 2001.

Césaire, Aimé. "Letter to Maurice Thorez." *Social Text* 28, no. 2 (Summer 2010): 145–52.

Chakrabarty, Dipesh. "Legacies of Bandung: Decolonization and the Politics of Culture." In *Postwar: Art between the Pacific and the Atlantic, 1945–65*, edited by Okwui Enwezor, Katy Siegel, and Ulrich Wilmes, 74–79. Exhibition catalog. London: Prestel, 2016.

Chambers, Emma. "Prototype and Perception: Art History and Observation at the Slade in the 1950s." In *The Concept of the "Master" in Art Education in Britain and Ireland, 1770 to the Present*, edited by Matthew C. Potter, 189–214. New York: Routledge, 2016.

Chan-Magomedov, Selim O. *Pioniere der sowjetischen Architektur*. Dresden, Germany: VEB Verlag der Kunst, 1983.

Chiem, Kristen, and Cynthia S. Colburn. "Global Foundations for a World Art History." *Visual Resources* 31, no. 3 (2015): 177–99.

Christ-Janer, Albert, and Mary Mix Foley. *Modern Church Architecture: A Guide to the Form and Spirit of 20th Century Religious Buildings*. New York: Dodge Book Department, McGraw-Hill, 1962.

Clark, Jane. *Sidney Nolan: Landscapes and Legends*. New York: Cambridge University Press, 1987.

Clark, Jennifer. *Aborigines and Activism: Race, Aborigines and the Coming of the Sixties to Australia*. Crawley: University of Western Australia Press, 2008.

Clark, Paul. *The Chinese Cultural Revolution: A History*. New York: Cambridge University Press, 2008.

Cohen, Joshua. "Locating Senghor's École de Dakar: International and Transnational Dimensions to Senegalese Modern Art, c. 1959–1980." *African Arts* 51, no. 3 (Autumn 2018): 10–25.

Colomina, Beatriz. "Le Corbusier and Photography." *Assemblage*, no. 4 (October 1987): 6–23.

Constant. "Manifesto." In *Cobra 50 år*, edited by Anna Krogh and Holger Reenberg. Ishoj, 167–71. Denmark: Arken Museum for Moderne Kunst, 1997.

Constantine, Mildred, and Jack Lenor Larsen. "Sheila Hicks." In *Beyond Craft: The Art Fabric*, 173–93. San Francisco: Kodansha International, 1973.

Cooper, Frederick. "Possibility and Constraint: African Independence in Historical Perspective." *Journal of African History* 49, no. 2 (2008): 167–96.

Cortes, Rosario Mendoza. "Tan's Devoted Presidency (1951–1956): A Campus Shaken by Strife until Redeemed by Sobriety." In Alfonso, Oscar M., ed. *University of the Philippines: The First 75 Years (1908–1983)*, edited by Oscar M. Alfonso, 295–337. Quezon City: University of the Philippines Press, 1985.

Couturier, Marie-Alain. "Religious Art and the Modern Artist." *Magazine of Art* 45, no. 7 (November 1951): 268–72.

Cruz Porchini, Dafne, Claudia Garay Molina, and Mireida Velázquez Torres, eds. *Diplomacia cultural en México durante la Guerra Fría: exposiciones y prácticas artísticas, 1946–1968*. Mexico City: Secretaría de Relaciones Exteriores, 2021.

Curtis, William J. R. *Modern Architecture since 1900*. London: Phaidon, 2005.

Dadi, Iftikhar. "Calligraphic Abstraction: Anwar Jalal Shemza." In *Anwar Jalal Shemza*, edited by Iftikhar Dadi, 9–17. London: Ridinghouse, 2015.

Dadi, Iftikhar. *Modernism and the Art of Muslim South Asia*. Chapel Hill: University of North Carolina Press, 2010.

Daftari, Fereshteh. "Another Modernism: An Iranian Perspective." In Balaghi and Gumpert, *Picturing Iran*, 39–87.

Daghir, Sharbal. *Al-hurufiyah al-'arabiyah: Al-fann wa-al-huwiyah*. Beirut: Sharikat al-Matbuat lil-Tawzi wa-al-Nashr, 1990.

Daneshvari, Abbas. "Seismic Shifts across Political Zones in Contemporary Iranian Art: The Poetics of Knowledge, Knowing and Identity." In *Performing the Iranian State: Visual Culture and Representations of Iranian Identity*, edited by Staci Gem Scheiwiller, 101–20. London: Anthem, 2013.

Das, Kumar B. *Cement Industry of India*. New Delhi: Ashish, 1987.

Davis, Eric. *Memories of State: Politics, History, and Collective Identity in Modern Iraq*. Berkeley: University of California Press, 2005.

Davis, Whitney. "World without Art." *Art History* 33, no. 4 (2010): 711–16.

Day, Tony, and Maya H. T. Liem, eds. *Cultures at War: The Cold War and Cultural Expression in Southeast Asia*. Ithaca, NY: Cornell Southeast Asia Program Publications, 2010.

De la Cadena, Marisol, and Mario Blaser, eds. *A World of Many Worlds*. Durham, NC: Duke University Press, 2018.

Deleuze, Gilles, and Félix Guattari. *A Thousand Plateaus: Capitalism and Schizophrenia*. Translated by Brian Massumi. Minneapolis: University of Minnesota Press, 1987.

Deliss, Clémentine, and Catherine Lambert, ed. *Seven Stories about Modern Art in Africa*. Exhibition catalog. New York: Whitechapel Art Gallery, 1995.

Demos, T. J. *The Exiles of Marcel Duchamp*. Cambridge, MA: MIT Press, 2007.

Denis, Maurice. "Definition of Neotraditionism." *Art et Critique*, August 23 and 30, 1890.

Derrida, Jacques. *The Beast and the Sovereign*. Vols. 1–2. Translated by Geoffrey Bennington. Chicago: University of Chicago Press, 2009, 2011.

Desai, Prajna. "Other Than Nation." *Art in America* 107, no. 2 (2019): 50–57.

Deshpande, Satish. "Imagined Economies: Styles of Nation-Building in Twentieth Century India." *Journal of Arts and Ideas*, no. 25–26 (December 1993): 5–35.

Diagne, Souleymane Bachir. *African Art as Philosophy: Senghor, Bergson and the Idea of Negritude*. Translated by Chike Jeffers. London: Seagull Books, 2011.

Diop, Alioune. "Niam n'goura: Ou les raisons d'être de *Présence Africaine*." *Présence Africaine*, no. 1 (November–December 1947): 7–14.

Diop, Alioune. "Notre politique de la culture." *Présence Africaine*, no. 24/25 (February–May 1959): 5–7.

Dioquino, Corazon C. "Kumintang." In *CCP Encyclopedia of Philippine Art*, edited by Joi Barrios and Nicanor G. Tiongson, 92–93. Manila: Cultural Center of the Philippines, 1994.

Documenta '59: Kunst nach 1945; Malerei—Skulptur—Druckgrafik. 3 vols. Exhibition catalog. Cologne: Verlag DuMont Schauberg, 1959.

Douglas, Mary. *Purity and Danger: An Analysis of Concepts of Pollution and Taboo*. London: Routledge and Kegan Paul, 1966.

Dower, John W. *Embracing Defeat: Japan in the Wake of World War II*. New York: W. W. Norton, 1999.

Doyle, Laura, and Laura Winkiel. *Geomodernisms: Race, Modernism, Modernity*. Bloomington: Indiana University Press, 2005.

Doyle, Laura, and Laura Winkiel. Introduction to *Geomodernisms*, 1–16.

D'Souza, Aruna. Introduction to *Art History in the Wake of the Global Turn*, edited by Aruna D'Souza and Jill H. Casid, vii–xxiii. New Haven, CT: Yale University Press, 2014.

Dubuffet, Jean. "The Initiatory Paintings of Alfonso Ossorio." Translated by Richard Howard. In *Angels, Demons, and Savages: Pollock, Ossorio, Dubuffet*, edited by Klaus Ottman and Dorothy Kosinsky, 115–28. Exhibition catalog. Washington, DC: Phillips Collection in association with Yale University Press, 2013.

Dunn, Michael. "The Enigma of Gordon Walters' Art." *Art New Zealand*, no. 9 (March–April 1978): 56–63.

Dussel, Enrique. "World System and 'Transmodernity.'" *Nepantla: Views from South* 3, no. 2 (2002): 221–44.

Economist. "A God Dethroned." August 31, 2000. www.economist.com/books-and-arts/2000/08/31/a-god-dethroned.

Eder, Rita, ed. *Desafío a la estabilidad: Procesos artísticos en México / Defying Stability: Artistic Processes in Mexico; 1952–1967*. Mexico City: Turner/UNAM, 2014.

Ekpo, Denis. "Slaying Négritude's Last Shadows: Post-Africanizing Senghor, Dakar, and Dak'Art." *Obieg*, June 24, 2016. https://obieg.pl/en/7-slaying-n-gritude-s-last-shadows-post-africanizing-senghor-dakar-and-dak-art.

Elkins, James, ed. *Is Art History Global?* New York: Routledge, 2007.

El Popular. "Siqueiros y Diego apelan el buen criterio del rector." June 15, 1954.

El-Salahi, Ibrahim. "Chronologue." Unpublished manuscript, n.d. Typewritten document.

El-Salahi, Ibrahim. "The Artist in His Own Words." Translated by Mustafa Adam. In *Ibrahim El-Salahi: A Visionary Modernist*, edited by Salah M. Hassan, 81–91. Seattle: University of Washington Press, 2012.

Emami, Karim, and Peter Lamborn Wilson. *Saqqakhaneh*. Exhibition catalog. Tehran: Tehran Museum of Contemporary Art, 1977.

English, Darby. *1971: A Year in the Life of Color*. Chicago: University of Chicago Press, 2016.

Enwezor, Okwui. "Mega-exhibitions and the Antinomies of a Transnational Global Form." *Documents*, no. 23 (Spring 2004): 2–19.

Enwezor, Okwui. "The Postcolonial Constellation: Contemporary Art in a State of Permanent Transition." *Research in African Literatures* 34, no. 4 (2003): 57–82.

Enwezor, Okwui, ed. *The Short Century: Independence and Liberation Movements in Africa, 1945–1994*. Munich: Prestel, 2001.

Enwezor, Okwui. "Travel Notes: Living, Working, and Travelling in a Restless World." In *Trade Routes: History and Geography; 2nd Johannesburg Biennale 1997*, edited by Okwui Enwezor, 7–12. Exhibition catalog. Johannesburg: Greater Johannesburg Metropolitan Council and Thorold's Africana Books, 1997.

Enwezor, Okwui, and Chika Okeke-Agulu. *Contemporary African Art since 1980*. Bologna: Damaini, 2009.

Enwezor, Okwui, Katy Siegel, and Ulrich Wilmes. *Postwar: Art between the Pacific and the Atlantic, 1945–65*. Exhibition catalog. London: Prestel, 2016.

Enwonwu, Ben. "The African View of Art and Some Problems Facing the African Artist." In *Premier festival mondial des arts nègres: Colloque sur l'art nègre, Rapport*, vol. 1, edited by Société Africaine de Culture, 417–26. Paris: Présence Africaine, 1967.

Enwonwu, Ben. "Problems of the African Artist Today." *Présence Africaine*, no. 8/10 (June–November 1956): 174–78.
Eshun, Kodwo. "Further Considerations of AfroFuturism." *CR: The New Centennial Review* 3, no. 2 (2003), 287–302.
Evenson, Norma. *Chandigarh*. Berkeley: University of California Press, 1966.
Eyène, Christine. "Sekoto and Negritude: The Ante-room of French Culture." *Third Text* 24, no. 4 (2010): 423–35.
Fabri, Charles L. *Bhagat*. New Delhi: Lalit Kala Akademi, 1964.
Falvo, Rosa Maria, ed. *Zainul Abedin: Great Masters of Bangladesh*. Milan: Skira, 2012.
Fanon, Frantz. *The Wretched of the Earth*. Translated by Richard Philcox. New York: Grove Books, 2005.
Faraj, Maysaloun, ed. *Strokes of Genius: Contemporary Iraqi Art*. London: Saqi Books, 2001.
Fazila-Yacoobali, Vazira. "The Making and Unmaking of a National Artist." In *Sadequain: The Holy Sinner*, edited by Abdul Hamid Akhund, Farida Munavarjahan Said, and Zohra Yusuf, 54–67. Exhibition catalog. Karachi: Mohatta Palace Museum, 2003.
Feldman, Hannah. *From a Nation Torn: Decolonizing Art and Representation in France, 1945–1962*. Durham, NC: Duke University Press, 2014.
Findlay, John M., and Bruce Hevly. *Atomic Frontier Days: Hanford and the American West*. Seattle: Center for the Study of the Pacific Northwest in association with University of Washington Press, 2011.
Fodor, Nandor. *The Search for the Beloved: A Clinical Investigation of the Trauma of Birth and Pre-natal Conditioning*. New York: Hermitage, 1949.
Forty, Adrian. *Concrete and Culture: A Material History*. London: Reaktion Books, 2012.
Foster, Hal. "I Am the Decider." *London Review of Books*, March 2011.
Foster, Hal. *Prosthetic Gods*. Cambridge, MA: MIT Press, 2004.
Foster, Hal. "What's Neo about the Neo-Avant-Garde?" *October*, no. 70 (Autumn 1994): 5–32.
Fosu, Kojo. *20th Century Art of Africa*. Zaria: Gaskiya, 1986.
Fox, Claire F. *Making Art Panamerican: Cultural Policy and the Cold War*. Minneapolis: University of Minnesota Press, 2013.
Friedman, B. H. *Alfonso Ossorio*. New York: Harry N. Abrams, 1973.
Friedman, Winifred H. *Boydell's Shakespeare Gallery*. New York: Garland, 1976.
Galimberti, Jacopo. *Individuals against Individualism: Art Collectives in Western Europe (1956–1969)*. Liverpool: Liverpool University Press, 2017.
Gaonkar, Dilip P. "On Alternative Modernities." *Public Culture* 11, no. 1 (1999): 1–18.
Gassmann de Sousa, Bea. "Decolonizing Nigerian Modernism: Ben Enwonwu's 'Identity in Politics.'" *Tate Papers*, no. 30 (Autumn 2018). https://www.tate.org.uk/research/publications/tate-papers/30/decolonising- nigerian-modernism-ben-enwonwus-identity-politics.
Gauchet, Marcel. "Primitive Religion and the Origins of the State." In *New French Thought: Political Philosophy*, edited by Mark Lilla, 116–22. Princeton, NJ: Princeton University Press, 1994.
Gerber, Michele S. *On the Home Front: The Cold War Legacy of the Hanford Nuclear Site*. Lincoln: University of Nebraska Press, 1992.

Gerschultz, Jessica. *Decorative Arts of the Tunisian École: Fabrications of Modernism, Gender, and Power*. University Park, PA: Penn State University Press, 2019.
Getsy, David J. "Tactility or Opticality, Henry Moore or David Smith: Herbert Read and Clement Greenberg on *The Art of Sculpture*, 1956." In *Anglo-American Exchange in Postwar Sculpture, 1945–1975*, edited by Rebecca Peabody, 105–21. Los Angeles: Getty Research Institute, 2011.
Giedion, Sigfried. *Architecture, You and Me: The Diary of a Development*. Cambridge, MA: Harvard University Press, 1958.
Gifkins, Michael, ed. *Colin McCahon: Gates and Journeys*. Exhibition catalog. Auckland: Auckland City Art Gallery, 1988.
Goeritz, Mathias. "La integración plástica en el C.U. 'Presidente Juárez.'" *Arquitectura México*, no. 40 (July 1952): 419–25.
Goeritz, Mathias. "Manifiesto de la arquitectura emocional (1953)." In *El Eco de Mathias Goeritz: Pensamientos y dudas autocríticas*, edited by Mathias Goeritz, 27–30. Compiled by Leonor Cuahonte. Mexico City: Instituto de Investigaciones Estéticas, Universidad Nacional Autónoma de México, 2007.
Goeritz, Mathias. "The Sculpture 'The Serpent of El Eco': A Primary Structure of 1953." *Leonardo* 3, no. 1 (January 1970): 63–65.
Goldman, Zoe. "Imagining a City of Plastic Integration through Guía de Arquitectura Contemporánea Mexicana/Guide to Contemporary Mexican Architecture." *Caiana: Revista de historia del arte y cultura visual del centro argentino de investigadores de arte*, no. 13 (Second Semester 2018): 62–76.
Gombrich, Ernst. *Art and Illusion: A Study in the Psychology of Pictorial Representation*. Millennium ed. Princeton, NJ: Princeton University Press, 1960.
Gombrich, Ernst. *The Story of Art*. New York: Phaidon, 1950.
Gómez Mayorga, Mauricio. "Sobre la libertad de creación." *Arquitectura México* 10, no. 45 (March 1954): 37–45.
Greenberg, Clement. "Avant-Garde and Kitsch." In *Art and Culture: Critical Essays*, 3–21. Boston: Beacon, 1961.
Greenberg, Clement. "Modernist Painting." In *The Collected Essays and Criticism*. Vol. 4, *Modernism with a Vengeance, 1957–1969*, edited by John O'Brian, 85–93. Chicago: University of Chicago Press, 1995.
Greenberg, Clement. "The New Sculpture." In *Collected Essays and Criticism*. Vol. 2, *Arrogant Purpose, 1945–1949*, edited by John O'Brian. Chicago: University of Chicago Press, 1986.
Greenberg, Clement. "Sculpture in Our Time." In *The Collected Essays and Criticism*. Vol. 4, *Modernism with a Vengeance, 1957–1969*, edited by John O'Brian. Chicago: University of Chicago Press, 1995.
Grohmann, Will, ed. *Art since 1945*. New York: Harry N. Abrams, 1958.
Grohmann, Will, ed. *Neue Kunst nach 1945*. Cologne: M. Dumont Schauberg, 1958.
Grossman, Daniel. "Hanford and Its Early Radioactive Atmospheric Releases." *Pacific Northwest Quarterly* 85, no. 1 (January 1994): 6–14.
Groys, Boris. *History Becomes Form: Moscow Conceptualism*. Cambridge, MA: MIT Press, 2010.

Guha-Thakurta, Tapati. *The Making of a New "Indian" Art: Artists, Aesthetics and Nationalism in Bengal, c. 1850–1920*. New York: Cambridge University Press, 1992.

Guilbaut, Serge. *How New York Stole the Idea of Modern Art: Abstract Expressionism, Freedom, and the Cold War*. Translated by Arthur Goldhammer. Chicago: University of Chicago Press, 1983.

Gupta, Atreyee. "Dwelling in Abstraction: Post-partition Segues into Postwar Art." In "To Draw the Line: Partitions, Dissonance, Art—a Case for South Asia," edited by Alice Correia and Natasha Eaton. Special issue, *Third Text* 31, no. 2-3 (2017): 433–57.

Gupta, Atreyee, and Sugata Ray. "Is Art History Global? Responding from the Margins." In *Is Art History Global?* edited by James Elkins, 348–57. New York: Routledge, 2007.

Hales, Peter B. *Atomic Spaces: Living on the Manhattan Project*. Chicago: University of Illinois Press, 1997.

Hales, Peter B. "The Atomic Sublime." *American Studies* 32, no. 1 (Spring 1991): 5–31.

Hall, Stuart. "Black Diaspora Artists in Britain: Three 'Moments' in Post-war History." *History Workshop Journal*, no. 61 (Spring 2006): 1–24.

Hammill, Graham, and Julia Reinhard Lupton. Introduction to *Political Theology and Early Modernity*, edited by Graham Hammill and Julia Reinhard Lupton, 1–20. Chicago: University of Chicago Press, 2012.

Hamoudi, Jameel, ed. *Al-fikr al-hadith: Majalla shahriya lil fan wa al-thaqafah al-hura* 1, no. 4 (1949).

Handberg, Kristian. "The World Goes Modern: New Globalized Framings of the Postwar Era in the Contemporary Exhibitions *After Year Zero* and *The World Goes Pop*." *Journal of Aesthetics and Culture* 8, no. 1 (2016). https://doi.org/10.3402/jac.v8.30925.

Harney, Elizabeth. "Constellations and Coordinates: Repositioning Postwar Paris in Stories of African Modernisms." In *Mapping Modernisms: Art, Indigeneity, Colonialism*, edited by Elizabeth Harney and Ruth B. Phillips, 304–34. Durham, NC: Duke University Press, 2018.

Harney, Elizabeth. *In Senghor's Shadow: Art, Politics and the Avant-Garde in Senegal, 1960–1995*. Durham, NC: Duke University Press, 2004.

Harney, Elizabeth. "Narratives of a Reluctant Modernist: Rethinking William Fagg's Africa." *Res: Anthropology and Aesthetics*, no. 77/78 (Spring–Autumn 2022): 1–14.

Harootunian, Harry. "Disciplining the Enemy: Area Studies and the Relocation of Japan." Unpublished manuscript, ca. 1998. Typed document.

Harris, Jonathan. *The Global Contemporary Art World*. Oxford: Wiley-Blackwell, 2017.

Hashim, Muhammad. *Hashem al-Khattat* . London: Iraqi Cultural Centre, 1978.

Hassan, Ijaz Ul. "The Way It Was: Cutty Patang." *Daily Times* (Lahore, Pakistan), March 15, 2006.

Hassan, Salah M., ed. *Ibrahim El-Salahi: A Visionary Modernist*. Exhibition catalog. Seattle: University of Washington Press, 2012.

Hassan, Salah M. "The Khartoum and Addis Connections: Two Stories from Sudan and Ethiopia." In *Seven Stories about Modern Art in Africa*, edited by Clementine Deliss and Catherine Lambert, 105–25. Exhibition catalog. New York: Whitechapel, 1995.

Heathcote, Christopher. *A Quiet Revolution: The Rise of Australian Art 1946–1968*. Melbourne: Text Publishing, 1995.

Heidegger, Martin. *The Fundamental Concepts of Metaphysics: World, Finitude, Solitude*. Translated by William McNeill and Nicholas Walker. Bloomington: Indiana University Press, 1995.

Heidegger, Martin. "Letter on Humanism." 1947. In *Martin Heidegger: Basic Writings*, edited by David Farrell Krell, 213–66. New York: HarperCollins, 2008.

Heidegger, Martin. *Parmenides*. Translated by André Schuwer and Richard Rojcewicz. Bloomington: Indiana University Press, 1992.

Hitchcock, Henry-Russell. *Latin American Architecture since 1945*. New York: Museum of Modern Art, 1955.

Ho, Christine I. "The People Eat for Free and the Art of Collective Production in Maoist China." *Art Bulletin* 98, no. 3 (2016): 348–72.

Ho, Denise, and Jie Li. "From Landlord Manor to Red Memorabilia: Reincarnations of a Chinese Museum Town." *Modern China* 41, 4 (July 2015): 1–35.

Hobbes, Thomas. *Leviathan, or, The Matter, Forme and Power of a Commonwealth Ecclesiasticall and Civil*. London: Andrew Crooke, 1651.

Hoek, Lotte, and Sanjukta Sunderason. "Journeying through Modernism: Travels and Transits of East Pakistani Artists in Post-imperial London." *British Art Studies*, no. 13 (September 2019). https://www.britishartstudies.ac.uk/issues/issue-index/issue-13/two-east-pakistani-artists-in-post-war-london.

Holledge, Richard. "The Myriad Aspects of Ibrahim El-Salahi." *Gulf News* (Dubai, United Arab Emirates), June 27, 2013. https://gulfnews.com/general/the-myriad-aspects-of-ibrahim-el-salahi-1.1202632.

Holt, Claire. *Art in Indonesia: Continuities and Change*. Ithaca, NY: Cornell University Press, 1967.

Holt, John. "Anwar Jalal Shemza: A Search for the Significant." *Third Text* 12, no. 42 (1998): 104–8.

Holzhey, Christoph F. E. Introduction to Holzhey, *Multistable Figures*, 7–21.

Holzhey, Christoph F. E., ed. *Multistable Figures: On the Critical Potentials of Ir/Reversible Aspect-Seeing*. Cultural Inquiry 8. Vienna: Turia + Kant, 2014.

Hongoh, Joseph. "The Asian-African Conference (Bandung) and Pan-Africanism: The Challenge of Reconciling Continental Solidarity with National Sovereignty." *Australian Journal of International Affairs* 70, no. 4 (2016): 374–90.

Hoopes, Townsend, and Douglas Brinkley. *FDR and the Creation of the U.N.* New Haven, CT: Yale University Press, 1997.

Hua Junwu. "Zhide xuexi de diaosu hao yanbang." *Renmin ribao* (Beijing), October 31, 1965, 4.

Hughes, Jeff. *The Manhattan Project: Big Science and the Atom Bomb*. New York: Columbia University Press, 2003.

Husain, Intizar. *Chiraghon ka dhuan: Yadon ke pachas baras*. Lahore: Sang-e-Meel, 2003.

"Interview with Shakir Hassan Al Said." *Al-Aqlam* 1, no. 3 (November 1965): 89–102.

Irele, F. Abiola. *The Negritude Movement: Explorations in Francophone African and Caribbean Literature and Thought*. Trenton, NJ: Africa World Press, 2011.

Irele, F. Abiola. "'1956 and After': Cinquantenaire du 1er congrès des écrivains et artistes noirs." *Présence Africaine*, no. 175/177 (2007): 229–33.

Iriye, Akira. *The Origins of the Second World War in Asia and the Pacific*. Abingdon, VA: Routledge, 1987.

Isaac, Allan Punzalan. Introduction to *American Tropics: Articulating Filipino America*, xv–xxx. Minneapolis: University of Minnesota Press, 2006.

Issa, Rose, Ruyin Pakbaz, and Daryush Shayegan. *Iranian Contemporary Art*. London: Booth-Clibborn Editions, 2001.

Jabra, Jabra I. *Al-rihla al-thaminah: Dirasat naqdiyyah*. Beirut: Al-Moassasah al-Arabiyyah lil Dirasat wa al-Nashr, 1967.

Jabra, Jabra I. *The Grass Roots of Iraqi Art*. St. Helier, Jersey, Channel Islands: Wasit Graphic, 1983.

Jabra, Jabra I. *Iraqi Art Today*. Art Series 15. Baghdad: Ministry of Information, 1972.

Jabra, Jabra I. *Jawad Salim wa-nusb al-hurriyah: Dirasah fi atharih wa-araih*. Baghdad: Wizarat al-Ilam, Mudiriyat al-Thaqafah al-Ammah, 1974.

Jachec, Nancy. "Léopold Sédar Senghor and the Cultures de l'Afrique noire et de l'occident (1960): EuroAfricanism, Negritude and the Civilization of the Universal." *Third Text* 24, no. 2 (2010), 195–204.

James, Paul, and Manfred B. Steger. "A Genealogy of 'Globalization': The Career of a Concept." *Globalizations* 11, no. 4 (2014): 417–34.

Javed, Yunus. *Halqa-e-Arbab-e-Zauq*. Lahore: Majlis-e-Taraqqi-e-Adab, 1984.

Jeanneret, Pierre. "Incidences des techniques locales et du climat sur la construction à Chandigarh." *L'architecture d'aujourd'hui*, no. 67–68 (October 1956): 180–82.

Jolles, Adam. "Stalin's Talking Museums." *Oxford Art Journal* 28, no. 3 (October 2005): 429–55.

Jones, Amelia. "Writing Contemporary Art into History, a Paradox?" In *A Companion to Contemporary Art since 1945*, edited by Amelia Jones, 3–16. Malden, MA: Blackwell, 2006.

Jones, Caroline A., and Steven Nelson. "Global Turns in US Art History." *Perspective*, no. 2 (2015): 2–14.

Jorn, Asger. "Discours aux pingouins." *Cobra*, no. 1 (1949): 8.

Jorn, Asger. "The Human Animal." Translated by Niels Henriksen. *October*, no. 141 (Summer 2012): 53–58.

Jorn, Asger. *Lettres à plus jeune*. Paris: L'Echoppe, 1998.

Jorn, Asger. "Peinture détournée." In *Vingt peintures modifiées par Asger Jorn*, n.p. Exhibition catalog. Paris: Galerie Rive Gauche, 1959.

Josten, Jennifer. *Mathias Goeritz: Modernist Art and Architecture in Cold War Mexico*. New Haven, CT: Yale University Press, 2018.

Joyeux-Prunel, Béatrice, ed. "Art History and the Global Challenge: A Critical Perspective." Special Issue, *Artl@s Bulletin* 6, no. 1 (2017).

Juneja, Monica. "Global Art History and the 'Burden of Representation.'" In *Global Studies: Mapping Contemporary Art and Culture*, edited by Hans Belting, Jakob Birken, Andrea Buddensieg, and Peter Weibel, 274–97. Ostfildern: Hatje Cantz, 2011.

Kamel, Adel. *Al-harakah al-tashkiliyah fi al-Iraq: Marhalat al-Ruwwad*. Baghdad: Ministry of Culture and Information, 1980.

Kamola, Isaac. "A Time for Anticolonial Theory." *Contemporary Political Theory* 18, no. S2 (2019): 67–74.

Katō Etsurō, *Okurareta kakumei*. Tokyo: Shōwa 21, 1946.

Kee, Joan. *Contemporary Korean Art: Tansaekhwa and the Urgency of Method*. Minneapolis: University of Minnesota Press, 2013.

Keshmirshekan, Hamid. "Saqqa-Kana School of Art." In *Encyclopaedia Iranica*, online ed. Article published August 15, 2009. www.iranicaonline.org/articles/saqqa-kana-ii-school-of-art.

Keswick, Maggie, ed. *The Thistle and the Jade: A Celebration of 150 years of Jardine, Matheson and Co*. London: Octopus Books, 1982.

Khullar, Sonal. "Parallel Tracks: Pan Yuliang and Amrita Sher-Gil in Paris." In *Eurasian Encounters: Museums, Missions, Modernities*, edited by Yoshiyuki Kikuchi and Carolien Stolte, 73–102. Amsterdam: Amsterdam University Press, 2017.

Kieckhefer, Richard. *Theology in Stone: Church Architecture from Byzantium to Berkeley*. New York: Oxford University Press, 2004.

Klassen, Winand W. *Architecture in the Philippines: Filipino Building in a Cross-Cultural Context*. Cebu City: University of San Carlos, 1986.

Knöfel, Ulrike. "Es ist eine Beleidigung, ja." *Der Spiegel*, August 17, 2018. www.spiegel.de/kultur/okwui-enwezor-ueber-seinen-schmaehlichen-abschied-aus-muenchen-a-00000000-0002-0001-0000-000158955211.

Koselleck, Reinhart. *Futures Past: On the Semantics of Historical Time*. Translated and with an introduction by Keith Tribe. New York: Columbia University Press, 2004.

Krauss, Rosalind E. *The Originality of the Avant-Garde and Other Modernist Myths*. Cambridge, MA: MIT Press, 1986.Kubler, George. *The Art and Architecture of Ancient America: The Mexican, Maya, and Andean Peoples*. Baltimore: Pelican History of Art, 1962.

Kubler, George. "Renascence and Disjunction in the Art of Mesoamerican Antiquity." In *Studies in Ancient American and European Art: The Collected Essays of George Kubler*, edited by Thomas F. Reese, 351–72. New Haven, CT: Yale University Press, 1985.

Kubler, George. *The Shape of Time: Remarks on the History of Things*. New Haven, CT: Yale University Press, 1962.

Kubler, George. "The South Coast Valleys." In *The Art and Architecture of Ancient America: The Mexican, Maya, and Andean Peoples*, 283–301. New York: Penguin, 1975.

Kupka, Karel. *The Dawn of Art: Painting and Sculpture of Australian Aborigines*. Sydney: Angus and Robertson, 1965.

Kurczynski, Karen. "Ironic Gestures: Asger Jorn, Informel, and Abstract Expressionism." In *Abstract Expressionism: The International Context*, edited by Joan Marter, 104–24. New Brunswick, NJ: Rutgers University Press, 2007.

Kurczynski, Karen. "No Man's Land." *October*, no. 141 (Summer 2012): 22–52.

Kurczynski, Karen, and Nicola Pezolet. "Primitivism, Humanism, and Ambivalence: Cobra and Post-Cobra." *Res: Anthropology and Aesthetics*, no. 59/60 (Fall 2011): 282–302.

Kwami, Atta. *Kumasi Realism, 1951–2007: An African Modernism*. London: C. Hurst, 2013.

Lachenal, Guillaume, and Aïssatou Mbodj-Pouye. "Politique de la nostalgie: Restes du développement et traces de la modernité en Afrique." *Politique Africaine* 135, no. 4 (October 2014): 5–21.

Lachica, Eduardo. *Ayala, the Philippines' Oldest Business House*. Makati, Philippines: Filipinas Foundation, 1984.

Laing, Ellen Johnston. *The Winking Owl: Art in the People's Republic of China*. Berkeley: University of California Press, 1988.

Lambert, Michael C. "From Citizenship to Négritude: 'Making a Difference' in Elite Ideologies of Colonized Francophone West Africa." *Comparative Studies in Society and History* 35, no. 2 (April 1993): 239–62.

Larkin, Brian. "The Politics and Poetics of Infrastructure." *Annual Review of Anthropology* 42, no. 328 (2013): 327–43.

Larkin, John. *Sugar and the Origins of Modern Philippine Society*. Berkeley: University of California Press, 1993.

Latham, Rob. "Our Jaded Tomorrows." *Science Fiction Studies* 36, no. 2 (July 2009): 339–49.

Lebovics, Herman. *Bringing the Empire Back Home: France in the Global Age*. Durham, NC: Duke University Press, 2004.

Le Corbusier. *Le Corbusier Sketchbooks*. Vol. 3, *1954–1957*. Notes by Françoise de Franclieu. Cambridge, MA: MIT Press, 1982.

Le Corbusier. *Towards a New Architecture*. London: Architectural Press, 1927.

Lecznar, Matthew. "Weathering the Storm: Ben Enwonwu's Biafrascapes and the Crisis in the Nigerian Postcolony." *Tate Papers*, no. 30 (Autumn 2018). https://www.tate.org.uk/research/tate-papers/30/weathering-the-storm.

Lee, Christopher J. "At the Rendezvous of Decolonization: Final Communiqué of the Asian-African Conference, Bandung, Indonesia, 18–24 April 1955." *Interventions: International Journal of Postcolonial Studies* 11, no. 1 (2009): 81–93.

Lee, Christopher J. "Final Communiqué of the Asian African Conference." *Interventions: International Journal of Postcolonial Studies* 11, no. 1 (2009): 94–102.

Lee, Christopher J., ed. *Making a World after Empire: The Bandung Moment and Its Political Afterlives*. Athens: Ohio University Press, 2010.

Lee, J. M. "Commonwealth Students in the United Kingdom, 1940–1960: Student Welfare and World Status." *Minerva* 44, no. 1 (2006): 1–24.

Lee, Pamela M. *Chronophobia: On Time in the Art of the 1960s*. Cambridge, MA: MIT Press, 2004.

Lee, Pamela M. "'Ultramoderne': Or, How George Kubler Stole the Time in Sixties Art." *Grey Room*, no. 2 (Winter 2001): 46–77.

Lelyveld, Joseph. "Modern U.S. Art Stirs New Delhi; New York School, Pop and Op Get Mixed Reactions." *New York Times*, April 10, 1967.

Lenin, Vladimir Ilyich. *Imperialism: The Highest Stage of Capitalism*. London: Penguin Classics, 2010.

Lenin, Vladimir Ilyich. "On Proletarian Culture." In *Lenin's Collected Works*, vol. 31, 4th ed., edited by Joseph Lelyveld, translated by Julius Katzer, 316–17. Moscow: Progress, 1965.

Lenssen, Anneka, Sarah Rogers, and Nada Shabout, eds. *Modern Art in the Arab World: Primary Documents*. New York: MoMA Publications, 2018.

Lévi-Strauss, Monique. *Sheila Hicks*. London: Studio Vista, 1974.

Lewis, David Levering. *W. E. B. Du Bois: The Fight for Equality and the American Century, 1919–1963*. New York: Henry Holt, 2000.

Li, Hsiao-t'i. "Making a Name and a Culture for the Masses in Modern China." *Positions: East Asia Cultures Critique* 9, no. 1 (2001): 29–68.

Li, Vivian. "Redefining Artistic Value in Communist China: *Rent Collection Courtyard*." *Oxford Art Journal* 39, no. 3 (December 2016): 377–98.

Li, Vivian. "*Rent Collection Courtyard*, 1968, Palace of Culture, Tirana." In *The Handbook of Socialist Exhibition Cultures: International Art Exhibitions in the Socialist World 1947–1989*, edited by Sven Spieker with Polly Savage, Bojana Videkanic, and Christene d'Anca. Toronto: University of Toronto Press, forthcoming.

Li, Yan. "Lun Wang Zhaowen wu liu shi nian dai de meishu pipin—shi yi daxing nisu 'Shouzu yuan' weilie." *Guancha* 3 (2004): 85–87.

Lico, Gerard. *Arkitekturang Filipino: A History of Architecture and Urbanism in the Philippines*. Diliman: University of the Philippines Press, 2008.

Lifshitz, Mikhail. "Why Am I Not a Modernist? [*Estetika*, 1963]." Garage Museum of Contemporary Art, accessed July 30, 2024. https://garagemca.org/en/exhibition/i-if-our-soup-can-could-speak-mikhail-lifshitz-and-the-soviet-sixties-i/materials/pochemu-ya-ne-modernist-why-i-am-not-a-modernist#.

Lindqvist, Sven. *A History of Bombing*. Translated by Linda Haverty Rugg. New York: New Press, 2003.

Lindsay, Jennifer, and Maya H. T. Liem, eds. *Heirs to World Culture: Being Indonesian 1950–1965*. Leiden: KITLV Press, 2012.

Liu, Zhaoquan, ed. *Sichuan meishu xueyuan xiaoshi*. Chongqing: Sichuan Meishu Xueyuan, 1990.

Llewellyn, Nigel. "Histories and Contexts." In *The London Art Schools: Reforming the Art World, 1960 to Now*, edited by Nigel Llewellyn and Beth Williamson, 9–25. London: Tate, 2015.

Locsin, Leandro V. "Directions for the Building of a Church." In *The Poet of Space: Leandro V. Locsin,* edited by Augusto V. Villalon and Rodrigo D. Perez III, 16–17. Manila: Cultural Center of the Philippines, 1996.

Loeffler, Jane C. "The Architecture of Diplomacy: Heyday of the United States Embassy-Building Program, 1954–1960." *Journal of the Society of Architectural Historians* 49, no. 3 (September 1990): 251–78.

López, Paula Barreiro. *Avant-Garde Art and Criticism in Francoist Spain*. Liverpool: Liverpool University Press, 2017.

Los Angeles County Museum of Art. *Four Abstract Classicists.* Exhibition catalog. Los Angeles: Los Angeles County Museum of Art, 1959.

Lukács, Georg. "Expressionism: Its Significance and Decline." In *Georg Lukács: Essays on Realism,* edited by Rodney Livingstone and translated by David Temback, 76–113. Cambridge, MA: MIT Press, 1980.

Lyford, Amy. "Noguchi, Sculptural Abstraction, and the Politics of Japanese American Internment." *Art Bulletin* 85, no. 1 (March 2003): 137–51.

Malaquais, Dominique, and Cédric Vincent. "Entangled Panafrica: Four Festivals and an Archive." *Mezosfera*, May 28, 2018. http://mezosfera.org/entangled-panafrica.
Manahan, Liliane R. "This Is Not an Angry Christ." In *Victorious: 100 Years Victorias Milling Company, Inc.*, edited by Felipe F. Salvosa II, 28–47. Victorias City: Victorias Milling Company, 2019.
Mane-Wheoki, Jonathan. "The Class of '66." *Off the Wall*, no. 1 (March 2013): 1–4. http://arts.tepapa.govt.nz/off-the-wall/4130/the-class-of-66.
Mansoor, Jaleh. *Marshall Plan Modernism: Italian Postwar Abstraction and the Beginnings of Autonomia*. Durham, NC: Duke University Press, 2016.
McCahon, Colin. "Beginnings." *Landfall* 20, no. 4 (1966): 360–64.
McLean, Ian. "Aboriginal Modernism in Australia." In Mercer, *Exiles, Diasporas and Strangers*, 72–95.
McLuhan, Marshall. *The Gutenberg Galaxy: The Making of Typographic Man*. Toronto, ON: University of Toronto Press, 1962.
McMahon, Robert J., ed. *The Cold War in the Third World*. Oxford: Oxford University Press, 2013.
Medosch, Armin. *New Tendencies: Art at the Threshold of the Information Revolution (1961–1978)*. Cambridge, MA: MIT Press, 2016.
Mercer, Kobena, ed. *Cosmopolitan Modernisms*. Cambridge, MA: Institute of International Visual Arts/MIT Press, 2005.
Mercer, Kobena, ed. *Discrepant Abstraction*. Cambridge, MA: Institute of International Visual Arts/MIT Press, 2006.
Mercer, Kobena, ed. *Exiles, Diasporas and Strangers*. Cambridge, MA: Institute of International Visual Arts/MIT Press, 2008.
Mercer, Kobena, ed. *Pop Art and Vernacular Cultures*. Cambridge, MA: Institute of International Visual Arts/MIT Press, 2007.
Mérida, Carlos. *Escritos de Carlos Mérida sobre arte: El muralismo*. Edited by Xavier Guzmán Urbiola. Mexico City: Instituto Nacional de Bellas Artes, Centro Nacional de Investigación, Documentación, e Información de Artes Plásticas, 1987.
Mérida, Carlos. "La pintura funcional." In *Escritos de Carlos Mérida sobre arte: el muralismo*, 133–34. Mexico City: Instituto Nacional de Bellas Artes, Centro Nacional de Investigación, Documentación, e Información de Artes Plásticas, 1987.
Mérida, Carlos. "Self-Portrait." *Américas* 2, no. 6 (June 1950): 25–27.
Meyer, Richard. *What Was Contemporary Art?* Cambridge, MA: MIT Press, 2013.
Mignolo, Walter D. *The Darker Side of Western Modernity: Global Futures, Decolonial Options*. Durham, NC: Duke University Press, 2011.
Mitter, Partha. *Art and Nationalism in Colonial India, 1850–1922: Occidental Orientations*. New York: Cambridge University Press, 1994.
Mitter, Partha. "Decentering Modernism: Art History and Avant-Garde Art from the Periphery." *Art Bulletin* 90, no. 4 (2008): 531–48.
Mitter, Partha. "The Paradox of Ernst H. Gombrich." In *Art and the Mind—Ernst H. Gombrich: Mit dem Steckenpferd unterwegs*, edited by Sybille Moser-Ernst, 315–32. Göttingen: V&R Unipress, 2018.
Monsiváis, Carlos. *No sin nosotros: Los días del terremoto, 1985–2005*. Mexico City: Ediciones Era, 2005.

Mount, Marshall W. (Marshall Ward). *African Art: The Years since 1920*. Bloomington: Indiana University Press, 1973.

Mphahlele, Es'kia. "Paris in the 1960s," In *Seven Stories about Modern Art in Africa,* edited by Clementine Deliss and Catherine Lambert, 254–56. Exhibition catalog. New York: Whitechapel, 1995.

Munif, Abd al-Rahman. "In His Own Words: Nasb Al-Hurriya / The Monument of Freedom [1998]." Translated by Karam Nachar. "Jewad Selim Notes," Modern Art Iraq Archive, accessed August 6, 2024. https://artiraq.org/maia/files/original/jewad-selim-notes_d5531df32b.pdf.

Munro, Eleanor C. *Originals: American Women Artists*. New York: Simon and Schuster, 1979.

Munroe, Alexandra. "All the Landscapes: Gutai's World." In *Gutai: Splendid Playground,* edited by Ming Tiampo and Alexandra Munroe, 20–43. Exhibition catalog. New York: Guggenheim Museum, 2013.

Munroe, Alexandra. "Introducing Little Boy." In *Little Boy: The Arts of Japan's Exploding Subculture,* edited by Takashi Murakami, 240–62. New York: Japan Society and Yale University Press, 2005.

Munroe, Alexandra. *Japanese Art after 1945: Scream against the Sky*. New York: Harry N. Abrams, 1994.

Munroe, Alexandra. "Postwar Japanese Photography and the Pursuit of Consciousness." In *Daido Moriyama: Stray Dog,* edited by Sandra S. Philips, Alexandra Munroe, and Daido Moriyama, 31–40. San Francisco: San Francisco Museum of Modern Art, 1999.

Murakami, Takashi, ed. *Little Boy: The Arts of Japan's Exploding Subcultures*. New York: Japan Society and Yale University Press, 2005.

Murata, Hanako. "'The *Choshu* Five' in Scotland." *History of Photography* 27, no. 3 (Fall 2003): 284–88.

Muzaffar, May, ed. *Al-Qassab: Art Memories*. London: Dar al-Hikma, 2007.

Muzaffar, May. "Iraq." In *Contemporary Art from the Islamic World,* edited by Wijdan Ali, 166. London: Scorpion Pub, 1989.

Muzaffar, May. "Iraqi Contemporary Art: Roots and Development." In *Iraq: Its History, People, and Politics,* edited by Shams C. Inati, 63–89. Amherst, NY: Humanity Books, 2003.

Naef, Silvia. *À la recherche d'une modernité arabe: L'Évolution des arts plastiques en Égypte, au Liban et en Irak*. Geneva: Editions Slatkine, 1996.

Naef, Silvia. "Reexploring Islamic Art: Modern and Contemporary Creation in the Arab World and Its Relation to the Artistic Past." *Res: Anthropology and Aesthetics,* no. 43 (Spring 2003): 164–74.

Naqqash, Sadequain. *Ruq'at-i Sadiqaini*. Karachi: Matbu'at-i 'Irfani, 1979.

Nashashibi, Salwa Mikdadi, Laura Nader, and Etel Adnan. "Arab Women Artists: Forces of Change." In *Forces of Change: Artists of the Arab World,* edited by Salwa Mikdadi Nashashibi, Laura Nader, and Etel Adnan, 12–37. Exhibition catalog. Lafayette, CA: International Council for Women in the Arts, 1994.

Nelson, Robert S. "The Map of Art History." *Art Bulletin* 79, no. 1 (1997): 28–40.

New Gallery. *Carlos Mérida: Paintings, 1948–1951*. Exhibition catalog. New York: New Gallery, 1952.
"The New Sculpture, a Symposium: The Museum of Modern Art, February 12, 1952." Typewritten manuscript. Museum of Modern Art, New York, 1952.
Newton, Eric. "Zainul Abedin: Pakistan Artist Studying in London." *Commonwealth Today* l, no. 10 (1952): 15–17.
Nietzsche, Friedrich. *The Birth of Tragedy and the Genealogy of Morals*. Translated by Francis Golffing. New York: Doubleday Anchor Books, 1956.
Njami, Simon, ed. *A Useful Dream: African Photography, 1960–2010*. Milan: Silvana Editoriale, 2010.
Noelle, Louise. "La integración plástica: Confluencia, superposición o nostalgia." In *(In) Disciplinas, XXII Coloquio del Instituto de Investigaciones Estéticas*, edited by Lucero Enríquez, 537–51. Mexico City: Instituto de Investigaciones Estéticas, UNAM, 1999.
Ockman, Joan. "The War Years in America: New York, New Monumentality." In *Sert: Arquitecto en Nueva York*, edited by Guido Hartray and Xavier Costa, 22–45. Barcelona: Museu d'Art Contemporani de Barcelona ACTAR, 1997.
Ogbechie, Sylvester Okwunodu. *Ben Enwonwu: The Making of an African Modernist*. Rochester, NY: University of Rochester Press, 2008.
Okeke-Agulu, Chika. *Postcolonial Modernism: Art and Decolonization in Twentieth-Century Nigeria*. Durham, NC: Duke University Press, 2015.
Okeke-Agulu, Chika. "Questionnaire on 'The Contemporary.'" *October*, no. 130 (Fall 2009): 44–45.
Oles, James. "Noguchi in Mexico: International Themes for a Working-Class Market." *American Art* 15, no. 2 (2001): 10–33.
O'Rourke, Kathryn E. *Modern Architecture in Mexico City: History, Representation, and the Shaping of a Capital.* Pittsburgh, PA: University of Pittsburgh Press, 2016.
Oshima, Ken Tadashi, "Characters of Concrete," In *Crafting a Modern World: The Architecture and Design of Antonin and Noémi Raymond*, edited by Kurt G. F. Helfrich and William Whitaker, 65–78. New York: Princeton Architectural Press, 2006.
Oshima, Ken Tadashi, and William Whitaker. "Portfolio." In *Crafting a Modern World: The Architecture and Design of Antonin and Noémi Raymond*, edited by Kurt G. F. Helfrich and William Whitaker, 79–264. New York: Princeton Architectural Press, 2006.
Ottmann, Klaus, and Dorothy Kosinski. *Angels, Demons, and Savages: Pollock, Ossorio, Dubuffet*. Exhibition catalog. Washington, DC: Phillips Collection in association with Yale University Press, 2013.
Oyobe, Natsu. "Human Subjectivity and Confrontation with Materials in Japanese Art." PhD diss., University of Michigan, 2005.
Paltridge, Blair Allen. "Carlos Mérida's Integration of Art, Architecture and Ideology in the Multifamiliar Juarez." PhD diss., University of California, 1992.
Parker, Michael P. *The Saybrook Arras*. New Haven, CT: Eastern Press, 1984.
Parrish, Sarah. "From Collectives to Corporations: Sheila Hicks's Transnational Air/Craft." *Journal of the Design Studies Forum* 8, no. 1 (2016): 79–99.
Patel, Geeta. *Lyrical Movements, Historical Hauntings: On Gender, Colonialism, and Desire in Miraji's Urdu Poetry*. Stanford, CA: Stanford University Press, 2002.

Patel, Gieve. "The Decades and the Seminar." *Contra'66*, no. 5–6 (June 1967): 5–6.
Patriot. "Two Decades of American Paintings." March 2, 1967, n.p.
Pezolet, Nicola. *Reconstruction and the Synthesis of the Arts in France, 1944–1962*. London: Routledge, 2018.
Pile, Steve, and Nigel Thrift. "Mapping the Subject." In *Mapping the Subject: Geographies of Cultural Transformation*, edited by Steve Pile and Nigel Thrift, 13–51. London: Routledge, 1995.
Piotrowski, Andrzej. "Le Corbusier and the Representational Function of Photography." In *Camera Constructs: Photography, Architecture and the Modern City*, edited by Andrew Higgott and Timothy Wray, 35–45. Surrey: Ashgate, 2012.
Plekhanov, Georgi V. "Ibsen, Petty Bourgeois Revolutionist." In *Henrik Ibsen, a Marxist Analysis*, edited by Angel Flores, 35–92. New York: Critics Group, 1937.
Polites, Nicholas. *The Architecture of Leandro V. Locsin*. New York: Weatherhill, 1977.
Prakash, Vikramaditya. *Chandigarh's Le Corbusier: The Struggle for Modernity in Postcolonial India*. Seattle: University of Washington Press, 2002.
Prashad, Vijay. *The Darker Nations: A People's History of the Third World*. New York: New Press, 2007.
Pue, A. Sean. *I Too Have Some Dreams: N. M. Rashed and Modernism in Urdu Poetry*. Berkeley: University of California Press, 2014.
Pye, David. *The Nature and Art of Workmanship*. [1968.] London: Bloomsbury, 2008.
Quirino, Carlos. *History of the Philippine Sugar Industry*. Manila: Kalayaan, 1974.
Rabemananjara, Jacques. "The Foundations of Our Unity Arising from the Colonial Epoch." *Présence Africaine*, no. 24/25 (February–May 1959): 73–88.
Rasmussen, Waldo. *Two Decades of American Painting: An Exhibition*. Exhibition catalog. New York: Museum of Modern Art, 1967.
Raymond, Antonin. *Antonin Raymond: An Autobiography*. Rutland, VT: Charles E. Tuttle, 1973.
Raymond, Antonin. "Antonin Raymond: Interview by Tange Kenzō (1960)." In *Crafting a Modern World: The Architecture and Design of Antonin and Noémi Raymond*, edited by Kurt G. F. Helfrich and William Whitaker, 307–12. New York: Princeton Architectural Press, 2006.
Raymond, Antonin, L. L. Rado, and Paul Weidlinger. "Alternate Designs for a Church, Negros, Philippine Islands." *Progressive Architecture*, January 1948, 46–48.
Reed, Robert. "The Iglesia ni Cristo, 1914–2000: From Obscure Philippine Faith to Global Belief System." *Bijdragen tot de taal-, land- en volkenkunde / Journal of the Humanities of and Social Science of Southeast Asia* 157, no. 3 (2001): 561–608.
Rent Collection Courtyard Collective Sculpture Team. "Shouzuyuan nisu chuangzuo de gousi sheji." *Meishu*, no. 5 (1965): 4.
Rent Collection Courtyard Collective Sculpture Team. "Xian ge sixiang de ming, zai ge diaosu de ming." *Renmin ribao* (Beijing), July 20, 1966, 1.
Rent Collection Courtyard: Sculptures of Oppression and Revolt. Peking: Foreign Languages Press, 1968.
"A Revolution in Sculpture." *China Reconstructs* 15, no. 3 (1966): 30–33.
Rhodes, Richard. *The Making of the Atomic Bomb*. New York: Simon and Schuster, 1986.

Rilke, Rainer Maria. *Duino Elegies*. Translated by J. B. Leishman and Stephen Spender. London: Hogarth, 1939.

Ross, Alex. "The Frankfurt School Knew Trump Was Coming." *New Yorker*, December 5, 2016.

Rousmaniere, Nicole Coolidge, ed. *Kazari: Decoration and Display in Japan, 15th–19th Centuries*. New York: Japan Society, 2002.

Sadequain. *Ghalib*. Karachi, Pakistan: Elite, 1969.

Said, Edward W. *The World, the Text, and the Critic*. Cambridge, MA: Harvard University Press, 1983.

Sakaguchi Ango. "Discourse on Decadence." Translated by Seiji M. Lippit. *Review of Japanese Culture and Society* 1, no. 1(October 1986): 1–5.

Santner, Eric L. *On Creaturely Life: Rilke/Benjamin/Sebald*. Chicago: University of Chicago Press, 2006.

Sanyal, Sunanda K. "'Being Modern': Identity Debates and Makerere's Art School in the 1960s." In *A Companion to Modern African Art*, edited by Gitti Salami and Monica Blackmun Visonà, 255–75. Malden, MA: Wiley-Blackwell, 2013.

Sargeant, Winthrop. "Great Simplicity: Dr. Daisetz Teitaro Suzuki." *New Yorker*, August 31, 1957.

Sartre, Jean-Paul. *Essays in Existentialism*. New York: Citadel, 1965.

Sartre, Jean-Paul. *Existentialism Is a Humanism*. [1946.] Translated by Carol Macomber. New Haven: Yale University Press, 2007.

Sawaragi, Noi. "On the Battlefield of 'Superflat': Subculture and Art in Postwar Japan." In *Little Boy: The Arts of Japan's Exploding Subcultures*, edited by Takashi Murakami, 204–5. New York: Japan Society and Yale University Press, 2005.

Scarry, Elaine. *Thinking in an Emergency*. New York: W. W. Norton, 2011.

Schimmel, Annemarie. *Calligraphy and Islamic Culture*. New York: New York University Press, 1984.

Schmitt, Carl. *Political Theology*. 1922. Translated by George Schwab. Chicago: University of Chicago Press, 2005.

Scientific American. "Improved Triple Expansion Engines." October 22, 1887, 262.

Sekoto, Gerard. "A South African Artist." *Présence Africaine*, no. 14/15 (June–September 1957): 281–89.

Selim, Jewad. "The Renewal of Art (1951)." Translated by Dinah El Husseiny. In *Modern Art in the Arab World: Primary Documents*, edited by Anneka Lenssen, Sarah Rogers, and Nada Shabout, 152–54. New York: MoMA Publications, 2018.

Selim, Rashad. "Diaspora, Departure, and Remains." In *Strokes of Genius: Contemporary Iraqi Art*, edited by Maysaloun Faraj, 47–62. London: Saqi Books, 2001.

Sembène, Ousmane. *Les Bouts de bois de Dieu*. Paris: Pocket, 1960.

Shabout, Nada. *Modern Arab Art: Formation of Arab Aesthetics*. Gainesville: University Press of Florida, 2007.

Shakespeare, William. *The Tragedy of King Richard III: The Oxford Shakespeare*. Edited by John Jowett. Oxford: Oxford University Press, 2000.

Sheikh, Simon. "Towards the Exhibition as Research." In *Curating Research*, edited by Paul O'Neill and Mick Wilson, 32–46. London: Open Editions, 2015.

Shemza, Anwar Jalal. "Artist's Statement, July 1963." In *A. J. Shemza: Paintings Drawings 1957–1963,* 2–4. Exhibition catalog. Durham, UK: Gulbenkian Museum of Oriental Art, 1963.

Sherwood, Marika. "Pan-African Conferences 1900–1953: What Did Pan-Africanism Mean?" *Journal of Pan African Studies* 4, no. 10 (January 2012): 106–26.

Shih, Shu-mei. "Comparison as Relation." In *Comparison: Theories, Approaches, Uses,* edited by Rita Felski and Susan Stanford Friedman, 79–98. Baltimore: Johns Hopkins University Press, 2013.

Shiraga Kazuo. "The Establishment of the Original." Translated by Reiko Tomii with Ming Tiampo and Alexandra Munroe. In *Gutai: Splendid Playground,* edited by Ming Tiampo and Alexandra Munroe, 279. Exhibition catalog. New York: Guggenheim Museum, 2013.

Siddiqui, Ayesha. "Shemza: The Lahori Artist Who Juggled Symbols." In *Lahore: Paintings, Murals, and Calligraphy,* edited by Barbara Schmitz, 140–51. Mumbai: Marg on behalf of National Centre for the Performing Arts, 2010.

Siegel, Katy. *Since '45: America and the Making of Contemporary Art.* London: Reaktion, 2011.

Simms, Gretchen. "The 1959 American National Exhibition in Moscow and the Soviet Artistic Reaction to Abstract Art." PhD diss., University of Vienna, 2007.

Siva Kumar, R. *Santiniketan: The Making of a Contextual Modernism.* Exhibition catalog. New Delhi: National Gallery of Modern Art, 1997.

Skinner, Damien. *The Carver and the Artist: Maori Art in the Twentieth Century.* Auckland: University of Auckland Press, 2008.

Skinner, Damien. "Indigenous Primitivists: The Challenge of Māori Modernism." *World Art* 4, no. 1 (2014): 67–87.

Skinner, Milica Dimitrijevic. "Three Textiles from Huaca Prieta, Chicama Valley, Peru." In *The Junius B. Bird Conference on Andean Textiles,* edited by Ann Pollard Rowe, 11–18. Washington, DC: Textile Museum, 1986.

Smith, Bernard. *The Antipodean Manifesto: Essays in Art and History.* Melbourne: Oxford University Press, 1976.

Smith, Terry. "Art History's Work-in-Pro(re)gress—Reflections on the Multiple Modernities Project." Prologue to *New Histories of Art in the Global Postwar Era: Multiple Modernisms,* edited by Flavia Frigeri and Kristian Handberg, 12–24. New York: Routledge, 2021.

Smith, Terry. "Rethinking Modernism and Modernity Now." *Filozofski Vestnik,* no. 35 (Summer 2014): 271–319.

Smith, Terry. *What Is Contemporary Art?* Chicago: University of Chicago Press, 2009.

Smith, Terry, Okwui Enwezor, and Nancy Condee, eds. *Antinomies of Art and Culture: Modernity, Postmodernity, Contemporaneity.* Durham, NC: Duke University Press, 2008.

Snyder, Timothy. *The Road to Unfreedom: Russia, Europe, America.* New York: Tim Duggan Books, 2018.

Solnit, Rebecca. *Secret Exhibition: Six California Artists of the Cold War Era.* San Francisco: City Lights Books, 1990.

Soto Soria, Alfonso. *Carlos Mérida: Su obra en el Multifamiliar Juárez; Nacimiento, muerte y resurrección*. Edited by Roger Díaz del Cossío. Mexico City: ISSSTE, 1988.

Soto Soria, Alfonso. "Sus aportaciones técnicas a la plástica mexicana." In *Homenaje nacional a Carlos Mérida: Americanismo y abstracción*, edited by Mario de la Torre, 62–66. Monterrey, Mexico: Museo de Monterrey, 1992.

Stallabrass, Julian. *Art Incorporated: The Story of Contemporary Art*. Oxford: Oxford University Press, 2004.

Steele, Elizabeth, Sylvia Albro, Scott Homolka, and Chantal Bernicky. "Materials and Techniques." In *Angels, Demons, and Savages: Pollock, Ossorio, Dubuffet*, edited by Klaus Ottman and Dorothy Kosinsky, 129–41. Exhibition catalog. Washington, DC: Phillips Collection in association with Yale University Press, 2013.

Steil, Benn. *The Battle of Bretton Woods: John Maynard Keynes, Harry Dexter White, and the Making of a New World Order*. Princeton, NJ: Princeton University Press, 2013.

Stokvis, Willemijn. *Cobra: The Last Avant-Garde Movement of the Twentieth Century*. Aldershot: Lund Humphries, 2004.

Sullivan, Michael. *Art and Artists of Twentieth-Century China*. Berkeley: University of California Press, 1996.

Sunderason, Sanjukta. *Partisan Aesthetics: Modern Art and India's Long Decolonization*. Stanford, CA: Stanford University Press, 2020.

Sunderason, Sanjukta. "Shadow-Lines: Zainul Abedin and the Afterlives of the Bengal Famine of 1943." *Third Text* 31, no. 2–3 (2017): 239–59.

Supangkat, Jim. *Indonesian Modern Art and Beyond*. Jakarta: Indonesian Fine Arts Foundation, 1997.

Tabish, Zulfiqar. "Anwar Jalal Shemza." *Mah-e-Nau*, no. 2 (February 1986), 1026–30.

Tanaka, Stefan. *Japan's Orient: Rendering Pasts into History*. Berkeley: University of California Press, 1995.

Taylo, Donata V. "Bartlett as First President: Laying the Foundation of the University." In Alfonso, Oscar M., ed. *University of the Philippines: The First 75 Years (1908–1983)*, edited by Oscar M. Alfonso, 1–46. Quezon City: University of the Philippines Press, 1985.

Thomas, Daniel. "Australia's Most Important Exhibition." *Sydney Morning Herald*, July 15, 1967.

Tiampo, Ming. *Gutai: Decentering Modernism*. Chicago: University of Chicago Press, 2011.

Tōmatsu Shōmei. "Christ in the Nuclear Age." In *Nagasaki 11:02: August 9, 1945*, n.p. Photographs by Shōmei Tōmatsu. Translated by Linda Hoaglund. Tokyo: Shinchōsha Photo Musée, 1986.

Tomii, Reiko. *Radicalism in the Wilderness: International Contemporaneity and 1960s Art in Japan*. Cambridge, MA: MIT Press, 2016.

Toor, Saadia. "Culture/Nation/State: Cultural Nationalism and Moral Regulation in Pakistan, 1947–1971." PhD diss., Cornell University, 2007.

Torres, Leticia. *Integración plástica: Confluencias y divergencias en los discursos del arte en México*. Abrevian ensayos 6. Mexico City: INBA, CENIDIAP; Estampa Artes Gráficas, 2016. https://cenidiap.net/biblioteca/abrevian/6abrev-LeticiaTorres.pdf.

Trilling, James. *Ornament: A Modern Perspective*. Seattle: University of Washington Press, 2003.

Trotsky, Leon. "Futurism." In *Literature and Revolution*, edited by William Keach and translated by Rose Strunsky, 112–27. Chicago: Haymarket Books, 2005.

Troy, Virginia Gardner. *Anni Albers and Ancient American Textiles: From Bauhaus to Black Mountain*. London: Ashgate, 2002.

Tsutsui, William M. "For Godzilla and Country: How a Japanese Monster Became an American Icon." *Foreign Affairs*, May 27, 2014. https://www.foreignaffairs.com/articles/united-states/2014-05-27/godzilla-and-country.

Twomey, Christina, and Ernest Koh, eds. *The Pacific War: Aftermaths, Remembrance and Culture*. Abingdon, VA: Routledge, 2015.

UNESCO. *The Artist in Modern Society: Essays and Statements Collected by UNESCO*. Paris: UNESCO, 1954.

Vaillant, Janet G. *Black, French and African: A Life of Léopold Sédar Senghor*. Cambridge, MA: Harvard University Press, 1990.

Vargas, Elvira. "Multicosas." *Novedades*, May 10, 15, and 17, 1954.

von Moos, Stanislaus. Introduction to *Chandigarh 1956: Le Corbusier, Pierre Jeanneret, Jane B. Drew, E. Maxwell Fry*, edited by Ernst Scheidegger, Maristella Casciato, Cerena Nievergelt, and Stanislaus von Moos, 15–19. Zurich: Verlag Scheidegger und Spiess, 2010.

Wagner, Anne Middleton. *Three Artists (Three Women): Modernism and the Art of Hesse, Krasner, and O'Keeffe*. Berkeley: University of California Press, 1996.

Wang Zhi'an. *Hongtian juechang: Shouzuyuan nisu qiguan*. Chengdu: Tiandi Chubanshe, 2001.

Weisgall, Jonathan M. *Operation Crossroads: The Atomic Tests at Bikini Atoll*. Annapolis, MD: Naval Institute Press, 1994.

Westad, Odd Arne. *The Global Cold War: Third World Interventions and the Making of Our Times*. New York: Cambridge University Press, 2007.

Wilder, Gary. "Eurafrique as the Future Past of 'Black France': Sarkozy's Temporal Confusion and Senghor's Postwar Vision." In *Black France/France Noire: The History and Politics of Blackness*, edited by Trica Danielle Keaton, T. Denean Sharpley-Whiting, and Tyler Stovall, 57–87. Durham, NC: Duke University Press, 2012.

Wilder, Gary. *Freedom Time: Negritude, Decolonization and the Future of the World*. Durham, NC: Duke University Press, 2015.

Wilkins, Lola, ed. *Stella Bowen: Art, Love and War*. Exh. cat. Canberra: Australian War Memorial, 2002.

Winther-Tamaki, Bert. "The Asian Dimensions of Postwar Abstract Art: Calligraphy and Metaphysics." In *The Third Mind: American Artists Contemplate Asia*, edited by Alexandra Munroe, 145–57. Exhibition catalog. New York: Guggenheim Museum, 2009.

Wollaeger, Mark. Introduction to Wollaeger and Eatough, *Oxford Handbook of Global Modernisms*, 3–24.

Wollaeger, Mark, and Matt Eatough, eds. *The Oxford Handbook of Global Modernisms*. Oxford: Oxford University Press, 2012.

World Festival of Negro Arts. *Colloque: Fonction et signification de l'art nègre dans la vie du peuple et pour le peuple (30 mars–8 avril 1966)*. Paris: Présence Africaine, 1967.

Wright, Richard. *The Color Curtain: A Report on the Bandung Conference*. 1956. Jackson: Banner Books and University Press of Mississippi, 1994.
Yoshihara Jirō and Nakamura Shin. "America no kindai kaiga." *Kansai Bijutsu*, no. 13 (May 1951): 12.
Young, Robert J. C. *White Mythologies: Writing History and the West*. London: Routledge, 1990.
Zarobell, John. *Art and the Global Economy*. Berkeley: University of California Press, 2017.
Zhou Enlai. "Wei zongluxian er fendou de wenyi gongzuozhe de renwu." In *Zhou Enlai lun wenyi*. Edited by Wenhuabu wenxue yishu yanjiu yuan. Beijing: Renmin wenxue chubanshe, 1979.
Zijlmans, Kitty, and Wilfried van Damme, eds. *World Art Studies: Exploring Concepts and Approaches*. Amsterdam: Valiz, 2008.
Zitzewitz, Karin. "Infrastructure as Form: Cross-Border Networks and the Materialities of 'South Asia' in Contemporary Art." *Third Text* 31, no. 2-3 (2017): 341–58.
Zúñiga, Olivia. *Mathias Goeritz*. Translated by Sonia Levy-Spira. Mexico City: Editorial Intercontinental, 1964.

Contributors

IFTIKHAR DADI is John H. Burris Professor of History of Art at Cornell University and a practicing artist who collaborates with Elizabeth Dadi.

PATRICK FLORES is professor at the University of the Philippines and chief curator at National Gallery Singapore.

HAL FOSTER is Townsend Martin '17 Professor at Princeton University.

BORIS GROYS is Global Distinguished Professor at New York University.

ATREYEE GUPTA is associate professor at the University of California, Berkeley.

ELIZABETH HARNEY is associate professor at the University of Toronto.

JENNIFER JOSTEN is associate professor at the University of Pittsburgh.

VIVIAN LI is Lupe Murchison Curator of Contemporary Art at the Dallas Museum of Art.

TARA MCDOWELL is associate professor at Monash University.

ALEXANDRA MUNROE is director of curatorial affairs at the Guggenheim Abu Dhabi and senior curator, Asian art and senior advisor, global arts at the Solomon R. Guggenheim Museum.

NADA SHABOUT is Regents Professor at the University of North Texas.

TERRY SMITH is Andrew W. Mellon Emeritus Professor of Contemporary Art History and Theory at the University of Pittsburgh; professor in the Division of Philosophy, Art, and Critical Thought at the European Graduate School, Saas-Fee, Switzerland; and faculty at large in the curatorial program at the School of Visual Arts, New York.

JENNI SORKIN is professor at the University of California, Santa Barbara.

MING TIAMPO is professor at Carleton University.

Index

Page references in *italics* indicate illustrations.